"All Will Yet Be Well"

A Bur Oak Original

"All Will Yet Be Well"

The Diary of Sarah Gillespie Huftalen, 1873–1952

By Suzanne L. Bunkers

University of Iowa Press   Ψ   Iowa City

University of Iowa Press, Iowa City 52242
Printed in the United States of America

Design by Karen Copp

Printed on acid-free paper

Library of Congress Cataloging-in-Publication Data
Huftalen, Sarah Gillespie, 1865–1955
"All will yet be well": the diary of Sarah Gillespie
Huftalen, 1873–1952 / [edited] by Suzanne L. Bunkers.
       p.   cm.—(A Bur oak original)
Includes bibliographical references (p.   ) and index.
ISBN 0-87745-421-3, ISBN 0-87745-422-1 (pbk.)
   1. Huftalen, Sarah Gillespie, 1865–1955—
Diaries. 2. Women—Iowa—Diaries. 3. Iowa—
   Biography. 4. Women—Iowa—Social
   conditions. 5. Mothers and daughters.
   I. Bunkers, Suzanne L. II. Title. III. Series.
          CT275.H76A3   1993
          977.7'03'092—dc20
            [B]   93-32516
                     CIP

97 96 95 94 93 C 5 4 3 2 1
97 96 95 94 93 P 5 4 3 2 1

Frontispiece: a composite photograph made by Sarah
Gillespie Huftalen. When the original photos were taken,
James Gillespie was seventy-one, Emily Gillespie was
forty-six, Henry Gillespie was twenty-nine, and Sarah was
twenty-four. State Historical Society of Iowa, Iowa City.

He comforts readily and sweetly with his words, and says:
But all will be well, and every kind of thing will be well.
—Julian of Norwich

FOR RACHEL

Contents

Acknowledgments

Many individuals and organizations deserve thanks for their contributions to this project. Mary Bennett, Special Collections librarian at the State Historical Society of Iowa (SHSI) in Iowa City, first brought the manuscript diary of Sarah Gillespie Huftalen to my attention. I am grateful for her assistance in locating manuscripts, discussing Sarah's life, and arranging for reproductions of photographs in the Huftalen Collection.

Gordon O. Hendrickson, State Archivist, secured permission to publish Sarah's diary. Christie Dailey, SHSI Publications Director; Marv Bergmann, editor of the *Annals of Iowa*; Ginalie Swaim, editor of the *Palimpsest*; Deborah Gore Ohrn, editor of the *Goldfinch*; and Mary Helen Stefaniak, editor of *Muses*, the Iowa Humanities Board magazine, shared many helpful insights into Sarah's life and diary. Vongchouane Mary Baccam helped copy materials in the Huftalen Collection. Jason Nado helped me proofread the edited typescript. Kathryn Cullen prepared the index.

Judy Nolte Lensink, whose superb research first piqued my interest in Emily Hawley Gillespie's diary, advised me throughout my work on this edition of Sarah's diary. Ann and Steve Baumgarn, who lived for many years in the Coffins Grove Stagecoach Inn near Manchester, graciously invited me to visit their home and talk about the Gillespies' lives. Trudee and Lynn Svaldi were kind hosts during my visits to Manchester, and Trudee located a good deal of biographical information about Sarah. Wilma Kehrli, Wilbur Kehrli, and Anna LaVerne Bockenstedt visited with me about their recollections of Sarah, Henry, Emily, and James Gillespie.

Tim Tutton shared a wealth of information about Manchester's history and many individuals mentioned in Sarah's diary. Gary and Micki Cline helped me locate places where Sarah lived in Manchester. Robert Nieman, Delaware County Clerk of Court, provided death and probate records. Gretchen Kuhlman and Lee C. Baker provided useful genealogical information, along with letters and reminiscences about the Gillespies. Helen English, Forrest and Charlene Scanlan, Neva Meehan, Lillian Hillers, Edith Coltman, and Gertrude Schmitz shared memories of Sarah.

In March 1992, Ann Baumgarn organized and facilitated a workshop, "In the Daily Course of Human Events," at the Stagecoach Inn. This workshop, cosponsored by the Iowa Humanities Board, the National Endowment for the Humanities, and the Lutheran Brotherhood Respecteen Program, gave me an important opportunity to discuss Emily's and Sarah's diaries with other teachers and local historians, whom I would like to thank: Ann Baumgarn, Judy Nolte Lensink, Steve Baumgarn, Trudee Svaldi, Marilyn Hageman, Gary Cline, Jill Vanderwilt, Carolyn Milroy, Peggy Johannsen, Tracy Potbury, Sharon Cook, Karen Wallace, Karen Klein, Jean Haas, Diane Hakler, Gladys Kell, Faith Meinzen, Delpha Schuster, Aletha Kramer, Clairabelle Baum, Norma Jean Zumr, and Mary Helen Stefaniak.

Over the past twelve years, I have been grateful for financial support for my research from the National Endowment for the Humanities, the American Council of Learned Societies, the Iowa Humanities Board, the Women's Studies Research Center at the University of Wisconsin-Madison, and Mankato State University. I have appreciated invitations to present papers on Sarah's diary at the Modern Language Association Convention, the Midwestern Modern Language Association Convention, the Congress of Historical Organizations Conference, and the American Association of University Women (Mankato, Minnesota, chapter).

James Olney, director of the 1983 NEH seminar, "The Forms of Autobiography," first encouraged me to consider the diary as autobiography and to study the writings of Julian of Norwich, a medieval mystic. The research of the following scholars has influenced my interpretations of women's daily lives and private writings: H. Porter Abbott, Emily Abel, Ilene Alexander, William Andrews, Elizabeth Baer, Virginia Beauchamp, Harriet Blodgett, Lynn Bloom, Jeanne Braham, Robert Burchfield, Helen Buss, Mary Hurlbut Cordier, Margo Culley, John Mack Faragher, Deborah Fink, Susan Stanford Friedman, Cinthia Gannett, Carol Gilligan, Dure Jo Gillikin, Minrose Gwin, Elizabeth Hampsten, Carolyn Heilbrun, Rebecca Hogan, Cynthia Huff, Steven

Kagle, Linda Kerber, Philippe Lejeune, Judy Nolte Lensink, Geneva Cobb Moore, Glenda Riley, Ann Romines, Paul C. Rosenblatt, Dorothy Schwieder, Elaine Showalter, Judy Simons, Trudelle Thomas, and Laurel Thatcher Ulrich.

I continue to be grateful for the support of colleagues, students, and friends who share my interest in diaries. I would especially like to thank my mother, Verna Bunkers, who gave me my first diary. Finally, I would like to thank my daughter, Rachel, for her contributions to this project. In summer 1992, Rachel and I went to Manchester, where we visited the old Gillespie farm and placed flowers on Sarah's grave. Then we went on to Iowa City, where we read Sarah's earliest diary, begun when she was just about the age Rachel is now. Rachel's presence in my life provides a unique perspective on the lives—and diaries—of mothers and daughters.

Preface

I first read the manuscript diary of Sarah Gillespie Huftalen in 1987, when I traveled to the State Historical Society of Iowa in Iowa City to study the manuscript diary of Sarah's mother, Emily Hawley Gillespie. Late one afternoon, after I had spent several hours poring over Emily's spidery and faded handwriting, I rubbed my eyes and walked gingerly toward the reading room's door. Mary Bennett, the archivist, sat behind her desk, studying a tattered photograph.

"How are you coming along?" she politely inquired.

"All right, I think. This diary is fascinating." I shook my head in astonishment.

"Oh," Mary smiled, "if you think Emily's diary is interesting, you ought to read her daughter Sarah's diary."

The next day I made a start. I've been captivated by Sarah's diary ever since. Analyzing over three thousand manuscript pages of diary entries has required determination, perseverance, time, and strong eyesight. It has required a certain degree of empathy for the diarist as well as a desire to keep turning the pages and not simply say, "Well, there's nothing more worth reading here." It has required more than sitting at a computer day after day, typing selected diary entries for this edition. It has required more than wading through the extensive collection of photograph albums, scrapbooks, and memorabilia in the Sarah Gillespie Huftalen Collection. It has required more than several drives from Mankato, Minnesota, to Manchester, Iowa, to talk with people who knew Sarah as a farm neighbor and to walk around the house and outbuildings on the old Gillespie farm. Most important, it has required a belief that Sarah's story is worth telling and a confidence that you will find it worth reading.

Editorial Principles

This edition contains selected entries from Sarah Gillespie Huftalen's massive diary, which she kept from 1873 until 1952. In all, this edition contains approximately 15 to 20 percent of the manuscript document; each chapter of this edition contains entries from a specific period in Sarah's life. As the editor of Sarah's diary, I have tried to select entries that will describe, analyze, and evaluate people and events in a life that spanned nearly ninety years. I have divided these diary entries into eleven chapters, each of which covers a certain period in Sarah's life. Sarah was a creative and a frugal diarist; she would write individual diary entries in bound volumes, on loose-leaf paper, in school record books, and on the backs of old letters and bills, as time and writing materials were available. Her method of composing her diary has required that I sort carefully through all of her diary entries, arrange them into chronological order, and select and edit individual entries for presentation in this book.

As a researcher primarily trained in literary theory and close textual analysis, I have striven to maintain the narrative flow of the manuscript diary, supplementing Sarah's entries with a general introduction to provide a context for the events described in the diary as well as a conclusion to provide commentary on the diary's significance. At the same time, I have attempted to set Sarah's words into a context bounded by critical theory in the fields of autobiography, social history, and psychology.

I have presented the diary entries as Sarah did, with the date in the left-hand margin and the entry beginning immediately following it. I have used ellipses to indicate where I have deleted portions of entries and ellipses in brackets to indicate where entire entries have been deleted. I have retained the original spelling, punctuation, capitalization, and phrasing, even in the case of misspelling or misphrasing; I have used *sic* only to indicate an unintentional error made by Sarah. I have added information in brackets when necessary to clarify meaning and to add pertinent information to individual diary entries. I have used italicized notes where appropriate to add commentary on persons and events described in the diary.

The annotative notes included for each chapter are often explanatory and interpretive. Some notes provide biographical information about persons mentioned in Sarah's diary, while others offer comparisons between Emily's and Sarah's diary entries for the same date. Still other notes speculate on possible reasons for and/or repercussions of specific incidents recounted by Sarah in her diary.

Above all, my objective in preparing this edition of Sarah Gillespie Huftalen's diary has been to create a text that will reconstruct one woman's life, a life about which you may know little when you open this book, yet a life that I hope you will find hard to forget after you have closed it.

"All Will Yet Be Well"

Introduction: The Diary as the Tapestry of a Life

Keep well this book and bear in mind
A constant friend is hard to find.

Sarah Gillespie made this entry in her diary on January 1, 1877, when she was eleven. It would set the tone for many more diary entries during the next seventy-five years.[1] As a girl, Sarah lived on the Gillespie family's farm near Manchester, Iowa, fifty miles west of Dubuque. As an adult, she became a well-known and highly respected leader in the rural education movement in the American Midwest.

My interest in editing Sarah's diary grew out of my study of the diary of her mother, Emily Hawley Gillespie.[2] Taken together, these two women's diaries, spanning nearly a century, provide a wealth of materials for learning more about how rural American women lived, wrote, and interacted. Emily's and Sarah's diaries are especially rich in their chronicling of daily farm activities, interactions with relatives and neighbors, educational pursuits, and family dynamics. Sarah's diary, which she kept throughout the late 1800s, the turn of the century, World War I, the Great Depression, World War II, and the early 1950s, reflects her self-consciousness as writer and historian.

In many respects, Sarah Gillespie Huftalen led an unconventional life for a rural midwestern woman of her time. She was a farm girl who became a highly regarded country school and college teacher. A gifted writer, she crafted essays, teacher training guides, and poetry while continuing to make lengthy, introspective entries in her diary. In addition, she devoted her energies to chronicling and preserving the history of her family. She compiled extensive genealogical files on both her mother's and her father's ancestries; and she prepared her mother's ten-volume diary, covering the years 1858 to 1888, for donation to the State Historical Society of Iowa. Had it not been for Sarah's efforts, Emily's diary would probably not have been preserved, and it would not be in print today.

At the same time as she worked to trace her genealogical lines and preserve her mother's private writings, Sarah Gillespie Huftalen wrote in her own diary about her multiple roles as daughter, sister, wife, teacher, family historian, and public figure. Her diary reflects her growing consciousness of the ways in which these roles intersected. Not only does her diary embody the diverse strategies used by one woman to preserve her life story for future generations, it also offers ample evidence that the diary can become a primary form of autobiography for a woman whose life, work, and writing did not lend themselves to traditional definitions of autobiography.[3] As Judy Nolte Lensink has observed about both Emily's and Sarah's diaries, "By crossing many of the formalist boundaries of published autobiography, I would argue, diarists both tell their truth *and* create female design—a supersubtle design, similar to a quilt's, made up of incremental stitches that define a pattern" (*A Secret*, 380).

Along with many other scholars, I continue to examine the ways in which women's diaries constitute life stories. Such texts break canonical rules by not conforming to the pattern prescribed for "autobiography proper." Yet scholars have demonstrated that diaries are not haphazard, shapeless, or directionless. Rather, a diary's shape represents the diarist's creation of a pattern, a design, characterized as much by its omissions as by its inclusions. Elizabeth Hampsten cautions readers of diaries to "interpret what is not written as well as what is, and, rather than dismiss repetitions, value them especially" (*Read This*, 4). Margo Culley explains that a diary "is created in and represents a continuous present" and that many diarists "reread previous entries before writing a current one, creating a complexly layered present to which a version of the past is immediately available. From entry to entry, the text incorporates its future as it reconstructs its past" (*A Day*, 20). Rebecca Hogan notes that the diary's "valorization of the detail, its perspective of immersion, its mixing of genres, its principle of inclusiveness, and its expression of intimacy and mutuality all seem to qualify it as a form very congenial to women life/writers" ("Engendered Autobiography," 105).

Bettina Aptheker's analysis of the patterns inherent in the dailiness of women's lives resonates with scholars' analyses of the dailiness of diary keeping. Aptheker explains:

> By the dailiness of women's lives I mean the patterns women create and the meanings women invent each day and over time as a result of their labors and in the context of their subordinated

status to men. The point is not to describe every aspect of daily life or to represent a schedule or priorities in which some activities are more important or accorded more status than others. The point is to suggest a way of knowing from the meanings women give to their labors. The search for dailiness is a method of work that allows us to take the patterns women create and the meanings women invent and learn from them. If we map what we learn, connecting one meaning or invention to another, we begin to lay out a different way of seeing reality. This way of seeing is what I refer to as women's standpoint. And this standpoint pivots, of course, depending upon the class, cultural, or racial locations of its subjects, and upon their age, sexual preference, physical abilities, the nature of their work and personal relationships. What is proposed is a mapping of that which has traditionally been erased or hidden. (39–40)

Aptheker's emphasis on "mapping," on searching for patterns within this dailiness, is central to my analysis of Sarah's diary. Sarah did not write in her diary every day, and she did not write about every aspect of her life. She did, however, create patterns of meaning in her diary by defining themes and developing them over the months and years, eventually shaping her diary into a "map" by which readers can traverse the landscape of her life.

In her recent study of the relationship between gender and diary-keeping, Cinthia Gannett explains that most women's diaries render the experience of female life in "three distinct and critical phases for the vast majority of women, in accordance with the primary cultural roles they are assigned: maidenhood, marriage and motherhood, then often widowhood. Their lives seem to be centered on the cycles of birth, maturation, courtship, marriage, pregnancy, child care, illness, and death. Indeed, women not only wrote about these critical shifts in their status and experience, they often start, stop, or shift the nature of their diary keeping in response to these changes, so that the diaries themselves begin to take on the shape of the women's lives" (127).

Several recent editions of American women's diaries illustrate Gannett's theory about the many ways in which diarists shape their texts into life narratives. Minrose Gwin describes the Civil War diary of Cornelia Peake McDonald as "a diary, a memoir, and then another memoir constructed out of lost portions of the diary, specifically lost books on whose pages McDonald squeezed her writing literally between the printed lines" (8). Gwin explains that the text "circles and recircles itself as it incorporates the spatial dailiness of the diary form along with the diary form *as remembered* and subsequently as reshaped through memory" (8–9). In the introduction to *A Midwife's Tale: The Life of Martha Ballard, Based on Her Diary, 1785–1812*, Laurel Thatcher Ulrich comments that "it is in the very dailiness, the exhaustive, repetitious dailiness, that the real power of Martha Ballard's book lies" (9). P. A. M. Taylor notes that Elizabeth Rogers Mason Cabot used her diary as a means of "defining thought, shaping experience, imposing a pattern on the confusions and contradictions of the real world" (30).

My study of Caroline Seabury's Civil War diary indicates that it became what Robert Fothergill calls a "book of the self": "As the diary grows to a certain length and substance it impresses upon the mind of its writer a conception of the completed book that might ultimately be, if sustained with sufficient dedication and vitality" (44).[4] As Caroline Seabury continued to write in her diary over a period of nine years, it began to "take shape as a life narrative which recorded her experiences and reflected upon their significance" (Bunkers, *Seabury*, 16). In her edition of Madge Preston's diary, Virginia Walcott Beauchamp recognizes the importance of the diary as a "quintessentially female form": " . . . for nineteenth-century women—cut off from the means men drew on in the larger world of commerce, government, and the arts to develop their individual potential—the diary was the quintessentially female form: no document could be more private and therefore modest. Yet in the very tangibleness of its form, it could preserve for an unknown posterity the record of a life lived, of thoughts registered on a living mind. It could outlast the oblivion of death" (xxxiv–xxxv).

Judy Nolte Lensink deftly analyzes the ways in which Emily Hawley Gillespie used "diary time" to shape a "coherent world formed by the writer's perceptions" and "populated by reappearing characters; mappable, even if only the size of a household" (*A Secret*, 382). Although Lensink acknowledges that writing a diary "demands everyday immersion in the text that parallels one's immersion in life" (383), she asserts that Emily's diary could be called a "meta-autobiography" in which its author created the personae of the "striving sufferer," the "perfect mother," the "unappreciated wife," the "misunderstood daughter," and the "maligned sister" (387–389). The diary of Emily Hawley Gillespie, Lensink concludes, is "a book incrementally written to frame an author-ized version of life—selective, immutable as the self-image driving it, eventually vocal and judgmental" (389).

As scholars continue to investigate the significance of noncanonical literature in the expansion of generic perimeters, diaries like Sarah Gillespie Huftalen's elucidate how one woman's recording of the minutiae of everyday life helped her chart a course for her life. Just as important, such texts challenge us to re-examine our own "private" writings and analyze how we use such "household words" to generate, sustain, and alter our ways of looking at the world.

Sarah Gillespie was born to Emily and James Gillespie on July 7, 1865. Her twin brother was stillborn. Sarah's older brother, Henry (born on September 4, 1863), was almost two years old at the time. Their mother's diary entry for July 7, 1865, reads: "ah. ah. can it be possible that we have a little daughter born this morning—that weighs 5 lbs. 7 oz—her twin brother did not live to even breathe—I do not know but it was right—however we would have done the best we could had he have lived—may our little girl be in the world as virtuous & pure as has been our prayer for little Henry . . ." (Lensink, *A Secret*, 128).

The year of Sarah's birth was a tumultuous year in American history; Abraham Lincoln had been assassinated three months earlier, and the Civil War had just ended. Sarah's parents, married nearly three years, were struggling to make a living on a 100-acre farm. Now they had two small children to raise.

Sarah's mother, Emily Hawley, had been born in Lenawee County, Michigan, on April 11, 1838, to Sarah (Baker) and Hial Newton Hawley.[5] In 1861, Emily traveled west to Manchester, in Delaware County, Iowa, to live with her widowed uncle, Henry Baker, at the Coffins Grove Stagecoach Inn, and care for his daughter, Susan. There Emily met her future husband, James Gillespie, the son of Hiram and Lorindia (Rawden) Gillespie, other immigrants from Michigan to Iowa.

Twenty-four-year-old Emily and twenty-six-year-old James were married on September 18, 1862, in Manchester. Their first home was a wing in Hiram and Lorindia's house. In 1862, James's parents deeded him 100 acres, where James, Emily, and their children lived.[6] Hiram and Lorindia Gillespie continued to live in a small house on the farm until their deaths in 1867 and 1869, respectively.[7]

The Gillespies' lives were like those of many other midwestern farm families during this era. All four family members contributed to the daily operation of the farm. Their social, economic, and ideological network of exchange with relatives and friends brought them aid and support.[8] While James was primarily responsible for crops, livestock, and farm repairs, Emily was primarily responsible for childcare, household matters, and the poultry operation.

James and Emily Hawley Gillespie, ages thirty-seven and thirty-four. Photo taken February 14, 1873, in Manchester. SHSI.

In *Open Country, Iowa*, Deborah Fink analyzes the interdependent nature of men's and women's roles in the "dual economy" of farm life. While men handled the "market sphere," women handled the equally important "household sphere" and contributed a good deal of the daily economic support for the family:

> They raised poultry, gardened, and helped their husbands with livestock chores and fieldwork; they produced chickens, eggs, butter, potatoes, and other foods eaten in the homes; their egg money or egg trade bought flour, spices, cloth, and school pencils. As household partners, they were doing an immediate, material, and essential part in reproducing the farm labor force. Women's rights to benefit from their work were upheld through the social sanctions of their extended families and public opinion within the moral community. The bonds among women were central in maintaining the social consensus which, in the absence of legal rights, protected women's interests. (230–231).

Along with Emily Gillespie, her children Henry and Sarah were indispensable links in the reproduction of the farm labor force described by Fink. Sarah's earliest diary entries tell of feeding the chickens and turkeys on the farm, pulling weeds in the strawberry patch, helping her parents dig potatoes, sewing on a new dress, piecing a quilt, and studying her lessons. At first, Sarah wrote brief daily entries in her diary; as she grew older, she often wrote lengthy periodic entries, sometimes covering five or six diary pages at a time. Many of these entries document the often harsh realities of nineteenth-century farm life.

As young children, Sarah and her older brother Henry were tutored at home by their mother; then they attended the Sub District No. 6 country school a mile and a half from their home. Many years later, Sarah reminisced about starting school: "Plump and chubby at four years of age I trudged one and a half miles to Sub District No. 6 to a new school house for a four months term it being taught by a younger sister of my mother [Harriet Hawley] who lived with us and who led my brother and me to and from daily. . . . My mother coached us during vacations so that by the time we finished the Common School Course in this school we had received some advanced subjects in mathematics and grammar."[9]

On November 10, 1879, Sarah and Henry began attending the newly established Manchester Academy. Their mother's diary entry for that date reads: "They Commence to day, to attend an Academy, tis new to them. there is 68 students, mostly young Ladies & gentlemen.

Henry and Sarah Gillespie, ages nine and seven. Photo taken February 14, 1873. SHSI.

They are to attend the last half of this term, their studies are Arithmetic; Grammar, reading & spelling. . . . Henry & Sarah are much pleased & had good lessons to day" (Lensink, *A Secret*, 234–235). The siblings studied at the academy for over two years, until a measles epidemic forced it to close in the spring of 1882.[10]

Attendance at such an academy was unusual for farm children at that time, but Emily Gillespie wanted Henry and Sarah to have a good education, even though James Gillespie objected to their attendance, complaining that he could not afford to send them to the academy. James and Emily's disagreement over whether their children should attend the Manchester Academy no doubt had to do with their financial difficulties, but the dispute was also indicative of their ongoing power struggle. In early January 1880, Sarah had written in her diary that she and Henry would not be able to attend the academy and that their mother was helping them study at home. On April 2, however, Emily wrote in her diary that she had paid the children's full tuition for twelve weeks out of forty dollars that James had earned bailing hay for Uncle Henry Baker.

On September 4, 1880, Emily spelled out the nature of the disagreement in her diary: "Henry is seventeen years old to day. James & I go to Town. Henry & Sarah at home. they felt *very* much disappointed this morning because James said he could not pay their tuition (16.00) to go to school. they feel all right this evening however—as he changed his mind & paid 12.00. Henry pays 4.00 (1/2) for himself" (Lensink, *A Secret*, 250). That same day, Sarah wrote this diary entry: "Henry 17 to day, gave him his card. Pa said at breakfast ~~that~~ to Ma 'If you send them children to school, *you* will have to borrow the money somewhere.' Ma told us we would have to give up going to school. . . . Pa changed his mind I guess because we *are* to go to school after *all*. . . ." The Gillespie children continued to attend the Manchester Academy, and Sarah appeased both parents by attending school and doing her full share of chores on the farm. Her mother helped her study at home in the evening.

During her early years, Sarah's diary entries continued to recite a litany of household and farming chores: doing the wash, ironing, cleaning house, making beds, helping make fences, feeding the chickens and cattle, and occasionally doing fancy work such as embroidery. Like many other farm families, the Gillespie family was struggling financially during the depression that gripped the country in the 1870s. On at least two Christmases, Sarah wrote in her diary that there were no presents.

Sarah's diary entries also reveal her recognition that her parents' marriage was deteriorating rapidly during the late 1870s and early 1880s. By March 5, 1881, Sarah wrote: "Ma & Pa went to town. they had a '*spat*' I guess. ma told me about it." Eventually, the situation reached the point where her father regularly threatened her mother with bodily harm. Like her mother, Sarah wrote in her diary about James's abusiveness. On May 1, 1883, Sarah explained: "Pa have a mad fit. Henry & I are enough for him though." In her diary entry for May 15, 1883, Emily wrote: "Henry has felt grieved all day. James must misuse him or some one else about every week. He told Henry he was here living on him—and he must leave . . ." (Lensink, *A Secret*, 264). On June 1, 1883, Emily commented on her husband's increasingly erratic behavior: "It is indeed trying to my nerves to live as I have had to for years. I am sorry it is so but I think something will have to be done. I do hope & pray it may be for the best. . . . yes I have not dared to go to sleep many a night, and it wears me out—I feel tis not right to live so . . ." (Lensink, *A Secret*, 268). As Sarah's and Emily's diary entries indicate, during Henry's and Sarah's teenaged years, their alliance with their mother grew stronger, as did their sense of estrangement from their father.

Despite the Gillespie family's involvement in a network of relatives and friends, it is unclear whether Emily or Sarah confided in this network about James's attitudes and behavior or, if they did, whether they received support from members of this network. It does not appear that Emily's sister Harriet (Hattie) McGee provided much support. Hattie lived on a nearby farm, and she and Emily visited regularly. Yet Hattie, whose marriage was troubled, lived in abject poverty with her children. The arrival from Michigan of Hial Hawley, Emily and Hattie's widowed and indigent father, compounded the economic difficulties; he expected his daughters to support him, and Emily and Hattie disagreed about whose responsibility it was to take their father in. Their dispute led to Emily's estrangement from Hattie. Emily also wrote in her diary that she felt James had turned members of the Gillespie family against her.

In Christie Dailey's assessment of the Gillespies' situation, "families internally divided and torn by external forces could not maintain cohesion and lost the core of personal relationships that contributes to the successful function of their farm as a *family* farm" (28). However complex the reasons for the difficulties in the Gillespies' relationships with their relatives, there is substantial evidence in both Emily's and Sarah's diaries that James's potential to be verbally, emotionally, and physically abusive contributed to the family's difficulties in maintaining a cohesive family unit and a successful farm operation.

Abusiveness was not uncommon among farm families, where wife abuse in particular appears to have been sanctioned not only by vagaries of personal psychology but also by social and environmental features such as patriarchal concepts of the family, rigidly defined gender roles, and societal pressure to preserve the family unit. According to Linda Gordon, few abused women kept the problem entirely to themselves (276). They often tried to get help from other family members, neighbors, and friends. Although such forms of help could prove important, even more important was "the influence of others on how victims defined the standards of treatment they would tolerate" (278). Betsy Downey observes that "victims of domestic violence could expect little help from legal institutions unless they were willing to resort to divorce, which an increasing number of women did as an escape from abuse they could no longer tolerate" (34). Unfortunately, abused family member(s) generally got little tangible help from others.[11]

As a girl growing up in an abusive family, Sarah Gillespie had few places to turn to for help outside her immediate family. Societies for the Prevention of Cruelty to Children (SPCCs) were being developed in the 1870s; yet, as Gordon points out, the reformers who founded such organizations often did not see the family as the source of the problem: "They saw cruelty to children as a vice of inferior classes and cultures which needed correction and 'raising up' to an 'American' standard. Their emphasis on cruelty made children's mistreatment seem willful rather than structural, a view which in turn grew from their unexamined confidence that their own family patterns were better because they practiced self-control" (27–28). Elizabeth Pleck observes that outside intervention in a family dispute was considered a violation of the family structure and that many public policies and programs advocated family reconciliation at any cost (12–13).

Despite the growing problems within the Gillespie household, Sarah continued her education by attending six-to-eight-week normal training institutes held in Manchester each summer. By 1874, a normal institute was required in every county in Iowa, and such institutes were to be held when classes were not in session. The registration fee for an institute was one dollar, and each teaching certificate issued cost one dollar. The State Teachers' Association suggested that all institutes adopt the same course of study and that teachers who conducted the institutes be appointed by the State Board of Examiners. By 1879, two additional state normal institutes were being held annually to prepare superintendents and instructors who taught the institutes for teachers.[12]

In November 1883, at the age of seventeen, Sarah began teaching at the one-room McGee country school not far from her home.[13] At that time, country schools suffered from a dearth of qualified teachers. Many, like Sarah, were young women still in their teens, who had not gone beyond secondary school. Teaching was not a lucrative career; it offered no job security; and many teachers saw it as a temporary stopping place en route to something better. Because it was assumed that female teachers would eventually marry, leave teaching, and not have to support families, their salaries were lower than those of male teachers.[14]

Sarah's diary entries reveal that, despite the many challenges of being a new teacher, she enjoyed her work. She taught reading, writing, spelling, grammar, literature, arithmetic, and geography. She was also responsible for disciplining her students. Many years later, Sarah looked back on her first teaching experience:

> There were 35 pupils with eight grades, one third of whom were of my age and whom I knew well. As I reflect upon it I believe there was more disciplining in that first term than in all subsequent years of service. In my previous visits to this school I had seen the teacher chase the large boys around the building and across the road around the shed to get them into the room but failed. The pupils talked out loud and sang whenever inclination prompted. Truancy was a weekly occurrence.[15]

Over the years, Sarah would teach in many country schools in townships throughout Delaware County. Typically, she would be hired term by term; she would board with her students' families during the week and return home on weekends.

After Emily Gillespie suffered a stroke in 1886, however, Sarah took time off from teaching to care for her mother. Sarah's diary for those years contains many entries like the one dated June 20, 1886:

> Ma had a sinking spell yesterday. She has been to weak to sit up much for 2 or 3 days. But has to be rubbed & hot flannels kept on & hot teas & a great deal of care. I've just been out to feed the turkeys. It rained to day but they did not get wet for I covered them with boards & turned the "boxes," as Joe says, rainward. . . . I cook nights. Seems as though Ma must get better soon

for we are all worn out. I took a bath this morning. . . . Now I must wash the dishes & get ready for to night. . . .

In August 1886, Sarah, Henry, and their mother moved off the family farm, shortly after James Gillespie tried to kill Henry. Emily's August 28, 1886, diary entry reads: "Orson Adams has been here two weeks. we hire him to stay here on account of James having grown so much worse & having such fits of insanity. Three weeks tomorrow he tried to choke Henry to death and declared he would kill him; chased him with the pitch-fork—& a club too; he declared he would be the means of him & of all the rest of us . . ." (Lensink, *A Secret*, 335).

Emily consulted an attorney about a legal separation. Then she and her children rented rooms in town. For a time, they moved back to the farm while James lived elsewhere. By November 1887, however, she and her children had rented rooms from A. R. Loomis in Manchester. Sarah gave up teaching altogether to care for her mother, a difficult task that required intense effort and the negotiation of conflicting emotions.[16]

On March 24, 1888, Emily Hawley Gillespie died at the age of forty-nine. In her diary, Sarah wrote: "O, my poor dear suffering Mother. I loved her when she was here, but I believe I love her more now." Grief stricken, Sarah wrote only sporadically in her diary for some time.[17] She kept on renting rooms in Manchester with Henry. Her father visited her on occasion; however, as her diary entry for July 22, 1888, reveals, Sarah continued to fear James until his death in 1909: "He seems to be in a serious condition some times. I really feel afraid of him. I hope he may not come when I am alone. . . ."[18]

Tucked neatly into the pages of Sarah's diary is a tiny yellowed newspaper clipping of a poem entitled "Mother's Love," written in the characteristic style of nineteenth-century popular verse and attributed only to "D. W." It presents a ritualized, highly stylized, and sentimentalized mourning ritual; the fact that Sarah preserved it indicates that it spoke to Sarah about the nature of her loss. Perhaps it also helped to shape the directions that expressions of her grief took in many diary entries to follow.

M O T H E R ' S L O V E

by D. W.

No love like the love of a mother,

When trials are gathering fast—

Though fond is the care of a brother,

Sometimes it will fail at the last.
Should you turn from the pathway of duty,
A sister's affections may fade;
But mother-love shows its best beauty,
When her child to sin is betrayed.

A father may speak stern and coldly,
If his son has wandered astray;
But mother will stand forward boldly
And help him regain the lost way.
And speak to him kindly, in warning,
With just as tender a tone
As she did in childhood's pure morning,
Ere sorrow and crime he had known.

Ah, no! There's no love like a mother's,
So noble forgiving and true;
We may trust it to many another's
And value it, that it is new,
To find, when life's sun is shrouded,
And our pathway enters the gloom,
Their love for us, too, will be clouded,
While hers follows us to the tomb.

Emily Gillespie's death was a watershed event in Sarah's life. It marked the end of the intact family and the end of Sarah's experience of daughterhood, since James Gillespie could in no way function as a father to Sarah. It marked the beginning of Sarah's attempt to define herself as an adult woman and to engage in a life-long process of reckoning.[19] For Sarah, this process involved reconstructing and chronicling her own version of her mother's life, an integral aspect of which was reading and interpreting her mother's diary. Just as important, the process of reckoning involved Sarah's commitment to keeping her diary for over sixty more years.

Emily Gillespie's legacy to Sarah was a complicated one. It was the legacy of a caring, loving mother; at the same time, it was the legacy of a demanding, troubled mother.[20] That legacy was reflected in Sarah's eventual work as a teacher and citizen and in her sense of duty to create a home for other family members. As we shall see, that legacy was also reflected in Sarah's dedication to her diary, her "constant friend," her own "book of the self."

Sarah's diary opens a fascinating window on late nineteenth- and early twentieth-century midwestern American life. More important, it completes a unique mother/daughter record of daily work and thoughts; interactions with neighbors, friends, and colleagues; and destructive family dynamics. Sarah's diary adds significantly to our understanding of mother/daughter relationships, domestic and religious ideologies, and abusive families. The rich tapestry of diary entries offers us insights into the importance of female kinship networks in American life, the valued status of women as family chroniclers, and the fine art of selecting, piecing, stitching, and quilting that characterizes the many forms of women's autobiographies.

"I Am a Good Girl": 1877–1879

Tis better far to learn while we are young
Than to wait till we get old for our
Learning is better than gold.
—from Sarah's diary, January 1, 1877

January 1877

MONDAY 1. New years. I commence to keep a journal to day.
Sarah L. Gillespie

> Tis better far to learn while we are young
> Than to wait till we get old for our
> Learning is better than gold.
> Sarah

MON. JAN. 1. I have not done very much to day. I whittled a little. Henry went to town and got five cents worth of herring for our New Years supper. Ma washed and Pa chopped. Henry and I worked some examples. Cold. [. . .]

WED. 3. It was so cold we could not go to school. making a whip stalk. Henry, Pa, and I took some hay down to Uncle Jerome's and saw the new bridge.[1] It is a very nice one and rests on bars of iron. I got a spool of black thread for me. Henry got the papers. Ma worked on her Sofa cushion. Warmer. [. . .]

SAT. 6. In the forenoon George Trumble was here, he did not come in went down town in the afternoon.[2] Ma got Henry a new suit of clothes, & ribbon necktie. Ma a new comb & hair ribbon. Pa a necktie & herself one, they are very nice. we went down to Willie Scanlans in the evening.[3] The tree's were covered with snow or mist. Chilly. [. . .]

FRIDAY. 12. We went over to the north schoolhouse to visit the school where Nettie Barnard teaches they have from 23 to 25 scholars.[4] the

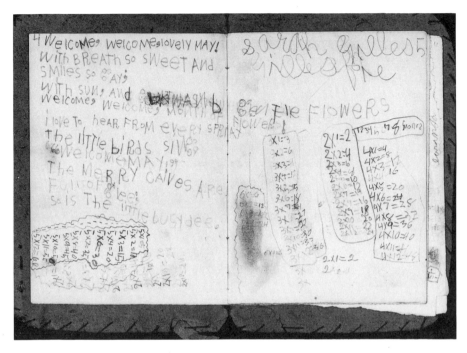

Pages from Sarah's earliest diary, hand-sewn by her mother in 1873. SHSI.

scholars whisper a little more than what is necessary, and make considerable noise for such large schollars as they are. they wrote Essay's the most of them were copied, either out of their books or News-Papers, I know the most of them. Cold. [. . .]

THURSDAY. 16. I helped all day so she [Ma] could finish Pa's Pants to go to the "The Old Settlers Society" to-morrow. I washed all of the dishes, got supper & dinner & made a first-rate jonnie cake. Cold & Snow. [. . .]

MON. 22. We are not going to School any more it is so lonesome up there with only 4 or 5 scholars. Ma worked, she has got a very sore toe, we are going to study at home the rest of the winter. ma says as soon as we get through this arithmetic she will get us another one. Pleasant but Cold. [. . .]

February 1877

[. . .]

WED. FEB. 14. To day is St. Valentines day. I did not send any Valentines nor did not get any. To day was the last day of our school. there were a good many there. Mr. & Mrs. Chapman, Mr. & Mrs. Van Alstyne, Mr. & Mrs. Sellens, Mrs. Morse & Pa, Henry & myself.[5] Ma did not go.

March 1877

THS. 1. To day is Pa's 41st anniversary, we did not have any Party. I made a cake for supper. Pa go to mill. we got our lesson. Pleasant. [. . .]

MON. 5. We cipher, Ma wash, Pa do chores. Pleasant. [. . .]

FRI. 16. get our lesson. go up to Mr. & Mrs. Morse's in the evening on a Surprise. it is their fifteenth anniversary. we had a good time. there were 16 Persons, we gave them a set of glass dishes. they were very much pleased with their presents, it was a surprise they did not have the work done up at all. We had them married over again. we had a splendid good time. Pleasant. [. . .]

April 1877

TUES. 3. I done 24 examples to day. Henry done 19, we go to town, it is very muddy. Sunday evening Barrs livery Stable, the Agricultural Depot & the Blacksmith shop was burned. they saved all of the horses but none of the carriages, he says that his loss is about $3000.00. Dr Barr feels pretty bad over it, all that was left was a buggy-wheel & cook stove & they were all burnt, the stove was cracked & broken, too, it is to bad, me & I thought shure we would tip over in one place. Mud, Mud, Mud. [. . .]

WED. 11. to day was ma's birthday. I went up to Mr. Morse's to spend the afternoon. had a good time. Ella & Victor Esty were here.[6] visitor rented 10 acres. Warm.

THS. 12. get our lesson. ma said her 39th Anniversary was yesterday. Pa says it was a lucky thing that she kept it to her-self begin to wear sun-bonnets. Warm. [. . .]

TUES. 17. go to school we had 12 scholars, the boys act real mean. the teacher said that there was not but 1 boy in the whole school that tended to his own business. Warm. [. . .]

May 1877

[. . .]

FRI. 10. Go to school. kill 2 snakes. a beggar was here. [. . .]

July 1877

[. . .]

SAT. 7. To day I am 12 years old. Warm.

SUN. 8. Did not do much of anything. Read. Warm.

MON. 9. Help ma all day. pick 19 strawberries. Warm. [. . .]

SUN. 15. I will write Now see here ma is going to write in my journal. I wonder what she's going to write. I guess I shall have to ask her. Warm. [. . .]

SAT. 28. Went up to Uncles get some butter stay to supper.[7] I have been sick with the belly-ache.[8] all day yesterday & 2/3 of to day & feel some better. Mr. Camp here to dinner. Camp help load hay. Very warm. [. . .]

August 1877

WED. 1. Henry is makeing him a stand. Help pa. Warm. [. . .]

Written in the upper margin of this page in darker ink are these words, referring to Henry's washstand: "he has it yet 1951 good as new."

MON. 6. Help ma & pa pull weeds in the strawberry patch. I just touched a little young Bird in the nest & all the rest jumped out. I am so sorry. If it would do any good I'd cry. Cool.

MON. 26. Go to School. have 4 scholars. get wet. Miss McCormic teacher.[9] Rain. [. . .]

September 1877

[. . .]

SUN. 2. Go up to Uncle's & over to Aunt Harriets. we got a letter from Uncle Dennis. "He says he is going to the far west across the Missouri into Nebraska."[10] Cold. [. . .]

TUES. 18. Go to school. Ma has been married 15 years to day. We have a surprise party here this evening there were 23 in all. they were married over again. we had supper all kinds of cake pie & best of all water mellons & musk mellons. they presented ma & pa with a set of glass dishes a real nice time we had. moonlight evenings now. Warmer. [. . .]

THURS. 27. we all go to the fair. we had a good time. I got 2 premiums 1 on cake & 1 on bread. Ma has the first premium on a great many things but a few in town are trying to make a fuss about it & say they are not worthy of a premium. ma is a little spunky about it. Foggy. [. . .]

October 1877

[. . .]

SUN. 14. Go and take a ride. pa is quite mad about something. I do not know. Beautiful. [. . .]

FRI. 19. Go to school to day is the last day. speak dialogues pieces & read essays. we had a good time, we went up to Mr. Berry Smith's 25th Anniversary. There were over 50 there. (their silver wedding). we presented them a silver Cake Basket—sugar shell & Castor. they were well pleased with their presents. uncle married them said the ceremony. Rain. [. . .]

December 1877

[. . .]

TUE. 25. got a motto on CardBoard & a pair of slippers, but the slippers were too small, ma is going to exchange them. Henry got a purse pair of clippers & perforated motto. Ma got pa a book "The Royal Path of Life," & ma got herself a morocco pair worth 2.00. they were very nice & a perforated board motto. We (H & I) got a small Christmas tree (A limb of our plum tree) & we hung the presents on it, it looked quite nice. so we did not hang up our stockings. work on my Motto. "What is a home without a mother." foggy, Rainy. [. . .]

MON. 31. To day we bid good bye to our old year & wish that our journal will be filled with pleasant & bright hopes. Pa chopped. we started to go to school, but when we were about half of the way we met Charlie Chapman & he said there was no school until Wednesday, so we turned around & came home. so Henry came home & I stayed at Mr. Morse's until about half an hour then I came home. Henry went to town in afternoon. peace on my calicoes. I help ma some & read etc. froze some last night. Colder. [. . .]

March 1878

FRI. 1. Pa is 42 years old. Henry give him a whipping piece. Help ma. Pleasant in the day in the night Rain. Pleasant. [. . .]

SUN. 17. I am perfectly ashamed of my journal there are so *many* blob & goose tracks (or as pa calls them hens tracks) all the way through. I *must* write better.

Last night the moon had a golden ring
To-night no moon we see.

MON. 18. help ma. work on motto. It looks very nice. I think I will take it to the fair. I forgot yesterday we went to sabbath school we (that is Henry & I) joined the school at the Universalist Church.[11] Henry went in one class & I in another. Henry looked as if he wondered what was coming next & when it did come he looked as if he took a short breath. I know I felt so & to take it all into consideration we were perfect greenies, we each got a book to read until next sabbath. Pa is setting trees along the garden fence & plowing the garden in fact—cleaning up generally. Warm. Pleasant. [. . .]

April 1878

[. . .]

TH. 11. do not feel very well. make syrup. ma & pa went to town leave H & I at home. a beggar stop & a tin smith. I got awful lonesome. ma get some licorice. ma's 40 years old. Windy. [. . .]

FRI. 18. got our lessons. Pa go to town, get a letter from Mrs. Wood wanting me to learn a piece to speak next Sunday. Easter we are to have kind of Exhibition get some herring, hog Cholera Medicine, the papers, and a 10 cent piece changed into pennies for ma get caught in a rain storm. Saw Mr. H. D. Wood. I took off my hat & then my Apron & covered up so as to keep it dry, just as I got home it began to just pour down & then hail (this large around O) If I had not run about 3/4 of the way I would have got soaked through & through. X X X X Rain. [. . .]

May 1878

[. . .]

THR. 3. get lessons. our nice little colty died. pa cried. Betsy felt very bad. we are all so sorry. Warm.

Forgot to say all our little goslings were taken this morning very sudden. pa said they were just going down to the slough & all of a sudden the old goose flew up in the cow yard & made a great fuss. pa looked out of the stable but didn't think much about it, until we looked & looked & looked again, but could not find them. too bad.

Henry & I went up to Morses to see their little wolves. (6) they look quite crabbed. Warm. [. . .]

WED. 22. did not get lessons. help pa build fence. we all go to aunt Hatties & see their nice baby & to uncles. while we were gone 13 of our nicest little turkeys smothered to death. ma felt so sorry about it. ma put an extra quilt over them & fastened with a stick. something she had never done before. Cloudy. [. . .]

FRI. 31. well I have had a pretty good time this month & hope the next I shall have no worse. help ma, etc., my legs ache. Cold. Rain.

June 1878

[. . .]

MON. 3. I am so sorry. those poor old Robins sit on the fence & cry for their little ones, which we think were killed in the hard rain. ma said in the night she thought she heard her turkeys but it must have been those poor little robins. I climbed the tree & ever one was gone. I think it is too bad, did not get lessons. Rain. [. . .]

MON. 10. I forgot to say that 1 of our little ducks got lost some where & we could not find it. I think that it either got stung & it ran in under some of the shrubbery or has got on its back & cannot get up. We are so sorry. that was yesterday. I mean (on sunday). it is too bad. help ma & etc. get lessons. Cold. [. . .]

SAT. 22. get part of lessons. help ma. I am tired ma is ironing & I cannot write very good. Henry go fishing. Quite warm. I forgot to say that pa fell out of the Carriage & hurt his head. [. . .]

July 1878

[. . .]

SUN. 7. I am 13 years old to day. go to Sabbath school wear my new Pink Chambree dress. in the evening we all take a ride & drive way over to Maggie McCormicks, & this is the way I have celebrated my 13th birthday. Very warm. [. . .]

SUN. 28. we did not go to sunday-school. pa got mad at a cow this morning & hurt her very badly & got dragged around through the brush by her it did not hurt him very much. He took & tied a rope around her under jaw & thence her leg so as to bring then very nearly together & then chased her it made her very lame. Willie was here most all day & had a good visit. Cloudy. [. . .]

WED. 31. To day is the last day of July. I help ma. Willie Scanlan commence to cut oats just as we got the turkeys & ducks in under some boards & in a box it began to hail & rain I tell you it rained so hard that we could hear it over two miles. pa said if it was a tornado that we must go down cellar. it is blowing real hard & raining now. Rain. [. . .]

August 1878

[. . .]

SUN. 4. did not go to Sunday School but I wanted to. ma gave me a back-comb. it is made of horn & is very pretty. Ma done my hair up very nice. ma has got the blues. [. . .]

THR. 8. go blackberrying. A wolf caught one of the little lambs but he had to let go of it & pa caught & carried the little lamb down here. he was sure that it would die but we (ma & H & I) in got him & put some tar on every place that it was bitten, & washed the blood off its little head & eyes. the wolf bit it in the places that is where the teeth went in. the worst places were very near the throat & on the eyelid. we tried to feed it some milk. when the sheep came in the yard we carried it out & it found its mother & tried to eat but he acted as if it hurt him & he is so very weak too by losing so much blood. but I guess that he will get well. I hope so anyhow. go to town & gt a chance to ride both ways. Warm. [. . .]

SUN. 11. Ma, Henry & I go to sunday school afoot & we thought that we would go unbeknown to pa, (for he was watching Sheep), but just as we started he saw us & said: I think that that is great, Mr. Wood is minister. Warm. [. . .]

WED. 28. In the after-noon we all go to the Normal Institute it is very nice. when it closed Henry & Pa went home & ma & I went over to Mrs. Houghtons & stayed until time to go to the lecture in evening by Proffessor T. H. McBride of Hopkinton. he told us the earliest History of the world. Pa & Henry come down to the lecture & take us home. Cool Mornings & evenings. Cloudy. [. . .]

September 1878

[. . .]

WED. 4. Henry is 15 years old to day & Ma make a jelly cake & a common cake & put the candles on the motto was this: "When first I saw your face so fair; my heart was filled with anxious care."

I think it was very good. some movers were here to stay all night.
· 2 men is all. I go to town & get drawing paper, & walked both ways
every step. Very warm. [. . .]

MON. 9. work on Handkerchief. get part of lesson. ~~get~~ help ma, etc.
etc. Ma & Pa & I go up to Uncles & get some butter. there were
some movers here & so Henry stayed. when we got home Henry had
gone to bed & is asleep. it's 10:15 P.M. Now I must go to bed. good
night My Journal. Cold & Windy. [. . .]

TUE. 24. Ma help me make a necklace to take to the fair. a flea has got
onto me & I am just covered in blotches & they itch so I cannot
hardly stand it. A wolf came right down to the slough & caught a
sheep & I saw the wolf jerk the sheep until he got it down & then
we hollowed & made just all the noise we could & he left it but he
stopped every 2 or 3 rods & look around as if he were very much
disappointed. Henry go a fishing. I help pa sort out sheep & lambs
to take to fair a little Shorter. [. . .]

THR. 26. we all go to fair have a good time. Warm.

FRI. 27. " " " " " . I took 2 mottoes. straw-work Lampnet &
handkerchief. get the 2nd premium on my handkerchief & on my
straw-work. my Lampnet & all my things but the mottoes were the
only ones there I think I had right to have the 1st premium on them
all. ma got quite a no. of Red & blue Cards. we entered Betsy in the
wrong class or else we would have got the Red Card = $6.oo. we
entered her as a horse of all work & it ought to have been draft-
horse's because she is so slow. Pleasant. [. . .]

October 1878

[. . .]

WED. 2. ma go to town leave me all alone do up all the work in the
morning. Very Pleasant.

THR. 3. did not get lessons. help pa build fence all the afternoon.
Windy. [. . .]

SAT. 5. A wolf caught another lamb he caught it in the left side & tore
the skin off in a very large place as large as Pas hand. Pa & Ma took
it down & let Mr Thorp see it & the butcher would not buy so they
brought it back & done it up ma put the skin that was torn down
back in place & sewed the wool together then she sewed 2 thick-
nesses of cloth over it & sewed it to the wool. it looked like this as
near as I can draw it. [At this point in her diary, Sarah sketched a
sheep with a triangle on its side.] I hope it will get well. Henry took

the sheep up above the railroad & watched them for 2 hour's. while Pa & Ma were gone G. Trumble came & stayed an hour & the other hour I was alone. I done the morning work they gone just 2 hours the Wolf came right down east of the house. Help ma. Warm. [. . .]

SUN. 20. Mr & Mrs Wood our minister & wife are going to Colorado Springs Colorado next week so he preached in the morning & in the even he almost cried to think that they had tried to have a meeting here so long & now must we depart we went in the morn & even both. Warm. [. . .]

SUN. 27. we all go up to Aunt Hatties, she cried because she was so glad that we came. I believe that she & John will separate. he wants to go to Nevada & she will not go & if he goes she says she will never live with him again. we went by way of uncles. Chilly. [. . .]

November 1878

[. . .]

SUN. 10. ma got me a new cap yesterday it is real nice. I put on my new shoes dress & cap & I think they look very nice. I have got my books put up ready to go to school to-morrow all day. Rain. [. . .]

THR. 28. Uncle, Aunty Preston, Aunt Hattie & John & the children we had part of a baked pig for thanks-giving dinner. we expected Dan Ryan & his family but they did not come.[12] it was a very beautiful day just like summer. beautiful. [. . .]

December 1878

Pledge signed by Sarah L. Gillespie
in the village of Manchester Delaware
Co. Iowa. Dec. 5 1878
God—Home—Country.
Our Pledge.

I solemnly promise to abstain from the use or sale of all intoxicating liquors as a beverage & I invoke the blessing of god and the considerate judgment of my friends and neighbors to help me keep this pledge.

Sarah Gillespie

[. . .]

WED. 25. Christmas. go up to Uncles. Uncle John Aunt Hattie & the children Mr & Mrs Libby & Lizzie (their girl) & we were all there &

Susie & all 4 of the children.[13] we had a good time. I got a Cocoanut, China candle-stick, wax candle (red) A yard of satin Ribbon & some crackers. Santa Claus was very good this time. Henry got the same. Cool. [. . .]

TUE. 31. to day is the last day of the year. go to town get 10 cents worth of paper & 10 cents worth of envelopes & 3 cents worth of candy & a 10 ct salt cellar. I gave Henry & May each 6 sheets of foolscap & 6 envelopes for New Years, & Divided the candy equal. get a ride both ways. Warmer.

good bye old year
I am ready for the new.
Amen.

I hope I will have as pleasant a time in 1879 as I had in 1878.
Sarah

January 1879

WED. 1. Henry got me a very nice tooth brush & ma a tack hammer, & I gave what I said & got yesterday. I heard that Florence & Bertha Bailey were to be married to day. Loring R. Loomis son of A. R. Loomis & his nephew were here.[14] the little boy was very cold & stopped to warm. pa bought a black cow of Mr. Loomis. Real Cold. [. . .]

WED. 22. go to school. Henry & Pa & Ma go to town get some oysters & crackers. I walked all the way home, & got so very warm & tired I could hardly stand up. We had some oysters for supper & I found a very hard round kind of stone or something like this o & just about as big. these are the first oysters I have tasted in over a year. pa made ma a present of a pair of kid gloves. Warm. [. . .]

February 1879

[. . .]

SUN. 16. stay at home all day. play ball with Henry. I forgot to say that last mon. a creature stepped on one of the ducks legs & it is very sore it could not walk so I brought it in & put it in a basket with some straw in it, & kept it in the house all last week. let go with the rest Thr. evening. our cow had twin calves while we were gone yesterday & the hogs broke in where she was & ate one of the calves &

the other died this morning. Ma & Henry are ciphering. Pa is out doing the chores & I am writing. . . . [. . .]

March 1879

SAT. 1. stay at home all day I done all of the work up in the morn got dinner & helped ma all I could so as to have her finish my dress but could not quite. Cousin Sarah was over here to day.[15] Thaw.

SUN. 2. Pa is 43 years old to day & pa had a lame side all day. Pa & Henry go to Baptist meeting. ma & I stay at home all day. Rain. [. . .]

SAT. 8. I helped ma all day & got real tired. ma said if she got her work done up in time she would go to town with me. we started after 4 o'clock in the afternoon. we got a ride all the way. we went to Mrs Farlingers & then over to the lecture, H & Pa came down in the evening. I like to hear Mr Stolz talk, it was quite muddy when we got home there was not a turkey in the trees ma was scared & worried, afraid she would not find them. (15 we had) Cool, Wind. [. . .]

WED. 12. To day is the last day of school there were scholars & visitors 48 in all. we had a good many pieces. the north school (part of it) came over, & some of the south school. Hattie Beal & Luella Morse read a paper that teacher composed.[16] Cloudy in the forenoon. Cool. [. . .]

FRI. 28. help ma. Pa went up to uncle Johns when he came back fox (our horse she has been very sick & lame a long time) was lieing down broad side right by the straw stack & was breathing very hard, but after pa went up to A.P. Co. with the milk, we (ma, H, & I) got some hay & some water & bran & fed her it was pretty hard work for her to eat being down so flat but she did. then we went to the house when pa came in at night he said she would be dead in 2 hours. so we go to bed expecting to find a dead horse in the morning, but I hope not she seems to be so week that she can not raise herself. good night. Very Pleasant.

SAT. 29. this morning we sat at the table telling what we dreamed. Henry & I dreamed just the same thing that Foxy was in the stall standing up. Pa dreamed that he saw a black dot (which is a good sign) & ma could not remember what she did dream, when Pa went with the milk this morn we went down where fox was & was standing by her she raised clear up on her side, ma just braced with all her strength and held her until H & I got some straw & put it under her & she stayed that way until after pa came & we fed & watered her, this was before we done up the dishes & we stood there by her she tried to get up & pa helped her & sir! she got up but [pa] had to steady her or else she would fall as it was she had to lean against the stack. (this was about (10 A.M.)) & finally pa kindly held her & rubbed her legs & shoulders & she got up in the stable with Betsy. We all said, Good! & So you see our dream came to pass, arter! all! Uncle John [McGee] was here to dinner pa & him went to town this afternoon he (Pa) told Kinney (horse doctor) he would give himself $10 if he would cure Fox. help ma. I am tired. this morning the sun shone very! very! warm but this afternoon about 5 o'clock it rained & lightened & thundered real hard. Pleasant Rain. [. . .]

April 1879

[. . .]

WED. 2. help ma, get lesson, Aunt Hattie was over stayed 3 1/2 hours had a good time. I got a letter from Mary Tyler Sat she said that she got a good necklace & a writing desk. wish I had some I think I might have too. Cold. A little snow. Cold. [. . .]

FRI. 11. gave ma her shawl pin. she is 41 yrs old to day. I spanked her. 42 times stay out doors all-day ma & I build hen & turkey nests & trim up evergreens. Very warm. [. . .]

May 1879

[. . .]

SAT. 31. last day of May

> Spring gentle spring has ended
> Summer, tomorrow, will be here
> With all her glory and beauty blended
> Thrice welcome with hearty cheer

help ma all day am tired

June 1879

[. . .]

• FRI. 27. go to school. I got sopping more than wet this morning the rain ran off in a stream on my face for all the parasols. But it cleared off by night some so teacher came home with us to stay all night &

till morning. When we went past Mr Chapmans Fred Charlie & their hired men (2) were all snickering & talking about me. I hope they saw all they wanted to. Rain. Warm. [. . .]

July 1879

[. . .]

THU. 3. go to school. tis the last day Speak pieces etc. The teacher gave prizes. she gave Henry in the A Spelling & Grace Ferry in the B spell for leaving off head most times each a Chrome all framed. they were real nice. & those who did not miss a day were Ida Beal & me we each got an Autograph Album mine was Green & hers Red. then she gave nice Cards all around. Pa & Ma & Mr B. Beal, were up to school. Rain. [. . .]

SAT. 5. I feel kindeeye s-i-c-k—t-o—t-h-e—s-t-o-m-a-c-h to day. I am tired, help ma some. Warm. [. . .]

MON. 7. Well! I am 14 yrs. old to day, pretty near sick, finish Braiding that Chemise tho. Warm.

Almost sick, in the fournoon But I help ma Fry cakes in the afternoon I got very warm & so did ma. Very Warm. [. . .]

THU. 10. Henry & I waded in the slough we had a good time. help ma she made & cut out for me a new pair of Drawers & skirt & made me a new part of a chemise for me & sewed on my white Dress. they are very very nice. Cool. [. . .]

SUN. 13. I went to S. School Congregationalist & wore my new suit of clothes. Pa went with me as far as the hill & then watched me the rest of the way on acct of tramps. Pooh! what do I care for Tramps, Cousin Sarah went with me & stopped at Aunt Hatties & got my dinner ma said I must not stop there much. I wont Aunt Hattie has enough work to do without my there I walked there & Back I am very tired & warm. [. . .]

THU. 31. Piece on quilt. I intend to take it to the fair if I get it done I think it will be nice. Warm.

August 1879

[. . .]

WED. 6. Help ma all day In the afternoon I made another Apron for myself. Mr Farlinger Here My Ears are very sore. Ma opened one next to my ear but not where it was pierced & squoze an awful lot out. Cool evening. Warm. [. . .]

WED. 27. There was a man stopped that rode with Mr. McGee & gave us a letter that Aunt Hattie sent up containing the sad news that Grandma had Broken her Arm & that Doc's Chapel & Elley came twice a day to see her. they are in hopes of her getting Better ma feels sorry & so do I. It will go pretty hard, on an old lady like her But I think she will get well. I hope so any way. Sarah. [. . .]

September 1879

[. . .]

THU. 4. Henry is 16 yrs old to day Aunt Hattie Susie & all the children, except Ada & Baker were here. Uncle here to supper I went with Betsy all alone & took Aunt Hattie & the children home. ma & I took milk to the creamery. Freddie fell off of the porch & knocked his tooth all loose. he walked off the Porch a purpose & then he would cry. Aunt Harriet was awful Fidgety all the time. I never saw the ~~Beat~~ she was afraid that Betsy would run off the Bridge when there was no more danger than a shrimp running off of the ground. ma killed a turkey that got hung in the fence last night. Chilly. [. . .]

SUN. 21. Got into trouble all day H nearly broke my Back & hit my head with a walnut & I won't know what I done to him I know I hit him & ma said I always hurt him worse than he did me, but I know Better than that I feel like flying some times & wish I could. . . . [. . .]

SUN. 28. ma & Henry & I go up to Uncles after some butter. Uncle gave me a puppy that is nearly a year old his name is Jack his mother is pure blood shepherd & came from Scotland. Oh! he is a nice fellow some movers stayed here last night 2 men & 2 horse, there were some Emigrators went past here to day with 5 Jacks & Jennies just as high as the wagon box some were very nearly black & some a very light drab & there was one little young one not any higher than the table & about as big as a good sized dog but his Ears & tail was all of him about he looked funny enough & they asked $100 for him. Real Windy. [. . .]

Last of September:
I shall always Remember.
S. G.

October 1879

THU. 2. did not go to school on acc't of rain. Henry wanted the Umbarella & all I said was that if Henry did not want it I did & he would not take it on that acct, when I told ma he could take it if he wanted to, she did not believe me, & she dont believe what I say but if Henry says any thing she believes him. do some examples Chas Chapman goes to the Academy. I wish I could. 3 loads of movers here to stay all night. one of them played on an accordian it is real muddy H got wet through. Rain.

FRI. 3. go to school. Warm.
> The Autumn leaves begin to fall
> I can hear the winters call. [. . .]

FRI. 10. Go to school. The Boys act like very bad boys. Henry was sitting astride the fence & (the boys have been making fun of H & I ever so long) Will Vanalstyne & Fred Chapman come up 1 on 1 side & the other on the other side & caught hold of his legs. H did not like that so he hit Fred on the head & that made him let go & Will still hung on so Henry went after him & told Wm that if he did not want to get into trouble to leave him alone & then Will pitched onto him & I told the teacher & she started out there but they ran & H went to the steps & sat down. we stood where we were a few minutes, & then we (teacher & we girls) started back to the schoolhouse & then those boys went back where Henry was the teacher said it would not be well for them to touch Henry, & every time the teacher would start to go out there & call to them they would Run. But after awhile teacher & we went in the schoolhouse, & the boys (after awhile) came too, & Fred C put Dees hat down in the Privy & made "[Dee] cry, & the teacher" [made] Will & Mat & Fred take their seat's & sent Dee after whips down to the Willows. when he got back it was time for school to call, so teacher gave the boys a little speech & then she called them out one at a time & whipped them over the head & legs & she whipped little Charlie Vanalstyne in his seat. O but the boys were mad. ma came to school she was so disgusted with those boys that she wouldn't make any remarks. [. . .]

TUE. 14. go to school. this forenoon Mrs Vanalstyne came to school & called the teacher out on the stoop & had a real talk with her & when the teacher came in the schoolroom she was crying. little Charlie said that "his mother was going to give that old teacher a regular blowing up" & I guess she did. Charlie acted just as bad as could be

& the teacher didn't say a word to him only once, or the rest of the boys either. [. . .]

November 1879

SAT. 1. go to school last day Miss Thompson gave me one prize of box of stationery .50 cts. she also gave Susie Stewart the same in B spelling & Dora Millet got a nice knife. very pretty in C spell. Besides giving cards all around & very very nice ones too. Hurrah for the first snow storm. Hurrah for the 1st Snow Storm. [. . .]

THU. 6. help ma! help ma!! help ma!!! all day Pleasant

FRI. 7. ma & I & H & pa go to town, ma & H & I go over to the Academy to see about going Mon. ma got some New Appletons 5th Readers for us. ma took her premium money to send us & I was awful sorry, too. Mr Kissell asked us to read from them new Readers & I faltered more than I ever did before I had Rather Read before 500 than just him alone. help ma. Rain. [. . .]

MON. 10. commence to go to the "Academy" to school.[17] we study "Appletons 5th Reader" "Robinsons Progressive Arith" "Read & Kellog" "Gran and Sumtoms Spelling" & that all. like it very well, but seems a little different from our school up here. Rain. [. . .]

WED. 26. Go to school they did not have only 1/2 a day of school because Mr Kissells was not there & also Thanksgiving. I had the colic the worse kind all the forenoon so I stopped to Aunt Harriets they have a new store table. Ring for Aunt H & a Watch for Uncle John. when both teachers were down stairs hearing classes, Mr. Cananda & Amsden turned the clock ahead 13-, tied the thumb Bell so it would not ring, lit the lamp sat it on the table & put Mr. Denios Cap & coat on one of the pointers & put it on the stage. & then Amsden run but Mr. Van stayed. It has been a stormy day. 1st Snow 2nd Rain 3rd sleet & Rain. [. . .]

December 1879

MON. 1. go to school. last night there was some great mischief done the pedulums to the clocks were both hidden, & the one the clock upstairs we dont know anything about, & then the chairs were all inverted & the organ meddled with so they could not play on it & a light of glass was broken also. at 2.30 P.M. Mr Kissell called the school to order & gave out these questions No 1 "was you in

this Academy building anytime between 5 o'clock P.M. & 7 o'clock
A.M. between the 1st & 2nd of December. No. 2. do *you know*
of anyones being in this Academy Building between the above
time mentioned." and everyone answered no Sir to both questions
except Mr Kusay Clark & Avery Amsden & then Mr Kissell told
them to take the C room down stairs & then he followed them.
Foggy. [. . .]

SAT. 6. it snowed last night but has melted now, sloshy. Ma & Pa go to
town, Ma got Henry a Collar Button, 35 cts & to Day a peddler
stopped ma got a pair of linen table cloths & a pair of very pretty
handkerchiefs for H & my Christmas present. Henry dont know it
though. the foundation is White dotted with red in the center a
wreath of Red leaves & Roses around the border. they are linen or
silk finish. I have a cold & a sore throat. Sloshy. [. . .]

FRI. 19. Go to school. It is the last day. they had the society nearly all
day had a trial of Mr Blair & Wolcott for not paying a fine. Wolcott
payed his fine but Blair's was suspended for one term. we had but
one class all day. Reading. Ma was there she has a New Hat & a
Dolman. they look nice. we had exercises in the evening from 7 till
15 min after 9 P.M. then retired to our respective homes. Mr Kissell
is going away from Manchester he wont stay in such a *bad* place &
I dont blame him any. I am sorry to have him go, but they will have
school next term just the same only Different teachers. I think we
shall stay at home. Henry & I both had a declamation, some Essays
& Music. finished or made the exercises of the evening.[18] It is Cold.
[. . .]

THURSDAY 25. Christmas. Santa Claus was a very decent kind of
a gentleman this time he-she brought me an Acc't Book or journal. 4 handkerchieves one silk & linen finish with a very nice
wreath of flowers around it. & 2 white ones & H & I traded a
white one for a red one. so I have 4 & then the *best of all* was
a set of cuffpins they are very nice they are a plain body with 2
tinted leaves on it colored & then I got a journal. 240 pages in it.
we went down to Aunt Harriets Ma. Henry & myself to spend
Christmas. Mr & Mrs McGee were there. Frankie got a drum &
Sarah got a trunk & Fred got a 2 wheeled bell & Mr & Mrs Farlinger were there also. Henry got a shirt, set of studs 4 handkerchieves & journal. I had my first sleighride With Mr McGee home.
I am totally bankrupt. −24 below Zero at sunrise this morning.
Oh! pa got a check of $3.37 for Ducks from Ma for *his* Christmas
present. 24 below Zero at sunrise. Cold.

TUES. 30. Stay at home all day. Warmer.

WED. 31. 1879 last day of 1879 very Pleasant. help ma some ride on
sled same as Monday.

> "Good Cheer." "Good Cheer."
> "For the happy New Year."
> "Is smiling gladly before you"
> "And merry Bells ring"
> "And Happy Hearts sing"
> Good Cheer, Good Cheer
>   To the Chorous."

CHAPTER TWO

"A Perfect Woman Nobly Planned": 1880–1882

A perfect woman nobly planned,
To warn, to comfort and command;
And yet a spirit warm and bright
With something of an Angel's light.
—from Sarah's diary, January 1, 1880

A Christmas present to
Miss Sarah L Gillespie
Manchester   Delaware Co.
Iowa
December 25th 1879
By her mother
Mrs E. E. Gillespie[1]

January 1880

THURS. 1. We go up to Uncles to spend New Years. Pa did not go just because he did not want to & they all thought he might have come. Mr. Griffin & his wife & children Lizzie, Clement, Mary, Sadie, Burdette, Simeon & Ethel. Mr & Mrs Bailey. Susie & Florence. Clement, his wife & 2 children Belle & Joel. 27 in all. they had splendid dinner, Oyster Cakes cookies. Pies & An English Plum pudding. I had a splendid good time. Pleasant. [. . .]

TUES. 6. The Academy commenced yesterday, we did not go. study at home, tho. I began on Page 30 in Arith & Henry on 250. ~~help ma some~~ help pa on Barn, and Help Henry shingle on woodhouse. Misty.

WED. 7. Ma is sick has been all day is a little better to night. Mr. Farlinger helping pa on Barn I made some bread 3 loaves, a pie & a cake & done all the work only pa help set supper table & brought in an armfull of wood. I am nearly fatigued. ma has a nervous head-ache. Pa says the Weather is Foggy. ma says Rainy & Henry says Wet & I say it was All of them. Mixed. [. . .]

WED. 14. did not get lessons. ma could not help both of us at once so I couldnt get only 4 examples in Arith & 1/2 lesson in Algebra. & Henry is about 100 pages in arith ahead of me & in algebra 15. & I dont think that is fair play. ma dont believe what I say either this morn ma helped me in algebra I got about 18 pages then this afternoon Henry was 5 pages behind me. (Henry studied in Arith in the forenoon & ma helped him whenever he asked it) so ma & Him sat down & told me that she would help Henry get his algebra lesson now & I could study my arith. so I went to work & ma would not listen so I went at *my* algebra she would not listen to that neither so I went down to the ice. & I had the head it was after 3 o'clock, & I did not feel well & cried. But ma was very willing to help me but I could not study. & now good Night *dearest* Journal. a slight *chilly* wind. Pleasant. [. . .]

WED. 28. Ma & I went to town in the afternoon. Pa went & took us. got Henry a new pair Boots $3.50. Henry & I went to Literary in the evening. Ma & Pa stay to Aunt Hatties until we arrived. Aunt Hattie is in a sputter with Mrs. Collier its too bad. Saw most all the girls I new, & Mr Butler But not to speak to. He is not Mr Kissell, I do not think But guess he is a good man & Instructor.[2] Mertie Sherman I thought had the best piece and spoke it best.

February 1880

[. . .]

WED. 18. (I did not write in my journal Wed nor Thu. Will write now have pretty near forgot what I done.)

Pa & I went to town & stayed at Aunt Hatties 'till noon. Then I went over to visit the Academy. Saw the New Professor. think he is real good looking & generally has a smile on his face. He gives a good explanation. The Scholars laugh & play more than they did last Term. Still think I shall like him. no danger but that we will do. Walked home. A *cold chilly* wind. [. . .]

FRI. 20. Ma made a party for "Uncle's Birth day party"

There were 14 her. namely: Uncle, Susie, her children, Ada, Baker, Clifford, & Cora, Aunt Hattie & her Children Sarah, Frankie & Fred, & then Ma Pa Henry & myself. had a good dinner. 2 turkeys tarts 2 kinds of cake (Pork & Common) Butter, Etc. Pa has just gone to Carry Aunt Harriet & her Children home it is 20 of 9. time I was asleep. It is real pleasant out doors. Moonshiny. Uncle has sprained his hand said he fell off the fence on the frozen ground. & then the other day he fell off a load of hay his hips strck the fence. Pa's just come home Did not get lessons. Chilly. [. . .]

SUN. 22. Ma & Pa went to Church. We stay at home all day it is just Beautiful. Pleasant.

MON. 23. Done some examples in Algebra. tried to study my Book Keeping. have got to Copying the memoranda in "Ledger." & it is a perfect puzzle. O. Dear is what I feel like saying. ma says I stink of the Barnyard have been cleaning horse stable & Etc. with horses to day. Old Nellie has got a lamb 5 days old. a real pretty creature. Still & Bright & Calm & Beautiful. [. . .]

March 1880

MON. 1. Pa is 44 yrs old to day. help ma some. Chilly. [. . .]

TUES. 16. Ma & I went up to Mr. Benj. Smiths in the morning staid till after 4 P.M. I got some of Mrs. Millers & Mrs. Smiths hair to put in some hair flowers. In the Evening when we were getting ready to go to bed had boots & shoes off & our Clothes unfastened at 8 o'clock there came a knock at the door & in came about 30 visitors. there was a perfect surprise 6 loads. there were Mr & Mrs Fred Durey, Della Durey William Durey. Jennie Stewart (Mrs Fred Dureys daughter) her husband Pratt Stewart & their two children Lillie & Pearl. Thad Smith & his wife. her daughter "Emma" her husband & baby. (I dont know her nor his (her husband) Sir name) Mr Harris, Mr Freeman Smith, & his 2 sisters. Flora Graham & her sister, & I dont know the rest. They staid till 3 o'clock. A.M. they had a Mask which caused a great deal of fun with Mr Dureys Plug hat to put on with it. Mrs Durey had the most & made the most fun with it they had pepper & *other* kinds of Candy & we popped popcorn. O! What a looking floor! & then at 1 o'clock A.M. they spread the table with many delicious kinds of victuals & chicken they had a splendid time I hope. But they had all just gone 2.30 but Pratt Stewart & his wife & baby & he stepped out to get his horses they had broken loose & gone home too. Pratt came to the door & said "dont be frightened, my team have run away but I will go right after them stay here till I come etc. so he went, & caught them away beyond Mr. Bird Beals. the team caught up with the rest had passed one team & ran into the next when 2 of the boys who came horse back though there was no driver stopped them & one of them (the boys) came back with Mr Stewart. they didnt break a thing. ~~Jennie~~ Mrs. had let her mother take Pearlie home with her. Mrs. Stewart was just as tired as she could be & nervous too so it was after 3 when they had all gone. they said there didnt over 1/2 come that they had invited I dont know what we would have done with them because the room (kitchen) was crowded as it was & they couldnt go into the other rooms at all. *hope they will come again.* Good Morning. Pleasant. [. . .]

April 1880

THURS. 1. Pa was going to town this morning. ma & I got ready & then ma made up her mind not to on acc't of the mud. So we staid at home. Mr. Waite an Agent (has been here several times) was here to day. ma sent for a Dictionary (Websters Unabridged) & pa bought a Book called "The American Stock book & Farrier" of him. so I guess it was all right we did not go. Pa said that East of here a horse would go in the mud nearly to his body. it is very Cloudy.

FRI. 2. Ma & Pa went to town. Henry & I stay at home. Muddy. [. . .]

THU. 8. Did not go to school. have the "Belly" ache, & headache. Pleasant.

FRI. 9. go to school. I did not get my lesson in BookKeeping because I hadn't any ink at the school. Professor Sells "wanted to know if there wasn't any ink in town." why I told him I supposed so. "well" he said "that was no excuse" I *must* & had *got* to *have* this lesson & also Mondays lesson, & I dont know whether I can do it or not. We got Websters Unabridged Dictionary by express to day. Rode home with Uncle. Chilly. [. . .]

SAT. 17. Mr Alcock here yet Studied some.[3] I'll tell you just what I think. I think that I have got to many studies (6) I can not get any of my lessons, all the way I do in Arith, is just to set the statements down in another book & copy the figures on the board. & thats all I know about it. O Dear! I feel like not going to school some times. & my book-keeping I dont half get it I can't nor any of the rest of my studies.

> O what weary world this is
> I think it's a pity that I ever is (Rose)
> E'er the sun shall set twice
> I'll feel as if I were in a vise.
>
> S.G.

(Isn't that lovely) Windy
    composed by my
    own self in the
    Evening [. . .]

MON. 19. Go to school. Ma said I might give up ~~Arithmetic~~ (here what am I thinking of) Book-keeping. I awfully hated to but think it is best. I will now go in the penmanship class. Chilly. [. . .]

May 1880

[. . .]

SUN. 9. Ma & I & Henry went up to the woods I got a small boquet of flowers violets, cowslips dandelions & other yellow flowers. Ma got awful mad at pa she told him she would leave him just as soon as H & I could take care of ourselves if he did not do different. Warm. [. . .]

FRI. 14. Went to school. Professor Butler said that he thought it was a pity that I could not come yesterday & that I had to stay out at all. I had such good lessons when I was there & it took off so much when I stayed out. I think so too. Pa might have taken us yesterday. Pleasant. [. . .]

SAT. 29. Well Sarah you was at home all day trimming, or rather making ruffles for collars etc. Rained.

The following entry is in Emily's handwriting.

SUN. 30. Do not neglect to write in your journal every day.
        'A stitch in time saves nine'
        Then write every day, for an incident lost
        now & then, you might sorely repent
        A day once forgotten can be gained at no cost.
                      E. E. H. G.

June 1880

[. . .]

WED. 9. Went to school. We thought there was a Lyceum so we stayed I was mad they didn't even give it out that there was not to be any I said I would not go to another one this term you see my things were all locked in there. ma laughed. Muddy. [. . .]

Sarah with books and lunch pail while a student at the Manchester Academy, ca. 1881–1882. SHSI.

FRI. 25. Went to school in the morning on purpose to see Mr. Butler surprised. We could not get the books there before Mr Butler did so one of the girls told him he was wanted out doors and just as soon as he was out Lizzie Allen went and put the present on the table so when he came in he saw them his face turned red & then he laughed & Etc. He told me *that we need not be examined in* Arith. I went up to Aunt Hatties in the forenoon & in the afternoon I went over to Alice Wilson's but they had company and Alice didn't say very much to me so I went over town where ma was and we went to the "Contest" in the evening Miss Genevieve Parker got the prize a $10 gold medal. Good. Pleasant. [. . .]

WED. 30. Ma went to town at 10.30 A.M. and got back 4.30 P.M. Pa & Henry were above the rail-road in the hay field so I was here all alone all that time when I saw a tramp coming I would lock up the house, go down back side the garden a [*sic*] watch them until they had gone then I would go back again and watch for ~~another~~ ma. ha! ha! I didn't get lonesome ma got me a nice bird cage. Mr Loomis brought her home. many thanks. Warm.

July 1880

[. . .]

MON. 5. Ma & Henry & I went to the Celebration. Pa was to work above the R. R. He said. he saw some fellows down here around the house so he came down and when he got here he saw that the cellar door was open and thought he had them down there & went to fastening the door with stones etc. then he started down back-side the garden to call Sellens (But he did not come) when he got back they were down in the slough going toward the R. R. with coats over their shoulders. Pa started after them they ran, and he chased them to the RR when both stopped. (Pa he caught nearly up with them) drew razors and the big one took a large stone and threw at pa's head it was as large as his two fists he was about a rod from Pa when he threw it and with all the force he had. Pa dodged it fell on his knee's they both ran. pa chased them across the R.R. to the other gate and then came into the house. they broke the bolt on the inside cellar door to get in. pulled the catch part off and then screwed it back on only that one screw was left on the shelf they took $3 and Henry's shirt stud from him a 50¢ from ma & a 5¢ and 2 ore piece (pocket) from me. it came from Ireland Luke Scanlan brought it from there when he came dated 1858.[4] [. . .]

FRI. 9. Am not very well ah! Warm.

SAT. 10. Will Scanlan here ma went to town am not well to day either ah! Warm. [. . .]

SAT. 17. Ma & Pa go to town ma got Henry some things to peddle, a Satchel, Buttons, needles, pins, towels, combs, thimbles, h'dk'f's, hose, shoelaces, pipes, fishlines, Etc. got me a yd. of Ribbon 25¢. Warm. [. . .]

FRI. 23. Henry went peddling Fri. got $1.11¢ Ma is making her a new dress. it will be very pretty when it is done. Warm. [. . .]

August 1880

SUN. 1. stay at home all day. Warm.

MON. 2. Ma & I went after black-berries in the forenoon did not get any. Ma & Pa went to town stayed from 1 until 6 P.M. I washed and done the work. Ma got me two new dresses Poplin & Gingham and also an apron (calico for one) & another dress. and some for herself. a suit of Clothes for Henry, pants for Pa. towels thread Etc. Pleasant. [. . .]

FRI. 6. Sick all day had a sick-head-ache and dysentery. Warm.

SAT. 7. Was *better.* Sewed on dress all day. tired. [. . .]

THUR. 12. Ma & I went to town, got Henry a new stock of goods also the mail which brought sad news. 2 letters from Tylers, One from Nellie to Ma & one from Mary to me. The sad death of their mother. She was sick but 2 week's, Nellie said. "O! My Dear Poor Ma! I loved her so and to think I can never see her again almost kills me some times" She died July 23rd 1880 5 o'clock 5 min in the Evening. Mary said it seemed so odd to see Nellie dressed in Black trimmed with crepe walking around the yard, and theres poor dear little Mable left to her care. she sent 2 pansies out of her ma's flower garden, and told all about it.

Oh! its awful for them. I hope I & H will never be left so. I thank the Lord that we have been spared! Mary said they could scarcely bear. I *pity* them. I wish I could go out there & see them. ~~also got a letter~~

Also got a letter from Grand-Ma. she's well said Aunt Mary is Married. again. Real warm. [. . .]

MON. 23. Did not do much of any-thing. Pa is going to work his own farm next summer. has commenced to plow.

O! Dear! Warm. [. . .]

THUR. 26. Henry went to town I sew on my dress. have had a stitch in my side all day. Pa tore Floras blanket in about 20 pieces I am mending it [sketch of torn blanket]

Ma tired out Baking & washing. Pa was mad at Ma because I wrung part of the clothes for her, did not come in to eat supper till 9:10 P.M. it was cold. Mrs Smart is dead. Mrs. McGees mother. [. . .]

September 1880

[. . .]

SAT. 4. Henry 17 to day, gave him his card. Pa said at breakfast ~~that~~ to Ma "If you send them children to school, *you* will have to borrow the money some-where." Ma told us we would have to give up going to school. . . . Ma & Pa went to town 9.30 A.M. got back 3.30 P.M. Ma got Henry a new hat & rubbers. made his pair of pants finished them 12 Mid-night. I sat up & waited, she got some peaches 1 box $1.00 canned the most of them, i.e. (preserves & pickles.) to night (4 qrts). Pa changed his mind I guess because we *are* to go to school after *all* Pa and Ma went to Aunt Hatties they all say that boy looks just like ma. Rev E. R. Wood is back But his name is E. R. Wood M.D. or Dr. Wood. Ma & Pa saw him he is at Clarence hotel. He gave Ma some of his cards. Pleasant. [. . .]

FRI. 17. Went to school in forenoon. Went to fair in afternoon did not cost us any-thing. I got premium on my beans 1st premium too, I'm going to give ma 1/2 for shelling them, then I let her keep the beans too. The boys had a bicycle race on the 1/2 mile course. Their names were Wm Foster, Frank Abbot, & J. Toogood I think or else J. White. Will Foster won. 2 min & some seconds. Real Warm. [. . .]

October 1880

[. . .]

SAT. 9. In fore-noon help ma do up work. In afternoon I was helping Ma sew on my new poplin dress. Mr & Mrs Walt H Butler came to make us a call. Henry was off fishing. Pa was in field plowing. Ma & I were here. I was *kindy* surprised, tho was *very glad* they came. I was sorry we had not any carpets, nor did not have it cleaned up better. well may be we will next time they come. hope so. Henrys got sore throat. Pa about sick. "And all the trees are stripped & bare." Chilly. [. . .]

SAT. 30. Ma & Pa went to town took stove pipe so we had no fire. It is getting Winter. I chrocheted me a mitten. Cold.

November 1880

[. . .]

SAT. 20. Henry go skating. When pa went over to Mr Beal's to husk corn (at noon) I went with him, It turned cold & began to snow at 3 o'clock so we started home when we got to Wm. Scanlan's we looked back & there pa had spilled 3 or 4 bushels of corn all along the road. He went back to pick it up. I came home. (I expected to find ma gone she said as soon as we went at noon, she was going to town) We could not see 5 rods it snowed & blew so fast & hard. When I got home, Ma had just got a good fire. she had gotten Henry a new cap, new boots, Etc. Me a new flannel dress (mostly blue & black) Henry froze his ear. Snow. [. . .]

THURS. 25. ThanksGiving. Uncle was here had turkey Etc. Pleasant. [. . .]

SUN. 28. at home all day. Read. Henry went to church. Congregation-alist. Pa make some pudding. the weather is getting colder & colder. fire burns like snow, & "what will the robin do then." Pa says the weather was mild. Ma says lowery. Henry says cool. I think it was Pleasant but cold. Sew on my new dress. Ma sew on it too. help ma. I made me a new pair of drawers. Chilly. [. . .]

December 1880

WEDNES. 1. Winter brings cold frosts & snow's. Yet still I help in natures growth, With snow I warm the grass & grain Till Spring shall bring it back again.

Ma & Pa went up to Uncles. Pa got a calf of Uncle. Don't see what he wants so many calves for, Mr Chapmans have moved to town. Glory. (good-bye). I made me a new cotton-flannel chemise comes below my knees. I've got a canker sore mouth. John McGee has got back from railroading he went 7 mos ago. got back Thursday. Snow last eve a little Cold. Wind. [. . .]

SAT. 25. Christmas. I got a portmonaie a Red Morroco with 4 pocket. Henry got a collar button Pa a purse & Ma a portmonaie. We all go to town. Pleasant. [. . .]

January 1881

[...]

FRI. 7. Go to school. I couldnt hardly get home would not I guess if I had have not got a ride part way. My head felt as If it would break. my throat was sore from ear to ear & I had the ~~regular~~ stomach-ache. Did not eat only a little breakfast. had cold dinner etc. Is what made it, ma & pa went up to Vanalstynes & to Benj. Smiths. Real Cold. [...]

TUES. 18. Go to school. In the evening we went to the play "Merchant of Venice" at City Hall. It was for the benefit of the Academy Library. Pleasant. [...]

February 1881

[...]

SAT. 5. Finish one strip of my embroidery for my new muslin apron. Heres the way it will be when it's done. red floss. At home all day. Cloud. Wind. [...]

SAT. 26. ... My new dress (debage trimmed with red) is done was finished Mon or Tues. We (Pa & Ma & I) went up to Billy Williams 3 or 4 mi. west of Masonville. It rained *awful* we were wet through when we got there. They were all well. we got home 6 P.M. Henry stayed at home. He must have been lonesome.

March 1881

TUES. 1. Pa is 45 yrs. old to day. had oysters & Crackers. Rice puddings Etc. bad cold. Cold. [...]

SAT. 5. Ma & Pa went to town. they had a "spat" I guess ma told me all about it. Oh! drifts. Pleas.

SUN. 6. at home all day. Read Etc. The cars have not been past for 3 days. They went to day though. they had 2 engines each with 6 drive wheels, & on the head one had a D——l's Bunter. Then there was one Engine with two cars to carry the men (60). For all the force they had they got stuck out in the curve. came from the East. The snow is about 12 ft deep, & 16 or 18 ft on the sides. Right straight down to the rails. Oh! It looked grand! Very Bright. [...]

FRI. 11. I was nearly sick abed with the sick-head-ache. Ma gave me *cat*-(nip) tea. Etc. (Ma aint any better.) Very Blustery. Couldnt see to the Barn hardly. Snowing too. Blow Snow. [...]

SAT. 27. I help ma paint my room the hall & other bedroom. the stairs
Etc. Am tired. head-ache. ate too many prunes for supper. [. . .]

April 1881

FRI. 1. April fools day. We did not go to school on acc't there was none
to day. Mr. Butler could not get wood in town. Aunt Hattie & Uncle
John have moved into the Carpenter house right near us.[5] Hummy!
Hum! Pleasant.

SAT. 2. Help ma paint my room & the chamber yesterday & am about
sick to day. we have been putting down carpets in Henry's & my
rooms. My head aches. Snow very deep in the road yet. Cold. [. . .]

SAT. 9. Go to school to make up for last week Friday drill. Henry spoke
to day in Elocution Class! One little bird has hatched. Pa took &
Came after us. Ma grained the hall yesterday. We have got 5 turkey
eggs. Botany will be interesting when we get the flowers. Amy
Boggs, Lizzie Allen & I went out in the hall to study. (rest much.)
Sweet sixteen Mr. Cates said. that Susie Brayton was not going to
teach after all. I told her her mother wouldn't let her. Damp.

MON. 11. Go to school. Jennie Wood's sitting with me now. good. Algebra & Geometry are dull someway lately. in A 331, just in Solid
Geom. —frill. Ma was 41 to day. I would have gotten Ma something
if I had had the money. Snow. [. . .]

MON. 25. Go to school. Uncle John is helping pa. About 2 doz. of the
scholars have left school. Mr. B—— suspended 3 boys for playing
quoits after he had forbidden them not to, namely Jerimie Rundell
(too bad), E. J. Healey & Lawrence Doggett. Rain in night. [. . .]

May 1881

[. . .]

WED. 4. Uncle Henry Hawley & Grandpa & folks have sold out. H
[Henry Hawley] is going to Cheboygan to buy him a place. Ma &
Aunt Harriet think Grandma is insane.[6] hope not. go to school. have
head ache. Warm.

   ~~ma & I go down to Aus~~ [. . .]

MON. 30. Decoration Day. go to school. Alice Eldredge & I went over
to the grave-yard, looked around until it rained in the evening. Very
Warm & Sultry.

TUES. 31. Last day of May. Examination in University Algebra. Guess I was about 50%. Dont know. I am not feeling well at all. Rain hard. Warm.

June 1881

[. . .]

THUR. 2. Go to examination, in Analysis & Botany. Henry was 88% in Botany, I dont know how much I was. At 3 P.M. Arbuckle read an essay (a real good one) on "Habits."[7] then we parted for this term. He said "Good bye Sarah" & the smile on his face I shall never forget. Mrs Webster was not there on acc't of head-ache. I went & staid with her over an hour I guess. then I bade her gooydbye, as also Miss Randall, I like her *very* much. I wonder why Mary Tyler does not write to me. I am getting to begin to think she has forgotten me almost. Rain. [. . .]

THUR. 16. help ma. done up the mornings work. Clement Griffin (& his dog) was here about 1 1/2 hrs.[8] Ma was strawberrying that plaguey dog caught one of ma's little turkeys, right before my eyes & hurt another. do not know whether he caught any more or not. Ma declares she will tell Griffin to keep his ~~doggie~~ d-o-g-g-i-e at home or else have him killed. Henry is making some door-screens for Uncle John. 2 @ 50¢. I made me a new apron out of some of the stuff that Ma makes the window curtains of. Quite pretty though. Pa & Henry have gone to bed. 10.30 P.M. sleepy. hoe in garden. Why does not Mary write to me? I wonder. Extremely warm, in shade 88 above zero. [. . .]

TUES. 28. Ma & Pa go to town in the fore-noon. Ma got me a Bunting dress real pretty, nearly corn color. Henry a pr. pants. & Hat. Pa a pump etc. some Huckle-berries. an Umbrella. In the afternoon Pa drag. up by R.R. He tried I guess to work himself & team both to death. He is sick, cross. Horse's dripped with sweat. Too bad. If he works so (in that way) he wants every one else to around him. Sultry. [. . .]

July 1881

[. . .]

THURS. 7. At home. Uncle John is here cutting hay.—Emma Brook & children (Maud, Gail & Bertie) were here in afternoon. They had not had any dinner I know by the way they acted. I had a queer dream last night: Dreamed as I was coming home from School. I caught 2 doves. Hattie Beal helped me. It seemed when I went past the P. O. I got a letter, too. When I got home thought I would read my letter while holding the doves with white top to their heads, white on tip of tail. & half the wings white yellow eyes. I read. (It was from Mary Tyler.) She wrote & said she dreamed I had 2 doves white top of head, white on tip of tail. Etc. Well! Well! I have told that dream. Wonder what it will reveal. Rain last night . . .

Am 16 yrs old to-day. Sweet sixteen. s-w-e-e-t. Warm.

FRI. 8. We heard last Sunday that Pres. Garfield was shot, not dead hopes of recovery.[9] was shot 9.30 A.M. Sat. morn. was shot by an Italian lawyer of Chicago. the man was caught on the spot. Too bad.

Rake & hay for Pa all the forenoon.

pick rasp-berries all or nearly or half nearly the afternoon. Will Denton is serenading this part of the country with his mowing machine. tis after 10:30 P.M. moon-shiny, nights. Skeeto bites. Very Warm. 91 in shade. [. . .]

WED. 13. Ma is just about sick abed to day. feels better to-night. Help Ma. got supper. It is arter 10 o'clock & I'm sleeper. We can see the comet yet.

The Great Bear ✶ ✶ ✶ ✶ ✶   ✶ North Star
(Ursa Major)
or
Big Dipper ✶ ✶ ✶ ✶ ✶   I'm sleepy. *Warm.* [. . .]

August 1881

[. . .]

FRI. 12. Ma & Pa go to town in forenoon. In the afternoon Pa, Ma & I went over to the river. Pa to wash the buggy. Ma caught 11 fish I caught 2 doz or more grass-hoppers, ugh! I let one fall in the creek. Pa carried Ma & I across the river he tho't I wasn't as heavy as Ma. I tho't sure he would set me down in the water. He found out that I weighed 100 lbs he said ha! ha! Henry is not very well to day. I guess. He's as cross as a a —— what? [. . .]

TUES. 16. Threshing. Help. Henry & Wm Len are drawing away. Pa's mad all the time scolding Ma & Henry, saying they don't do anything but Ma said she couldn't endure it always so she told him a *good*-many things. He couldnt say a word. Ma's half sick any way her face was white as a sheet. Its too bad. I'm sorry. Ma cried & sobbed until after 10 then I went to sleep. she said her head ached so hard on top. Mrs Spencer was here canvassing for a book a good one. I wanted it very bad. don't know tho. Warm. [. . .]

FRI. 19. Help Ma, etc. Clean door-yard. Aunt Hattie & children here in the afternoon, a short time what a woman she is. I dont believe she has been here once without saying something about I dont know what. Its "Henry & James kindy hinting around to John that they were afraid he would steal Henrys melons" "You needn't hide your melons, I dont want any had the children eat all they wanted before they come on purpose," etc. etc. I dont see any use in talking so— Uncle & Beatty stopped Aunt Hattie went straight home. we gave them some melon to eat & a musk-melon to carry home. Aunt Hattie has not tasted one mouthful of our melons & says she wouldn't for a $1000. what foolishness! Harvest home to day. Henry went fishing. Pa help Uncle John McGee. Henry caught 3 fish & 3 turtles. Cool.

Normal in session this wk & next. I would kindy liked to have gone. . . .

WED. 31. Last day of August. I went down & got Mrs Walt H. Butler & little Walter & brought them up here. had a good visit. I started 10 A.M. & Pa didnt come to or in the house until after Ma carried her home 6.30, not even to eat. I went down & asked him to come & he said *we were always & forever getting some such company here, & he did not want us to do it again either.* Well he's apouty—& I hope he'll get over it, he'll have to any-way. Mrs. B—— said to tell him when he came up that It was lucky for him not to come while she was here for she was dangerous & would bite him. ha! ha! Rain.

Done some of the washing.

September 1881

[. . .]

SUN. 4. Henry's 18. Ma & I went plumming. Pa is cross as bedlam, Ma not well. Henry sleeps in barn to watch his melons (199). Warm. [. . .]

MON. 19. Go to school get along nicely. some one has shot 2 bullet holes through the 2 panes of glass in the north window of the Academy Building. Mr. Butler offers to give any-one who will find out his or her tuition in the Academy for a year. Uncle John & Aunt

Hattie have rented this place ie the Carpenter farm, for another year. [. . .]

FRI. 23. At school, We stay to organize a Library society after school. (my head aches) I am to be one of the 3 leaders of the Divisions. Henry is Treasurer. Mr. Butler-Pres., Florence Chapman-Vice Pres, Austin Brown Secretary & Mrs. E. J. Congar Critic. Rain.

Mrs. Webster made me the neatest little present of a crystal cube as a letter holder she also brought one to Nellie Flint, I did not see it, she got it a while ago. Hers is a Lions-head, I think mine is very nice Mrs W brought them from Chicago when she came here from her summers vacation. Rain. [. . .]

MON. 26. Pres. Garfield was buried to day. They have celebration at Manchester. Henry went. It rained nearly all day & thunders extremely hard. I commence me a pr white woolen mittens. Made Ma & I each a new neck-tie. Warm.

October 1881

[. . .]

SAT. 8. At home. the Carpenters done all they could So Henry could finish. After they had all gone Ma says "James what made you tell Mr Alcock (a man digging potatoes for pa & who owed Ma $2 for pickles) that you would pay him any-way & let it run any length of time," At which Pa said, "*Now* Emily, do for heavens sacke dont bring up every little nasty thing & commenced to tell Ma to pack up & leave" etc. the same story he always tells her—& Ma would not hear a word of it, & spoke about his paying Henry etc. He was more than mad & went out doors, "He wouldnt trouble us anymore. Well, after awhile he came in & swore & got his pocket-book & laid $20 on the table & said with a harsh oath that that ended all earthly accounts with Ma & Henry & went to the barn crying & talking. I asked him to come back, Henry was out door & saw him, & ran for him to find him with a rope in his hand & crying, when I made an appearance. Henry & I after a *good deal* of work & pleading got him in the house which he said he would never more enter. Its no use to repeat here what he said. But it was a great deal. He almost despises the ground that Ma walks on, & its too bad, I was afraid of her dear life last night (to day is Sunday 9). Well, we got to bed, at 11.30 nearly tho we did not sleep much.

Ma, Henry & I have slept up stairs all summer & Pa down stairs in the Bed-Room. Ma cant say *any*thing "She grabs every cent of money I get." & plans & O dear, I cant write what he said. He does not seem to think that Ma has any feeling or wants to make a visit, or do any-thing. Ma works extremely hard (So does Pa). Its been a very hard job for him to take care of & make the butter & climb up & down that cellar way & its been equally as hard for Ma to do all the work raise 120 turkeys & over 90 chickens. 26 canaries, besides the sewing & Ma is just as & more saving than pa. she *"must not"* & dare not ask him for a cent & has not for a no. of yrs. & if he sells any-thing. He says it all goes for us. But if Ma does buy the groceries & what we have to wear, I dont see the difference. Ma allmost starves & goes naked now. I dont see how he can say-any-thing any-way. Im O so sorry. Have as much as we do But its all an old & true saying, That "the more any one has the more trouble it is to keep it." "Dear Lord spare us to night. guide us all to do right." Amen. the least noise woke me. I & Ma rose at 6. Pa little befor 6 & Henry 6.30. Henry & I told Pa that we would not trouble *him* very much longer. As the 1st chance we got to earn & support ourselves we would not hesitate to accept. Henry said "not another summer will *you* support *me* & you remember it." I will not do wrong for any-man as you wanted me to over load & Flora came & used up in Hay & Harvest. "etc.etc." O tis too disheartening to think of it further. But I will never forget *humm*. Amen. the House looks very nice. Beautiful.

SUN. 9. Well I guess I have written nearly enough for a week. The sun is shining very bright. Pa is churning. Ma & Henry are down stairs. Ma's all a tremble & nervous, any-way at this period of life. When I go away I will take Ma with me, as she says "she could not live when Henry & I go away."—In the after-noon Ma & I took the team & went up to Uncles. Stayed awhile. Mrs Gardener came home with us & her boy took her home. Henry staid with Pa. Pleasant. [. . .]

THUR. 27. Went to school, I had my tooth pulled at noon, never ate any dinner before going, & I did not sleep much last night. Its ached for 2 days steady. Dr. Abbott broke it all too Smash (& it made me so nervous) in 5 or 6 pieces. He left the Root in there said it would work up in a couple of weeks, & then he would pull it. How it aches I can scarcely stand it, Its so tender I can reach it even with saliva. I was excused at Recess. We just commenced to have Recess this week. The students kept going out & in so much during class time. Mr Butler tried locking the door But that didn't work at all for they kicked it & every-thing else. Cold & Disagreeable. [. . .]

November 1881

[. . .]

SAT. 5. Ma & I cut my new dress, Navy blue Brilliant. Real pretty over skirt. [sketch of dress] looped up high on the sides & comeing to the pleat Ruffle of the underSkirt. & where it shows in front & at the side putting on shirred pieces. I think it will be nice. dont you? It cost $3.00 12 yds. @ 25¢. Henry went down & had a tooth pulled He's just sick to night, Pas o a grunting so hard with neuralgia & tooth-ache they both have their heads done up. its comical for all it is such pain. I have 4 more rotten ones, one has to be pulled I guess the others may be filled, I hope so anyway. Chilly. [. . .]

THUR. 17. At school; Henry went yesterday afternoon; but did not go to day. We have both the whooping-cough. Mrs. Walt. Butler has a girl baby a we born last Saturday, the scholars had a subscription, and got a box of toys for it (a rattle box, bedstead, tooth-brush, etc. A.B.C.) and in order to have him open it before the school Merton Brown delivered it, but when he went up to Mr. Butler they all clapped, Mr. B—— suspicioned and would not open it. So they are getting up another subscription to get it a gold-necklace & Autograph Album. Pleasant. [. . .]

TUES. 22. Examined in Latin. I wouldnt give my paper & Mr. Butler feel awful mean. Cant help it. Students social at the Academy this evening. Henry & I stay, had a good time; Austin Brown made the presentation of the necklace & album to Professor Butler, Mr Butler said he would take them home & see what *Baby* Butler said about it & tell us to-morrow. The Album cost $1.75 and the necklace $5 or $6 I think. The autographs of the donors were inscribed. Well, Henry says "they never made such a fuss when he was little," nor me either.

I went over to Lenas in the forenoon & stay until we came to social. next time I will advance some plays I believe. We got home just 11 P.M., *walked all the way.* Dark. [. . .]

December 1881

THURS. DECEM. 1 Whoop,—whoop—whoope, My Belly aches me head aches, my tooth aches a little. I vomit. [. . .]

THUR. 22. go to school we are in a hard place in Trigonometry. seems so any-way. it is to prove by the figure that sine c = sine a sine C etc. & I can not do it.

FRI. 23. At school Mr Butler expelled Susie Bailey & Ernest Platt for bad conduct. whispering & Laughing. Susie was mad. The boys after vacation are to sit on the two outside rows leaving the two middle rows for the girls. Colder.

SAT. 24. At home, help Ma. Chilly.

SUN. 25. At home it does not seem much like Christmas, no presents, no company. Ma & I went down to Aunt Hatties in the evening. Very Muddy. [. . .]

FRI. 30. No news from our turkeys yet. Ma also wrote two stories to the Companion, for a $1000 prize. Im a little afraide she wont get it tho. She did not tell Pa yet. Sun Dogs & Cold.

Am getting over the whoooopiiiing cough some. We had had a weeks vacation.

SAT. 31. At Home, Uncle was down & spent N. Years. He is getting old. 68. Cold.

January 1882

[. . .]

SAT. 7. At home, We heard last night that Uncle was not expected to live, a breaking in his head. he jumps up & down & hollows at the depth of his voice tho he can not be made to hear any-thing. Ma & Pa went up this morn. at 8.31. Pa came back 6.30. Ma stays all night. O Dear! Cold. [. . .]

MON. 9. Go to school. Standing.

Latin, Carrie Ruggle, Nell Flint, F. A. Norris. were best. Tressie Gately & Eunice Norris next. That only left Ben Keller, Will Colemans & myself and I dont think that I had had a bad lesson yet, And have not missed any-days. But I have found that crying does no good.

> Trigonometry: Carrie & Amy 1st, Henry 3rd
> Well that was all right.
> Algebra. J. Arbuckle.
> > Alice Eldredge all first
> > Henry & I
> Rhetoric.

The following entry is in Emily's handwriting.

TUE. 10. Tis snowing. Sarah you say crying does no good. I think it does, for I too, often find relief to an over burdened heart in tears. About the standing in your lessons, *Im sure you* was one of *the best*.

justice is sure to be meted out to whom justice is due. if Nell gets this partial *praise* now, you will at the end get your *reward*—& they—well they may have a chance to cry for that they never were worthy of.

> We will never give up. No. Never. Ma
> I found this Book right in my way,
> And thought I would see what it did say.
> I only read that just one day
> And here is the rhymeing of it, Sarah.

WED. II. Thanks—thanks to you Wonder how it would scan.

> u-/u-/u-/u-   Iambic
> u-/uu-/u-/u-   Tetrameter
> u-/u-/u-/u-
> u-/uu-/uu-/u-   With some anapest. [. . .]

THUR. 19. Go to school. When I came home there was two were two men ahead of me and they kept acting so bad & hollowing at me, so I stopped at Mrs Mattox & staid an hour or so. I got home at six P.M. Ma & Pa were to Mr Wellmans on a visit. Henry came at half past six, & Ma & Pa at seven, I had supper all ready. Ma has a new hat. I bought me a new one too. Ma paid me a $10 gold piece the other day I paid a dollar & a half for Artics [sketch of boot] $1.25 for my hat. .25¢ for a journal My hat is a white soft high crown felt. [sketch of hat] turns up all around a bought about a half or 1/4 inches. then I got red shaded plush ribbon 3 in wide to trim 1 1/2 yds at .50¢ = 75¢. which added to the frame = $1.25. Pleasant. [. . .]

February 1882

[. . .]

SUN. 26. At home all day. I wrote my essay in the afternoon & we all went down. Henry spoke "The Loom of Life," & I read my essay, "Union Mission Work." We have neither of us attend S. S. there and tho we took part in the Concert. A full house & good programme. I did not like it as well as I did Fri. eve Lyceum. Hattie Beal was there with Everet Smith. Some Muddy.

March 1882

[. . .]

SUNDAY. 5. At home all day. I have not done any thing on a/c of my cold. I went down to Aunt Hatties, when I came home John was here after water and Aunt Hattie is waiting so that she may wash the children all over. Pa & him are talking horse and blabbing. Chilly wind. Cold. [. . .]

THURSDAY. 9. Henry in bed all day with the measles. he's all broken out. looks bad. Dear & to think that I shall have to have them. I do not much like the idea. My nose is real sore. my throat is sore too. I have a caker [canker] sore lip, a sore on the end of my tongue and my head aches to night. Ma & Pa went to town to day in the cutter. Extremely blustery. Snow very fast all day. Uncle John sallies down to the other well after water and shoots way round as if he were afraid of something, but I guess he's all ready got them for he has been here every evening, this week and planned to kill time. Stephen McNett here but wouldnt come in. Yesterday Pa thought that Henry could plane some pickets for the fence just as well as not, and monday he wanted him to turn grindstone, with that high fever burning. well. I dont see why some dont know anything any-way. I feel real bad myself to night, but the work has yet to be done for the night it is 10.10 but the clock is 1 1/2 hrs too fast. so it is 8.20. Isnt it? In this weeks Democrat it says the "Manchester Academy students are enjoying a weeks vacation." well! Its all right. Ma heard that Mr Meads had the small-pox. we'll surely have to abide with *that* the next thing we know. whopping-cough, measles, ———, ———, ———, when will this panic stop. I imagine seeing myself wrapped in comforters with my feet in a teakettle no! no! not teakettle. Dishpan. no! mop-pail there thats what I mean I guess. You must excuse me I'm light-headed to night. I must close with saying that I am very sleepy and my throat is getting worse. Ma brought home lemon oranges, apples & opened her quinces, and I dont know what else. Cold. Snow. [. . .]

SATURDAY, APRIL 8, 1882. 2 weeks ago to day I felt bad. the next day Sunday I knew I was coming down with the measles. did not go to bed until Wed. stayed abed only 2 days. Wed. & Thur. But Oh how thick the measles were. Henry was in bed just one week to a day, and he was very sick. Ma made his bed in the kitchen then when I was sick she made a bed in the bedroom with her & pa so that we would not take cold. Well I thought I was going to get well but getting up so quick & being unwell. It turned it into a Bilious or intermittent fever. then one night Pa got mad (mean) & took the horse blankets & robes & went up stairs & Ma & I never slept a wink hardly & that made me worse. when he came down in the morning he said to Ma, that he would learn her to talk to him so of course he just done it for meanness.

I am gaining very fast, but I walk like a baby (just about) Polina Shaw is working here. 2 wks Monday night since she came. Dr. Hines & his wife were here a short time. Fred Davis came in a few minutes & brought Prince off Pa for $85. Ma has bo't her a new sewing machine with here bird money of last year. "Domestic" is the name. Rec'd a letter from Amelia Randall of Epworth, also one from Lena of Anamosa. 2 from my friend Hattie Riggs. Hattie is going to teach our school, she is to board here. school commences 17 Apr. and I must go to her.

Ma has some little birds. "2 pr." Pa is breaking Minnie the colt. he puts her right into hard plowing etc. & last night he left them standing. Minnie was so tired & they went 2 or 3 times around the plow before he caught them & then he kicked Minnie just as hard as he could & just as fast. Ma went out there & he said "Did I ask any of your assistance?" i.e. after ma had said "Dont you kick that colt again" she ans: pa by saying "No! nor I dont ask any of your assistance either." Cool! wasnt she.—but nervous & trembling as an autumn leaf. got a new bedstead & mattress $10. Uncle John is sick with the measles. but not so sick as Henry & I. He keeps drunk all the time. Pa does his chores & its a real task too: Aunt Hattie came up here to see me for I had to go to bed again a week ago yesterday, as I had a chill Wed. & thur. before & then the fever. then I got up again day before yesterday so as to be dressed all day. that was Thursday I cut 119 half squares to finish my quilt to day, am all tired. Polina washed yesterday & ironed to day. Ma's real tired to night. Well! this is all I can think of at present. as to the weather it has been Raining & is changeable. Rain. [. . .]

TUESDAY, 11, 1882. I went down to Aunt Hatties & back got kindy tired. Uncle John didn't have them hard at all the measles. Ma & Pa went to town. Ma got a Pr of vases, for Lena Cunningham 20¢. She & I bargained last winter that I should get her a birth day present of 25¢ ~~each~~ and she is to get me one for the 7th July. hers is the 4th of May. Ma also bo't me a new blue & white fine check gingham dress. 13 yds. 2 12 1/2 ¢ . . . $1.62.

Got 8 new chairs. some other things. More Pleasant.

Sideways in the margin alongside this entry, Sarah has written:

Ma 44th birth day. Wish I could have bought her a present. but there are other birth-days coming. [. . .]

SATURDAY 22. Chrocheted on cover.
Pa is about sick with a cold.
He will get well though if grunting has any-thing to do with it. "If I live I will and if I dont Ill do something else." "uh!" "uh!" "O dear" "Well it's well enough to tell you have much to feed & what to do for if Im sick and I will be tomorrow." "O" "uh" has been continued from last week Saturday till this. He is all right to night, and I cant see whats the use of trying to be sick. Henry has an extremely bad cold. mine is loose. Cold Wind.

May 1882

[. . .]
FRIDAY 19. R. W. Emerson, Henry W. Longfellow and Darwin the scientist are dead. also Jessie James the bandit. poor man. I would not be ashamed to have him for a relative, no! indeed. I don't know why, but I cant hardly keep from tears when I read it about "Billy the kid," and Jessie also. I can see their dispositions. They are always ever true to those who are true to them. His horse would lay his head on his shoulder and follow him. his wife & children loved him and he loved them. I had rather be in his place than in Fords who shot him. too many false stories have been brought against him. He had suffered much. [. . .]
SAT. 20. At home help Ma. Pa is mad & has & is all the time. at noon we were speaking about the millinery trade and Ma said if she had not ever been hindered from doing any-thing she might have been rich. That fired Pa's fury & he said it was her selfishness and began his lingo & when Ma would commence her work he told her not to make up any lies & tell him that he never hindered her—, but he did. when Mr Thorp brought hats up here for Ma to trim Pa swore & said "Bringing that d. . . . trash up here" etc to ridiculous to think of. He has always hindered her always says she never does anything. But I guess she does as much & that which amounts to as much as he does. Well Henry couldnt stand it any longer & said to Pa in a fierce tone *"you needn't tell Ma she tells stories for she does not"* Pa said; "None of your sas young man, I wont take a word of it. now." "Well!" Henry said, *"you just neednt say that Ma tells lies for she dont"* at which Pa rose threw down his paper & said "we'll see who's master of this house now sir you keep still etc" & his eyes like peeled onions. Ma said "now stop right there that's enough." Then I

stepped between them & Pa turned toward Ma & said "Henry had no right & he'd put him out of the house." Ma said, "He has a right dont you dare touch him" and then with Ma's saying that nothing only prayer had saved her for her children her prayers are being answered" Pa went out saying "we (H & I) had a pretty bringing up" "The horses are all harnessed & if you want any more of me" & then the rest was finished after passing through the door. I think it looks pretty I'm actually ashamed of him & always will be. Cold Rain.

SUN. 21. In the morning after breakfast Pa went out and was cleaning the horses. We heard them haveing an awful time & Ma & I went out there.

He was swearing at Flora & trying her head up so high that it nearly took her off her feet. She is such tender skin and has a ring gone on her hind leg so that it hurts to curry it and she would naturally step around and that made him mad and he was tying her up there & knocking her on the nose & going to slip knot it around her under jaw & saying " G——D—— you, I'll take your hide now we'll see" but there is when we arrived Ma snatching the rope & I pulling back his hand. Ma was perfectly beside herself not really that but insane she *could not endure it* to see him so ugly. we had a bad time of it with him out there too bad to write. so I will omit it.[10] But we told him that if he did not stop being so ugly to his team that would complain of him and if he does not stop *we will. no jest.* Such a man to tie so innocent as Flora or Minnie and make them throw themselves is shameful.

The Punishment of the Highest will fall upon him. yea, he shall reap a bitter reward.

I'm sorry that I have such a father I cant relish to call him a real friend. no! he is not a father. Ma's head has ached all day, and she grows old too fast if she can only live through it and see a score or two of bright sunny years of life I may thank the good Lord with all my heart. In the afternoon Pa was going to Uncle's with the plow & Ma said she guessed maybe she had better go. Henry told me to go & insisted upon it so strongly that I went, & I knew why. The last time Ma rode up there with him he said so much & got Ma so worked up that she declared that she would never ride with him and hear such ugly demonstrations as he issued she would get out & come home & I do not blame her. He is too slick tongued to strangers and they *know him—not.*

Hattie home to night. Cold.

MON. 22. Dear Lord I pray we may never have any more such trouble may we have happy days grant us this week to be a week of pleasure & cheerfulness.—amen.—

In the forenoon I washed in the afternoon I done up the dinner work made 4 beds and then went up to school at arrived 10 min of three.

Hattie is a good teacher I guess. The men came and built the kitchen chimney. Pleasant. [. . .]

TUESDAY. 30. Decoration day. Ma & I went to town but not to decorate. Ma bought some cabbages etc and herself a new hat, and I had my picture taken I guess they will be all right. I hope they will suit Ma. I don't believe I shall like them at all my hair was crimped very nice (by Hattie) but Ma pinned it high on top of my head so as she said to look like her friend Lora Rose of Cal, but I think my face is too long. I felt just full of fun & was all right until it came to comb my hair and I then wished it had not have been crimped at all. But I knew I looked sour, although I tried not to. You see I'm so poor, my dress was made full breast and it hung down and looked very bad but the gentleman said he'd fix it all right, and said I had nice sharp eyes and made a very good negative. I thought it looked rather cross and unnatural. But if they suit Ma all right I don't care.

Ma's hat cost $2.75 mine $2.30. Rain. [. . .]

June 1882

[. . .]

SUN. 11. Ma & I & Henry go to Union Mission S.S. Childrens day. I spoke "Through death & Life. We also go in the evening. Henry had an essay "Temperance" and I spoke "The Millers child." got home a little after ten. Pa came after us. he was *mad*. Warm. [. . .]

MON. 19. Washed in forenoon. I had 8 sheets 8 pillowcases a doz towels Mas & my under-clothes 2 pair for me & one pair for Ma 5 prs stockings. Pa's shirt, my dress, etc.

We learned that there was a hurricane of wind here. Ma & I & Pa go to town in afternoon I got some silvered paper & zepher to work for Hattie. The paper cost 10¢ for 2 sheets for which Hattie paid she is to furnish zepher for us both. I bought 10¢ worth of zephyr myself. Ma gave me a quarter. Am tired as Ma & I missed Pa & had to walk all the way home. Uncle went to Dubuque races last week was robbed of $90 by ruffians. too-bad. Real Warm. [. . .]

FRI. 30. Poor Guiteau—was hung at 12–5 to day poor assassin of Pres. Garfield. It seems to bad to hang an insane man. I went to school this morning with Hattie. Stayed all day. Heard the A reading. Ma carried us on a/c of heavy rain last night. about two o'clock in the night the wind blew so hard that it woke me. I roused the rest. we kept watch of some very wild dark-black-clouds in the north sweep east as if their fury was excited. It seemed as if ~~they~~ it broke loose & it rolled & plunged along to the east. I & Hattie stayed up until the blackest of the clouds had passed to the eastern horizon. [. . .]

July 1882

[. . .]

FRI. 7. At home. help Ma all day. She cook for Hatties school picnic to-morrow. I have a real lame back all the time. I fell from the fence awhile ago & then mowing rasp-berry-bushes with the brush scythe made a bad stitch. It is nearly eleven I guess & we are all going to bed. Ma did not think of my 17th birth-day until to-night & she brought up a glass of lemonade. Am tired & sleepy. "Time flies fast" is a true saying I guess. [. . .]

SAT. 15. Hoed in the garden, Help work.

We have learned from Aunt Hatties letters that Grandma had a stroke of Palsy. very bad. she can not speak, nor move her right side she was taken Sunday. Aunt Hattie gets a letter every day. they think she is beginning to realize a little. Will Woolcott came after Hattie this morn.

I take my old room back now. She left a lot of her things here. Blows fall. Cool. [. . .]

MON. 17. Washed. Done some of house-work. Ma & Pa go to town. Henry got his discription of character it is splendid.[11] He can be a jeweler, keep a variety store, a furniture store, or a book store, could be a carriage trimmer, make inside finishing of house, or a piano-forte maker. could be a no 1 Doctor or Dentist. His Hope is like the head light of a Locomotive & illuminates the distance, though like the Locomotive you may travel in darkness. [. . .]

TUESDAY 18. To day brought the sad news of the death of Ma's mother. She died this morning.[12] Uncle Henry telegraphed to Aunt Hattie. It is too bad when Ma wanted to go & visit them, had saved her bird money to go last fall & then spent it for a sewing machine. She can hardly endure it seems so. Ma cries & cant do any-thing.

I wanted her to go to the funeral but she said she *couldnt* see any of her folks dead if she couldnt when alive. Grand-ma has been failing a long time.

Ma might have gone home many times but she is afraid of Pa, afraid of his wicked threats though she would not dare to let him have the first idea of such a thought. I helped Ma. Am not well myself. Warm. [. . .]

WEDNESDAY. 26. Pa said he had some home made beer up to Smiths in haying now. Ma ask him how it tasted? he said "*good.*" "Yes" ma said just like any other whiskey. I dont think much of Pa now I tell you nor Smiths either. Help Henry cock hay. Rain. Warm. [. . .]

SUNDAY. 30. Rained all day & is cold.

Henry went to town.

Ma rec'd a letter from her bro Henry asking her opinion as to the division of Grand-Ma's things. Aunt Aggie is to send me her (Grand-Ma's) ear-rings that she said I should have when she came here visiting in '76.[13] I'm so glad. I rec'd a letter from Jennie Wood asking Henry & I to go to school with her to Oskaloosa. (thats where Ma's Cousin Elijah lives) I hope We can go. Rain. [. . .]

August 1882

[. . .]

TUES. 22. Go to Normal. Very dusty.

WED. 23. Same as yesterday. Hot. 100 in sun.

THUR. 24. At the Normal. Jennie Williams came home with me is to stay all night. Warm. [. . .]

September 1882

[. . .]

WED. 6. Help Ma. Ma & I go to town. When we went down we stopped at Aunt Hatties to pin up my dress & O my what a "blessing" (pretty talk but can't help it) she gave us. Ma bought $10.66 worth of goods for Henry to peddle. They were real nice goods, & I hope he can sell them all for 3 times as much as they cost him.

He walked down, & when we started home we met Uncle & he brought us home. Dusty. [. . .]

SUN. 10. We are all at home alone together. It may be the last time, God knows only what the future may bring forth. Henry starts for Rose Hill & Oskaloosa, Mahaska Co. this state.[14]

He sells Yankee Notions, and canvases for the Phrenological Journal, I hope he will have good luck, health, wealth & gladness. Thats the best I can do. He intends to be gone 3 or 4 weeks.

Amy Boggs & Nora Mansfield were here a short time. Amy starts for Mt. Vernon this state. Wednesday. & she tho't she must see me. Hattie Beal & Anderson went past here to shuck—an—run—. Henry says *"Shoot him,"* & laughs. Ma is "Card marking" for fair. She says "dont you joggle me now."

Henry rec'd letters from Prof. Butler. Mary Yeoman, Fowler & Wells, Phelps of Colesburg & I dont know who else. I guess I will write to my old love Mary Tyler to night. Chilly.

MON. II. Henry started this morning for Cous Elijah Dear me! How hard it was to see him go As you might say. Shored off without a cent into the cold world to starve or live. Ma said she done all she could & she did. But Pa ah He never has once asked a question or said a word. In fact just Glories at the idea. Glad that Henry has gone. He will repent yes dearly repent for his meanness to his family.

Henry's valise weighed 25 pounds & was all together too much for him to carry. He went South across to the woods to the South Road. Ma went out after he had gone & watched him. Pa said to me he "bet Ma would cry before she got through with it." I said "she did & couldnt help it, that it was pretty tough to see boy as small as Henry & as young go off so."

"Well" he said "We'd got to earn our own living and the sooner we learned the better" that "Henry was not obliged to go." I told him. "He thought he did any-way." And how can we help it. We want to go to school. Pa never intended to help us an atom, means to hinder us instead. He may be old some-time & need to be taken care of. But I pray to the Dear Lord that Henry & I (Henry the most) will be crowned with success, and we can *safely say* that Pa has never helped us in the least.

How lonesome it is. only 3 plates. only 3 beds. No pleasant and cheerful face to say good-night. It just about makes me so sad I cant hardly write this. We may never see him again. He said Good bye Sarah. Good bye Pa. Good bye Ma but the great bright tears were in his eyes.

His satchel was oh so heavy.

Well I *cant* write any more but think lots.

I washed & help Ma to go to fair to morrow. Ma go to town. Warm. [. . .]

MON. 18. Uncle here all day. Mas & Pas 20 Anniversary. Ma bake a turkey, we had potato, turnips, turkey, onion, melons, gravy 4 kinds cake, apple pie, a real good dinner, & good visit. In the evening Ma & I took 27 melons of Henrys down town. It looks like rain & thunders. Cool. [. . .]

MON. 25. Its nearly 10 o'clock. P.M. Ma is writing in her Diary. Pa is milking. Henry is:—well its hard to say *what* Henry is doing. Gone to bed likely. We are all tired. Pa cut corn.

Ma & I can tomatoes, make apple butter, do housework. It rained real hard this morning & I did not wash. Had Parsnips, carrots, sweet-potatoes, pickles, peachblow potatoes, Raspberries, Coffee, crackers & biscuit for supper. Cold. [. . .]

October 1882

SUN. I. OF OCTOBER: —"There comes a month in the weary year, When the ripe leaves fall and the air is clear. October the clear the brown the blest."

We got a letter from Henry yesterday. It seemed almost as if he was here. We are at home this morning. We go down to Aunt Hatties in the evening. Cool. [. . .]

WED. 4. We go to town. This morning, Pa & Ma had a fuss well it was not a real fuss, but some time ago Pa lent John McGee some oats to be paid when he threshed, & Pa said he was afraid he never would get them so he has spoken to John several times about it. Ma said, "She knew it all the time & thought he'd never get them, the only way to stick to him but she did not believe John meant to pay any of the time." Ma spoke just as pleasant as she ever did, Pa spoke up as ugly & said *"I'd like to know who you are talking to. You had better talk a little better to me."* Ma said she was talking to him & I believe repeated what she said. "Well" Pa says "You'll find you dont have a right to say just what you want to. pretty bringing up you have had." Ma says "I *have a right* to say just what I want & to say it just *when* I want to." Pa said "If shed had any bringing up at all etc. I shant say any more about it but I am quite certain that he is the ugliest mortal that I am personally acquainted with. We go to town Ma & I stayed went to Mrs. Heimes. Took Henry Smiths cage bird to him. Ma bo't a nice bottle $1.00 of perfumery. *"Verbena"*. It poured down while we were in town. We walked home. Rain. [. . .]

SAT. 21. At home. knit & work on card-board. Pa dig turnips, 3 of which fill a half bushel. nice, large, grand. big whoppers, "ain't they?" Ma walked to town, walked back rather for she rode down with Mr Gardner. Got a card from Henry. He has a sore throat he wrote it last Sat. I am very sorry. I think that Ma ought to go down to Elishas with him he has wrote so much for her to come and has sent $6 & said "now come you can as well as not." I think so too. But its all in that man. "we must sell the turkeys, the birds, dry up the cows, get a covered buggy & rent the farm & pack up & travel & visit this next winter & summer.

O! what a bluster. I never got personally acquainted with any one yet that has so little sense. may be I dont see it right, but It would be splendid for Ma & I to take Minnie & a spring board and drive down to E Hawleys & see Henry & have a little pleasure trip. For we cant all have the things at once. I am going to try to have Ma go anyway. Wind Blows. [. . .]

MON. 30. All Hallow Een to morrow night. I tried no tricks. Ma washed the wood work in sitting & sewing rooms. I helped her a little. I sewed the carpet. did not wash. Had the head ache. Rain. Cold.

November 1882

[. . .]

SUN. 12. Shall have to enumerate the things I done during the week. It has rained 3 or 4 times & has been nasty weather. Monday I washed. Tuesday was election. Ma & I went up to Mrs Alcocks to visit. We had a good visit. Jerome has graduated at the Ia State Normal School and is going to teach in Ackley.[15] Wednesday. We put down the sitting room carpet. Pa helped us. Thursday Pa & Ma went to town & got a new stove very nice. West Point Base Burner. $44. Fri. Ma & I fix the doors over the threshholds had to take every one off & plain it. on a/c of the oilcloth. We also put a glass door in the parlor. Sat. I swept & cleaned the chamber. also down stairs. Have a sore throat and cold. Ironed. Ma can apples. I knit. Pa went to town. Did not hear from Henry this whole week. It rains & is growing cold. To day is cold. [. . .]

MON. 27. I washed sewed on cloak (Pelisse) Just as we sit down to Supper table who should come in but Henry & say that he heard us call Pa to supper & tho't it was time to come in. We were very glad to see him. He has gained 10# since he went away & is fleshier but tanned & brown hands. Cold.

He walked from Marion since Sunday morning. [. . .]

December 1882

[. . .]

TUES. 12. Sewed on Pas overalls most all day. Ma says I learn her to scold when there is so much to do & no one careful about the things I dont think it scolding to ask them to be careful. Warmer. [. . .]

SUN. 24. In the morning Henry & I went to church & S.S. Fred Hines is home for the holidays. Pet Chapel is glad to see him. Mrs Hines is too. She thinks lots of Henry & I & wants Fred to. He does of Henry but is too afraid of me. In the evening Henry & Pa & I went down they had a little programme. But done very well. We walked. Beautiful moonlight. Ma wants to go to but has no new clothes. Mrs Hines invited her class to spend the evening with them at their house for Fred. There are about 20 of us. I guess we can go. Moonlight.

MON. 25. Christmas has come but with it no presents. The snow is fast flying. I guess it has snowed most all night. The snow is real deep, & getting deeper. Its about 2 in deep on the limbs of the trees. We had an invitation up to Uncles, dont know whether we will go as Pa is as usual obstinate. The wind is getting in the North. I hope we can go down to the C—— tree to night but don't know. We went after Pa had done the chores, about 12 M. In the afternoon Lucy & Jas Parker & Nora Gardner & Henry & I went on a sleigh ride 3 mi. North of Masonville. am sorry but we did not get home until so late 9 P.M. Snowed all day. 6 in. [. . .]

SUN. 31. Last day of 1882. Henry & I went to Church & SS. Its too hard a walk. Henry has a cold. Ma is tired and has worked from 6 till now 9.30 & is going right along. she's awful tired. Im sorry but I burnt the bread all up. It was real nice & the wood was green & I never thought to watch it, only to keep up the fire & I burnt it all to a crisp all over. Ma has got supper & done up the work, dressed a turkey, made bread pies cakes etc for tomorrow. But the bread is spoiled & I am so sorry, that does no good I suppose. I dont see that I was thinking of. Ma says that I may say that she does not blame me but I do not see who else she can blame for I was the one she asked to do it & then to think Id go & neglect it. when she is so tired. Pa hmmm He does not care, Ma has just this minute sat down & its

the first time since she got up & Pa wants her to go out & get coal &
fill up the stove. (She cried about the bread.) She wont go & get the
coal & he is sponky about it. I guess by the way he slams doors etc.
Mrs. Heims gave Henry a mustache cup & saucer & me a pr vases
& a shell box. Laura Doolittle kept them for us. Thanks. Cold.

DEC. 31. Sunday evening, my head aches for walking down there &
back in a cold West wind. I dont think I shall go many more Sundays
for Im so cross & tired after it & Ma's so tired too. Pas grunting. to
bed. Henry has gone to bed. Ma & I have yet to go out. It just struck
10 P.M. Cold.

> "Full knee deep lies the winter snow,
> And the winter winds are wearily sighing
> Toll ye the church bell soft & low
> And tread softly & speak low
> For the old year lies a dying.
> Old Year you must not go
> You came to us so readily
> You've lived with us so steadily
> Old Year you shall not go."

CHAPTER THREE

"I Question Myself":
1883–1884

I question myself.—is it right for us to live with

such a person.

—from Sarah's diary, November 1, 1884

Received this much needed treasure book Christmas 1884.

Will copy from old diary and have it all in one book. It was kept in a "December plow book" for a part of 1883 & consequently will not be much.

1883

JANUARY. MONDAY 1. Had company. Cold.

TUES. 2. Knit & help Ma. Cold. [. . .]

SUN. 7. Henry got a bean in his throat; It is all right now. Cold. [. . .]

SAT. FEB. 3. Rev. E. R. Wood is dead. He died Jan. 23, at their home in Colorado. Only Mrs Wood & one son Stanley are left. Blow. [. . .]

MON. 12. At a party to Gardners. Birthday party. Have a splendid time. (Frank Paige of Masonville) Moonlight.

TUES. 13. Washed. Sewed on dress. Nice weather.

WED. 14. Got a very dainty valentine. Think Frank Mead sent it. It is pretty. Mop.—Thaw. [. . .]

MARCH 1ST. Pa is 44 to day. Ma go to town. Get knife (silver) Thaw.

FRI. 2. Ma & Pa go to Crosby's with a bird. Thawing.

SAT. 3. Help Ma make a birdcage all day. Cooler. [. . .]

SAT. 24. Ma & I went to town. I had Dr. Ames fill two teeth and then went to Mrs Estys when found Ma. We made a visit & then walked home. Ella has some fine paintings. Chilly.

SUN. 25. Pa have a mad fit. Snow all day.

MON. 26. Wash. Pa mad. Snow.

TUES. 27. Help Ma.—Poor woman.—Snow.

WED. 28. Mop. Bake cake & cookies. Ma to Meads. Cold. [. . .]

SAT. 31. Have the blues. It is very muddy.

April 1883

[. . .]

WED. 11. E. R. Congar here.[1] Carrie came with him and they bought my saddle. Gave me $8.00. Ma & I & Henry are painting blinds. Mrs. Geo. Crosby here. Warm and Sunny. [. . .]

FRI. 13. We went to Universalist meeting in evening to hear an able discourse. Pa watched horses. Moon.

May 1883

[. . .]

TUES. 1. Pa have a mad fit Henry & I are enough for him though. Henry helping take out chamber windows & I washed them. Mrs Smith & Bertha came & stayed a little while.

SUN. 6. Ma & Henry & I go to church. Pa mad again. Warm.

MON. 7. Wash. Mop chamber. Warm. [. . .]

WED. 23. Go to town. Very Warm. Paid Ames 3.00 for filling teeth. [. . .]

THURS. 31. In the morning early Ma & I took Henry over to Lawrences where he & Mr Parkhurst are to build a piggery. When we came back just Ma went home & I stayed to visit Beals & in afternoon Maud & I went to Hatties & visited. I got impatient to come home about four o'clock but Hattie was hurrying to get supper & so I stayed & did not get home till quite near dusk. Ma came to meet me at the gate & I then knew as soon as I saw her that Pa had been having a time. She said she never had a worse time with him in her life. He is bound to have a deed of the place he swore at & shook his fist to Ma, & she was afraid He would take hold of her. He did not eat any supper to night. Not much sleep or rest.[2]

June 1883

FRI. 1. Pa is mad won't speak & does not eat with us. Waits until we're through & then snoops to the cupboard or cold table & takes a bite. Ma & I are at work. Windy. [. . .]

MON. 4. Wash, went to town. fishing. Warm. [. . .]

THUR. 7. Cleaning. Henry to Epworth. Warm Rain. [. . .]

SAT. 16. Am not well. Sew. Warm.

SUNDAY 17. All at home. Rain. [. . .]

MON. 25. Wash. Go strawberrying. Chilly. Turks peep.

TUES. 26. Work hard all day. Go to town. Warm. [. . .]

July 1883

SUNDAY 1. Went to meeting. Warm. [. . .]

WED. 4. Ma & I go to Celebration. Amounted to "not much." Warm. [. . .]

WED. 11. Work. Pick berries.

SAT. 21 & SUN. 22. Help Ma do the work. Rain. [. . .]

August 1883

WED. 1. Attending Normal. Like it. [. . .]

SAT. 4. Am not well. Sun. 5. Feel better. Warm.

MON. 6. 7. 8. 9. 10. 11. 12. 13. 14. 15. 16. 17. Am going to the Normal. Help Ma what I can.

SAT. 18. Ma & I pull beans. I went to town. Johnnie Arbuckle came up & stayed all day. Ma's cousin E. S. Hawley & wife of Rose Hill, Mahaska County came in a buggy. tired some from the ride. [. . .]

MON. 27. They started for Home this morning.

September 1883

SUN. 9. Henry starts for Adrian, Mich., to night. He is going to attend the "Adrian College."[3]

We all went down rode on the hay-rack. Frost.

MON. 10. Knit on Henrys sock. Tues. 11. Help Ma. Wed. 12. Feel real mean.

THUR. 13. Ma & I go to Fair in Afternoon. Fri. 14. Am not well. [. . .]

November 1883

THUR. 1.2.3.4.5.6.7.8.9.10. Help Ma to get Falls work done. [. . .]

SUN. 25. Rain & Mud. At home.

MON. 26. Commence to teach in No. 1. C. Grove Twp. in McGees. District. . . .[4]

Frank Porter is director, and did not ask me to teach the school until Fri. 23. when Pa & I met him & Ma & I went up Sat. 24. & I signed the contract. Have a large school. [. . .]

DEC. 21. Taught. nothing usual or unusual. I can only say I think a great deal of my school & I hope & trust in Him that they may think as much of me. Snowed.

DEC. 22. Saturday. At home. Pa came after me last night. Ma & I go to town. Get presents for scholars etc. Snow & cold. They had a surprise dance at Uncles last Tues. night. thats the place I board. Sun. 23. At Home. [. . .]

TUES. 25. No school. Christmas. Ma & I went to town: I bo't a silk handkerchief for Henry $1.50 and Ma Bo't Henry a pair of Gold cuff buttons 3.50 to send to him.

WED. 26. Pa took me to school in the morning. Snowed hard all day. 10 in deep. Walked to Uncles in snow over shoe tops.

THURS. 27. Have a bad cold. taught school.

FRI. 28. Taught. had a time with the Preston boys. While I was shaking one for talking loud in School the other came at me & then when I went for him Alvah took up a stick of wood & came at me.

I sat Charlie down so hard that he stayed there & then I sent Alvah out door "hooping," & did not let him in till he begged like a good fellow. made them mind though.

SAT. 29. SUN. 30. At Home. Bad cold. Mon. 31. Taught school.

January 1884

THURSDAY 1. No school. Ma & I go to Uncles. He was down with a load of hay & we rode back with him. Snow blow & drifting all day. Pa came after Ma in the evening & I stayed. Snow. [. . .]

FRI. 18. Was at Uncles last night. "Well," he said, "You get around home once in a while dont you Sarah." & he seems to think everything of me. But those Quinns that are there "*such* people" I think of changing some of the pupils seats which I very much dislike to do. Mild. [. . .]

THURS. 31. Last day of Jan. A nice day. Johnnie & Russell were trying to put the other little boys in "the jail" & I had to have them stop it. I told them that if they came to school to me they would have to do as I said. I was real sorry for Russell & had him stay after school when we had a talk, & cry & a kiss & a good night. I told him I think everything of him & depended on him to be my best scholar. I went home with Charlie Anderson last night. Oh! Gee! the smell! ugh! Although Charlie is a nice swede boy.

If Johnnie comes any more I will change his seat for he is spoiling Russell one of my best boys.

February 1884

FRI. 1. Has been thawing all the week. Four Tripps children took their books home to night. Guess they will be back again. The reason was because the teachers before me have always sided in with them & Susie Cook and "pounded" the other scholars & I will not be partial. That makes 11 that have quit school. . . . 5 Well it makes my school small, but they must do right. Those who were said to be my best scholars are my worst and vice versa. Pa came for me. Sploshy. [. . .]

WED. 26. Well its a long time since I opened this book but will try to write the most that has taken place in the past three or four weeks.

My school closed the 15 on Saturday. I gave some gifts in the way of books. Clarence Gifford one book $1.75. Bertie McGee two books 75¢. Claude Gifford one book 25¢. Reward cards 3 doz. 60¢. Mrs. Grey & daughter Susie & Mrs Haines came to visit. It was a nice day & I & the scholars rode down hill. Gave Autograph albums that cost 25¢ each to 6 or 7 of the scholars. It [entry stops here]. [. . .]

FRI. 28. In the forenoon I washed & Pa churned & after dinner we went to town. got a letter from Ma. She is at Adrian with Henry & is well. Oh how good it seemed for I was so lonesome last night—oh! oh! Pa is better. Misty. [. . .]

April 1884

[. . .]

TUESDAY 8. Ironed—went to town. Cold. It is very muddy. Henry received a letter & I tho't that maybe I had better open it for it might need answering. But imagine my surprise when I saw the beginning—cant quote exact words, but was "loving" & it being Leap Year etc. I hastily concluded to reseal it and vowed ne'er to open another letter of his that comes while he is gone.

O how sorry I am but I didn't dream of such a thing. I supposed some relation sent it of course. Well he may read the whole of Frank Meads letter, that I, naughtless, never answered. Wonder what Frank thinks of me. If I were a young man & a girl treat me so, I'd box her ears so she'd remember one better. Cloudy. [. . .]

TUES. 15. Ma & Henry came home. we looked for them in the morning & went to the train. Rec'd a card from Henry that they would be here Tues. evening. 9.18. So we went down in the evening. Roads muddy, but deep. horses went in to their knees. Yes they came & we got home all right. Was oh so glad to see them well. Ma was sick on the cars, though. Henry looks just the same. Cold.

WED. 16. Pa & Henry go to town. get trunk, & box of goods & we opened them & the tool chest. Ma brought me the most wished for & acceptable present of a stereoscope & 15 views. And Henry gave me a book & an ink pencil, & clothes broom. Ma brought Pa a heavy china mustache cup & saucer. I wanted to give them some presents but could not as I did not have my money yet. Aggie—auntie—sent me a glass pickle jar & Aunt Edna sent a gold bracelet. Ma got some stones—specimens from Idaho etc. for me. I am commencing to make a collection of such things. Was very thankful. Ma's about sick.

THURS. 17. Same as yesterday—Ma brought some relics in shape of an old fashioned pitcher her grandmothers which she gave to me to keep with the blue one which was also my great-great grandmothers which was sent when grandma Hawley died. Ma also got the little old fashioned flaxwheel which maybe 200 yrs old. Its 150 anyway. Henry got a box which was carved & made in 1714. It is my delight to keep such treasures. Warmer. [. . .]

MONDAY. 21. Picking up—forgot that last Friday Pa & Ma & I went to Sarah McGee Carpenters funeral, & Ma & Pa went over to see Mr Richmond—who lives by the Quaker Mill—to settle for the calves which Pa wintered, Pa said to Ma coming home, "Emily, I believe you mean to kill me sometime" etc. Ma could not make him tell why though. I don't see what makes him have such thoughts. Am sorry he is so.—he hardly speaks for two or three days, or perhaps a week, just as sour as he can be. Ma is better—Diet is what she needs most of any thing I think. I went to town in the forenoon. Saw Alfred & Julia Brower. also Willie Dean. He is a nice young man. Is at present in to Gemmils Grocery Store. He likes to talk about as well as I & to day we had quite a visit. I just as soon visit with nice young men as with girls they are not so soft & flabby—have more general news, current items of interest & dont bother about folderol laces or any other dresses as girls do. Wind.

TUES. 22. Pa's been cross or melancholy for all day, said the old hog ate the nice black lamb—Its too mean—I had not seen it yet. We have over 80 turkeys eggs. Hens do not set yet. Help Ma. Hope Pa will feel better before long. Windy. [. . .]

May 1884

[. . .]

SAT. 3. Henry's coming home to night. I am washing. Ma has a cold. Ma & I plant strawberries all the afternoon and melon seeds by lantern.

Clement Bailey came & took some gooseberry & Raspberry vines. We now have about 1000 strawberry plants set out. Mrs. Carpenter was up in the evening. Looks like rain. [. . .]

THURSDAY 8. Well I have not written since Monday and we've got it a little mixed, Pa *knows* that its "so and so" I think differently. To day I dropped potatoes nearly all day. Ma's cold is better. Aunt Hattie brought down some gladiolus bulbs. She is terrible jealous dispositioned. But the mean stuff she has written home to Uncle Henry, which Ma saw and read, she ought to be ashamed.

Mrs Carpenter & May Duton were up. Ma & I rake off the dooryard—we are tired. Very Warm. [. . .]

THURSDAY 15. Ma paid me 50¢. Last night just as we had retired, and were about to enter in the sweet slumbers of 10 o'clock: we were quickly awakened by a loud knock, and who should appear but Grandpa Hawley. Pa got up and let him in, & then Ma & I got up. I made the bed & we took the poor-old-man in. Uncle Henry is in Idaho. Left Aunt Aggie & children & G-Pa. in Mich. So Grandpa came to live with us, he walks with two canes. Its too bad. He gave all his property to Henry who has "squandered" it all.[6] He said his goods were coming. So ma should have all he left. I went & had Aunt Hattie come down. She said,—"You never told me Emily he was coming." Well, how could we? we did not know he was coming. Said he was surprised to find me thick & short. Do general housework. Ma can scarcely speak above a whisper she has such a bad cold. Henry & I went to town in the forenoon after pickets. I paid 10¢ to Mr. Keller to have the heels taken off my shoes. Breezy.

FRIDAY 16. Ma is some better to day is unwell for the first time since December. I've got the "toupad" too.[7]

Grandpa was 77 yrs old to day. can see to read without glasses. Pa told him that "Ma didn't like work, that Aunt Hattie did etc."

I'd like to have him count up the hours and the hrs. Ma's worked, & what each has amounted to.

But what is the use of grieving over such speeches.

Henrys thumb is sore. I mopped, cooked, & washed dishes. etc. Am tired. Have a bad cold to night.

Aunt Hattie came down and said to Grand-pa that she was going to have him come down & stay a week or to night any-way. He told her he wouldnt do it. At that she started off crying and I dont know what all she said, said that Ma wouldn't let him come & that he didn't come to see her etc.

Ma never said a word to him about it. supposed he'd go when he wanted to. She Aunt H. said she'd never darken our doors again. My nose is sore. Henry & Ma & I set the skunk trap again.

The other time he got caught but when Pa hit him he ran in his hole, leaving one toe.

Henry said "that's too bad, it must hurt him real bad." Guess there's 5 or 6 by the way they sound. It's under the barn and we've dug a great hole there. Mrs. Crawford Hutchinson called. We've 5 little chickens babying in the house. Cool Breeze. [. . .]

SUNDAY 25. Got up at 5. Prepared breakfast. Went to Congregational meeting & S. S.[8] Saw Lottie Dunham and quite a number of others was in Mr. Morriseys class. Carrie Congar and Lottie & I.

He said he was thankful for my intelligent answers and wanted me to come every Sunday. Said he was just selfish enough to want me to be in his class etc. Maybe he'd change his mind if I went every Sunday. Then went over to Mr. Boggs & him & his wife and I went to Chas. Chapmans funeral.[9] It was a sad occasion. A large attendance. 42 teams, beside foot passengers in the procession. The text was Genesis 42-36. "All these things are against me." Rev. Evans, the Presby. minister, preached the sermon.

Charlie was 19 Yrs. 2 mo. 4 da. old. He had the Consumption. Looked as natural as could be. I felt sorry for them. But thats the way we all must go. "He who hath given, must taketh away," therefore weep not. Henry & I drove over to Mr. Beals & take a saw to Mr. Parkhurst to sharpen.

When we came home I helped unhitch in the barn and Beauty's tug was hooked when I went to lead her out and it took that buggy out of the barn & me too rather lively. no one hurt. just a little scare all around. Rain. [. . .]

FRI. 30. Grandpa came home. Ironed. Ma went to Decoration and got tired. See to the turks. Work. am fatigued. Dusty.

SAT. 31. Work like a "beever." Patch, cook, etc. etc. Mrs. Carpenter up. Warm.

June 1884

SUNDAY. 1. JUNE. 1884. Got up at 5.30. got breakfast, mopped. Changed & made 5 beds, swept, washed a cartload ? of dishes, made jelly cake. Picked up. Took a bath. put on clean clothes, went to Cong. meeting. & M. E. S. S. walked back. helped get supper. Look after turkeys. Do up work. walk up to Aunt Hatties. Walked back in a hurry to keep out of the rain. Help cover turkeys. Henry gave me 10¢ to mend his pants. Retired. [. . .]

THUR. 5. Was just about sick and am stiff yet to day. Do work. Ma has a cough. Pleas. [. . .]

MON. 16. Ma & Pa went to town. Pa got up on his ear coming home. I am sorry. nothing serious. He gave me $5. & I'll cancel Ma's debt of 48¢. Mr. & Mrs. Hines called to scold me for not coming to their S. S. Pooh— [. . .]

FRI. 20. Ironed, & do house work. am tuckered out. Ma wrote for Sat. the 21st, & so I will clip it out and paste it on the other clean side—Poor Ma. [. . .]

July 1884

JULY 2, 1884. Henry came home tired and hungry, worked on the M. E. church in P.M., he will board at home now for some-time. I am not going to get up at 4 and get warm breakfast for him but am going to get a ~~warm~~ ready cold breakfast at night. Have missed a week but can remember. Wed. 25. Ma & I went to Mrs. Carpenters to the social. Thurs. 26. washed. Fri. 27. work in general. Sat. 28. Iron I think. Sun. 29. went to meeting. Cong. Mon. 30. worked hard all day. Tues. 1. do, do. Wed. 2. Thats to day—Rain, warm. [. . .]

SAT. 5. Was just as sick as a horse. had the head-ache and stomach-ache and spewed up my breakfast.—Washed along toward night but did not wring the clothes—could not. Ma pick berries all day & did the work and is about bushed. [. . .]

MONDAY 7. Am 19 to day. It is quite chilly and I am going to do general house-work & iron to day. Grand-Pa is out sawing. Ma is hoeing in the garden. Henry has gone to town to work on the church. Pa is sprinkling potatoes & I am going now to do the dishes & make the beds, sweep. etc. Picked berries. Ma & Pa went to town. Ma sold some berries 10¢ a quart. Ma got me a new tooth brush 50¢. Rain. [. . .]

FRIDAY 11. Got woke up by the turks at 8.15 A.M. and have not slept any since. Henry came home earlier tonight and went up to Sellens' where Mr. Parkhurst is working and brought him down to stay all night. Ma & I came up to make the bed. Henry came up & said Ma would have to get up early or Mr. P. would see her as he has to pass her bed. Ma says—"You ashamed of Ma?" And he said—yes in the morning—she did not look very handsome in the morning. And she cried & felt so bad about it. He did not mean any-thing wrong. But he and Mr. P. think a good deal of each other and he wanted every-thing all right—I suppose.

So Ma put down some quilts at the foot of my bed in my room on the floor & has just retired & will not sleep in her bed in the hall. I feel real sorry. Ma takes every-thing to heart so. Now I cant half sleep & it spoils our visit though Mr. P. knew nothing of it. Pa is helping John hay it. Ma & I pick berries. Pa took down ten quarts. He would not have gone had he not told John he would come after him and take his butter down. It rained extremely hard and blew the dust down the road and across over the fields like monstrous clouds. Saw our Agt. Logan this morning. *we* passed the compliments of the day this morning. Well I guess he's honorable enough but I lookout for strangers. Well its after 10 o'clock & I must go to bed whether I sleep or not. I am tired enough. Washed to day. Will rinse and hang out clothes in the morning. Ma is tired too and I am sorry she can not sleep in her own bed when I made it up so good. Rain. [. . .]

WED. 30TH. Am not well. Ma & Grandpa & I have an argument on Woman Suffrage. He is beat but wont give up. He & Pa have their talks.

THURS. 31. This morning at breakfast Ma & Grandpa were talking about being rich & poor, & Ma was speaking that if she could have it as she would, like to that she could raise 500 (turkeys, I suppose, not in book. Jan. 10 1893) GrandPa asked her, why she didn't then, & she said surrounding circumstances hindered her. At which GrandPa & Pa laughed & said "You've owned right up now, don't say any more, just keep still" etc.

Pa has been so ugly to Ma all summer. Has not answered her decently once. Ma said so & then Pa began his lingo. she'd figured him out of every cut etc. I can't tell all they said but Grand-Pa & Pa just look to each other to sanction their talk and it is more than we can endure. Ma cried. Pa went away to help harvest & then GrandPa

& Ma & I had it, he siding for Pa: because Pa has told him his pitiful story. It got around to the deed of the farm "where did you get that? & how? to Ma. Ma told him a good deal & I helped her all I could. I feel so bad to think Pa is such a man. I think some-thing ails him. Everytime he gets a chance he's at Ma for a deed of the place, & she declares he shall not have it. He'd turn us all out door. Well, we'll try to live through it. Went to town after meat. Warm.

August 1884

[. . .]

SUN. 3. All at home all day. Ma & I went berrying they are not ripe yet. After supper as Ma was feeding some little turks by the well, Pa came up and said—that it seemed they were dying every day. Some other little things were said when Pa stated that he was not going to live & work another year as he had this. If Ma was going to give him some of the property, he wanted her to do it. Ma asked him to tell how much money he wanted but as for "dividing" & splitting up as he wants to she never would, & also she had the place & she should keep it. Then I went out and he never said another word.

Is pleasant and talkative at times. But now he is "O humming"— "O Dear" & "Well, well" all the time. I can hear him. Ma is waiting. The rest have retired 9 o'clock & I must also for I am to go to the Normal tomorrow. I pray that all will be well—Good night. Beautiful moonlight. [. . .]

SAT. 23. Ma & I wanted to go up to Meads & Underwoods to find out if Susie Sloan was examined, if she does not receive a certificate I am to have the school. So I said we'd go. I expected Pa would be mad for we have not taken the team in over a year. And he thought he had them so we could not drive them & we'd have to stay at home only when he said we could go. Of course the buggy is old but there's always some excuse. Well he was mad—so mad he wouldn't harness. Thank the Lord I know how. I harnessed & hitched up & we went. Pa said if we got killed or run away with we needn't blame him & that he'd "like the team once in a while." We got up to Meads at 11 A.M. & stayed until 3.30 P.M. & then drove up to Underwoods. He said he'd let me know as soon as possible whether she rec'd a certificate. We got home about seven—same time Henry did. He rode with Mrs. Morse. We had a good ride & a good visit and Pa &

GrandPa I hope will feel better. They had a *good* ? talk I guess. Pa never said a word but G-Pa told Ma when we first came in that he knew no one could drive "that horse" without her jumping & getting nervous etc. They can if they treat her half decent. I can do anything with them & they do not jump to the other side of the stall when I enter the stable. Warm. [. . .]

THURS. 28. We have taken up honey twice or thrice. Sold 4 lbs to Mr. Esty for 50¢. Ma gave me 25¢ as my share. Do general work. sew on my gingham dress. Ma's hands are quite numb & I am afraid it is *palsy*. She thinks it was from the sting of a bee on her finger.

FRI. 29. Cut down limbs, trim trees. Ma & I did. Mr. Seger came & stayed the forenoon.[10] He said he thought I'd make a pretty good second wife. Melons are ripe. work. am tired. Pleasant.

September 1884

[. . .]

WED. 3. Ma is in town. she went with Pa when he took the butter down this morning.

I have got the kitchen work done, mopping etc. & GrandPa is reading. Pa is hauling manure. Henry is working on the church. I washed yesterday. It is 3.30 P.M. I must make the beds & clean up the rest of the house. My head aches. Have a sore ear which aches. A *strong* wind but *warm*. Pa is mad I should judge by the way he jerks the horses around. Yesterday a man came to look at Minnie. Pa talks of selling her & she is not his to sell. She belongs to Ma. Its awful mean he has no feelings but for himself. Ma visited Mrs. Houghton and Mrs. Cunningham all day. I drove down & got her & Henry. Pa was mad because I would go. Warm.

THURS. 4. Help Ma. Henry is 21 yrs. old to day. Ma gave him a nice album for a present. I wish I could get him some-thing too. He went to Dubuque—will be home tomorrow night. Ma & I could not go. Mopped etc. Pleasant. [. . .]

SAT. 6. Washed. Dropped the boiler of hot water—suds—& it slopped in my face. I was pretty deluged, it wetting my dress & garments through. The heft of it went in my open eyes & nostrils. My face & eyes are some scalded—it makes them ache & smart. Mr. Seger stopped & stayed to supper. Said he had made 6 applications for me a school said if he could get me one he would & it should be a *good* one.

he stayed till nearly 9 o'clock—we all talking. After he went Grand-pa & Pa made some remarks that "How would it look for *me* to be away from home talking to a mess of women" Ma said "if it had been a mess of men talking a week it would be all right and never be mentioned or thought of." "Yes" said GrandPa—"Well"— ma said "women wanted to talk as well as men" & that stopped it. Grandpa can't bear to see a woman be anybody only just as he tells them himself. [. . .]

SAT. 13. . . . Cora Brook boards with Geo. & Emma & teaches our school. Mr Clute sent me an offer of $95.00 for 3 mo. & board at $1.50 per wk. to come & teach his school near Edgewood. 12 mi. n. of Manchester. Cora said she had to apply for her schools & asked me if I was going to teach (they think I can not get a school).

I told her if a Director came for me I would but otherwise I should not & they think I will not be very apt to teach. I have my school engaged and wrote Mr. Clute when it was to commence.

Ma is not very well. Her hands are so bad, and her mouth sore. We came home about 8 o'clock & had supper to get for the men. Pa nor Grandpa never spoke once. Henry said he did not know what to do. Ma was tired and nervous and went out door and cried—no cry ever sounded so pitiful and moaning—oh how it rang in my ears. I was so sorry.

I got their supper and—well I guess it did not hurt them any. Pa claims to do all the housework & has told such to the neighbors— "But where is he"—Like Emma said to day. "Why, Mr Gillespie can get supper" just as if she thought he always did. I told her he know nothing about it no more than her baby Bert. 5 yrs. old. "well she thought that was queer." Because Pa washed 2 or 3 milk pails once in a while he thinks he "does all the house work" He is trimming trees & cutting some down, cleaning in general. Pleasant. [. . .]

SAT. 20. . . . It wears on Ma & she is so sickly. No man that I ever saw we'd think of working if he were half so sick as Ma.

—But we do not live with "woman" "suffragists = men." They believe in man-grunt-ism & women-wait-on-us-ism—That's their platform. I hope Ma will be better & stronger right away. Hope Henry is getting along all right. its so lonesome. They have all gone to bed but me & I must go its after 9 and I am tired. To day is the first pleasant sunshiny day this week. Pa has a lame shoulder—its the spine between the shoulders. Dan & Mary are coming over Sunday. Moonlight.

October 1884

FRIDAY OCT. 3. 1894 [*sic*] ought to come here as it was the 2nd. I last wrote but have been so busy that I could not write until to day. Sun. 19 Oct.

SUNDAY OCT. 19. So much has happened too that I can not begin to write only particulars.

FRI. OCT. 3. Henry fell from the church spire 75 ft. to the ground: at 10 min. past 1 P.M.[11] I had just started to go to town when I met Morse the liveryman coming for us with the news that Henry was hurt—was just gasping & it might be possible we would see him alive if we got there as soon as we could—well we got there in about 20 min where we found him conscious—no bones broken but badly jammed up.

It is impossible to describe my feelings. Ma did not cry but was as white as a corpse. She is almost sick at best. Well Fri. night Oct. 3 was the worse night I ever experienced, for the first 4 dy & nights he was fanned & rubbed every second by myself and Ma. He was taken to Mrs. Nell. Smiths where he boarded. Drs. Graves & Bradley & Sherman examined him. He was literally covered with black & blue spots and had to be bathed in hot water—and cold clothes kept on his head. O such pain and suffering as he endured. He was light headed a couple of times at night and we had to work so hard to keep him alive.

Pa came for me every morning and I would come home and do the work & then he would take me back in the evening & I wld sit up nights, some nights not sleeping a minute. Everybody was so kind. Austin Brown helped us some. All the girls & boys & people seem to feel so bad. we had to fasten the doors for a week & not allow any one in to see him. Why there was a perfect line coming & going all the time the first few days. Dr. Sherman said he never see any one have so many friends in his life. Sat. Oct. 11. Henry was brought home. Mr Morse (liveryman) brought him in the omnibus & Ma. & Dr. Sherman rode with him.

It jarred him up considerably & I sat up alone with him. Had 20 out of each hour for myself devoting the rest of the time to Henry. Since then he has gained rapidly & to day Oct. 19th he can get to the barn and back on crutches. One leg being almost useless. The heft of the blow was on his hip so of course it effects his whole leg. He was shingling the hip as it is called. was perched on a stool 1 ft.

one side of a rope and the other the other side—the rope was fastened to a hook that projected between the boards farther up the spire. just as he sat down on his stool the hook turned just enough to let the rope off & as a natural consequence Henry went down.

. . . But oh how thankful we are. he is going to get all over it. that is if he will not strain it too much. It must have time. Dr. Sherman just called & was well pleased with his treatment. Thinks Henry will come out all right.

As to the work I can't tell how many washings & ironings I have done. But a doz. pillow slips had to be changed each day besides sheets & clothes. & I rem. of washing & ironing 23 slips one day when I came home & then baking a doz. pumpkin pies, & making cake & washing all the dishes making the beds & to see to every thing else. Why I am stronger than I tho't I was. I wrenched my back lifting & turning Henry & now my left wrist is "gun" out. He can not turn or get on or off the bed without lifting and—well a great many offered to & were bound they would sit up with him but I couldn't trust such a care to any one. Ma is tired too. Her hands are so near raw that she can do nothing with the housework. I have not undressed since Henry was hurt. think I shall to night.

Pa & Ma have gone to Mr. Beals to see Ida who is nearly dead with quick consumption. Those absesses have eaten her all away in front exposing the ribs, pericardium, pleura, breast bone, etc. & she is so poor. I sent her a boquet of pansies. Henry is lying down. Grandpa is reading. . . . [. . .]

MON. 27. Do gen. work. Harry came up & spent the evening.[12] Said he fell 16 ft. with a scaffolding. raked his shin a little—fell Friday. Is not able to go to rink, says he does not think it pays. Henry steps on his foot a little for the first to day. Pa said he wanted Henry to take down seed corn from the top of the cupboard. It is queer some folks know so little about anything. Henrys leg & hip are so sore he can scarcely sit down on cushions and then tell him to do that? Moonshine. [. . .]

FRI. 31. Help Ma. We have a time with GrandPa. Pa & Aunt Hattie have set him up against Ma, & he is capable of being mean and abusing anyone. He seems to think it is Ma's duty to support him—told her she lied etc. I would have turned him out door had I been in Ma's place.

And then Pa is so mean. I do not know what it will amount to.

Grandpa finally said he had no demands to make of Ma.

November 1884

SAT. 1. Ma & Pa go to town. Ma got me a pair shoes for winter 2.50. flannel for underwear 4.35. Pa tho't I did not need them. He & Ma had an argument when they went to town. I thought they would when they started—I could see the mad in Pa for the past week. He went over the same lingo (ma said) that he was coming to want & he wished he was dead—that lots of times he thought he'd ~~get~~ put himself out of the way. what kind of a man is he any way to make such speeches.

I question myself.—is it right for us to live with such a person. He waits every time to take Ma alone & then misuses her why he told her he'd given her $40 this summer & he couldn't see for the life of him what she had done with it—so much. well he said she took every cut and there was not a penny paid out for him. Ma simply told him that when they went to the woolen mills the other day—she got him clothes to the amt. of—I've forgotten—that she spent $8.00 for him for his clothes & $5.00 for groceries & $10.00 to Ansel Henderson for sheep. that "every penny had been spent for him & him only." When he wishes he was dead etc. I should too if I'd done such mean things as he has. GrandPa will have to leave here. He needn't tell Ma she *"lies"* I can't stand that. . . . [. . .]

TUE. 18. Made two pair woolen drawers for myself. Help Ma. knit. Am going to knit Henry, Harry & myself a pr. of mittens (blue). Grandpa came down and wanted his things & the bureau which is ma's. Said he had taken council & had a good backer etc. Ma told him his things were ready any time he would call for them. That the bureau never was his and he should not take it. He said he acknowledged that and went away mad. After Pa came home from husking corn Ma told him about it, & then *he* was mad & said he better put himself out of the world & well—I don't know what all.

The thing of it is Grandpa would not have turned against Ma so if Pa had not so slandered her to him and Aunt Hattie. Ma told him he was at the bottom of it all. *And he is*. I do not think it is right to live with a person that makes such threats & speeches as he does. Why this makes the second time, to my knowledge, that he has told Ma that he believed she intended to kill him yet. He also said if he had what he thought belonged to him he would leave us all.

I suppose that means he'd turn us all out door which he has so many times tried to do—but thank the Lord has failed. Henry is getting so he can walk a little without a cane. He had not ought to do it. He is lame. He said he'd hate to live with such a man (as Pa) alone. He would want to make his will first. Now you see Henry intends to work in the shop with Trenchard again as soon as he can, in 2 or 3 weeks, & I will be gone teaching. So I dont see what Ma will do. I shall worry about it. Colder. [. . .]

SAT. 22. Rained all day. Ma covered grape-vines with straw. I sewed—finished up my underwear. 4 underwaists, one skirt. 3 pair drawers. They look nice & are made good. Rain. [. . .]

December 1884

MON. 1. Commence teaching in sub. District No. 2. Honey Creek Township. 20 enrolled. Think it will be a pleasant school. Mostly germans. The stove smoked extremely much all day which left us all crying. Nice weather. [. . .]

WED. 24. Pa came for me. My face was chilled going home. They are quite well. GrandPa took the bureau and his things.[13] I feel very sorry for Ma. Cold.

THURS. 25. Christmas. Had turkey etc. Harry was up and stayed all day. He let me read his chart. It is quite good. Said he was coming up to school. Sleighing. Cold.

FRI. 26. Am *unwell*—very much so. Ma and Henry go to town. Rec'd through P. O. Byrons poems & a "note" for me. & Ma & Pa & Henry each a nice Xmas card. They were marked—"Compliments of Harry." It is a nice present. I made the curtains for the school-house which the scholars & I bought.

SAT. 27. At home. Do a small washing. Help Ma a little. Grunt a little. Cold. [. . .]

MON. 29. Have a good school. Mr. Millen came to visit my school—stayed from Recess until noon. Was much pleased. Said he liked my methods very much—especially in spelling & arithmetic. That which so many teachers neglected I had taken up. He was at our house a week ago and stayed over night.—& said he enjoyed his visit very much. Said I had improved the appearance of the school-room—a great deal. Rain. [. . .]

CHAPTER FOUR

"This World Is Not So Bad a World": 1885–1886

"This world is not so bad a world as some would

like to make it

But whether good or whether bad depends on how

you take it."

—lines copied into Sarah's diary, July 15, 1885

January 1885

THURSDAY. 1. Happy New Year. taught school. Wesley said "Teacher you always get ahead of us." when I said "Happy new year" to each. Mr. Alcorn had a chance to trade me for the teacher in No. 1.[1] Mr. Fenner. Hear from all around that I am well liked as a teacher. Nathan Croyle—a pupil of No. 1 came all day. Cold. [. . .]

FRI. 9. Taught school—The scholars seem to think a great deal of me. No one came for me. Feel disappointed for it is a beautiful day. [. . .]

FRI. JAN. 23. Taught. Henry & Harry came for me. It is beautiful moonlight. we had a nice ride home. 8 o'clock P.M. Am not well. Ma had worked too hard. I took her some glass sauce dishes. Snow.

SAT. 24. At home. cold & Snowy. I feel real mean. washed etc. [. . .]

February 1885

[. . .]

FRI. 13. One of Jud Breeds scholars left the Edgewood school & comes to me. She is a large girl 17 or 18 Yrs. old. It works Mr & Mrs Alcorn terribly. You see this Breed is their daughters husband and he taught in 1883,—I think—, the school where I am teaching. And well theres no one can beat him teaching in their estimation. I hope

I may never brag of what I may or may not do. Wesley built the fire. Snow. [. . .]

SUNDAY. 15. Wonder what Ma & Henry are doing. Am lonesome to day. Andy & his wife & babies & Jud Breed & his wife & babies were here to make a visit.[2] I made some (4) wings for Lori & Maud who are to be dressed as angels. They are very pretty. Snow, blow & Cold. [. . .]

THURS. 19. It is 10 below zero and I am almost freezing while writing this in my room. Am sitting on one foot beside my trunk. Commenced school at half past eight & had a half hours nooning so as to recite lessons & go once through the programme for tomorrow night. Warmer—Cold. [. . .]

SUNDAY. 22. We got a little uneasy and it being Beautiful. sleighing. Mr Alcorn hitched up & we started with my satchel for Manchester. When we reached Dan Ryans Pa was there and so I & my satchel parted company with our friends & entered Pa's ???ng. & after calling on Dan who is sick a bed we were soon on the road home, or rather to Mr Meads where found Ma anxious to see Sarah. We stayed there till almost evening & then came home. May gave me her picture. Was glad to see them all. . . . Reached home where we found Brother Henry keeping house, was gladded to see him. He is getting over being lame quite a considerable. Am glad. Am sorry that his hip troubles him though.

We have 16 lambs. Pa has sold Minnie to Bailey for $100. Expect he feels better now. He drives Comet & Beauty. A beautiful day. [. . .]

TUES. 24. At home all day. Help Ma wash. swept, made beds knit etc. Ma & Pa went to town. Pa is mad to night. Hope he will get over it. Uncle stopped. Jay Smith is moving to town. . . . [. . .]

March 1885

[. . .]

TUES. 3. Started to Manchester at half past seven in the morning: ran part of the way to catch the train. Rode on the "Accomodation" to Delaware Center where I had to wait till nearly noon to take the Northern train. Arrived at 9.10 A.M.

Visited the school. Amy Boggs teaches in the Primary room. She does not have good order but seems to put all her spite on one little urchin. She nearly pulled the tongue out of what seemed to me, to be a bright, industrious boy. He took his books home & nearly 2/3 of those who commenced the first day are not coming now. . . .

WED. 4. Inauguration of President Cleveland.[3] Now we Democrats are happy. I suppose.

Sarah went by train to visit the Greeley school, but she was stranded when the Delaware Center train did not come to take her back to Manchester. She wrote in her diary that she had to sleep that night in a bed with a family, including a child. The wife had spasms and fits in the middle of the night, and Sarah was terrified that her reputation would be ruined. She wrote of shivering and crying in the bed. At daybreak Sarah walked home.

WED. MARCH 11. 1885. . . . Pa said he went in to see the Lawyer about Grandpa & that the law is that after a person becomes a resident of this state, & a year will make him so, that his or her children can be compelled to take care of & support him & even the grand-children.[4]

If that is the case we will have to do something about it. Of course it brings up a great deal, & as Aunt Hattie was passing Pa went out & called her in to talk about it. She said she would not let her father go to the poorhouse but that she could pay nothing for his support (& that would throw it on us). She said many things. Said that GrandPa is intending to sue Ma for work done here last Summer & for a pillow & linen table cloth. Now I did not know that he had a pillow here & he gave the cloth to Ma when he came here. He can have all that belongs to him in welcome. & then she went on to tell how we misused her & how Pa was & is a perfect waiter & slave to his family. how we treat him worse than the niggers of the south & I dont know what all else. She never would have told all these things if it had not been told her by Pa. He's the one & I think he knows it too. Thats just the way he talks just as bad & worse than I can think. It's pretty tough to have one of a family do such shall I say, wicked, acts. We were all talking about it to night & Pa said "if the property had been in his hands it would be different & if he was obliged to support GrandPa, before he would do it, *he* knew what he could do and he should do it too but it would cause a terrible contention etc. But he'd not tell now it was not necessary." I suppose at least I can not think aught else that he means unless he means to sue either for a divorce or a deed of this place.

I'm so sorry that we have to have so much trouble but it might be worse & all I hope & pray is that we may live & enjoy ourselves better & that we may see our enemies vanish from our sight & hearing. Thawing.

THUR. 12. At home all day. Pa went to town again to see the lawyer & when he came home he said that the only way Ma could clear herself of Grandpa's support is to deed back the property to him that she could go down & do it tomorrow or any day as soon as she pleased. Dear me! That means that if he has a deed that we (Ma & H & I) have no home here any more. I believe Henry takes it worse than I for he said "Here I am not able to work & all I shall ever try to do is to make a living & can never go to school any more" Thats the way I feel too. Ma is going to see Lawyer Bronson & get his advice what to do, & what not to do. It seems like a very serious affair to me. I can not believe that Ma could live with him any more than Henry & I. For he has tried & threatened time and again that as soon as the children were of age he'd show her what she'd have to do. Henry work on secretary. Ma sew on Pa's clothes & I help do housework & straighten my things in my trunk. Pa now thinks that we are in his clutches. O Lord we pray that it may not be as bad as we contemplate. to put it at best it is very very bad. Henry had a real cry I feel so sorry for him for I'm certain that he never can come on this place or in this dear house if Pa has a deed of it for I do believe that Pa hates him & also his family & when he puts on his flattering talk once in a while like his saying he "is going to help us to go to school" etc. He's always *"going to"*—and its only deceit. Dear Father in Heaven I only trust in thee & with tears I ask that we may be protected: that it may all be for the best & to the end I'll watch & wait & hope and pray. Chilly wind. [. . .]

SAT. 14. Pa went to town again & said he had seen Bronson & Ma could have till Wednesday & then she could go down. He feels terrible upstrapulous and talks as if no one knew anything beside himself. Ma feels very bad. She told Pa that she felt as if she would be in the streets just as soon as he has the place & told him of the threats he has made as the reason. Now we are in more trouble. It was time for me to be unwell last Wednesday & I have not yet. Ma said Could it have been possible that I was chloroformed in Delaware Center.[5] I don't see how for I know I was not asleep at any time. Dear me what wicked thoughts I have run over lots of times think I will come around all right & think the reason I did not was because I got my feet damp. My head was full & I felt just like it until I got my feet damp. Took some pepper tea & soaked my feet in hot water. Stormy.

SUN. 15. Have not come around yet. My head aches all day. Pa does not say much. Ma & I & Henry have talked it over & it may be that Ma can reserve some in some way. I dont know but I believe in less than six months we will not be enjoying the comforts which surround an undivided home. We have wanted Pa to get his picture taken for ever so long but no he was "too poor." To day he said he is going to have his hair cut & put on his new suit (Ma finished yesterday) & have his picture taken & give one to Mercelia one to Marguerite one to Dennis & keep one.[6] I must be that it will all be for the best but it looks like darkness with not a ray of sunshine in our path. Ma got a real good supper, I helped her, she said she felt it was the last Sunday we'd be together & feel it is our home. It will not be long & we will have *no home—No Home.* Those words which will almost chill ones heart I fear will too soon be made real & perceptible.

Henry went to church. He is real lame from the walk. How I wish I knew he would get sound & strong. My head is aching real hard. Snowing.

MON. 16. Have a severe ache in the lower part of the abdomen & came around all right. Ma cried for joy when I told her. I *was glad too* and so Help me I will never endanger myself again. . . .

Ma had the blues pretty bad to day but feels some better to night. There is a place somewhere in this world, I know, where we can live if it be not here, but I feel as though our home is broken & the ties which have bound us shall soon be rent in twain & can never be united again. O, sad thought! . . . [. . .]

April 1885

APRIL 1, 1885. WEDNESDAY. We uncovered bees & have a live swarm. Just the same we had a year ago and also 2 yrs ago now. . . . Henry took Ma down [to see Mr. Bronson, the attorney]. She wanted to take some old trumpery down to the pawnbroker to pay for the mink skins she bought. . . . Now Pa knows that Ma can't get along with him and it looks to me as if he is trying to wear Ma out "kill her in fact, & it plainly shows he does not care for her, or her feelings. I do think he is the meanest of any one I ever saw. Here Ma looks like a ghost cant do up the dishes without being all used up & has to sit down & rest so often—I feel so sorry for her. Shower.

THUR. 2. Ma took down the birds & sold them to the pawn broker yesterday. It seems so lonesome without them. Pa kept speaking about the paying for, of Ma's mink furs which she bargained for of the pawn man & Ma was determined he should not pay a cent on them so we gathered up our old traps (things we could not use) old fruit cans my clock, parasol, old photo album etc.etc. The big bird cage, old sewing machine & such things. I disliked to sell the birds. They are beautiful nutcrested singers "Harry" & "Peter." Harry is dark all but his throat which is orange. Peter is all orange color. & they are such nice singers.

Well Ma & Pa went to town to day & Ma gave Pa a deed of the place.[7] I do hope it is all right. we must think its for the best anyway. Ma never would have done it if she had not been compelled to. I can think so much but can not write it to night. But I do think that Pa is a poor specimen of what a husband & father should be.

I feel as if we had no home, Henry & I & Ma—what may we— what *can* we do. May our Father in Heaven have Mercy upon us & his will not ours be done,—amen. . . . Dear me! I do hope Ma will be better soon for I am anxious about her she looks so bad—"so pale & careworn as she sits before me there," May she live many years & I do hope they will be happy years. Henry & I talked to day of going to the Phrenological Institute in N.Y. & we *will* too if we can, as soon as we can. We will have to read & study some first. One feeling with which we can retire to night is that Ma is not obliged to support GrandPa. That wasn't the reason at all that Pa wanted the deed. To day Ma said that Bronson told Pa they (He & Ma) had better make their will—Pa wouldnt even reply—kept reading a newspaper. Its as I tho't—He only has said he wanted it so he could make his will & made other harsh threats only so as to get the deed. He's got it. O may it be all right at last? Cold & disagreeable. [. . .]

WEDNESDAY 22. Done the work & Ma has got so she can talk a little better so we visited all day. Mr. Seger stayed all night with us. We did not retire till nearly 11 & arose at 5 so I did not get much sleep. In the morning before Ma & Henry rose and when Pa was at the barn Mr. Seger had a great chance to express his feelings I think for he smothered me with kisses & actually put his arms around my neck and "hugged" me. I told him he must not do so for its not right—He said if I was his girl I should never want for anything. He'd give $100,000 this minute for me if he had it & he'd have house built before night.

He'd like to help me do something some time & if I wanted to if I'd come to him he'd do anything he could to help me. Pa is digging a trench for his hedge along the road. Ma made an attempt & found two turkeys nests: too much for her. [. . .]

May 1885

In May Sarah began teaching in No. 2 Honey Creek Township School, the same school where she had taught the preceding winter. Twenty-seven students were enrolled.

[. . .]

FRI. 22. Expect to go home to night. Let out school 10 of 4 for I thought that if Pa did not come by 15 of 4, he would not come at all and then I'd have to go on the cars & wanted to get home early—But had not gone 20 Rods when I looked back & *Ma* & Pa coming for me. Pa hired a double covered buggy so Ma could come. Poor Ma—How glad I was to see her. She couldn't get out of the buggy, nor into the house without help & then would have fainted if had not had camphor & cold water instantly. She looks very very bad & has the dropsy so bad in her feet & up to her knees. She laid down awhile & then we ate supper and started for home. Mrs Ryan rode as far as Dan Ryans with us. He is gaining. Then when we got to Meads we stopped at the creamery & got a fresh drink of buttermilk & that rested Ma considerable.

Had to stop & change buggies in town. Pa lifted Ma from one to the other. Seems so bad for she's always been so spry. Arrived home in due time. Was glad to get home & see Henry. The hired girl (Ada Haskins) has to be told every-thing to do & I tell you she does not work the way I do when Im at home. Not *half* as hard. Wish I could find a real good girl & then there is nothing done for Ma at all. She said she had not slept any for two or three nights. Her feet pain her so & her heart beats faster & faster, about nine when we got home. Moonlight.

SAT. 23. *Sarah wrote that her parents had argued about her father's refusal to give Sarah money; Sarah was angry as well.*

. . . But I can stay at home & work just like a slave & if one cent is wanted he's mad & acts ugly as he can for a week & says "You've got the money & if you want any-thing—get it" He wants Ma to give him the note of Mr. Bailey's for Minnie—for a covered buggy—I told Ma to keep it—Its all she's got or will get. He told me once that I ought to take my money & buy one if I wanted it.

I told Ma I'd not bother about it—but she is so weak that it gets her heart to beating so bad that I fear it will not stop. . . .

Mr. Seger called—kissed me—was so glad to see me. I was glad to see him but do not think it right for him to think so much of me. Henry & I had a wrestle. fun for him. Moonlight.

SUN. 24. . . . I tell you I've cried more than once since Fri. evening when I first saw [Ma] this time. Something must be done for her. I kept a wet cloth on her head & rubbed her feet a while last night & she thought she could sleep a little which she said she did this morning. . . .

June 1885

[. . .]

FRI. 5. Taught school—The children were playing school and Flora got hurt. Lonnie Phelps was the Prof. & whipped her—too hard. He said he did not mean to hurt her & with tears in his eyes. He is trying to do right. But its hard work for one who has been in such a rough school as he, to get sobered down—It can't be done in 3 wks. nor 3 mo. . . . [. . .]

THUR. 11. I see by the Democrat that one of our horses fell in an "open ditch" & almost killed it—also that Ma's Silesian Lambs 1 yr old sheared 21 lbs of wool. . . . [. . .]

THUR. 25. *Sarah began by writing about a visit from Mr. Seger.*

. . . "Dear Sadie" he said "if I was single you'd not be here long—I've been so home-sick to see you." I told him it would not do—(when he asked me if he should take me home Fri. night)—for he knew what such things lead to & it was worse for me than him. He said he knew it and "Sadie—you need have no fear that I would do anything to harm you or hurt your good name." That if I was ever in trouble or wanted any assistance of any kind to come to him—He would befriend me. And I know he would. He fairly worships me. The worst of all he said to me was this. "Sadie—if your mother dies—you must be our girl & come & live with us." "We *must* have you." I am sick to night. Very warm.

July 1885

WED. 1. Taught school. Have a nice school. Milton is helping me to make badges for the scholars the 4th. Warm.

SAT. 4. Celebrated at Edgewood. the 1st time I was ever away from home the 4th. Almost always have been to Manchester. My scholars—most 2/3 of them were there and marched. They had the 13 original states represented. then the York school passed behind them. Sherd Robinson told me where to have them march. I took red and white cambric for the Banner. On the white side in silver letters "In God we trust" and a wreath of evergreen. On the red side York No. 2. Then had silver fringe on both. Their badges we made of red cambric & silver letters. They looked real nice. Took dinner with Ray Adams & family at Mrs Homans. Had ice cream at Jud Breeds. He never mentioned my school. They also had rag-muffins and a more ridiculous affair, *parading*, I never saw.

Stayed to fire works in the evening. It rained about an hour which made the roads muddy. Rode up and back with Ray Adams. Saw Wesley several times. He told Mr Graham (of whom he hired the buggy) that he was going to take me to Manchester—So Mr G told Mr. Alcorn. Thats all I know about it. Now if he knows anything— he must surely know that a Lady would go in no such manner. It makes me out of patience any-way. Got a pair of rubbers of Mr Beyer 50¢. Saw Mr Vint Hubbell with whom I had a pleasant chat. He is of the same temperament as Mr Seger. Andy & Helen & children & Jud Breed & Sallie & we were all together. Had two Balloons. Pleasant. Rain. [. . .]

MON. 6. Have the head-ache this morning. Its *muddy*. Now Im ready for school. To day I made Mamie Adams read after school because she refused to at class time. She took her books home. And Ray came up to see about it. I told him what I thought about it. Do not know what his conclusion was, but think perhaps he felt no better. . . . Sent Ma a letter to day. Hope she feels as well as I do. Mamie & Frankie are both bastards. (Do not care about putting that word in my journal) and are nearest the dumb animals of any human beings I ever saw. Warm. [. . .]

WED. 15. Have the sick head ache & stomach ache. am not well to day which was the cause. Had to give up hearing B & A spelling which Jennie heard for me. They did very well only she had to ask the scholars how to pronounce the words. Felt better in the afternoon. In the evening Milton & I walked down to Mr Croyles. Had a good visit. Mr C. is Sub Director in their district & if there teacher goes back on them he wants me to teach 2 1/2 mo for them.

Feel better—Not much like walking though. Warm.

This world is not so bad a world as some would like to make it
But whether good or whether bad depends on how you take it.
—From Anna's piece.

MON. 27. Help Ma. Ma is very poor. 90 lbs is all she weighs. wash the white clothes. Warm. [. . .]

WED. 29. Washed, mopped & scrubbed both porches & the kitchen. Did up breakfast work all by 11 A.M. Was tired. am trying to fix over old white dress into a skirt. Mr. Seger here to supper. Iron some. I think he says things to me which he has no right to say & Ill tell him what I think if he continues. Harry came home with Henry & stays to night. He looks sick. . . .

August 1885

[. . .]

THURS. 4. Ma is quite nervous to day. this morning she fell down over on that bank across the road & hurt herself quite badly. She cried. then lay down & fell asleep. I mopped & scrubbed & tugged around the work & got dinner. After noon I cut my pink calico that Ma gave me. Cut the top from a night gown pattern. pointed yoke. full waist with a deep flounce. opens at the back. The skirt will have 2 deep ruffles on back & one narrow one at foot in front. Made nearly all the waist to day. Then did the washing after night. Am tired. Cooler. Warmer.

WED. 5. do general housework. I nearly made my dress. Ma very sick to day. It seemed as though her head would burst. Is a little better to night. I was frightened. She seemed sick to her stomach & went to the henhouse. She called me & I hastened to where I found her holding her head & sobbing ~~that~~ out "My head will burst" "Do rub my head & neck Sarah." I felt of it it was burning & I hastened for water & camphor—Relieved her so that my my [*sic*] assistance she managed to reach the couch. It is perfect grief & despair & trouble. Poor sick woman who has worked so hard & to be ill treated & abused almost makes my heart "fly" sometimes. What can I do? I question my self again & again. What can be done. Henry is quite lame. Now I hope all will be better in the morning & that I may rise early. My back is lame to night & my knees shaky from sewing. There goes the train so Good-Night. Blows like fall. [. . .]

MON. 10. . . . I can't begin to think of all [Pa] said. Would dislike to mar these pages with such thoughts. It will be no pleasure to read them in the future. He was just raving & said he'd "divide up" For Ma to "get in" & go down. Ma told him that she should not leave without having something that she had earned. That if he wanted to go down & give her what belonged to her to do it. She would not go with him this morning. I got in & then he commenced at me. Its the 1st time I ever talked back to him. But I couldn't help it. To think there is my mother so sick she can scarcely get around yet striving to work & for him to abuse & talk to her & then to me about her is more than I can bear. He wants Henry & I to leave home entirely & I guess we'll have to but we'll not leave Ma to his abuse.[8] why he told her several times "When the children get big enough to take care of themselves then you'll see you'll come to tune" etc. Said we did not help him at all that we would not that we'd run him through 2 or 3 times & all most drove him to despair. Said He was kind & good to his family—"Yes" I said "It is kind to see Ma wearing herself out & when she asks you a civil question what you buy? what you sell? how much you pay out etc. for you to sit as dumb as a stump never replying any more than as though she did not speak." I was mad a little.

He said He chased around night & day for us. He would like to know what he was doing now "*a taking you down there?*" "Why" I said I asked Ma "what you were going to town for that I did not know you were going" She said she asked you "you said you had "biziness." "Well" He said "I have got "biziness" (?) I am after a man to help me in hay" "Well" I said "You are surely not coming down on my a/c then" "Dear Im just driven to despair if I tho't you folks could take care of yourselves Id leave this world" "I dont know what to do with myself." So he kept at it till we got to Grants where he stopped for him to help in hay. Would go no further. I told him he better go over after the girl [Vira Philips]. He said "Girl or no girl I'll have my hay taken care of." I went over & saw the girl & told her we would be there about 4.30. So when Pa came down town He was going right past. I said "why didnt you turn here" He'd like to know "what for" he said. Then I told him for the girl—He was mad & scolded all the way there. Henry rode home too. The girl has a baby but its the best I could do. Got home all right. Ma sick. Pleas.

TUES. 11. Go to Normal. Large attendance, worthy instructor.[9] Think I would like Prof Stookey quite well. red hair & mustache. Pa does not eat with us. He declares he won't. He may be glad to—Am sorry he acts so queer. Ma a little better. Am not well. Pleas. [. . .]

WED. 26. It's a long time to miss writing; but this is my first opportunity. Have been so busy. To night I feel so bad for Pa has again commenced his meanness.

Vira was in the sitting room rocking the baby and Henry was washing his feet. Ma & I went to the henhouse. Soon I heard loud talking and went in. Pa went out just as I came in saying "you can't get it by setting around thats sure." I then asked Henry what was the matter. He said Pa told him he'd have to leave or work enough to pay his board & I know they had severe words. Am so sorry. Henry is so lame and I think he has done well this Summer. & to think that Pa'd turn him out doors.

Vira (they have gone to bed) said she was frightened, that she was a mind to run down where we were. Henry is very nervous, He does more than he is able. Has moved a lot of weeds to day. Has asked Pa if he couldn't fix over the buggy, that is, have the team to get his tools home. Pa won't do it. I think things are in a terrible state of affairs & something must be done. . . . [. . .]

September 1885

[. . .]

SUN. 13. Looks nice & bright this morning. My eye-ball aches. Ma, Pa & I went up to Uncles. Vira went home. Henry alone. He is going away to work in the morning. New moon. [. . .]

TUES. 15. Henry went this morning with 6 others (they came along) are going to build a house for Bethel M.W. of Masonville. Hope they'll get along all right. Each took a quilt & H took his coat for they will sleep in the barn. Vira got sponky because Ma asked her where 3 of the teaspoons were & she picked up & went home—stopped at Aunt Hatties 1 1/2 hrs. Ma sew on my green dress. It is the nicest dress I ever had I think. . . . [. . .]

FRI. 18. Am all alone. Ma & I cut out part of my new black cashmere & brocade dress. At nearly noon Mr. Parkhurst stopped for Ma to go home with him & spend the afternoon which she did. He said he would bring her home to night. Mr. Seger also came at noon.[10] I went to work & got dinner. He stayed till nearly three. Pa did not go back to the field until Mr. Seger had gone.

Had quite a visit Mr S—offered to help me to go to school—that was well enough but when he come to say I am the one of his choice & kissed me why then I told him it would do no more. Said he was glad I had checked him. he tho't more of me for doing it & he would guard himself closer in the future. Why! it makes me out of patience to here a married man talk so to me. Here it is 4 o'clock; I cant do anything. Seems sort o' lonesome like.

October 1885

[. . .]

MON. 5. Do some work. Went to town & back afoot. Ma is to pay me. Put $25 in Bank. Henry paid me a $11.00 which makes us even. Have $125 in bank at present, & $5.67 on hand. Called on Mrs Prof. Trowbridge. She is Miss Randalls sister. Miss R. desired me to. . . . [. . .]

TUES. 13. Wash in the forenoon a big washing too got it out at 11 A.M. Mr Joseph Hutchinson came at 11.30 to see Pa.[11] He is the very fellow I dreamed of seeing several days ago. He was a stranger & I dreamed he was my husband & we had a baby & then it fled. As soon as I saw him I recognized his features in my dream. How strange.

He is courteous in manner & pleasant in appearance.

Afternoon Pa & I went to town. Got 50¢ worth of black cambric. Met Mr H on the street & he said "Ah! *Good morning.*" Ma said he must have been upset & Henry laughed. Thats nothing. But it does appear as if he was thinking of something when he looks at me so closely as far as he can see me either way. la. la. Henry went with Mr. Atwater to work on a large corncrib 10 mi. N.W. from here. Get early breakfast. Dark-ooogh. [. . .]

FRI. 16. Sew etc. Cut my plaid flannel dress. [. . .]

SUN. 18. Went to Church & S. S. Henry & Harry came home together. Quite Pleas.

Harry has rec'd a patent on his Streetcar indicator thinks he'll soon be worth a Million dollars.[12]

Got a letter from Mr Alcorn. Mr Croyle in Sub. No. 1. wants me to come & teach there this winter. Am sorry I can not accomodate him. Rainy in Evening. [. . .]

November 1885

SUN. 1. November 1885. Too muddy to go to church. Harry came up in a carriage, after supper he desired me to take a short ride. I had no excuse so I went. We went west as far as Amos. Saterlees there turned round & drove back. Its mud, mud & cold. Harry said—"Well, Sarah I intend to come back here for a wife sometime. do you think I could find one?" "No sir not I" He seemed to feel very sorry said he was foolish. Then he said he wasn't. then he seemed to feel very sorry & said that settled it with him—he'd never get married to anyone. He is going to Cleveland in about two weeks to see about selling his indicator. Said his Uncle wrote him that he was well acquainted with 13 presidents of street-car companies in Cleveland and if it proved a success would purchase it. Id like to know what a fellow thinks I want to get married for. Here I am working as faithful as a school-mom can to earn enough to school myself in medicine & do aught else I desire. Then to think of his wanting me to marry him. Why; in all the times he's ever been here I've had no conversation with him, he's almost what I consider a stranger. Cold.

SUN. 8. . . . I am solemnly thinking of Mr Seger to night. Why? I dare not scarcely tell.

A married man, demanding the esteem of the highest circle of society in Manchester, educated, a church-member & respected citizen. To be ingulfed by the few humble charms of a country school-mom. Seemingly desperate & so passionately fond. What does it all mean? Last evening when he called he said he could not pass he must see how we are getting along. When he started he forgot his gloves & had to come back after them. I handed them to him for I found them on the floor & as I did so he stole a kiss. Now I think considerable of Mr. Seger, as a friend. He has always kissed me but now I am older grown & the necessity of being a worthy woman forbids me accepting such warm friendship? from a married man.[13]

Is he not my worst enemy? Seeking to destroy my good name, my future welfare & happiness? What would the young men of M—— & vicinity think should one thought be lisped to their ears. would I ever enjoy their society or that of other persons of respect.

I am truly sorry—but I know one can control themselves far enough to do right if they seek. For my own passionate ? desires are strong as of some others & I can control them—So can they—They will have to.

Again must I pray for wisdom, health & strength. Give me wisdom, and may true womanly graces deck my brow. May Virtue Lead me in her narrow path may I faithfully follow being guided by her right hand of Justice and Truth and Love. Cold. [. . .]

SUN. 15. [Joseph Hutchinson and I] had a pleasant talk—I think he is a perfect gentleman as far as I have seen him. He has dark eyes & complexion & strong hair.

Is an agreeable talker & is to my ideas the best of my gentleman acquaintances. In fact I had to pray three times to night for I would be so interrupted by thoughts stealing in of Mr H——

Try my best to throw them off & in spite of my efforts they will return.

Seems to me he must have thought something of me or he would have passed me on so short an acquaintance.

Harry did not come up. am sorry if he feels so bad as all that. A Beautiful Day.

MON. 16. *Sarah went to see her new school, Sub. No. 6 Delaware County, the "Red Schoolhouse," four miles north of Manchester.*

. . . They have put up a new stove & cleaned the room which is commodious, pleasant, & conveniently arranged having all the necessary furniture, Broom (new) ash pail, poker, shovel, wood box, and library.

Enrolled 26 this morning—should judge they had been used to do about as they pleased. whispering, chewing gum, & a general shuffling noise—I shall never try to get along with. I do not want to be cross but we shall have to work diligently to overcome these formed habits. am tired. Hope Ma is well. Eddie is at home. Warm. [. . .]

WED. 18. I think they are a terrible noisy set—Why I supposed from what I had heard it was a model school. Chewing gum was the first attraction in the school-room and I quietly stepped down from the stage, and took a couple of "quids"—(Cuds I should call them) from the small pupils on the front seats. The older members took the hint I guess for I saw not another bit to day—The noise—O! Dear! So many pile-drivers. But they are all going to try to do better. Every one seems to be quite willing—They are careless with their slates. . . .

Prayer meeting to night—I have a severe head-ache. Pleasant. [. . .]

SAT. 28. Pa wanted me to wash & get the work done up—was exceedingly angry when I declined. I am willing to do that which I am able & all I can—Ma & I & Henry went to town in afternoon. I owe Henry 10¢ for blank paper. If it was not for Ma I'd not go home many times I can assure you. How it makes one feel to know that every mouthful they eat is begrudged them. Why! the other day he told Ma she must not buy a thing to eat or wear unless she paid for it & he knows she has not a penny—He got a bhl of apples, something Ma never eats, thats for himself but she must not get a qt of cranberries (12¢) or a 5¢ head of cabbage. Warm. [. . .]

December 1885

[. . .]

THURS. 3. I am feeling first rate to night. Have a splendid school yesterday and to day. And I feel much encouraged. Am so thankful that my efforts and earnest Labors are being appreciated. . . . [. . .]

MON. 7. Have another days work finished. Think I have a pleasant school. They are all so interested I think. If I can only keep them so.

Katie Peyton came & sat down by me this morning & said "Teacher I'm going to try & be a better girl this week & work more." May God bless Katie & give her strength & wisdom and power to overcome her weaknesses if she have any. Such expressions call forth my deepest sympathy. Edmund built a fire for me this morning and came over a little while to day noon when I went over for my dinner. . . . [. . .]

CHRISTMAS 1885. Up at 5.30—Breakfast at 6. Slept in chair from 6.30 till 7.30. Then Edmund & I went to school-house & prepared what we could. Then Willie & Horace went after lumber to make a stage. Worked all day; Am tired too. Mrs Hollister, Myra & a house full of others with myself as general sup't succeeded in building a stage putting up the tree and arranging scenery & so forth. they came in so early. House was cram full at 5 o'clock. Ma & Albert & Henry came up about 2 P.M. . . . [. . .]

THURS. 31. Have a splendid school—Scholars are extremely industrious to day—I give them New Years cards to night—they kiss me good-night.—I thought last year that if I could manage so as not to have the pupils kiss me good-night—for no matter who came they must all have a kiss & good-night from Teacher. Am I to encounter this same difficulty this term I wonder. It looks like it.

Went home with Ernest & Clarence Crocker to stay all night—He is a preacher (Regular quack, I should judge) He smokes & I think from appearances they are a rough religious family.

Mrs Crocker said she heard when I first came up there that I believed in dress reform & she tho't it sensible. She is going to give me painting lessons. Pleasant.

January 1886

JANUARY IST, 1886. Commencing of a Happy New Year I hope. I will briefly note my days Labors-pleasures? In the 1st place I slept a little and dreamed more last night—Dreamed I was married to a rich man. Listened to the gossip of Crockers—breakfasted on white Bread, buns, pork rinds "22 lbs for a $1.00 prunes" and sweet cake. It seems a pair of arctics were thrown to Rilla Holmes—Labeled Rhoda Williams & the donor has traced them up—But Rilla refuses to give them up—She is my "head-strong" pupil who says she will stand the pupils upon pegs in the corner & whom all the Boys & girls pick on. . . . [. . .]

SAT. 9. A very cold day. 22 Below Zero. Henry gone to town—Hope he wont freeze. He talks of going to Missouri. Blustery & cold. I washed some hdkfs stockings aprons etc. Ma is a little better I think. Am going to Commence grading my school next week. Wonder who sent my Christmas card. Ironed 3 hrs. from 6 till 9 P.M. Am tired out. Zero. 30. [. . .]

WED. 13. Last night I carried one of the Little Girls—Irene Hollister—to my boarding place—for she sprained her ankle so bad that she could not step on her foot. Never had such a "Lug" before quite. Have the tooth-ache all day—We set up later than ever last night—I have so much work & writing to do.

Have a Gum Boil and tooth-ache. . . . [. . .]

SAT. 16. Ma was awful bad off when we got home last night. Had worked herself sick. Here Pa sat reading—He wouldnt raise his hand to help her if she dropped dead in her tracks. Seems to me I can't get along this way—I'd rather hire a girl or stay at home myself. Ma can't bear up under it—She is so weak—I will be glad if only she can get well. Pa is so cross too & makes her worry & lots of trouble. Henry went to town this forenoon & got himself a pocket Revolver $10—Silver Plated. Hope he may never get hurt with it. . . .

SUN. 17. Not so cold—work all day—washed some & help Henry to pack up his things. Was just as tired as I could be. I never felt so bad to say Good-Bye before—

Henry says "Sarah be steady—be distant as necessary. Stick to school teaching & I believe you will be Co. Supt.—"if you are steady and keep doing as you now are."

He covered me up in the cutter & said "Bye-bye Sister." I tried not to cry but the tears would flow & I felt bad all the way. Henry will

have but $8 after he gets to Kansas City. But he said not to take
mine out of the bank. It never seemed so bad to have Henry go
before. *Snowed* for 2 or 3 hours. [. . .]

SUN. 24. Well I've got back to my boarding place at home to day. Help
do up the work. Albert was up in the afternoon. He used to clerk for
Loomis & said the Basket flannel sold for $1.20 a yd & the other
goods in same proportion. Dear me I wish I knew how Henry is
getting along & if he is comfortable. Albert rode to town when Pa
brought me. Pa said that next winter he was going to move to town.
He would[n't say] this if he'd known Henry was going away—& it
seemed awful lonesome over home now, & he got real nervous &
keeps looking for someone to come—

May be he'll have chance to regret his actions which have been
so barbarous to Brother & I.

He was so ugly to Henry that is impossible for him to stay at home
& then going away so sudden without a cent almost & to a far off
place—god only knows where—it makes him repent a little I guess.
He does not think Henry will ever come back—I do—& that in
April. Guess Pa'll wish more than once he had been a little kinder to
Henry, & I hope he will. How lonesome it seems. I must now write
to Henry, it is getting late . . . . [. . .]

Sarah burned her arm severely when it brushed against a stove pipe.
She didn't write in her diary again until February 6.

February 1886

SAT. FEB. 6. . . . To day is the Teachers Association—Pa took Ma & I
down just at noon. He is mad and scarcely spoke. Mrs Congar had
an essay also and in several places mine read word for word as hers.
Mine was "Theory." . . . I primped up & wore my best bib & tucker.
And managed to stammer off my essay to 150 Teachers. . . . Pa came
for us about 4.30—Was mad—When he came in he shook his fist
in Ma's face and said in a tremulous & savage tone "Emily you treat
me worse than I do my cattle in the stable." He then went out door
& Ma nearly fainted away. Her heart beat so I could hear it & she
trembled all over. I am so sorry—I believe Pa is insane he is all the
time telling suicide stories which he gleans from the Sun.

Ma & I were talking & Ma says she doesn't think she will live long and such shocks are so hurtful. Why her lips will even turn white. It makes me sad indeed. If its in my power this summer I'll get her away from that man. . . .

The following entry is in Emily's handwriting.

March 1886

MARCH 1. Sarah you said last night "Ma write in my Journal. *I* cant." I just thought I would write a line as I saw it in the Drawer. I tried to not read a word, but Sarah my eyes do take in so much that the above could not quite escape. I get lonesome every day—only that I think of Henry & you. how you are getting along so well. his letters and your sunday visits I should almost give up. I am so thankful that you are both all my heart could wish and can I really appreciate the blessing. You must never get discouraged with the annoyance which some pupils are ever ready to give. do only the best you can and their cutting words and misdemeanors will give them the most inconvenience. *they* will *not* forget. There is no use for me to worry or be made unhappy at the folly of others. just let them pass. I hope you did not get into a snow drift last night. my head does not feel very well to day—have to stay in doors too much. Pa is getting rats of Emma. by Ma. [. . .]

FRI. 19. Mr McNeil visited us. He said he felt like telling Rill, she need not come an other day that her presence was not needed.

The following poem, copied into Sarah's diary, is in Emily's handwriting.

Sarah. The following verse which just came into my head may be sung by "Rill" in years hence:
"Many a Miss feels favored with bliss,
When just sixteen a nice bean I ween
Has in advance asked her hand in next dance;
As years roll on—Changed; abused she has been.
Though, not like Rill, Sarah will be happy still.

Ma or
Emily Elizabeth Hawley Gillespie.
Manchester, Delaware Co.
State of Iowa.

On Wednesday, March 4, 1886, Emily wrote another lengthy entry in Sarah's diary.

WEDNESDAY 4 OF MARCH. Good morning Sarah. 10 A.M. I thought I would write a line in your Journal. I did not feel very well this morning, made some corn coffee, etc. a few crackers in it & now I feel better. Pa is throwing off a load of manure from the trucks so they can take them to help draw Emma Brooks hay & straw. he will have to load it again to draw it out. he *works* like a *nailer* to pick it up & off, *frozen solid, yesterday* him and John went and measured her oats & sawed her wood, took them 4 hours, and day before yesterday they were up there putting up oats about the same time. he was just ready to churn yesterday morning, left it, had to warm it again, churned 4 times, and all the chores to do, he *was* tired. I know. he came in last night *wishing he was dead, so much* to do & no help. went without his supper till most 9. I did not say a word and did not affect me much. Didn't pity him a bit—but when they came for him this morning I just said "we had enough of our own to do, we had to go to town. Sarah school closed this week and we had to go after her." he was washing the dishes and said not a word, but kept a good look-out to watch when they came for trucks. . . . (they the men seem to be . . . anxious for the well-fare of the charming young widow. Finally his aprobativeness run over "*I think* it would look very selfish indeed—for none of us men to not turn out and help a woman left in her circumstances." he preached. *I* think and *know* they neglect their own folks who are themselves to do it, and charity is, to not neglect nor injure ones-self to help those better able than they are. here *I* am can hardly get around, have not been out of the house for over a week, shut up here. it would have done me more good to go some where, than it did her. she has not lifted her finger to help herself since George died. but been waited on to curl & crimp her hair & be a lady, if they would try as hard to work for themselves as for her it would seem like something. Only sarcasm in reply. and he hurries about to help load her hay. "Yes and theres Harriet. *she* can chop her own wood, get water and work like a nigger for him, and he sit & smoke & read. and see her do it. she most dead with tooth ache. she looks like I do not know what, worse than a crazy person." I do not suppose it will do any good, but I guess he knows what I think about it—and would up with "well theres no use to say anything." I guess not either I have not been out doors since we went to Blanchards week ago to day, and we could have gone yesterday or the day before as well as not. Now do not be offended when you read this—for it is amusing after all to see how *silly upset and lose their sense some* do.

No Sorrow so great, but there is somewhere a pleasure mingled in. O yes Emma said to me "Ill show um what a *woman* can do." I think she will. Ma.

The next entry is also in Emily's handwriting.

MONDAY I. Pa's birth-day. he is fifty. Ma is cleaning furs. want to get them ready to make our cloaks. how glad I am you can come home for vacation next week. We can make our new clothes and do some other work. if I only can get well so I can get around better. I can not be too thankful. but Sarah I am weak. it seems sometimes I have no back at all, but as it is better sometimes I hope to get stronger when summer comes and I can get out into the fresh air. Blows but is warmer and thawing.

MARCH 6, 1886. School closed yesterday, am at home to day doctoring a cold. Shall have to write backwards from memory. . . . I composed a verse for each pupil & learned it but broke down when I had spoken but 4 or 5 stanzas. They all began to cry & then as I spoke a something rose in my throat & choked me & the tears would come. Edmund read then for me & he almost broke down too. Men & women & children—all cried. . . .

MON. 8. Pa went after Lizzie Beardsley to come & work for us. She is just 14. Have a bad cold. Cold wind. [. . .]

WED. 10. Ma & Pa went to Charley Babcocks to visit. Lizzie & I wash & I made 3 cranberry pies & a "stack" of fried cakes we are tired. I have a bad cold. This week so far I've made two chemise & a pair of overhalls. L—— is an awful girl to sleep with. She has eaten nothing scarcely since she's been here. Hope she wont get very homesick I know how to pity her.

She will put her arm over me in the night & nearly choke me & say "I like you teacher—you are the best person I ever knew—wished I was like you & Ma tho't it would be nice for me to work for your Ma and"—I'm choked again—Her father is dead & she has a Bro. Asa & sister Carrie (a short-hand writer). It is quite pleasant to day. My cold fairly stinks. Mr. Hutchinson told me to drink some hot lemonade & soak my feet in warm water at night. Bright, new moon true moon etc. etc. [. . .]

SATURDAY 13. Am better. We had dinner at 11 o'clock then Pa hitched on the cutter & we all, Lizzie too, went to town & then to Wattson Childs M.E. of M[anchester] & then to Mrs Wilcox's. I sent a letter to Henry. Mr Childs gave me an order for $120 I expected $35 a month, only 30—Never worked so hard in school & never received such small wages in the winter.—Paid Helen W—$28 for my board. Stopped at Lizzies mothers—saw her a few minutes. Guess she is willing to have L—— stay with us. Pa says Ma has got to pay the taxes. Isn't it too bad? Snow—Snow.

SUN. 14. At home. my head feels like a rotten squash. L—— is washing the dishes. Wonder if any one will come to day. hope not. It is one of those dismal days with a dreary, S. E. wind which whistles in a deep & solemn whisper, that steals in through cracks & crannies & finally enters ones soul & lulls & sooths the brain till one loses himself in a sea of sacred thoughts . . . . [. . .]

FRI. 19. Sew some. we all go to town. Ma paid the taxes. She paid me $10 on note & gave me $15. That makes with the eagle she gave me Christmas $25 the same as Henry. Before we went Pa said he wanted to straighten up Baileys note (for Minnie) so Ma went and Bailey paid $57 of it.—Pa went & pd the taxes out of it & told Ma to keep the rest handy so as to get a harness & *we* would have a nice buggy team. I don't know but I don't believe he intends Ma to have any use of her carriage at all. After she worked on her hands & knees to get it & then to be crowded right out of the use of it is almost unbearable. . . .

Ma says I must note the hail, rain & thunder shower of this morning—also how we saw the first robin yesterday—and the hive of bees are alive. . . .

April 1886

THURS. 1. April 1886. finish Henrys shirt. emb. it with white silk. Looks nice. sew on apron. am tired. Lizzie wash. Ma sew on fur cloak. Cold. [. . .]

SUN. 18. Have been working nearly all day & now will get dinner so as to go to my school. Ma is feeling very bad & has a fever to day. I am so sorry. I wonder if I ought to go & leave her. She can scarcely move to day.[14] It is beautiful & bright.

At Mrs. Wilcox's using Ed's ink. Pa brought me. I am very homesick to night for I had to leave Ma feeling so badly. She wants a horse to drive & it wouldn't cost Pa a cent more than to let them run in the pasture. I feel very sorry for Ma. Saw a lot of the young folks at Mr. Meads. Pleas. [. . .]

SAT. 30. In forenoon I & Ma painted the buggy—It was too much for her. She fainted away 2 or 3 times Sunday & I disliked to leave her very much. Sat. afternoon I went to town, rose there & back with Mr. Parkhurst & Maud. did not stay any longer than I could help, for I wanted to varnish the buggy but didn't after all on a/c of flies. I looked at a harness $9.00 & I'm going to get it. Ma is just dying for want of care. I'm almost a mind to give up my school. . . .

May 1886

MON. 3. it has been raining & is yet. I hope it has rained those little ——— all into the ground. Ma was discouraged yesterday, & I am sorry. I don't believe I'll try to teach any-more for I have to worry so much. I'm thinking of Ma every minute. Now I have made up Henry's cot & hope I may sleep better. Can't sleep with her, she touches me & then the smell too.

Had a splendid school to day. Set up quite late doing tomorrows work & commenced my essay for Saturdays association on "Writing in Primary Grades." Cliff. B. Irwin sent me a postal last Thurs. requesting me to do so & also I saw it in Democrat & Press Saturday. Pretty short notice. Sleep alone to night. Dark.

TUES. 4. . . . . Have just been writing some poetry for Ma and in spite of me I can not keep the tears back. I feel so sad to night. wish I could go over home & see Ma to night. I'm afraid she is worse. Just wrote to Henry also. I wish he might be nearer home. My head aches. I have half a mind to go to bed. Mrs. Wilcox has. The sun is just setting and its purple rays tinge the leaves with brown and white & fall in soft & mellow tints on the surrounding hillsides. The cat purrs in a quiet monotone & all nature seems hushed & is being lulled away to rest by a gentle breeze which stirs only the delicate plum blossoms & tender leaves. The croak of the frog is heard by the lazy brook & the low of cattle is heard at a far distance comes in undulating tones as it re echoes through the Grove. Warm.

WED. 12. Have a good school. Irene Hollister bothers me with telling falsehoods to the other little girls. I fear I shall have to punish her severely. Rena Allen went to town this forenoon & had Dr Trien cut out a tumor which was as large as a hazlenut above her eye. She came this afternoon. Alice Traner has a poisoned foot—She hobbles around on the other—I had her come home with me & stay till Amos McNeil came past with the milk, Charley Mead had the sick-head-ache so I have seen a Homeopathic to day. We went to Meads last evening. Looks like Rain. [. . .]

CHAPTER FIVE

"Murmur Not—It Must Be Right": 1886–1889

Fold those hands across her breast,

Close those lips so pale & white,

Clasp those hands they are at rest.

Murmur not—It must be right.

—from Sarah's diary, May 18, 1888

TUES. MAY 18. 1886. 11.30 A.M. Am sitting on the couch in front of Ma. She is resting a little for the first time seems so since Sunday morning. Saturday she sat in rocking chair & watched Dobson & I take up the carpet & clear house. Sunday morning (She teased me to sleep with her so I did) She did not realize any-thing. I had Pa telegraph Henry & go up & get Mrs. Mead & Albert Dobson & Dr. Fuller.—The Dr. managed to get her up & quite talkative & Sunday, Albert, Julia Brower were here & Mr & Mrs Mead & May, and Will Beaty & Mrs VanAlstyne, & all of Johns and Doolittles & she talked & laughed but it was only on the strength of the medicine. I have sat up both nights. Mrs Mead did also last night & we have had all we could do to keep her alive. I am so anxious about Henry. Its almost impossible to wait for him to come & Ma wants him so bad. She loses control of talking & can not talk right. Last evening she wanted to be drawn on the couch out on the porch & I could not tell what she said—but finally she said *"pocket-book"*—I'll go myself & raised up I got it & she looked at the things as I took them out & gave Henry the half penny to wear as a watch-chain & the "ten cent" & the "card" & I the penny & the English piece. She said that she wanted me to have the carriage & take care of it & Henry to have Baileys note of $50 I have cried 'till I can cry no longer. If Ma can only live to see & have a good visit with Henry I shall be so glad for she, I know, is fearful of dying.

May [Mead] was over Saturday, & I was so glad. She went up to school yesterday & got my things for I have to resign my school & brought them over yesterday. I do not see what keeps Henry so long. It rained last night but is bright to day. Ma's head gets so bad she is wasting away so fast. At times will be bloated & her eyes have grown weak for the first to day. so we darken the windows. I think she only lives on the hope of seeing Henry. I do wish he may come soon.

> Sad, more sad than heart can feel
> sadder yet than tongue can tell,
> I scarce can all my tho'ts conceal.
> In vain we make one last appeal.
>
> ———
>
> Spare her to us one day longer,
> Though her hands are cold & still.
> The hearts faint beat in vain dost linger
> God hath ordained it to his will.
>
> ———
>
> God has taught us thus to pray
> When we are clothed in darkest night.
> O may! He guard & kindly shield us
> Lead our wandering feet aright.
>
> ———
>
> Death will take so sadly from us
> The truest friend we had below;
> Friend in joy & friend in sorrow.
> She did all our feelings know.
>
> ———
>
> Mother dear we'll pray to you,
> you shall be our refuge still,
> for we know you're close by Jesu,
> As down at his feet we now will kneel.
>
> ———
>
> For we know that you'll be waiting
> Close beside the silent door,
> and the words you'll be repeating,
> Words so oft we've heard before.
>
> ———
>
> Fold those hands across her breast
> Close those lips so pale & white,

Clasp those hands they are at rest.
Murmur not—It must be right.

FRIDAY. 20. Embracing my first opportunity to write. Ma is sitting in the chair. I gave her a warm water bath & she slept. got up at 12 to dinner. Eats oatmeal gruel. Feels very well to day.

Tues. night it was all Mrs. Mead & I could do to keep her alive she vomited but has no strength. Her flesh is very sore at times. Tues. night I lay down an hour. Wed. morning Henry came on the 4.30 A.M. I cried for joy when I saw him come. I had just lain down & was asleep when Mrs Mead (she slept most of the night) woke me up saying "Henrys coming." I went to the door with eyes closed for I was so tired sleepy. He kissed me & said "Hows Ma." He had been up 4 nights last week & two on the cars. Ma was asleep but soon woke. I asked her if she was awake "yes" "Can you visit" "Is Henry here?" she asked & Henry said "Good Morning Ma & she just cried she was so glad. H & I worked all the forenoon. He then lay down & fell asleep from exhaustion till 5 o'clock. Mrs. Mead washed. was sorry to have her. Mr Mead & May came over. Mrs Mead went home with them. Alfred Brower & Albert Dobson & Mrs Scanlan here to stay over night. Ma did not have such a serious time Wed. night. I did not close my eyes. Mrs S— lay on the couch all night & slept part of the time. . . .

Last night (Thurs night) Henry took care of Ma & I lay down on a quilt & slept nearly all night. thats the 1st since a week ago to night. then I've been unwell since Tues. morning. Dr. Hines has been up twice this week, brought Ma a string of fish. Henry went to day & caught a nice mess. . . .

Miss Minnie Friend (a new beginner) is to teach my school—It makes me cry to think of them (my pupils). Helen said the children all felt so sorry for me & that I couldn't be with them. Warm.

WED. 26. Tho't I'd write in here yesterday but could not. Ma is a trifle better to day. She slept some last night. Aunt Hattie sat up with her last night. I lay down & got up when necessary. Henry commenced to work for Loomis yesterday. Have been seeing to the supper & writing in Ma's journal for her. She is now able to sit up awhile & feels a little better. I made two coops & have about 75 or 80 turkeys out for Ma.

After supper. Looking for Henry. Have been seeing to the turkeys. about 75 little ones.

10.30 P.M. Ma gone to bed on the couch. She said she did not know whether she would have patience enough to live or not. She says for me to keep the buggy. Henry is in the other room to bed. Lizzie is going to sit up with me & is now rubbing Ma's feet. . . .

I sat up all alone Sunday night & I was afraid Ma would die. There has not been a night yet but she would have died. I do not undress & my clothes are getting loose.

Pa does not seem to think but that I can work all night & all day. Henry brought home Dr. Aines horse to night & if Ma feels able Im going with her to ride to morrow. My eyes feel heavy but I dare not go to sleep for Ma has such terrible sinking spells. Warm.

THURSDAY MAY 27, 1886. Ma is improving slowly. Pa said Henry better go back to Garden City. He also wants to take Mas buggy & go to town. I have a lean on that carriage & he need not touch it. Lizzie & I sat up last night. I laid down at 6 & got up at 9 after Henry had arose.

Ma was very tired & I wish I c'ld keep awake better. I did work all night till 6 this morning. May be she can stand it to ride this afternoon.

FRI. 28. stayed last night. Ma slept 3 hours & think we can now manage to get along. Willie brought them [the Meads] & came for them. Thats the first nights sleep I've had for two weeks. I undressed & went to bed. Ma is helpless & her legs & feet are swollen hard.

11 o'clock. P.M. Have just got Ma laid down again.

11.10 Now Ill try to write again.

I took Ma to town again to day. Henry rode part way home. Willie Dean seems to be so glad that Ma is better. Ma slept nearly all day & had a stupid sinking spell this afternoon.

MONDAY MORNING MAY 31. Am sleepy. Slept 1 1/2 hrs last night. 2 hrs night before last & not any the night before. Sat. I went down after Henry. Got a hat frame for Ma 25¢. a balloon 15¢ 2 pair cotton hose for self 25¢ at Riddles. . . .

Ma slept some better last night. She is tired this morn. Henry has gone to work for Loomis again down E. on the hill. . . . aunt Hattie & children were here. She helped set up the stove. I got breakfast this morning. . . . Lizzie told me she would like to go that night but did not want to leave us at all. I told them she could go if she wanted to. I have to do all the work any way so it does not make much difference. . . . I sat up alone last night. got Ma out in the kitchen. etc. Beautiful.

June 1886

TUESDAY, JUNE 1, 1886. Another day has passed and another night has come.

> O! the nights are cold and fearful
> It seems not like our old dear home.
> See the watchers grim dark faces;
> Hear the whispers sad and low.
> Lightly tread the kitchen floor
> Softly step on carpets now
> For our mothers slowly passing
> Toward the sacred, silent door.
> Yes; the nights are cold & dismal
> As we watch that pale small face.
> Once those lips were full & rosy
> Once those locks were auburn curls
> Still they bear a sunny glow.
> Alike to those of younger girls.
> Now the breath is low & faint.
> Now the heart is throbbing fast;
> The pulses jerk & the dull harsh pain
> They will cease to longer last.

I trimmed a hat for Ma to day, got the hat of Miss Day 20¢ & the flower 35¢ of Thorpe. Albert Dobson here to day & to sit up to night. Ma came very near dying last night. I was so worn out that I fell asleep she got on her back & was nearly dead when I arose & turned her over. Warm.

THURSDAY 3. P.M. Ma asleep. Has been half asleep all day. . . . Ma is feeling very bad to day. Albert said she could not last long. Asked me what w'ld I do? I would have to go to my Father and pray for knowledge & wisdom & strength the same as I have done. There is always a way prepared & we must seek & find it.

O I feel so sad & lonely to think that our poor dear mother has to go & leave this world so young. never can look on these fields these groves, these flowers again. The breeze sways the pine trees in solemn remembrance, the doves are cooing in the barn. The little turks (150) are chattering on the lawn & "Peter" Ma's peafowl is spreading his tail in independent significance, but O how changed these scences appear to me—It seems as though they are all saying "Good-bye—Dear mother our only protection." The very trees seem to droop & the rose cups bow their petals to the sullen breeze. I set a coop on a little turkey—thats the 1st that has been hurt in any-way. [. . .]

MONDAY JUNE 14. After Dinner. Ma has been very very weak. My back gave out so I called Pa up for 2 or 3 nights. But he is so rough & wants it all his own way & says something & I think it puts Ma back. She would have nervous chills & Sat. night she sat up nearly all night. She just raised right up & told Pa to "Shut up" she looked wild enough. I never saw her look worse. He told her he knew how to lift her, & it hurt her so. She also had a sinking spell. I had to work faithful all night. So last night I called Henry & she seemed to get along better. She flowed some. Sunday (yesterday) Dobson was up. I went over & got a mess of strawberries & it seemed so lonesome Ma could not be there. . . . I do what I can to keep awake. Look over peas, set table, pick up things, etc. Ma is getting much heavier to lift. I have been washing her feet & rubbing them & it takes all the time to care for her. . . . [. . .]

SUNDAY 20. Henry & I & Ma in the parlor. I on the couch. Ma on the new lounge. Henry in an easy chair which he bought for Ma to try yesterday. She can not keep it. I slept from 7.30 till 2.30 to day. John sat up with me last night till 3.30 this morning. Yesterday I slept from 6.30 till 11. & day before from 8.30 till 12.30. I get very tired & sleepy. I am almost sick with my cold yet, & I have a severe headache. Aunt H—— brought Ma some Rice pudding. Ma had a sinking spell yesterday. She has been to weak to sit up much for 2 or 3 days. But has to be rubbed & hot flannels kept on & hot teas & a great deal of care. I've just been out to feed the turkeys. It rained to day but they did not get wet for I covered them with boards & turned the "boxes," as Joe says, rain-ward. Pa is just coming from Uncles. Mr & Mrs Chapman were here yesterday. Uncle stops, & Aunt H & John come 1 or 2's a day. Albert was up nearly all the week hoeing corn for Pa. Then Pa had another man. I cook nights. Seems as though Ma must get better soon for we are all worn out. I took a bath this morning. Lizzie went home last night. we look for her to night. Mr Parker called other day. Frank Smith & several others. Now I must wash the dishes & get ready for to night. Pa is going to have men next week. I just have the cooking to worry over all the time. Mary Griffin was up yesterday forenoon. The rain makes every thing look nice. [. . .]

THURSDAY, JULY 8, 1886. Have been sick abed a couple of days. yesterday I was 21 Ma gave me her velvet dress. Henry got a miller as large as a fly in his ear. I took him down to the Dr. [illegible] who chloroformed it & H—— had it washed out to day. Pa is grumpy. He is helping John in hay. for the past week have gone to bed at midnight & had to get up from 1 to 8 times till 6 o'clock in the morning & Ma & I went to town Monday to spend the 4th. Henry was in a booth. We lifted Ma out & she enjoyed herself very well. But I brought her home at 3 o'clock & worked with her every minute—till 6 o'clock Tuesday morning. I & Ma have taken the berries down nearly every night. Ma likes to ride. It has been very warm. Ma had a sinking spell Sat. P.M. & another Sunday.

WEDNESDAY, 14 JULY 1886. It seems almost impossible for me to write in my Diary. Ma is very poor I can lift her alone. She & I; sometimes Lizzie, take the berries to market. we get 11¢ & they sell for 15 for 2 nights I have only had to get up once with Ma. I sleep on the Lounge. . . . Harry Jeffers was her Sunday he is to have $20,000 for inventing a street car indicator; I am real glad for I wish Harry well. I somethings think; I think more of him than he thinks I do. He is so nervous when I am near—he did not stay long. I am sorry but then I do not want to marry him. It is hard to decide. Pa has been having another mad spell. Am so sorry for Ma; she can not help herself at all. Have 189 young turkeys. Joseph [Hutchinson] thinks I ought be proud of them he is haying & asked me if the men over here worked well? His conversation is easily listened to. I do wish I could throw away all thoughts of him: why I keep myself out of his way all I can but in spite of me the tenderest thoughts of affection will stray back. Why is it? I never saw any person before that had such a power over me, and I hope I never will for it bothers me. I am unwell this week. have been regular for 4 or 5 months & am so glad. [. . .]

August 1886

AUGUST 1. SUNDAY. In the Library. Pa skimming milk. Ma & Henry gone to Frank Smiths in the Grove. I am nearly tired out. Was so tired I fairly stagger. Henry & I have great times getting along with Pa. I have cleaned the lower part of the house & it is quite respectable. . . .

Wednesday evening Ma & I drove downtown. Joe Hutchinson invited us in to eat water-melon. we "invited" & had a pleasant tete-a-tete. Well—well I wish "Joe" didn't run in my head so much. Sarah is pleasant. I have cut & partly made a blue calico for myself. Mother

Hubbard front. tied from side seams with ribbon. Have cut ma a wrapper, myself a pair of drawers. made & cut myself an under-waist & ironed & mopped & cooked & done half the washing & help take care of Ma, & the turks run away up to Morris & over north & I have to chase—*chase*. Now I must go feed them.

Sarah made no more entries in her diary during 1886.

January 1887

JANUARY 10, 1887. A new year has dawned and with it sadness as well as blessing. We will not enumerate our griefs, they are bad enough to think of. I am teaching a pleasant school of 22 pupils 7 mi. N.E. of Manchester. Am boarding with Mr. Underwoods 3/4 mi N.W. of school-house in the field; edge of the timber.

They are a queer family—always in a jangle. I commenced Nov. 15, have not had my journal so could not write in it. . . .

MY PUPILS.
If I could keep them away from wrong,
or evil thoughts, or speaking guile,
T'would take the grief from off my heart.
O in joy & peace I'd rest the while. . . .

This is one verse of a Poem which I composed for our paper "The Banjo."

February 1887

SUNDAY, 6, 1887. At Mr Underwoods. And it would be a lonesome day if I had not had so much writing to do. . . .

FEBRUARY 21, 1887. Its been a long time since I wrote in my journal but I have no pen and ink and as I've been using theirs so much tho't I'd wait until I went home. So now I can write. . . . [. . .]

SUN. 20. Went over home. Kate said Pa was there one day and wanted a con her & Henry & Katie & himself to go down & have a consul of Doctors to see what was the matter.[1] Henry & Ma also said he did. I wonder what will be the end of this; if I only knew he would never injure us, But I am afraid he will kill some if not all of us some time. Ma is feeling first-rate—if she could only walk & wait upon herself. I hope she may by warm weather. But I'm sure it is the palzy. She has my crocheted cap nearly done. Henry is not so well he can not endure the dust and hay very well . . . . [. . .]

FRIDAY, 11. finish Ma's chemise. It is quite pretty. commence one for myself.

Took care of Ma. her foot is very bad she has cold in it. I put on a poultice of potato, changing it often during the day and have just put on bread & milk & sugar for to night. I get supper, make beds and ironed an hour. Katie gets along all right—she washed this afternoon & is on the bed. Ma's shoulder & hip are very sore where she sits down & lies down. The bones fairly come through. I give her catnip tea & bathe her hip in smartweed water. The snow is going fast to day. Now I must put Ma to bed & cover the fire and go myself. . . .

SUNDAY, MAR. 13, 1887. At home—Yesterday was quite warm & the teachers had an association in town. Henry took me down. . . . Went to see Jessie Gibbons & had the best visit. She thinks Ma is sick in the same way her Ma was. She said Lucy spoke of me so often. Lucy is in Nebraska teaching. we just talked about our Mothers and our lives & our innermost feelings seem to mingle in smiles, in tears, in words. . . . [. . .]

TUES. 29 MARCH 1887. At home. Have not been very well since Saturday. Pa was down Sunday & we were alone. This is the first time we were alone. It seems as though he wanted a "time" but every time he would commence in such a strain we would change the subject in one way or another. He went back up to Uncles—He talks different when we were alone than when some one is here—If it wasnt for his being around & bothering & the fear I would stay at home & not hire a girl. But as long as we have to have some one with us & She will take good care of Ma I might as well be earning something. Her foot is better and I am so glad. It has to be bathed 3 or 4 times a day. . . . It takes me most of the time to care for Ma and I sometimes fear she can not be with us long. I am tired to night. Mended Henrys coat to day—patch—patch. [. . .]

April 1887

SUNDAY, APRIL 3, 1887. Another weeks work is done & another Sabbath come. "Bless the Sabbath day" I have just felt sick all through to day; but feel a little better to night. I finished painting the kitchen last evening, painted the casings & large cupboards blue and the floor yellow ochre. Of all the lifting & tugging—I fully appreciate the fullness of the meaning thereof: especially those large cupboards & the stoves.

Mr. Seger called in his carriage Thursday I believe and he appears to have his same old malady come on again—"Courtin in the Country" I dont suppose I ought to laugh that way—but the idea to think of a married man falling in love, apparently with me. He said that was the reason he did not come here; it would not do. I think he had better stay away if he is wise. . . .

School commences in a week for 3 mo's Spring term @ $20 a mo. . . . My back has been so painful. Ma retired between 11 & 12 and when I work all day scrubbing it takes the energy partially away. Henry is tired too for he is up in the night an hour or two or three. Then we are up at 6 in the morning Pa fairly ached for a regular raving talk and appeared to be surprised to see any one here. I am fearful of his doing something desperate. He says he is coming home to stay. Then he said he wanted the old buggy to have to use at Uncles this summer. Then he said he guessed he'd go west in the Fall. He is a desperate wild looking man and I fear we will have more trouble with him. It blows & is cold again. Good night to all—if I could only go to bed. [. . .]

FRI. 8 APR. They have all retired except me & I sit by the kitchen table alone.

Dr. Munson the magnetic Dr. of Maquoketa is here.[2] I drove to the train for him. He said he could tell better in a day or two about Mas paralysis. He said Pa is a poison to her & it is no wonder she is paralyzed. Mr. Seger told us of him & I wrote him and rec'd a reply yesterday that he wld be here. Yesterday afternoon Henry & I went to town I saw quite a number I knew & had short chats. Pa brought a ham, a doz. oranges & a cherry can. He never brought home things that way before & does it for the name and outside show. He is so cunning. Well I do hope Dr. Munson can cure Ma. I took her to town day before yesterday it was so warm. I bot some things yesterday. Henry plowed the Garden to day. I shall have to defer my school a w'k the Dr. says. Pleasant. [. . .]

THURSDAY 20. My vacation is well nigh spent—only a few more days & then the Duties of the school-room will be around me. Ma is oh, so much better. . . . Dr. Munson is a free-lover. I do not believe in his doctrine. I dont see what's the reason he tells me such stuff for. Said he believed if he was a young man he would court me and get me. well I rather think not. He is not exactly the sort of a fellow I should admire. The idea of an old man wanting to kiss & hug me— Its surely unreasonable & below my dignity. If it was Joe I would be quite apt to appreciate his remarks or at least try to. But for an old married man I shall have to soliloquize. Henry has his barley in. it rains.

MONDAY. APR. 25, 1887. Commence teaching in No. 7 again. Have 12 enrolled. Am to board across the road with Mrs. Bush. Come over to dinner. Edith comes to school. She is 14. [. . .]

May 1887

SUNDAY, MAY 29, 1887. Am home to day. That woman Mrs. McFarland stayed 3 weeks. Then I drove back & forth to & from my school 8 mi. away & did most 1/2 the work at home for 1 week & 2 da. Then Delia Backard came & has stayed one week and is going away to-morrow to rest a week. But as we have no horse I can drive I scarcely know what to do. Mr. Huftelin is here he brought us up a lot of house plants, nice ones.[3] He

A break in Sarah's diary entries follows until November 6, 1887.

NOVEMBER 6, 1887. At home, if so it may be called. It seems rather a sad & happy lonesome. O how many changes since I last wrote. It almost makes me think of a whole life in one short day. I scarcely know where to begin in my recollections. we are living in Lu. Loomis's house in the N.E. center block in Manchester.[4] Henry & Ma & I & Mr Huftalen and Paulina Shaw has been working for us a week. Last Spring when I taught school, We had a girl 6 weeks & Henry & I managed the work the other 4 of the term. I drove back & forth, with a livery rig, 9 mi. & helped what I could. It was just in seed time & it seemed as though the strongest efforts were bound to be rifled & our greatest hopes must be baffled and driven from us. School closed the 25th of June. we had a picnic about 200 present. We had a splendid program and every thing passed off pleasantly. I worked very hard and walked from Manchester home; having rode to there with Mr. Matt. Hutson. I was very tired that Saturday night & thankful too, for I felt as though my school days were ended, not thankful for my own sake as much as Ma's & Henrys. Ma was so glad to have me with her again.

Sarah's next diary entry is dated Christmas 1887.

CHRISTMAS, 1887. Ah yes; Christmas has come at last with its bless-ings, its treasures, its bright sunlight and now we must once more sit down in the twilight and ponder over the past.

Some with joy & some with tears.
Some with hope & some with fears.
Some " life & some with light
Others with shade & darkness of night.

Several pages have been cut out of the diary at this point. Inserted are loose-leaf pages with the following entry, recopied.

JAN. 26, 1888. Half past 9 in the morning. Have just got Ma a little easier—She has lain very low for a week. She had a chill the 19th & had had chills and fever every other day since. She is very, very weak and faints away several times a day. Mr. Huftalen and Maggie are so kind to assist me since last Sabbath.

I went to meeting that day for the 2nd time in 18 mo. & Dr. Miller in his prayer said—"Oh, how blessed are the sick if they can be comforted and say "All is well." How often does Ma repeat those words "All is well." How I hear them to try to make myself believe their true.

For the past 4 wks. I have helped Ma up and down & she has sat up to eat with us. I lifted her from 10 to 12 times a day & she seemed to feel so well—was getting fleshy & had a splendid appetite.

I would retire about midnight and now she & I sleep in the middle room; we are much warmer.

Am up nearly all night but I do not mind it so much now that I have a good girl. Her name is Maggie Kruemple. we heard from Henry Monday and send him a letter to day. I feel so dull and eyes so heavy that I guess I will have to lie down a few minutes while Ma is resting.

Fading, fading day by day
Immortal life to tombless clay.

I some-times feel while I am watching by mothers bedside and listen to her heart beat and her breath so faint, Oh, what shall I do when Ma is gone, what would I do if she were taken away to night or to morrow. She has talked about it and she says "Sarah do not worry for Ma may get well again but if she does not she can believe that you will do all right, that you will stay by Henry." She tells me all about her things, how to do with them & her clothes and the tears will start and flow down my cheeks, though I strain to keep them back. She has two hip sores & they are very painful & as large as a cup top, one is 1 1/2 in deep & very putrid. I dress them often with poultice. Balsam of peru and arnica. Then her left arm is entirely paralyzed. It seems so bad to know one is dying almost by inches, and nothing can cure them. Ma is so patient and never complains. no matter how much pain she bears & she suffers all the time.[5]

I am indeed thankful to have assistance. Am scarcely out of the room & the odor makes my head ache I guess now I will lie down a few minutes as Ma has dropped off to sleep. I can not let her sleep long.

January 1888

1888. JAN. 27. Evening with its beautiful moonlight is here. And here again are we. Ma and I. Ma is better to night and we are oh! so thankful. She has been weak and faint to day but her voice is so much stronger. I was up nearly all night & my head ached so hard to day & then I let the lid to the flour chest hit it and in spite of me I couldn't help but cry. Pa was here a short time to day. Dr. Munson was also in and it seemed very good indeed to meet him again. He was on his way home in Maquoketa & was nearly sick with a cold. Isabelle Farlinger also called & Mary Schawb was here this evening. Ma has not sat up this week & it keeps me very busy to care for her. She went to sleep about 4 & so I lay down & took a short nap—It was so still & Maggie watched *us*.

> Quiet oh? so quiet sleeping here;
> Death our silent door is near.
> Peaceful dream, peaceful rest.
> Peaceful be—beyond the Blest.
> Sarah L. Gillespie

We heard from Henry this morning—he is at Onawa and is doing real well, & got the box of cooking we sent him all right. He says it is possible they may quit work 'till warmer weather & he come home awhile. It is a beautiful bright still day and not very cold.

THURSDAY, FEB. 2, 1888. To day is "Calamous day" and truly it has been a still, shadowy, and dreary day. Ma is much better. She sat up to dinner and supper yesterday & a considerable more to day. Those terrible hip-sores are much better or at least one of them is. The other is as large as a sauce place & filled with putrid flesh. I have to cleanse them so much & so regular. My side & back are very lame and, though I very much dislike to own it I feel very tired; a kind of tired sick; and if I make visible complaint, such as to lie down or go without a meal why, Ma will look so much worse & worry so that I dare not express an idea that I feel ill. Ma was so low & so very weak, Mr. Huftalen wrote to Henry Sat. to come home. Mr. Masden, Mrs. Huene, Sarah Ward, Mrs. Still, Mrs. Warner & others called the 1st & 2nd of Feb. Henry came home yesterday morning.

FEB. 3, 1888. To day I have been nearly sick, have a nervous headache. This forenoon after I had taken care of Ma and dressed her hips she dropped asleep and at 11 o'clock she is accustomed to get up I did not waken her. She woke up herself at 11.30 and then said it was too late & she was very much "all broke up." So when we were all seated at the table Ma was lying down she said "she overslept & when she woke she was in a terrible shape, one knee up & the other down; her head on the left side & her feet & knees turned on the right; & one foot at the head & the other down yonder." well—it spoiled my meal. I was choked & had to leave the table. I was hungry & had some nice mashed potato on my plate; but somehow I was not the least hungry in less than a minute. She gets so very tired. If she lies too long the blood fairly stagnates & it affects her all over to a greater or less extent when she is moved.

I do hope I will feel better tomorrow. Maggie helped me to make a corduroy vest for Henry to day. Pa came in a little while. My side is very painful. Henry feels proud of his Christmas Presents. 8 lbs turkey @ 8¢ to Mrs. Warner. [. . .]

MARCH 15, 1888. A Bright & beautiful Spring morning has unfolded its somber rays of sunlight & sheds hopes of pure, sweet sunshine around us. Ma is sitting up & dozing away & I hope resting a little. She suffers acute pain nearly all the time. Her bed-sores are very painful. one which is a trifle better now is 2 in. deep & the bone is visible. The other is 1/4 in. deep & 2 1/2 in. in diameter. I have to cut out the "puss" & cleanse them often & it fairly makes my veins refuse to carry the blood sometimes. Then she complains of her shoulders. Her left arm is entirely useless. I do hope she may retain the use of the Right arm & hand Ma had Chills & fever yesterday & seems very feeble. Then again at times she apparently feels better & talks so much & tries to be cheerful. Henry has been at Sioux Falls Dak. and is now at Primghar this state.

He wrote me "Now Sarah sleep day-times—do not try to do aught but take care of Ma & we can hire the swing done. And I will earn what I can to have what we need to eat and wear." —O, but it seems as though I must be earning some-thing too. I do so like to help what I can & then have a little spending money "all my own." . . .

MARCH 27, 1888. At Manchester, Iowa. Again do I find opportunity to write in my dear old Journal—friend—But 'tis with sad heart & heavy pen that I must pen these lines. Friday morning, Mar. 16, Ma said when we lay her down that Her hip sores pained her so badly that she guessed she would have to go to bed & stay awhile & not try to get up. So she did not get up to dinner & Sat. she did not wish to sit up at all but I insisted that it seemed so lonesome to eat without her so she consented to take tea with us for the benefit of my Comfort. All she ate was a few spoons of Oyster soup & that was the last meal we ate together. She commenced failing rapidly & I could see her life passing rapidly every hour. She did not talk much. She could not she said until "I am not so weak." But oh! she never was stronger. Henry was telegraphed Monday but did not receive the dispatch & another was sent Wed. morn. He came Thurs. morn. 10. A.M. Ma knew him but could not say much. She could not cry for the muscles of her face were paralyzed. Every second all night Wed. night & all day Thurs. she tried to talk but could not. She would say "who are all these?" "when will they come?" "How long?! How long?" "O! I can't tell you" & "write" & "paper," etc. I got her pencil & paper but she could not use her right arm.

O! how she suffered. No mind can realize. No pen describe. I sat in the chair by her bed & rubbed her hand & wet her brow & did as she had previously requested. Mr. Huftalen said she did not realize but I know she did 'till the very last. It Sat ~~night~~ morning that God call her spirit to him.

I sat up till 2 A.M. then called Henry & at 4.20 he said "Sarah come" then I was at Ma's side in an instant. she commenced to breathe fainter & slower & appeared to be in a sweet sleep when at nearly 5 she passed out of this cumbersome world into that Great realm where there is a shrine of Holy Light & we must all at last to kneel down together. . . .

I will try to write some more but when I feel a little better—It seems to hard to bear. . . . O, my poor dear suffering Mother. I loved her when she was here, but I believe I love her more now.

April 1888

SUNDAY MARCH —No to day is Easter—the first day of April. It is a long day. Ma is dead been gone a week—oh but it seems the longest week I ever knew. Henry & Maggie and Mr. Huftalen are here—

A portion of Sarah's diary entry for March 27, 1888, shortly after Emily's death on March 24. SHSI.

they all are lonely too. Henry will come in & look round the room—then go in the parlor—where Ma and I were all the fore-part of Winter,—and coming out says—Oh, Sarah You don't know how much I miss Ma.

Yes poor dear Ma—so good—so kind and I am so thankful that a harsh word never passed from me to her or from her to me. It is hard to decide what course to take when ones heart is aching so. —But Ma told me before she died that she wanted me to take care of the things which she has divided between Henry & I. Then Maggie wants to help us get moved & settled & Mr. Huftalen will need to find other rooms too—why Henry will soon be going back to his business & I will be here all alone. Little Daisy, my pupil, said she w'ld come & stay with me. But we must not think too much or get too anxious. [. . .]

APRIL 8, 1888. Another Sunday come and another week gone. What changes come and go.—We are moved, nearly settled. We are in rooms in the widow Brown house on _____ Street—It is a pleasant place—She has the two north rooms & one upstairs & we have one up-stairs a Sitting Room with double window—a bed-room & kitchen below, they are at the South & the sitting room faces the west—has a nice little Stoop & door corner.[6] Maggie is with us can stay until Wednesday. Effie Brown is also rooming here with me. I got a little anxious & so went & found some rooms at Mr. & Mrs. Ballards, & paid $5 in ad. for Rent—Then Mr. Huftalen and Henry were talking about it & its that "Old fellow" that left his first wife, & so Henry found more suitable rooms the ones which we are now occupying. Henry paid $9 Rent this time. The kitchen is small and we have two doors to go through & an "Cross old Maid Tierney" to go past—She has a room also & the cool draft is quite offensive to her. But we can put up a Sham partition if necessary. Mr. Huftalen has not moved yet—we paid rent there till the eleventh—So Henry sleeps with him for company. We took a lot of things out to the place and packed them there—two rooms full—Pa is there "overseeing" Says he is going to live with Henry & I. He is not going to work any-more, well I do hope he will not come here—I do not wish to see him at all. Joseph rented the place and has Mr. Spittler & family living in the house. They have 8 children. We are the 2nd block E of the Cong. church and our back door faces the Presbyterian, the Methodist and the Universalist (used for a schoolroom). Jack Browns are next door west—It is in the Aristocratic part of town. Mr. Huftalen so Henry says is going to room in his store. I would like to have bought his furniture they were heavy walnut $240 and new & he only asks $80. we have had beautiful weather all the week—we moved the 6th & are real tired and are wishing that no one will come that we may rest all day. It rained a little last night &

is cooler to day. I got a new red table cloth; and a piece of white oil-cloth to put on the shelf in front of the window. The room looks quite cheery & comfortable.

Sarah made no further diary entries until July 22, 1888.

JULY 22. SUNDAY 1888. Oh! How fast the time flies & so much tran-spires along with I regret not to have written every day in this dear book. . . . [Pa] seems to be in a serious condition some times. I really feel afraid of him. I hope he may not come when I am alone. Well, I must bathe & "prepare" for church. I am an "active Member" in the Christian Endeavor Society also Chairman of the lookout Commit-tee—And to day the Supt. requests me to conduct a teachers class whilst she is absent a month or two. I wonder how it happened he selected me I do not really feel competent to teach 15 or 20 Young Ladies. But I will pray for the Grace & Blessing of our Father to shine round about us & the members & teacher to-gether may we grow strong in well-doing.

> Many faces, many friends come and go;
> They cheer my hearth with warmth & Light
> They soothe my aching brow from pain.
> Yet into weary rest I sink again.
>
> No mothers love; no mothers hand entwining;
> Alike to hers with joy & tears combining;
> Yet, through the sacred, silent door,
> We know she's only gone before.
>
> I have a friend—a brother here;
> My mothers now in Heaven
> The only ones of kith or kin
> That God to me has given.
>
> And when he took her angel form
> All wrapped in angel robes of white
> He took her in his loving arms
> And bore her to his throne of light.
>
> 'Twas in the cold bleak March of Spring,
> The world was clothed in snow and ice
> With hoar frost each branch did bend & cling
> A lovely scene—no sin nor vice.

It seemed as though her spirit wafted.
Slowly toward that far off shore.
Wafted through a mist of zephyrs.
'Till we saw it then—no more.

O, how sweet the sleep she's sleeping
None to hers alike I know
None to me so pure—so holy
Mother dear—I loved her so.

AUG. 23, 1888. How I wish I could get along without neglecting to write in this book oftener. But time goes merrily on & I now & then grasp a moment of it for the purpose of penning an occasional line in my Diary.

Well, this is the 2nd. week of the Normal Institute and I have attended nearly all the time. To day I have a bad cold & as the bed-bugs in the chamber drove me out to sleep on the couch in my sitting room, It seriously aided in producing almost unendurable pain in some parts of my body—not the Thorax how-ever. Henry went to the western part of the state the 6th and has not yet returned. Heard from him yesterday & several times before, & wrote yesterday also sent some 4 clean shirts. Orpha Winkler who came to school to me at Little York is rooming with me & attends the Normal. The work is most too much for me & I can not study any, though I sho'ld like to. Have attended one chinese lecture & the Institute lectures, and last evening an Elocutionist Mr. May of Independence. He gave "The Bells" & "The Diver" remarkably well & also an original description "The Bouquet" of Hell's Forty, a sad and touching reminiscence.

Saturday last I went to the farm every-thing looks well—I will need to go again soon & sort & arrange our articles which are stored there & as Pa does not see to any-thing & Henry being gone it seems to fall on me to see to it in general. Pa comes here quite often & some-times he is apparently all right & at other times his nerves & mind are dangerously affected. It is really too bad. . . .

How we sketch & pencil & trace our steps through life. Plan after plan unfolds & you ravel out some of the most beautiful thoughts this world will allow. How high we build—if we could only climb half as high methinks 'twould be a bliss to live. Always may we do the best there is in us for we are all God had to give. He made us what we are then shall we not unfold our lives to our fellow being's on the stage of our short existence.

All is beauty; all is wealth; all is glory; all is health.

> One by one we all must sever,
> All the kindred ties that bind us.
> All the peace & beauty ever
> All the love links which unite us.

There is a break in entries until October 22, 1888.

MONDAY, OCTOBER 22, 1888. It is morning & the gray dawn ushers in the day on a field of snow. It has snowed since yesterday at three & the snow is 2 in. deep. But the rays of old Sol will soon roll up the white carpet & leave instead the highways full of mud and slush. I am alone again. Henry went to Ackley Thursday evening to be gone a month or two inspecting the water-tanks which belong to the I.C.R.R. He will travel all over this state & I received letter from him last night that he will probably be in Sioux Falls Dakota e'er I received as he was already on the way there.

He does not have to work unless he chooses this time. He had been here 3 weeks while we moved & have just got settled. We are with Mr. & Mrs. Tilton and have nice rooms. . . .

I feel quite tired to day. Rev. Crum gave 2 discourses in the Universalist church yesterday & I attended & felt a real satisfaction in hearing so able a speaker.

Pa was there in the evening and I did not know it until after services closed when he rushed up & put his arm around me & wanted to rush me up to the Rev. I had spoken with Crum in the morning & he was glad to see me.

Pa walked up with Mr. Crum he said so this morning. I feel sorry that Pa does talk & act so. I do really believe he will have to go to the Hospital for the insane if he does not cease his cunning and treacherous acts to me.

Albert Dobson was here yesterday.

He [Pa] was very angry this morning. He wanted to know who supported the family & I told him "My Ma did" & he wanted to know how we ever dont it—I said "There lies my poor dead Mother—that is the way she done it" He answered as he slammed the door "I *would be ashamed to mention her name—yes I wld*" He went to the farm then.

SUNDAY, DEC. 8. Henry & I at home. Henry is looking over Ma's writings. I have done up the work and just sat down 2 P.M. & will soon get the dinner. . . .

MONDAY, DEC. 31, 1888. The last day of another year has come & now as I have been sitting and sewing & thinking I thought it would be well to write a few lines in this dear book of mine.

Henry is at the store, and they seem to be doing well. I was nearly sick last week for all it is the 1st time in my life I have been so healthy, regular since March to an hour but I suffer such pain. it bears me down to the floor & I feel so weak after. Think it caused from being on my feet so much during the past 6 or 7 years. Feel very well to day. The ground was warm & muddy & Christmas day was like a day in June, but the 26th it snowed & blowed all day & kept on 'till the snow was 12 in. deep. It has been quite bright clear & cold since. Henry bo't me a pair of $5.00 glasses to wear to help my eyes. They are blue & *do not* magnify. Pa has we suppose gone to Michigan. I do really feel relief when I know he is no where near & I do hope he may not bother us any-more. Uncle was here Saturday to see us and was feeling very well—said he guessed he would come and live with us. all-right I wish he might. He said he couldn't tell what Pa did intend to do he never could tell by what he said.

I am so glad that Uncle found him out & we never told him a thing.

A year ago to night, this very hour I was sitting by the form of my poor sick Mother, and now she is gone. it seems as though if I could only have one more good visit with Ma, one more kind look or grasp of the hand—But no—no mother now is here to soothe my aching head; to brush away a grief or tear.

For our mother now—is dead.

I dream of Ma so often nearly every night & she always seems so cheerful and happy & looks so nice & good just as she used to. . . .

DECEMBER 31, 1888. Monday evening—I do not know that I ought to write any more but it is so still and lonesome here. I have been alone all day Henry to dinner at 2.30 & away at 3. and I have sewed & darned & mended and the sun is just sinking into a golden horizon.

I must build the fire, make the beds and write letters to Aunt Aggie, Mrs. Webster. Mrs. Webster has written such good letters to me—I wonder & only wish mine may do her half as much good. Mrs. Tilton & I went to the rink Christmas to see them skate—the 1st time I ever did and I would spend no more money to know how either. She & I & Henry went to the Cong. Tree & I helped decorate the church etc. [. . .]

MAR. 26, 1889. —And here I have waited this long time to write a line in this book—precious friend if ever any one should chance to get hold of you and read these thoughts, methinks they would have a medley of tales to relate. We have had beautiful weather and to day is warm and full of beauty and sunshine. . . .

A year ago to day our dear Ma was laid in the cold damp ground. And can it be? One year—A blank space of existence has my life been. Indeed I have felt so near dead the most of the time that it would almost have been a relief if I had not had to breathe. Not that I ever wish to die but that dreadful tired feeling, too tired to breathe and scarcely talking above a whisper.

And such pain—bearing me, dragging me out of my very existence. Well in January I took care of Mrs. Babcock one of Dr. Trien's patients—9 da. She had to have 2 stitches taken. Then our neighbors were sick and Mr. Hale died and I sat up all night and—well the 1st thing I knew I felt as though I knew nothing and one day the 2? of Feb. Dr. Munson came in (from Maquoketa, magnetic healer) and insisted on my taking treatment. I did—Some scrofula came out all over me and he also helped my head.[7]

He gave me 20 treatments for $10, as a present, and 7 or 8 beside.

He thought me to be in a critical condition & I would have died in less than six months. why he said I stayed in the house so close & had no strength, only tears and I would either have kept on & cried myself to death or have been a hopeless invalid all my life. well I feel better now. only I suffer so at my courses—and this time it was because I raked too much. I do not do my washing even. Had to stop for I can not lift a pail of water without pain. It really does seem too bad for me who was so strong and so young to have the female weakness. entire prolapsus of the womb. And I am so poor but am glad because I think my fat was scrofulus poor flesh. and what there's on my bones is good and I will eat & exercise & build on some good sound muscle. Osceola at the spiritualist meeting says it will take a year at least for me to be near well. I walk every day and am getting a good complexion. Have done some sewing etc. keep busy all the time. But do not try my nerves by getting too tired at any-thing like sewing or knitting. . . .

Henry keeps quite well and I hope he will not get too discouraged with me, for it takes so much time and patience. I only hope to get well and strong again. I sleep good from 8 to 6.30 breakfast 7. dinner 12. No supper. An indian Dr. & his wife were in M—— a week, and he pulled my tooth without pain. They have an infirmiary at their house in Janesville, Wis. and he said a nurse did not have hard work there. I do not care to nurse steady for I cant stand it now. I had rather give lectures as soon as I can go and study farther. Health 1st, Wealth and happiness after. Such a beautiful spring, crops mostly in. some gardens also put in. Dusty. wishing for rain.

JULY 11, 1889. Once in a while I think seriously enough of writing in this Dear book to get my pen & ink and collect my thoughts to write up for several weeks.

Time goes along so quickly and business and pleasure so smoothly that it scarce seems a week since I wrote on this page. I scarcely know where to begin as to telling what I have done is simply to say nothing.

Henry is out in Buchanan Co. putting up a house—he has been gone a week and I look for him home to morrow evening. He went because it is rather dull for a few months in the store. The most I do is church work. Sarah Hutchinson & I got up "*the* Sociable of the Season"—cleared $20.00. Joseph said he believed it was the "Two Sarahs." I cooked a Vanilla Cream Cake & it was pronounced delicious. Now we have formed a Literary Society & the Com. want a Bright girl, a bright subj. & a bright essay. well I wishes they had not asked me—thats all.

I went to Clement Griffins funeral yesterday—He died of consumption contracted by sleeping in a newly plastered house on his claim in Dakota.

Albert & Susan Hersey and Children are at Uncles to stay—I was out to see them all. Charley Baker (Ma's own cousin) was here two days & one night & we had a good visit. He & I took a ride around a mi. sq. & he I guess "fell in," he said he had never met any-one before that he would marry & he couldn't marry me—we are cousins. He is Henrys age only 6 mo. older. his birthday is in April, and he weighs 140 lb. just our height too. Has black hair & mustache & large brown expressive eyes and a good virtuous complexion. He was here Mon. & Tues. before the 4th on Thursday. He is traveling for a portrait Company, & went to Independence from here. Mrs. Tilton & I went there to the Celebration—which was the 1st time I was ever away. Well we had a splendid time. Saw the fastest 3 yr. old trotter in the world (Axtell). After he had done, a heavy garland of flowers was put over his neck & bouquest were thrown on the sulky seat while the band played a dirge & he walked to his cottage. Mr. Williams his owner held his watch in his hand while he drove him & has been offered 100,000 for him by "Bonner."

Saw Charley Baker in the eve. at the depot. He was with Ada Henry & the children. He promised to write & to come here again this summer.

About 20 children urged me to teach select school & finally I consented—but am not strong enough yet—my eyes failed me entirely and so I gave it up—Saw Dr. Sherman and he says it will take a year or two before I can do much of any-thing. He also spoke of Pa at some length—Said we were justifiable in preventing him getting in debt or any-thing of that kind in which he did not use good judgment, to be in the country & have proper exercise is the best thing for him.

But I do not think Pa will ever be well—I hope its all for the best—we can trust on & toil on with the thought that we have done all we could do. thankful our lives have been spared and that we are regaining health & vitality as fast as possible. I can see I am gaining but it seems as though I ought to be helping—Henry has to do it all. Of course I keep house and do all I can but it is different than working at a trade. I like it better too. I only wish I could keep house just as I would best like to—with a dinner set & tea set & extension table (with enough to fill it). And still I could not have an easier time or more enjoyment than I do at present. I only wish I might do more and hope Henry will get better out there—I believe it was being in the store so close that makes him look so poor and pale. Now I will go & distribute the S.S. sheets for the West Side S.S. (I have the pleas. ? of being Sec'y) then prepare to Lead the Christian endeavor Sun. evening. Take it all around Sunday is my busiest day—I feel most tired any-way.

Have made a green dress of gauze—It is very pretty but to bright and showy for me & I do not like to wear it for me one would think me so gaudy.

It is nice goods that we got 4 years ago though it cost us 5¢ a yard only 20 yd. & the lining—cream silesia was 90¢. So it did not cost much.

I was 24 last Sunday & Henry gave me a pencil. I had been thinking how Henry was at work and how every about so often I would get a little too ambitious to do a more than I'm able and then something keeps saying its all for the best do not worry—and I do not. some-way I can not.

Then to plan one's future seems vain—we have tried in vain & so earnestly did we work to gain a College education. I do not mind that though think we are just as well off. Sometimes I think I would like to go to the Institute of Phrenology & visit from here there as I went to & from. Henry says I may go as soon as I am strong enough & Cousin Charley says just go as far as mother & Lena & stay till I come by Christmas.

That is at Rochester, and would be nice indeed. But I fear he would court—cousin or no cousin? He said we could go to the beach a mile for our morning walk. I liked his looks well enough but then as to matrimony I have not yet aspired or rather reached my aspirations.

I dreamed I saw Joe night before last & he was in black though not mourning & I helped him put on his gloves. How nice they looked. He said (for it seemed I felt badly) "O never mind its all well with you & me & he put his hand in mine & said "What a good woman you are & how I like you." I do not see why it is if ever I am thinking seriously of teaching or any-thing worries me I will always dream of him & he will make it all right. It always seems to real—as real as life itself. And why is it? I don't think of him more like one generally does if they are going with a person. I don't care any-more for him than any-one as I know. And every now & then it's rumored he will marry but it never seems to me as though he would any of the girls. He now goes to see Miss Ratcliff a wealthy girl at Independence. Some-times I wish he would marry some-one—wonder if I would dream of him then in the peculiar way that I now do or not.

To resume—Yesterday I went to Clement's funeral and Joe was one of the pall-bearers & (well I did feel sad, could not help it. Clement looked so nice & only a few days before he died asked why I did not come to see him), he Joe did look sympathizing & gazed so intently for a long time right upon my face or at least my dream then came to mind what it had not before done—

DECEMBER 11, 1889. Evening and twilight and darkness are mingling their accents of rain & wind, and though some think it dreary it is to me a pleasant hour. We have had but little snow and now we are wishing it would freeze that we might go skating.

Farmers are plowing as there is no frost to speak of. Manchester is in general quite a dull place. Cousin Charley is with us Sunday yesterday & to day and we are indeed glad. He is so anxious to be working however that I fear he does not enjoy himself as he ought. He went to Dubuque Fri & Sat of last week and was tired out when he came home. I was quite sure he had been drinking for I smelled his breath and his eyes were inflamed. He had the blues seriously yesterday and talked of going back home—to the city. But I do hope he has given it up because he is better off, I know away from City life. I do not blame him for wanting to see his mother & sister, indeed the tears would swell in my own eyes when his chin quivered as he spoke of *home.* . . .

For we can not tell what time may do—but I do believe if he could be with me for a year or so on a farm that it would turn the whole course of his life. And as long as I do not teach I think it no more than a just duty for me to keep house for my Brother & cousin which I will do if they so desire until they are both settled. That is all I could do—then I could go back to my old trade again.

DECEMBER 1889. Charley & I went to Masonville to ride sunday. He went to see Mr. Childs about working—we found a horse-shoe going up to the Coffin Hill & Chas. picked it up—Good Luck. He was kind indeed to take me along for I enjoyed the ride. . . . I feel first-rate. Hope I may continue getting strong & I do pray to God that I may be capable of doing the duties that lie before me whatever they may be—I shall trust & hope to have strength & power of endurance to so fortify myself physically & mentally as to never again have to shrink & fail in such helplessness. Pa has been with us some lately but can put no dependence on what he says. He said he had $700 & all for me and that he w'ld pay my fare to Mich & ———

Henry feels quite well too. Some-times I wish he & Mr. Huftalen would dissolve partnership. For I do think it would be better. . . .

May we so live that our lives may be numbered among the blest, & may Charley feel brighter & happier and surely we will do for him all that a cousin could do—why when I look into his mellow pleading and expressive eyes & scan the panorama of his life as it reveals itself there I think perhaps it may be my lot to sustain & assist him now at the portal of life—I can trust Henry—I know he will never go astray & though we know not how long or short the time we are to continue together I feel as though Charley belongs to our fireside & our sympathy.

Yes, he is worthy & deserving the care & attention of his Iowa Cousin for so short a time & which in all kindness given & which from my pocket book of life would not be a trifle's expense—I do hope it if be right—this little act—this little deed may be as God thinks best.

It is growing colder and will freeze—I hope.

Sarah wrote the following on two loose-leaf pages which she inserted in the back pages of this volume.

M A, 1838–1888.

Well do I remember how my poor mother toiled and earned & saved and died that we might learn to live purer, higher, nobler lives. To her is due our all in all, and blessed shall her memory be even when the gray locks and furrowed brow shall be ours, when the gray shadows of the tomb shall be nearing

—yes even then may we look calmly back o'er the past and think of her kindly and thankfully for all we have done, for all we have hoped to be.

AT REST

For 8 long years she has known this dread disease of progressive paralysis would envelop her system & finally take her away from all earthly cares.

But oh how patiently, hopefully, & prayerfully has she been during her long period of suffering.

She often said she never knew a long dreary winter or a tedious summer. They were all so short to her.

For 2 yrs. she could not touch her feet to the floor & for 3 mo. has been unable to use her left hand or arm & the right but little.

Through her buoyant, cheerful disposition many were deceived as regards the real pain & fortitude she was enduring.

Always striving to make those about her happy & comfortable & even in severist pain—by her pleasant stories & bright hope clinging to her she would not let you believe she was sick. And at night her "All is well" would come so clear & pure & the thought would come to us, if we could only live like her apparently above trial or temptation or sorrow.

For 8 years that dire monster paralysis has been working with a slow, sure tread & at last has overtaken her weary form & crowded it from its path of mortal sphere where all human souls will finally find a resting place. . . . beginning with the lower extremities it has worked its way upward & stretched out its cold damp hand toward the central factor of life . . . and at last has enshone it like a rail for the tomb. Ma was born Apr. 11, 1838 at Medina, Lenawee Co Michigan and closed her eyes in peaceful sleep Sat. morning Mar. 24, 1888.

CHAPTER SIX

"Nobody's Wife": 1890–1891

1/4 of a Century.

1/3 of a Life.

Happy & content

& Nobody's wife.

—from Sarah's diary, July 7, 1890

SUNDAY, JAN. 4, 1890.[1] Rochester, N. Y. . . . I started from home last Monday morning at 5.30. arrived in Chicago 1.55 P.M. Then took the Lake Shore and arrived in Buffalo, N.Y. at 6.30 A.M. Tuesday morning. . . . The Lake looked beautiful and I for once & the 1st time really felt like "wading in." The waves rolled over so enticing it made me wish I could swim. . . . [. . .]

THURSDAY, JAN. 9. . . . I intend to go to the depot & prepare to "move on" to day. Heard from Henry twice. he has a bad cough yet from his influensa. I thought him about well when I left him. Why call the epidemic "La Grippe" it is a bad cold & some times causes pneumonia and death. A 100 cases in Boston. Nearly every one here & in the old County I have so far escaped & trust I may. I also rec'd a note from Charley in his mothers letter. He is yet at Mr. Childs.

> Rochester is a very nice place;
> And its Folk are beautiful too,
> But now the La Grippe has got them all,
> The Doctors have most of the work to do.
> (I did not have it—oh! no!)
>
> The street car lines are just the thing,
> When you are in a town like this:
> Get in—pull the strap—make it ring,
> Step out again to find you are amiss.
> (thats when I got lost)

It matters not how oft you slip
Nor own for a moment you have La Grippe.

MONDAY, JAN. 13, 1890. . . . I am truly home-sick. Because I did not bring the money with me—Henry is to send it as I need it and it is not a very good way and I will never go away again unless I have the money with me. For I feel so burdensome to be living for relations sake—It fairly made me sick last night & I cried & lay awake nearly all night. I enjoy visiting real well but I don't like to tire them all out.—and then one thing I think I feel so restless is because I never have been so idle before. . . . It snowed about 2 in. Friday and Saturday and rained all of yesterday. The wind has blown very hard all day to day & this evening it is snowing. Such changeable weather is very bad for sickness—I was glad the wind blew & felt thankful for, although it has done damage I think it has purified and cleansed the air. . . .

Yes I have enjoyed myself very much while here only I was so lonely among strangers. . . . Rain & snow. [. . .]

MONDAY, JAN. 27, 1890. Ripley, Chautauqua County, N.Y. am at Simeon Royces Ma's cousin. Left Rochester Thursday morning at 10.45 arrived in Buffalo 1 o'clock, & had to wait until 5.20 & arrived at Ripley Crossing 7.30—Simeon met me & we walked up a half mile to the house. . . . Simeon & Melvina have only two sons one is 17 Willis—named for his grandpa whose wife was H. Viletta Hawley (Ma's aunt) and Lee ten years old—is sick now. . . .

Can see over a mile of Lake Erie where I am sitting and I like the Country here real well. Warm. A little Rainy.

Ticket from Rochester to Buffalo   1.38
Ticket from Buffalo to Ripley Crossing   1.90 [. . .]

MONDAY 3. FEBRUARY—wash at Simeons. Newton took me to Westfield to call on their sister and Ma's cousin Mrs. Frank Wright—nee Miss Elizabeth Royce.

Went back with Newton and spent the P.M. with him & to Simeons over night. Windy. Misty. [. . .]

SUNDAY ? well I guess its the 2nd of March—Look about ?29?—Pa was 54 yesterday. Expect Henry is rather lonesome to day—Simeon says he need not be that he guesses I have not been here at all—does not seem a week—well it doesn't but I've been some-where since Jan. 1 anyhow. Aunt Aggie is getting anxious for me to come so I will make a brave effort to get off by another week any-way. Roads are very bad & its cold to day. Read—write—visit—help with dishes, etc. Cold. [. . .]

APR. 26, 1890. Saturday—at Milford Bakers in Morenci [Michigan]— came here day before yesterday.

Aggie Baker came up from Fayette Wed & stayed until to day. She is 20 yrs & a very good girl.

She & I & Chatty went to Morenci Thur. P.M. & yesterday P.M. I called on Dr. Stevenson and wife—they are nice people & I enjoyed it as well as any place I have been. they want me to stay a week. I also called on Chas. Blanchards—Ma's friends—they also want me to come & stay as long as I can. It rains to day and I am a trifle home-sick—I went to the depot with Aggie—& have written to Henry and Charley. I wonder why C. does not write, and Henry— Had a letter from him yesterday he is again working at his trade & said he can take care of him & me yet—Poor dear Bro. how glad I will be when I can help too—He also feels sorry about Pa—it seems he keeps such low Company. We can't help it as I see. [. . .]

JUNE 8. . . . Sent a letter to Henry yesterday.

Aunt Edna had letter from Pa which he sent the 7th—It is *very* melancholy and I judge he is again having one of his mel [melancholy] spells—I copied the letter and thought what a frame of mind must be he in to write such thoughts. I feel sorry for him & wish I might cure him.

Sarah included the text of her father's letter in her diary.

Manchester, Iowa. June 4th, 1890.

sister Ednas family although I have not had the pleasure of seeing you face to face

I still claim you as a sister and Brother & allways shall be you such to me

you speak of Sarah as looking like Emily I do not think so although she is very nigh to me now: yes so very nigh; she is my treasure and my hope. O my children Dear, it is all I have left to live for now. the world is so very dark now yes so dark. I can see no light only from above

Emily was my treasure my home was mi castle

my wife was my treasure

& my children was my Jewels, they are always so close to me I can see no one else, in my youth I thought i loved them twas only a dream a fancy now as the sands of life is running low they are a part of myself as were the reseon i did not come to see you when I was down there had not time nor money if i prosper i will come sometime, why not you and wallace come out—& make us a visit. I will entertain you the Best i can while you stay.

I received a letter from Harriet & John the 16th last month they are well & doing well. Uncle Henry past here yesterday & he is like a boy of 16 summers. Charley Baker is a hero of the first matter. I saw him to day we had a hard rain the 2nd & washed the corn some. it had 2 leaves, was looking fine. Oats is good & grass is heavy & milk goes by load. Butter by the turn & monney is plenty at 10 per cent now rite soon. J. Gillespie. [. . .]

THURSDAY 12. Aunt Edna wash & I help what I could about the house—they continue to quarrel so much that it makes me homesick. Warm.

FRI. 13. Aunt Edna got another letter from Pa—he had some one direct the envelope for him to Uncle Wallace & I see aunt Edna did not want me to read this one—so I told her I did not care to. But I think he got my letter that I sent to Henry Tues. & opened it for he spoke about what I wrote & then Henry has not answered either—I fear they are having trouble at home. [. . .]

WED. 18. Well I got home last night all safe & sound at 9.08 AM tired & glad and thankful. Henry had returned and this morning he left me to my slumber & went to his work—so I did not see him until to day at noon—I laid down & rest & clean the cupboard etc.

THURS. 19. Purchased a pr. of new shoes of Seth Brown—they were $4.00. He said Henry has looked and acted very lonesome since I was gone and he was glad to see me come home on his account. Uncle stopped for me to go home with him—Pa was along there would be no object for me to go on the farm with Pa. He w'ld be in debt at the end of the year and I w'ld have to support myself at best.

Henry has just gone to take our 3 yr. old colt to the pasture—Scipio is a nice looking animal and I only wish I could drive him. It is over a hundred in the shade. [. . .]

FRIDAY. JULY 4. I went on the excursion train to Edgewood to hear & see Prof. Butler deliver the oration of the day; and also to meet many friends whom I had not seen for a long time. My pupils have grown almost beyond recognition—but their pleasant smile & friendly greeting tell me so plainly how well they remember me—They all say if I will come back & teach this winter they will all come to me & they have not gone for 2 yrs.

Milton Alcorn & his mother are very lonely since Mr. Alcorn died & they did so want me to stay with them. I told them of their cousin whom I met as Conductor on the L.S. & M.S. R.R. from Hillsdale to Elkhart & of the good visit we had. Also saw Mr. & Mrs. Mort. Minkler and the girls—they are feeling badly because Orpha married a short time ago & she is sorry too.

Also saw Judson & Bertie Pogue & Mr. & Mrs. Schacherev and Ellis & Jo. & Josephine, and Mrs. Cox & Mattie & Horace Coon and Mrs. Doc Blair made a *charge* for me—really they all act as though they would like to eat me up—My arms fairly ache and Mrs. Mead & May & Aunt Mary Ryan and Clifford & Ida and Sam & Grace Wetterlen and so many they all are so glad to see me back & all wanted me to come & spend a few days with each of them. Why I don't believe they w'ld let me stay at home at all. . . . [. . .]

MON. 7. Am 25 yrs. old to day. Went over town. The funeral of Marshall Gardner is at 2 P.M. The oddfellows, Masons & fire Co's. all march & the engine out all dressed in mourning.

Berries 25¢

Graham 35¢

Eggs 11¢

Prunes 25¢   3 lbs.

Slop pail   60¢

Sent an order for Henry 1.03. He paid it. postal 1¢. Henry gave me a ¢. I let him take 5¢ the other day.

TUES. 8. The Democrat printed my article & were apparently glad to have it. "Home again" is what they headed it. Henry says yesterday was your birthday—such is poverty, no presents nor any-thing.

I am thankful to have what we really need & trust for more after awhile. Sew carpet rags & its amazing how so much hit & miss articles accumulate.

Bread 5¢, meat 15, crackers 15, radishes 5¢. [. . .]

SAT. 12. Sew rags & clean up—Mr. Trenchard is cross—Henry says. Pa was here to dinner & then he wanted me to go & select a tomb stone for Ma & said he w'ld like to get some-thing appropriate but the best he could get w'ld only be a marker & he just wanted "Emily" on it. He is rather disturbed in his mind I judge—I intend to attend the lecture this evening. washing 50¢. berries 15, cheese

& butter 20 celery 10 peas 5 tomatoes 5 eggs 10 meat 15 stamps 5 berries 10—95¢. [. . .]

THURS. 14. FRI. 15. attend the normal and I do enjoy it so much. Could have a position in the school here but Henry and I have talked about and conclude that I would feel much worse to have to stop on a/c of health than I do not to commence at all, and be patient this year—then I will try to be able by next fall to accept a good position. If it be possible I will try to review the branches at home & pass for a state certificate next year.

I succeed so nicely & get a trifle anxious but think with all I intend to do I can stand it another year. Henry is looking real well & is much fleshier than when I came home from the East. Beautiful. [. . .]

MON. 25. Examination—Am trying for a 1st Grade. Do not know how I will succeed—it has been so long since I have been examined.[2] And in keeping up my house work I have no time to study. Rather doubtful I think. [. . .]

SUN. 31. Attend Universalist Church & S.S. Rev. Wing is back and we all appreciate him so much. Have an interesting S.S. Last night at 9.08 we heard the bus & voices & very soon Mrs. Carpenter called me & I let her & Mrs. Denton in—was glad to see them & they breakfasted with us this morning. I walked up to N. Manchester & back & called at Giffords, and wrote "The Corn Palace Greeting." Have an extremely sore throat again. I do wish I might effect a permanent cure—It has troubled me over a year & its getting serious. Dusty. [. . .]

THURS. SEPT. 4. Henry is 27 to day and has gone to the Quaker mill—fishing. It rained last night all night. Mrs. Carpenter [their landlady] asked about Pa last evening & though I felt sorry to tell her I felt as though it was my duty to do so about him—recd a letter from Vina Royce to day and she said Aunt Edna wrote to her. Aunt Edna is treacherous—

Wish it was so Henry could have a nice present but such is poverty—if my health only improves how glad and thankful we will be. My throat is very bad but trust it may soon be better. May be by his next birthday we will be better able. . . .

FRIDAY. 5. Mrs. Carpenter and I finish cleaning up around. I mop, etc. Last night our large mirror fell down and broke all to pieces—Mrs. C—said she is superstitious about it that some one of the household may die. It made me think too of what Ma said when our other one fell down a couple of months before she died. Afternoon Mrs. C and I took our sewing and sat on the piazza—Mrs. Hitchcock—Mrs. Lynch, Mrs. Hines who now lives in Chicago also spent the P.M. with us. . . . [. . .]

MON. SEPT. 29. . . . Well the Dr. [Bradley] came as agreed and I went with him to Hempsteads—Ruthie the imbecile will most likely die. I assisted in chloroforming her. They wanted me to stay. Dr. B—I love thee. ["no I don't" was pencilled in here] why I can not tell—& I had a very good visit—Mrs. C. says it is too long to be gone—now for a genuine old folks party like ours—2 or 3 hrs. is a very short time when so pleasantly spent—But I wonder why his friendship turns on such a frail customer.

Sarah Gillespie and Dr. Bradley—stunning indeed—Still there must be an admittance in my behalf that I too have an inkling of love & trust or whatever you've a mind to call it—for him. Sport I guess. Mrs. Smith came to day but I use all my own victuals this week for Ada. Last day of September—how fast the months & days go bye. [. . .]

SATURDAY AGAIN—NOV. 1, 1890 At home or rather in our pleasant rooms at Mrs. Carpenter's corner. Gay and Franklin—How fast the days & weeks go bye—Mrs. C. and I have raked & swept the lawn & burned the leaves on the street. Mrs. Lynch and son Willie—aged 6—live in with Mrs. C—we will not be alone—Ada still remains with me and causes me a great deal of worry—this is 6 weeks and she has been out every evening but 6. I can not be imposed upon by her actions for I deem it unjust—Am sorry to be compelled to talk to her as I did last evening—

Well we 350 or 500 more or less went to the Hallow Een Party—I was too tired to remain or enjoy it however. . . .

NOV. 1. Waiting dinner—For Ada still remains with me—Henry went to the Rapids Wednesday to work for R. R. Comp. and a Mrs. Free-man of Earlville who endeavored to learn me to cut & fit dresses has been here a portion of the week until to day.

Mrs C. was dissatisfied to have her here & so I told her & she went this morning. Mrs. Dr. Fayles of Dubuque a *Christian Scien-tist* was here in M—— yesterday and day before & I had 2 pleasant conversations with her—She also called to see me—

It snowed Monday the 3rd—only a little however—The next day was warm & I washed windows—Dr. Bradley says I should not clean house or any-thing of the kind—He wanted to come to dinner but Henry says "How would it look to see any one so much older come to see you Sarah"—Can't help that—I am truly interested in Science and believe I will take treatment. [. . .]

FRI. 28. Yesterday was Thanksgiving and I had roast duck & dinner all alone—Mrs. C. ate just a luncheon a tin plate.[3] She laughed at my "big dinner." Ironed all the A.M. Called on Mrs. Huene in evening.

Had a letter from Henry in the morning. One of his good fatherly letters—so full of brotherly care. It was Beautiful and bright all day—The day before Charley was here & I had ordered a crayon portrait of Ma—Life size $9.00 Antique oak frame. He is agent & threw off his commission. . . .

Had letter from D. C. Falray one of the school trustees in Ripley N.Y. offering me the school—

Though I can not see for what though it must be for some good & best for me not to teach this year. I wait to answer the offer. Must say no to every good proposition that presents itself.

But if there is any-thing in dreams surely some good luck will follow. . . .

WED. DEC. 24. . . . Had a letter from Henry saying he would be home to day so I sat up and waited until 10.30 & retired. Received a package through the P. O. from Mr. Huftalen containing a gold watch & chain and the sentiments of the season. Last evening as I was in the store he asked if he might give me a Christmas gift and I answered no I did not wish any—and now that he has sent this I know not what to do.

There will be no pleasure in wearing it and if I keep it—It might stimulate him to think he could buy me with gold—and if I return it it will hurt his feelings—so I am loathe to know what to do under the circumstances. May God direct my thoughts.

THURSDAY 25—Christmas day and Henry came at 11 A.M. after I had given up his coming. We went to Sammie Collyers for dinner. Had a good visit. Henry go skating. He looks well and is studying hard—but says he is going to take his tools & work what he can.

He studies Greek—German. Themes. Rhetoric—Archeology—& Life of Christ. There are 125 students & Galesburg has over 20000 inhabitants. I fear he will overdo. Cold.

FRIDAY 26. Last evening Mrs. Denton and Ramy & May and Mr. & Mrs. Lynch & Henry & Mrs. Carpenter & I sat & chatted and May played for us. She is home from Sinsinawa Mound for the Holidays.

Charley drove Scipio down this P.M. and brought me a lovely toilet cushion from Lura. Pink satin with hand work cover of lace & baby ribbon drawn work.

I called on Mrs. Huene & Chas is home from Chicago—Bertha from Doon IA. for vacation.

Then I called at Mrs. Hadleys for my dress skirt—she had made over. Henry asked Mr. Huftalen up to dinner oysters & crackers— He appeared to enjoy his dinner—perhaps it was wrong but I could not thank him for the Xmas gift he sent me. The spirit did not stir me to mention it and so I did not. Cold & blustery to night—snow some.

Henry is preparing to go calling this evening & I am some tired think I will retire now. 7.30.

Henry will be with me yet tomorrow.

recd from 2nd Hand store $5.50 for the couch 4.50, shoes .25 & wringer 1.00. [. . .]

THURS. MARCH 12. 1891. Mrs. C. says she can not let the pupils come here after this month. She said they could before she went away— but now "she's changed her mind"—So it necessitates me to find a room for the pupils—They do no harm only she wants to stay in the kitchen all the time & fuss around. Its all right though—if I have enough pupils to do it. Perhaps I ought have taught for Mr. Coon when he asked me—but I thought it all right as she told me it was—The ways of *people are* changful—

SUN. 15. Let J. Brown for social biscuit 25¢.

Attend church—Pa was down last evening and I told him I had to find a room for my pupils and we were talking about the C. H. Carpenter brick on the corner.

He said he would buy it for me & give me the deed in my name. O, I do hope he will for that will be so much better for us all—I could pay the taxes on it & support myself as well as to pay rent.

Well—I also had a letter from Henry and he does not know what is best to do—Says that he & Mr. Huftalen talk of dissolving or at least of closing out the store here—that he may go to Chicago & work during vacation but that we will continue housekeeping & keep the rooms.

If I have 10 pupils I can keep up the expense all right even if I have to rent another room—which I shall have to do. And I think it best to close out the store if Henry can do better at any-thing else during vacation. He surely would get his share & that is some-thing. Seems as though we have to plan in so many ways. Pa wants a home & says he wants me to make it for him & take care of him. And Henry & I are determined never to forsake one another. And I can only hope & trust that we may plan well for the future; that whatever is best for us may be.

I am quite satisfied that my school will keep me just about even. But Pa said I could have next years rent from the farm and my fire wood etc if he could have a room & call it home with me & when he is in town to board with me—but that I would not be duty bound to do any-thing—only keep my school or teach where I see fit.

I have wished for some-time that Henry & Mr. H. would dissolve for it would be better for them both. Still it may not—I know not. I feel that he has wrongfully treated me at least. But Henry requests me to talk with Mr. H—and so I will & help him to decide what is best to do. I have written Henry to day and will again in a day or two. Thawing. [. . .]

FRI. MAY 8. Am still keeping school of 5 pupils at Mrs. Hadleys—I wish I lived there & feel so anxious to know if Henry is coming home. I have been trying to settle up in the store and will be glad when its accounts are balanced. It seems a hard deal for us—Mr. Huftalen pays Henry 200 i.e. 2/3 of what we put in & I can't think it just. However a little is most thankfully received. I paid Mrs. C.—on Rent—1.50. yesterday. Groceries of Graham .50.

Social 50¢. pictures 50 shoes soled .60. envelopes 25.

My pupil Susie Snyder has come to grief—because she did not heed her kind father—her Mother is dead & she stayed out nights etc. I told him I was sorry & we talked the matter over—he said with tears in his eyes it was a wonder the girl is not ruined. I think as long as he is away she ought to be sent to the Convent. [. . .]

JUNE 5.

> Work is pleasure—not pain.
> Pleasure is duty obtained.
> Duty is Love, and Love
> Is of God ordained.   s.g.

FRIDAY, JULY 31. again I am delinquent but time & events slip so noiselessly bye.

So may pleasures pass with the days of these fine summer hours that weariness is forgotten. Today finds me ready to rest & sleep.

Some weeks ago I undertook a scheme of having an Academy Reunion for & of schoolmates & professor—

It devolved upon me much time and labor but am repaid inasmuch as it was a success in every feature. Indeed we had a pleasant time a hundred of us banqueting & toasting in kindest of terms & familiarity.

Many came from abroad & faces once familiar but after ten years some-what changed soon beamed with gladness & recognition & cordial hand grasp & greetings were promiscuously scattered.

Will Clemans & I went across the way & rehearsed our "toasts" & Bro. Henry was much frightened as to my whereabouts & all were nervous, "Sarah out of sight 25 min"—terrible indeed—

My school closed July 23 & the Reunion was the 24—held in the Universalist church—"our old acad." I had quite a number of pupils. . . . [. . .]

WED. AUG. 12. Commence attending the Normal—Miss Graham of Dubuque introduces the Delsarte system of physical culture— Florence Gratiot who has been getting up Tennysons fair women is with us.

We gave it here 2 evenings and intended to go to Earlville but Henry & Florence went in advance and found there was no use & telephoned not to come—I was glad for I felt about famished— [. . .]

AUG. 19. Thursday—At home where I have been glad to stay since Monday morning. Last Fri. Earl Hutson stopped for me to go to his people & I went & rode back with him Monday morning—as he attends the Normal.

He & his sister Bessie came to school to me 6 yrs. ago at the Red 3 mi. N. of here.

I was nearly sick in bed both days & did just what I should not,—went to a social with them—they were ready & thought it w'ld be a treat for me—Mon. & Tues. I spent in sleep & to day in part also have commenced packing up the things. heard from Henry— he was at Uncle Henry's Sat. at Canandaigna, Mich.

Guess I'll try to get out a bit to morrow—that awful spiral & dis-agreeable sick-head-ache has been troubling me this week. So it necessitates my absence from Normal which I so much wished to take part in. Maybe I'll have to resign my position at W. Union but I trust in God & hope to soon feel better.

Mr. J. Roe came and we had a visit.

He must find a place for his little son Morris as Mrs. Wing is so disposed as to make it unpleasant. It is serious when a man like Wing marries a woman like Mrs. Wing—very much such a union as my parents. Pity them both and pity us all. He said he would have been on his knees to me if it were so I could take Morris—he also said that Mr. Hauger is desirous of marrying—but for me not to betray their secrets. I like Obadiah Staiegre [sp?] very well but I suppose he would wish some one a great deal my superior. I will betray no one I never do. Maud was over yester-morn & I told her that I could not take part at Greeley tomorrow night. Warm.

SUNDAY, AUG. 23. A cold dreary atmosphere—when a fire seems cheerful and friendly. Henry came home on the evening train 9.30 from Cleveland—somewhat tired. He attended the National J. P. C. U. and read a paper. He said many pronounced it the best paper read. It seems as though success surely awaits him in this new enterprise. O if we only had financial basis: but its all right—there is a divinity that shapes our ends—rough hew them as we will.—I feel better to day and hope & trust in God that my strength may increase day by day—then may I be able to help Henry at school.

Pa was here to day—nearly all day. He is so notional and changeable that one scarcely knows how or what to say. He says his nerves are all gone and that he knows not what he says or does half the time. We are sorry but know not what to do for him—He first wants me to come and then he don't want me; and then he wants to marry and 40 other wants and when you have planned in every one of these lines he is satisfied not.

Henry has gone to see Mr. Huftalen. He feels lonely to have us both leave Manchester.—

Our business relations have been pleasant and he appears to be a true friend.

Florence & Maud came to see me and to stay to supper last evening.

Maud returns to Dubuque tomorrow. She is indeed glad to get home. some-way she is not lasting with her friends.

Mr. Hutson left 2 boxes of honey from Earl & Bessie—and a bottle of patent medicine that they would have me take—they fear I will not stand it 3 mo. to teach.

Scrap book 40¢	.40
groceries 70 40	1.10
Paid Thorpe all to Bal	4.60
Rec'd of Jos. Skinner	3.50

Joseph—my pupil—may success crown his efforts. In him I admire many prominent traits which if rightly developed will make him a useful and honored citizen. Some-times when friends assail me for leaving Manchester, I begin to realize that the absence of a year will be apt to bring many changes but after all it seems best & right for me to go.

THURSDAY 21. Have been packing and tearing up all day. Henry went out S. of Masonville this morning to be gone until Sat. night.

_ Florence remained here until yesterday morning when she went to Mrs. Hadleys. I paid Mrs. Hadley to day for Henrys & my board $22.50. Henry gave me 15 to pay his part ($13). So he & I are just even. I let him have $7.00 he paid the rent $4 this month & as I have a $1 of his the remnant 3's bal.

groceries	2.00
Hat	3.00
Dry Goods boxes	.30

Pa was down Monday and wishes me to go with him to Riddells and get a dress—I was much surprised for this is the 1st. good dress he ever gave me. I did not think I could afford the making but had to promise before he got it that I would. So I took it to Mrs. Mills to be made—9 yds slate colored ladies broad-cloth—very fine @ 1.25. I got $1.06 trimmings and do not know how much the making will be.

SAT. 23. Paid Mrs. Allen for dress making 4.25
  that is all I owe her.
  Groceries & meat   .55
  Sleep nearly all day.

Tucked into the back pages of this volume of the diary is a poem, in Sarah's handwriting, on two pages of cream-colored stationery.

JULY 7, 1890.
July seventh eighteen ninety;
Heralds in a gladsome morn,
Tells to me the truthful story:
Twenty-five years since I was born.

God has given bounteous measure
Health and joy and peace combined
Mingled in some pain & sorrow
All around my heart entwined.

Yes, my journal tells the story
Of a portion of my life
Of my joys and disappointments
Of the victory and the strife.

O, the happy days of school-hood
Could I walk your paths again
Of the childish road of pleasure
Naught would I know of grief or pain.

Now my youthful years are ended
And the days go steadily on
Telling me of bud & blossom
Hence the fruit and we are gone.

He has filled my life with sunshine
And a few well scattered showers
May my days be bright & useful
Like his fragrant fairest-flowers?

And to you my friend; I tender
Warmest sympathy and love
Kindest thoughts for thee; & comfort
'Till God calls you from above.

1/4 of a Century.
1/3 of a Life.
Happy & content
& Nobody's wife. S. G.

CHAPTER SEVEN

"The Parent, the Pupil and the Teacher": 1900–1914

The parent, the pupil and the teacher form the trinity of the schoolroom—of excellence. Let us work together to raise its standard of excellence.
—Sarah Gillespie Huftalen, comments in 1908–09 Arbor Vitae Summit School schedule

From 1890 to 1914 Sarah made many changes in her life. Weary of the hard work and uncertain income derived from doing private tutoring, she accepted a full-time teaching position at the grammar school in West Union, Iowa, during the 1891–92 school year. The following summer, Sarah moved away from Manchester for the first time, going to Des Moines, where she worked as a secretary at the Mutual Insurance Company. Her life changed even more profoundly when, on September 14, 1892, she married William (Billie) Henry Huftalen. Sarah and Billie returned to Manchester, where he ran a second-hand store (pawnshop) and she tutored students and cared for friends' children.

The news of his daughter's marriage to a man older than he apparently came as a shock to James Gillespie, as evidenced by the letter he wrote to Sarah a month after her wedding.[1] As Mary Hurlbut Cordier notes, "Marrying Billie at a hotel in Des Moines in September 1892 was Sarah's most defiant act against the domination by her father and Henry's so-called protection. . . . Sarah's father and brother continued to disapprove of her marriage, and returning to Manchester did not mend this schism in the family" (218).

Although it is possible that Sarah continued writing in her diary during the rest of the 1890s, the volumes in the Huftalen Collection include no entries for those years. Sarah apparently resumed her diary-keeping around the turn of the century, at which time she was active in both the temperance movement and the women's suffrage move-

ment. In fact, she had just completed a term as president of the Man-chester Woman Suffrage Association. Her commitment to both move-ments was strong, and she wrote in her diary that she had arranged for Carry Nation, a prominent leader in the temperance movement, to speak in Manchester on August 11, 1902.

Manchester, Iowa, Jan. 1, 1900.[2]

Accounts etc of Mr. and Mrs. W. H. Huftalen
Household supplies—groceries provisions etc.
      "   "   —clothing
      "   "   —Fuel
      "   "   —Rent
Man must live and to live must labor.

I believe that it was intended for man to earn his bread by the sweat of his brow, whether it be for the body, the mind or the soul. Material things are vanishing things yet must man possess them and to become possessor must needs labor much, mentally, morally and physically.

JANUARY 1, 1900. Provision on hand—
    flour—white—50¢ whole wheat 3 lbs. 12¢
    sugar 15¢—granulated, brown and loaf.
    lard 20¢ butter 1 lb. 1/2 35 oysters 1 1/2 qt. 30
    honey 2 lbs. 25
    Left over from New Years dinner—a lot of suet pudding, beans, pies, cakes, lamb roast, etc.
    Wood.—3 cords, 10 lbs buckwheet flour 25¢ 9 1/2 lb. lamb .85
JAN. 5. Oatmeal 10¢. Cream wheat 15¢
JAN. 8. 2 bars soap 5¢ Jan. 9, bread 5¢   .10
JAN. 11 & 13. meat 8 bread 5   .13
JAN. 15. bread 5¢. rice 25¢. the 16th.   .30
JAN. 16. maple sugar 13¢ 17th oatmeal .10
   18TH BREAD 7   .30
JAN. 17–19. meat 14¢ goose 70¢ apples 25 maple 10   1.19
JAN. 23. pie 10 bread 25 24th meat & bread 15¢
   26TH APPLES 20 FLOUR 25 & W. 25.   1.00
JAN. 25. sugar 25¢ oranges 12¢. soap 5¢.
29TH. meat 20 kerosene 25 soda 10.   .97
JAN. 30. dried peaches, prunes, oatmeal, and oranges   .59
JAN. 31. bread and yeast   .07
                                    8.41

[. . .]

A brief account 'tis true but it means 365 days of labor, filled with mingled doubts & fears. 365 days unceasing toil for the needs of the material man. Ah! yes more than that—for is not the flesh the home of the soul for a time at least—only a short time.

JANUARY 1, 1901. A new year and a new century dawns. What may we do with the golden opportunities of time? How live? What do? "Man wants but little here below," but nevertheless man must needs "scrabble" to procure that "little."

Accounts for January 1901 follow. Then this note appears.

APR. 1. Please do not think we did not eat during Feb. & Mar.—we did, but I was too neglectful to keep a/c. No clothing or extra's. meat 5 onions 15 bread 10. [. . .]

JULY 8, 1902. Came to Greeley the 6th to Mrs. A. B. Holberts to remain as governess while they go abroad.[3] Came to Oneida on cars & the hired girl which made it uncomfortable riding. It seemed very hard to come away from home but we some-how promised and now we hope its all for the best. It was so rainy & muddy that the boys could not plow corn.

Jessie cut some hay in P.M.

Let Ben go to swim. Fred & I looked over mail—I scarcely know how to answer such letters as these call for—

I finished Charmions night-gown.

She tried to teach Louie to call me Mamma, it amused me to hear them in other room. Louie went to sleep at supper & I put him to bed—up several times in night to give him water & not bring used to the sleepers (resters) did not sleep much last night or the night before.

Mr. & Mrs. Holbert said good-bye at 7 A.M. going to Oneida in wagon—baggage. Ben took them. train 1 hr. later. they are to reach Montreal to night. Tues. 8 and set sail on the Lake Erie from there early tomorrow morning.

Hope they may have a safe and pleasant voyage and a happy homecoming all well and satisfactory. The children are good so far and no trouble to me.

I did errands yesterday (mon.) but more to day.

Telephones and telegrams galore.

Fred is to be head man or the man here said his papa. He is not to overdo. We ought to be up in the morning but it is raining now 3 A.M. after being so warm & sunny.

Men & boys at the farm—plow corn.

Children at Moffits a little while. Gusta [the family's hired girl] washing. Neither of the children have cried & Charmion says she calls me mamma and laughs.

Louie wanted to know this morning if his mamma had gone way off on the cars to Manchester & would she come back? I told him yes after a long time & he laughed & ran away. Have cleaned sec'y and sewing machine draws to day. mended some & taught Charmion "Jack's Tent."

JULY 9. Wake up before 2 every morning and cannot get to sleep after it. Am wide awake instantly if the children stir. they talk in their sleep. did not ask go to go Moffits to day. gathered stones, put up tent, played about. Louie set down in mud. Charmion stubbed toe a bit. They do not cry & Gusta says they are the best they have ever been.

I did errands in A.M. got groceries and saw Yatewan.

Look over mail with Fred and am sorry did not have the "know how" for a few days so can answer it. It ought to be.

Sewed on Charmion's drawers and mended.

Let Ben go to M—— and get pants. . . .

JULY 11. FRIDAY. Fred let me ride as far as Oneida & I went to Manchester. guess it made me homesick.

Have felt sad & cried—seemed couldn't help it. felt so good this morning. yesterday did errands for the house. . . . It has been very pleasant—both days beautiful. Hope 'twill be happier tomorrow. Ben & Fred wanted root beer and I thought not best a day or two ago when Ben wanted it and had Gusta throw it out supposing it was all right, but Fred spoke so severe to day threatening to have beer that it did not seem much like the Fred we have known and made me feel very down spirited. they find fault and scold at Gusta and Gusta at them continually. Keeping a perfect turmoil. Was sorry clear through to have such a day. [. . .]

MON. TUES. WED. JULY 28, 29. 30. three busy days. it is Wed. 30 evening. Boys up town. I don't know what for. I went to Manchester last ev. 5 P.M. & came back this morning. Billie has a cold—better tho. Had contest—g.g. Reba Spitter won the medal. Very warm.

Our folks are haying. I wish the children would do as they ought. Yate a man papering—paper too dark I think. Am afraid she won't like it—but she said she liked Mrs. Baker's all right & I guess its about same color.

Charmion and Louie are in bed. Gusta up town too. Well, we can't

Main Street, Manchester, ca. 1900. Courtesy of Tim Tutton.

have every-thing as would like but we could have them better in some ways than they are.

FRI. 1 AUG. Would like to go home—Fred and Ben went up town last night to see who guessed nearest weight of a horse & one to treat. I do not like this and the boys were up night before last also—no good in it. Thursday Ben did nothing it seemed to me but torment—he is very rude and rough and profane. It rained Wednesday night so he was not needed in hay. 3 men plow cane Thursday. Bright & Sunny. Gusta & I clean. Awful mess.

WED. AUG. 6. Have not felt very well to day. contest—last eve. very good.

Then Mr. Moffit chased a prowler down road & we were all up & out. Did not get to bed 'till 2 A.M.

Two fellows drunk came along & I believe had some-thing to do with it.

Had letter from folks Mon. Aug. 4. [. . .]

In fall 1904, Sarah began teaching at the Arbor Vitae Summit School in Oneida Township, where she remained for five years.[4] There she worked diligently with her pupils to beautify the school grounds and to institute a cohesive curriculum.

This book shall contain a record of the apparatus, books, charts and miscellaneous supplies, pictures, etc belonging to this district and also obtained.

PREFACE

It is as necessary to supply a child with all needful supplies, and to place him in the midst of pleasant and beautiful surroundings, if his soul is to grow and his mind develop, as it is for a carpenter to be supplied with tools for the building of a house; or for a plant to receive its quota of sunshine and rain that will help it to blossom and yield a fruitage.

"As ye sow so shall ye reap."—Bible

[. . .]

1904–05 Ash heaps, dirt mounds from the new building; sticks and stones, not a tree, grass & weeds. In Spring, cleaned the yard and basement. An extremely hard job. I never shall forget the boys—Wayne, Myron & John bringing up the ash barrel out of the basement. [. . .]

1905

SAT. FEB. 4. Henry came P.M.—he is taking care of pa who is having the gripp. Henry came Jan. 27th. they did not let me know & I was much surprised. Henry brought some eatables, white grapes, beets, apples, beans, meat, etc. He had to go back I sent pumpkin pie, jelly, genes and can of pears. Henry said pa was out of his head & very hard to get along with. Henry looks terribly worn. Seems as though Henry & I have had heavy burdens all the way. But we are ever prayerful and hopeful. God is good.

Billie went to Greeley to get horses' shoes set and some provision. It is cold but moderated a considerable. I was glad to see Henry—so glad. [. . .]

FEB. 15. Have studied all day. Mr. Cocking, the director brought 2 bu. of corn. 80. I walked part way one *cold* A.M. last week from hillsbridge hill. afraid to drive horse through. [. . .]

MAY 6, 1905. Saw pa. Pa looks old and wrinkled. Am sorry for him. He said Henry is in Halvermann hospital. Chicago. had been 2 wks. Dr. Trein had him go & have an operation for a breach [hernia]. Dear, ———. It seems so very hard for him to have had such a thing

Henry Gillespie working as a carpenter at the St. Louis Exposition, 1904.
SHSI.

done. It was done before the students—and that seemed worse to me. I have such a horror of operations anyway.

Mr. Simmons has hailed me as I was going to depot. He seemed a veritable Shylock.

This has been an exceeding dark day—I feel so bad I can not write & I do not know that there is any use anyway. Henry has had *such a hard time.* Taking care of pa—and pa—well its pitiful to make the best of it. [. . .]

JULY 10. . . . I picked up Henry's things and brought the cedar chest he made & had things in, the typewriter & his clothing etc. home with me. I feel that Henry must come here & stay until he is strong. I cleaned the cupboards etc & straightened up pa's rooms. Pa is very weak minded and it is pitiful so pitiful—he talked so cruelly of Henry—I just closed my ears. Mr. & Mrs. Hayden who live at fathers think him insane & she said he scolded Henry all the time & that they feared all day before Henry went. pa was vile & was vile all the week. Henry just packed his little grip & went away—not saying what he was going for. But I know he was very sick at heart & grieved and tho't to be able to work at his trade he would go & have it done—& then he could "work" as pa has always wanted him to. Pa is a terrible man. It kept me very busy to get the meals & do that which I did from 4.30 A.M. to 3 P.M. & so little rest and then I had walked out in the heat & had packages to carry the 7th so I was glad to get back to Oneida. I ate dinner at Mrs. Haydens—met Pa going to town after his & I had him go on. He wanted me to walk back with him and asked me: "where are you going?" I'm sure I do not know what the end of all our sorrows and trials and prayers will be. But God is good and we trust in his promises. I wrote to Henry Fri. 7th. Sun. 9th. & Mon. 10th & will write to day. I have written often but I can hardly endure the strain of not knowing just how he is and of not doing anything for him—it seems heart-breaking to me to have to wait and watch & pray without being with him and caring for him. . . .

In July 1905 Sarah wrote that Henry had gotten out of the hospital and was recovering. She then wrote about her father.

. . . Pa ought to have a guardian. I think his insanity comes from self-abuse and an uncontrollable temper. He is to be pitied & we always have but I will try to take care of him if he gets sick again & they let me know. when he is down he is glad to be taken care of. He said he would die some day & he wanted Henry & I to have the farm & the things & that he wanted to see us settled—poor man. And this is the way it is—you can't help feeling very sorry & doing all you can for him & at the same time he will kill you by inches. . . . [. . .]

OCT. 7. Have been teaching 4 weeks. 31 scholars. 30 seats. crowded for room.

Get along very nicely. There are a few strange dispositions—as much so as any I ever met. Ray Williams and Lyle Congers & Eva Michael, Verne Buchanan is low and dishonest.

OCT. 12. Pa came over between trains. Poor Pa. [. . .]

DEC. 27, 1905. Beautiful day. I am tired. Billie is ironing, he mopped & I sewed carpet which is ready to put down. Finish cleaning all down stairs except putting down kitchen carpet & washing outside of windows. I helped clean up the church Tues. afternoon. [. . .]

1905–06 FALL '05—Pupils & I set 2 box elders. Verne Buchanan. 1 rose bush, Lela Burbridge. also golden glow and iris. 1 five-leaf ivy, Maurice Struckoff. Lilacs, Lucy Boardman. 5 box elders, Director Geo. Meyer. [. . .]

MAY 10. also 7 catalpa I sent for, & 3 white ash & 2 mulberry. Mrs. Conger helped me set these out 5:30 P.M. we were tired. 1 five-leaf ivy—Mrs. Dickinson. we began at N.W. & think to cover fence all around yard. Mr. Dunn gave me a telephone pole. We set this last fall, & intend to make arbor with seats & cover with vines, post supports etc.

SPRING '06 10 scotch pine & 9 arbor vitae. I help Meyer & Mr. Dunham made flower beds. too grassy. [. . .]

1906. JUNE 13. Oneida, Iowa. Select-School-Oneida. The following young people met at my home in the evening to consider plans etc of select-school.

Wayne Bushnell. Miss Thomas.
Myron Bushnell. Nellie Michael.
John Michael.
Leslie Ausman.
Wallace Ausman.
Robin Cruise.
Arthur Cocking.
Clarence Jones.
John Rector.
Andrew Rector. [. . .]

JUNE 14. John Rowe called and wants to come. He is a poor scholar I know and slow and dull. 16 yrs. old. worked out from 12 yrs. at Lies one year—an uncle—so Rena Lie who took my pen is his cousin. She was a roomer and pupil in 1889.

JUNE 15. School-children picniced all day had a nice time. Beautiful day.

JUNE 17. SUNDAY—Children's day. on prog. com.

JUNE 18. MON. Leslie, Hazel & Wallace Ausman and Robin Cruise
8.30 P.M. to 11 P.M. fractions.
Nellie Michael 2.15 to 4.45 gram.

TUES., JUNE 19. Charmion & Louie started at 8, got here 10.30 ponies acted so. dinner & lessons. Fred is sick in hospital at Pomona. Ceal (my dream again) wreath of white flowers, large 3 qt. black center, thru the sky.—[. . .]

MON. 19. NOV. 1906. Would have whipped Ruth she speaks so ugly. I do not know what makes her. Mary says she has always been. Maurice began whispering again as soon as he entered the door.

Had a no. 1 school except for Ruth. Am sorry. I gave her same rules as last year.

TUES. Had a 100% school to day. Had Ruth come to the desk and talked to her and had her remain there until she promised the school she was sorry and would not speak that way again. I told her of:— habit and disposition forming—bitterness in the heart—patience and forbearance—endure it as long as could—punishment for betterment—being sorrowful turning a new leaf etc.

She seemed penitent and forgiven and all right until she went home at noon. Upon her return she went to her desk and out with the rest but never returned to school. Her mother certainly made a great mistake or could do nothing with her. She says Ruth gives her much trouble and she cannot manage her. [. . .]

JAN. 27, 1907. Water closet—Boys—morning clean. Recess—All say it was clean except Howard had wet the small one some.

Recess till noon. Howard, Arthur, Otto, Maurice. 11.57. Maurice said the large seat all right but the small one was wet some. Georgie went out at 12 before eating his dinner. (Edward, Henry and Charlie went skating and were tardy—did not go in closet at noon.) I went out and found both seats soiled so I thought George and Howard responsible (I believe Geo. most so) and had them clean it after school.

Chas. and Frank went in to hide and called Lyle and Roy to come and see and they came to me and said I ought to come and see.

I think Lyle and Roy soil it too by their manner.

Roy's mother believed a teacher had no right to watch the closets, had no authority over the children in regard thereto, and that a teacher had no right to punish her child if she said so—nor to strike a child. This made Roy haughty and disagreeable and boastful. Am glad the rest of the parents do not teach theirs such things. [. . .]

SPRING 1907—Pupils & I went to woods Arbor Day Apr. 26. get: 1 choke cherry which we named "Black Beauty," 1 wild crab, 3 poplar, 1 elderberry, 1 cottonwood & 7 yellow willows that died. I furnished 1 soft maple. 3 tame plums, 1 box elder, & 3 cottonwoods.

Graduation June 22, 1907

School closed June 7, but did not have program until the 22nd.

I invited Dists no's 2 and 3 to come also. . . . The Common School graduates from the Rural Schools deserve recognition in a public manner and I want to do my part—in behalf of the educational interests and moral benefits that our boys and girls merit.

SEPT. 2, 1907. School began.

Napier children came. Staid up quite a mess because of ruling of board that none child come from outside of the district. They only came the first day.

Smallest enrollment ever had. 12 pupils. 3 grades with two divisions in the 1st.

I felt like resigning because nothing had been put in shape about the building and grounds. The director said he would have the yard mowed and raked up, the doors and windows mended and put in shape, the roof repaired, the floor scrubbed and the coal put in the cellar—before school began—not a thing of which was done.

SEPT. 20. FRIDAY—at home yesterday and today with a sprained ankle. Sprained it Wed. A.M. at Mr. Dunham's. School has gone fine. Scholars good and helpful. We are hoeing & mulching the trees. Mr. Voelker mowed the most of the yard & the scholars and I will try to cicle the rest of it. George & Howard dug a hole for an arbor pole and Mr. Geo. Parker promised me 24 elms to set 2 rows in street. Wasn't that good, no expense either.

I staid to supper at Mr. Dicksons and he brought me home Wed. night. Mrs. Hood & Dora helped me from schoolhouse to Dicksons. foot is pretty lame, aches. . . .

SEPT. 30, 1907. Excellent days work.

Everybody busy & happy the whole day thru. Rather cool and cloudy—began keeping fire the 23rd.

OCT. 1. picked leaves from each kind of tree on grounds. "Morning dawns on the heights of Sedan Clear patient morn."

OCT. 2. "Twas a calm still night and the moons pale light (great round moon) shone soft o'er hill and dale."

Our school work has been so in keeping with the weather expressed in the above sentiments I feel heart thankful.

OCT. 7. Primer class had 1st lesson in book "Little Boy Blue" which we drill on words and dramatize—expression excellent. The 5th will read DeSoto in reading. Draw map of DeSoto's march in Geog. and recite about DeSoto, Coronado, Vaca and Narvaez in history—reciting from the maps.

In Geog. we started from the school-house & expect to travel all over the world from Oneida as a center.

We will make a map of the world.

"   "   " charts for 1st, Primary also.

"   " press leaves and collect curios & woods & specimens.

Library Books—I think it would be helpful to the sec'y. for each teacher to specify the needs of her school.

We have Geog. reader of Europe which have not been studying—but would have liked Geog. reader of America.

We are beginning history & w'ld like to keep 4 of the early books on history & Indians etc. [. . .]

THURS. OCT. 17, 1907. I gave each 10¢ = 30¢.

The boys are shoveling the coal and throwing it into the basement. It is a very disagreeable thing and I feel like giving up my school. I would not sign the contract until I knew it would not fall on me to put the coal in the basement or carry the ashes up the stairs. The director has not kept his word and keeps nothing in shape or repair as promised. The boys are only 10 to 12 yrs. old and would not want to do it without pay besides they are scarcely equal to it & it disturbs the schoolwork—cleaning them up & the dust of it drove us all out for 20 minutes yesterday, our heads ached and the afternoon amounted to virtually nothing. And then to make things worse a lot of earth caved in this forenoon—the boys & I tried to shovel it out the cellar windows—it is wet & heavy & I gave out. It makes me feel disheartened.

FRIDAY 18. Sent word to Mr. Miller who came up and appeared angry about it. But after looking at it, he said he would come up Sunday and dig it out. He did not. I had to hire a man myself. Beautiful weather. [. . .]

NOV. 12, 07. The fall term closed Nov. 8 and winter term began Nov. 11. no vacation. Excellent school. Jimmie and Howard are indolent, indifferent, and somewhat lazy. I try many ways. It seems sometimes as tho all they can understand is to be driven—to be made. Their home government is surely deficient. The whole 5 of them are dishonest. What a pity. Ed. Wilcox was in town and Billie saw him and he came up and shoveled the cave-in out of the basement and moved the coal into the furnace room. It seemed as tho the Lord sent him. Pd. him 33¢ all change had. He asked 50¢.

The scholars will haul the ashes and dirt away with a box. We made up our minds we do not like a path made of coal ashes—tracks and is unpleasant. . . .

NOV. 12, 1907. The 1st snow was Nov. 9. small round pellets, thick and fast.

Snowed again the 10th Sunday. I felt very much like resigning last night. By the time I carry 2 or 3 and sometimes 4 scuttles of coal up the stairs and empty them, and then go to Cole's place & get a pail or 2 *full* of water and carry it down stairs and put it in the furnace. then put in the amt. of coal and pick up etc. I feel about used up.

Now the coal being moved from the stairs and the door so it will open and the dirt out so do not have to climb over it—it is that much better. . . . [. . .]

1907–08 FALL. Pansy bed E. of house rocks form yard in a circle a foot high & a foot wide. filled with earth, hauled it in goods box with wire nailed to it.

Oct. 25, 1907. Sown Apr. 29, 1908. Blossoms June 1908.

Began drive and walk of ashes—did not like it. Took it up. Disagreeable for children's feet. Tracks in. Litters the yard. no good. [. . .]

Included in Sarah's diary is a copy of her letter to C. R. Scroggie, Des Moines, Iowa. The letter is dated July 19, 1909.[5]

Dear Mr. Scroggie: Thinking possibly you would like to know I am working on the articles I write to let you know that have them ready; that the only for September contains 3420 words; the one for October contains 2610 words; and the one for November about the same,—have not as yet counted. It was my intention to have each contain questions but fearing these are already longer than you might wish I withold the question feature for later articles.

I do not believe that any one teacher can lay out plans for any other teacher to follow; it is an impossibility. In listening to the remarks made by Rural teachers in regard to it they are invariably something like this: "Oh, yes, that is good but it won't fit my school

Sarah's students with their teacher in the Arbor Vitae Summit School classroom, 1909. SHSI.

a bit." And in answer to questioning them the sentiment is the same. As rural teachers, under present conditions at least, we find it impractical to attempt to follow in detail the many helpful and elaborate plans which educational Journals contain.

With these facts in mind it has been my aim to present those things which will aid the teacher in: First, the fundamentals required to grade and classify her school, and, Second, to keep it so under the varying conditions of rural schooldom, and Third, to give such an abundance of suggestive material as will aid her in applying the use of the Hand Book to these two things.

The things that have been helpful to me may be helpful to others, and our school is well enough classified and graded so that the pupils who have entered other schools from ours such as Chicago, Omaha, Nebraska, and others in different places in Iowa; have entered exactly where leaving off here as high second to low third: 4th to 5th, 8th to 9th, etc.

In the 4 1/2 yrs of my tutelage here there have been over 90 different pupils in attendance, the lowest attendance at any one time being 16, the highest 35. [. . .]

Sarah with her students at the Arbor Vitae Summit School's Graduation and Promotion Day, May 28, 1909. SHSI.

MAY 28, 1909. . . . I have been weaning myself from my beloved "Arbor Vitae Summit" all the year—In the early mornings before the children came I have gone from window to window & looked out long and silently on my little yard and trees. I planted my love in their rootlets. I felt sad but brave not to show it. Sunny Day.

JUNE 30. worked at school yard nearly all day, hoeing & weeding around the arbor vines & roses. Mr. Kephart & wife came & helped put 4 rafters on the arbor, & She & Dora helped stake some of the trees. Yesterday I worked in schoolhouse & yard all forenoon. Dora & Agnes & Adelaide helped me weed the flower bed. pansies & lily in bloom, Sweet Williams & mignouette up fine, roses in bloom. we trimmed off little branches that Lewis' horses had broken. It seemed too bad. Mrs. Dickson helped carry lawn seats over to their house. I took down all maps, pictures & charts & exhibits, arranged woods etc. etc. not a speck of litter anywhere.

I have also spent 2 days there since school closed—so the 6th could draw their maps for the state fair. As they did not get them done we brought all the materials to my house, where they are doing it.

I was at Mrs. Dicksons for dinner. *too tired to eat.*

I wrote 11 articles last week of over a thousand words each.

JULY 1. went to Manchester. Took the cover of Spec. book to [Frank] Joseph's office so I think every thing is about closed. He wanted to know how things were going?

They have circulated a petition to retain my services. Mr. Haight did it. He said Mr. Joslyn would not sign it although he had nothing against me as a teacher; that Cox's had been at him all winter to have Pearl get the school & if Haight would get Geo. & Jas. Cox to sign it, he would. He is going on Cox's farm another year. Haights are going on Geo. Mayers & Napers are going to Albany, Oregon. Dickson's intend to [go] away as soon as they can sell their property. It has stirred up a terrible bitterness in the neighborhood—The S. S. affair & the church vs. the school.

Mrs. Conger is the most curious & inquisitive gossip I've ever met. To think she would do what she has done.

JULY 5, 1909. Monday morning dark and rainy.

Mr. Hockaday, pres. of the board, came here Sat. evening July 3, to ask me if I would take his school no. 2. He was somewhat excited and appeared considerable angry. He said they had had a meeting that afternoon; that my duties have brought me in closer touch with the patrons.

We came here to teach the school, not to get into any church mixup. I scarcely know how I could have averted it. I've ever let them do whatsoever they would without protest or murmur and have done whatever I have been asked to do. Taught their Bible class for them 3 yrs. then to hear it said they allowed me to because I could not influence them any.

Just for the sake of memorandum I'm going to put their names down.

In a different color ink is this note, apparently added later by Sarah: "Factions that squabbled. I have liked & do like them all." Then Sarah's entry went on:

Sometimes I believe it all for the best and it does not worry me now at all. When I saw Mr. Joseph Thursday last, he said for me to get the wire of Mr. Legg & send the bill to him & to ask Mr. Burbridge to let Jimmie help me put it on, or get someone else.

He thought he could come and help some day this week.

Mr. Hockaday carried the idea to me Sat eve'g that "Mr. Miller had a teacher for this school." He said, "Miller says he's got one by the name of Beckman? from up Lamont way."

MON. JULY 5, AFTERNOON. Mr. Hockaday drove in to say he had "hired a teacher." He asked me Sat. eve. to take his school & said he would call Tues. evening to get my decision. That's the kind of a man he is.

Mr. Haight has just called. He said he asked what was done with the petition, how did the ballot stand & he was answered with "well, it was like this we either had to hire her or not hire her and we turned it down."

Mr. Hockaday, so Mr. Haight said, told him Sat. eve'g that he "wanted the 2 or 3 down here that was trying to run the board to shut up, to lay down and keep still or they would close the school and sell the property & compel his children to go down the track to the other school."

When rereading the diary in 1949, Sarah added another comment.

It is difficult & embarrassing for a teacher when neighborhood factions arise & the school is used to thresh each other. We were willing to resign as we had received a number of invitations from school officers in other places to teach.

Sarah added this entry on April 17, 1949.

EASTER (APR. 17, 1949) TIME. I've been collecting and organizing the school notes, this record, clippings, & photographs of the Oneida School Dist. No. 7 Oneida Township.

It brings many happy reflections in the school work and in our relationship to the community of which, being a resident, involved interest & cooperation.

We did everything we were asked to do altho sometimes hesitant in trying to please both factions.

And now I'm presenting this record book; the scrap book containing the columns I edited in the newspaper; and the photograph album to George Cox, who was ever a faithful pupil during my years of incumbency as teacher.

Really we were a happy school family in a school home every inch of which we all loved both inside and outside. We were a team in every project and endeavor. Harmony reigned on the hill.

We never worked for fame or reward but someway the work & joy of this school spread afar. we received requests for series of articles from State & National journals of Education; from State & World

Fair Expositions; from County Superintendents in different states to teach in their schools; from lectures for data; from visitors & from as far away as Boston, Mass.

It causes me a pang in my heart as I live over again the interest & activities of those days now gone to return no more other than in cherished and precious memories.—a pang at parting with these visible expressions so carefully preserved through the years. So clear & vivid do these pages recall the old scenes, the old days, the dear children, the happinesses, that we are loath to part with them. and yet:—

Knowing that such things are of no interest to strangers it is our thought that none other than one who was a pupil would care for the memoranda of that in which he was a part, a very substantial part, we have decided to present this ever beloved pupil these data.

God bless you and keep you, George, and your dear ones, and may His ever-abiding love sustain your faith & hope & trust in knowing His promises are secure.

Sincerely your old teacher friend,
Sarah Gillespie-Huftalen.

Should you not care to keep this record in your family do you not think it would be well to place it in the school library or with the Alumni Society for preservation & reference?

LATER. It was decided to present the album and the scrapbook to the Iowa State Historical Society, in Shaeffer Hall, Iowa State University, Iowa City, Iowa. This was in January 1951.

The scrapbook contained the columns of clippings written weekly for the Manchester papers and some record in the front pages of the school as it had newly been built and located in the village. The old building & school was about a mile SE close to the railroad & the citizens of the District voted the change—left the old building where it was. [. . .]

In August 1909, Sarah and Billie moved to Clarinda, Iowa, and that fall Sarah began teaching at the Norwich school in Tarkio Township, Page County, Iowa.[6]

SEPT. 27. John worked 1 1/2 hrs this A.M. on outbuildings. Jack Bloom dug pits 1/2 day 5 ft. 8 in. deep. They ought [to] be boxed. Lumber is high. I can only wonder some times why God sent me to this old neglected school yard and buildings. If I had the means I would

Sarah teaching country school at the Norwich school, ca. 1910. SHSI.

donate the whole thing because it costs such an effort for me to ask for anything. [. . .]

SAT. 31. Mr. Miller and Fred clean chimney, dangerous old pipe next to paper. Mrs. Hall & I paper boys closet in P.M. A severe week. Jno. gets $4.00 for the work on the outbuildings. am glad of it. They are going to be comfortable and substantial. we had old and very poor tools. I planned them the buildings. Miss Field approved. Mr. Miller ordered. The boys finished painting coal house. 24 New Ideal Adjustable desks and seats came today. Miss Field gave me Am. Seat. Co. Catalog. to select from. I chose these. She approved and Mr. Miller order them. I was going to get Kindergarten chairs as there were no small seats, but Mr. Miller thought, and so did I, best to get 24 Ideal instead of 30, as Miss Field said we ought, just as many as pupils less two at present, and make do. And he said I need not buy seats. [. . .]

On November 25, 1909, James Gillespie died at the family farm, with Sarah at his bedside. Sarah's diary entries continued to focus on her teaching.[7]

DEC. AND JAN. The boys help keep things up very well. Phillip Smith put screen around evergreens, latches on doors, hinges on outbuild-

Sarah and her students at the Norwich school, spring 1910. Sarah's caption reads, "The new teacher and her crew of happy, intelligent and industrious students. Just now making walks to well and fuel house out of old desks. Hard wood, hard nailing. Also spading for hyacinth and tulip beds." SHSI.

ing doors that had been put on wrong, etc. Jno. and Samuel put up bell rope.

The well went dry Monday Jan. 16.

FEB. 6. 1910. School goes very, very nicely. I praise God for the goodness He has done for me in this school—all clean and free from bad habits now.

I went to Page Co. Banquet Feb. 4. also Nellie Copeland, Mrs. Walter Lingo, and Mr. Miller and Vera. Mr. Miller is a veritable brother. . . . [. . .]

APR. 28. Arbor Day. impromptu program. Lulu Phillip & I went in evening and planted poppies, holly hocks, and verbenas by west fence near boys closet & staked around them to keep chickens away. Dallas spaded the bed. [. . .]

MAY 9.—Boys hauling the sand up to sand pile, girls help.

—1st, pick up sticks on their play ground.

Sarah's students followed by their teacher outside the Norwich school. Her caption: "The teacher and her flock eager for work or play." SHSI.

—Genevieve Phillip & Ada & I clean dirt piles from above wall.

I dug up cement flower bed—hard sod. Children put in some dirt on top of it. needs more. [. . .]

MAY 18. Have things in pretty fair shape. Boys mow yard with lawn mower. Boys scour outhouse, girls ditto, and hall, carry chairs etc. tired. [. . .]

During June I have gone almost every day to pull weeds or cut grass. Spent 3 days last week to lawn mow, then cut with sickle sweet clover as tall as my head in road way and large patch (short) on lawn, hoed all burdock as far as well and trained up vines and weeded flowers—too dry to amount to much. [. . .]

JULY 19. pd. Phillip Smith for helping lawn mow yard.   .25

Phil. King   .45

rest pd. boys is set down in the other book

the board paid me $3 for cleaning the schoolhouse & mowing the yard. [. . .]

OCT. 9. . . . We would always conduct our regular class work or should a visitor, patron or other call for a program we could respond with recitations, essays & stories by the Language & grammar classes;

poems & quotations by the poets & noted peoples, sing some of our school songs; show our art work, name the states & give their products, describe the mfg, exhibits, or give a dialogue of our own composing, all taken from our everyday work.

We always had plenty of visitors so we taught the children to meet them at the door & escort them to what is considered the proper seating place halfway up on the side of the room. They were never embarrassed or frustrated no matter who, or how many, came. [. . .]

Sarah's diary entries stopped at this point; they resumed on December 20, 1913. She and Billie were still living in Clarinda, and Sarah had just completed her first year as superintendent of the Page County schools.[8] Billie, in his late eighties, was in frail health, and Sarah had hired a Mrs. McKnight to stay with him while Sarah was working. Sarah and Mrs. McKnight had a disagreement about Mrs. McKnight's duties and pay.

DEC. 20. Mrs. McKnight for one week's house work. 4.00.

I do not see how she had it differently but she refused to accept it saying that Mr. Cook told her she was to do nursing. I told her on the day she came that all I wanted her to do was to get meals & keep the fires & I thought $4.00 a good price—no baking or washing & I would do all taking care of Mr. Huftalen—wanted no one to do it.

DEC. 22. Mrs. McKnight came for her pay. I had spent a part of the $4.00 she refused & so told her I would give her a five dollar bill but she wanted $16.00. So I telephoned Mr. Cook (Eliz) & Mrs. Cook came to the phone. I asked her what they had told Mrs. Knight. She said she told her she could help me out & thought Mrs. Knight and I would have an understanding when she came. I asked Mrs. Cook if she told Mrs. Knight that I wanted her to do nursing. She said she did not tell her so. She did not [do] what Mr. Cook told her.

I told Mrs. Knight very plainly the first day she was here that I did not want her to do nursing & I did not see what Mr. Cook said that led her to think it for I had phoned him asking him if he could come down Friday P.M. & keep the fires & he said he could not—that maybe he could find someone. I told him I wanted some one to keep the first & get the meals, that Mr. Huftalen was in bed & I did not want him left alone in the house but that I would do the nursing.

DEC. 22. Dr. Farrens 2 loads wood Dr.   5.00.

    Graham coal 1 ton   5.50 pd.

    Hill load of cobs. Excel Spices.   .75 pd.

2 buckets, vase, cards, 82 picture for Swanson   1.30
Ernest Squires in advance 1.00 he to cut other load @
    25¢ labor   1.25
DEC. 25. Have done office work at home on a/c of Mr. Huftalen being
sick in bed—bad. Miss Bower came Sun. P.M. & has been. I am
tired. Snowed Sat. A.M. & is 3 in. deep.—cold. (Thurs. Xmas) Rec'd.
from Ray and Cal $10.00 Xmas. plate from Amelia Driftmeier "Kings-
ley" from Faye Burt. cards, etc. [. . .]

1914

JAN. 23. Harold Bower has been here since Friday night—a wk. ago.
He & his sister Olive went to New Market to day at noon.
   I am entirely alone tonight. Have fuel in & am ready for bed. Very
lonely. Billie died 11.50 Jan. 7, after being in bed from Dec. 6. I can't
write it yet. I did all I could for him. Henry came at noon the 9th &
stayed until the 13th at noon. The funeral was Sat. the 10. 1:30 P.M.
[. . .]
FEB. 25. Harold Bower has been here off & on but went to day to Bed-
ford to remain, I think. He is a strange person.
FEB. 26. Olive Bower went to Sloan, took her trunk. I feel greatly relieved. They use so much fuel, & their talking and such personal
questions are very tiresome. I think them mentally unbalanced.
They have imposed upon me but I have endured.[9]

*Although Sarah's diary entries during the period from 1913 to 1915
tell little about her work, some of her reminiscences on loose-leaf pages
inside the back cover of her diaries and school notebooks add insights
into her outlook on life. Each of the two pieces below helps to illumi-
nate Sarah's philosophy of teaching.*

SEPTEMBER 25, 1914. "School Entertainments"
   People judge a place by the influence that goes from its door.
What the influence is that goes from a schoolroom door depends in
a large measure: first; upon the moral standard of the homes & community; second: upon the ideals and living example of the teacher.
   I am prone to believe that country people desire a high class of
social & literary entertainment for themselves & their children. I
believe they expect it of the school; that they want their children to
sing songs that are uplifting, to use proper language in original com-

Shambaugh School, Class of 1914. Sarah's caption: "8th grade graduating class & their Co. Spt." SHSI.

position to cultivate a good taste for reading; to have school programs that will uplift & edify those who take part & those who listen.

This poem is dated March 11, 1915.

SCHOOL NOTES, PAGE CO.
More efficient Teaching,
Better country schools,
This has been our slogan,
This has been our plea,
If you don't believe it,
Just you come & see.

Page is on the map to stay,
Our schools are in the van:
Every shoulder's at the wheel,
Every one is working;
Boys & girls & teachers, too,
Not one thought of shirking.

Patrons & directors all,
They have lent a helping hand;
Fixed things up in general,
Made the buildings good as new
So the children may be happy,
While their learning they pursue.

CHAPTER EIGHT

"I Do So Feel the Need":
1914–1917

I do so feel the need of a house and the house
spirit of gentleness and tenderness and
companionship. I miss the freedom of thought
and conversation that I've always enjoyed
so much. . . .
—from Sarah's diary, October 26, 1916

JUNE 28, 1914. Sunday. Clarinda Iowa. 341 16th Street.[1]

It is a bright and beautiful morning. I slept well and woke rested and refreshed after a week's arduous duties.

It is my privilege to be County Superintendent of Schools of Page County, Iowa since Jan. 1, 1913. I like my work always and am happy in the doing.

When I awoke I thought I would tidy the house, cook my own breakfast, bathe and go to church.

But when I began building the fire in our little kitchen stove and handling the things it brought the memories of loved days so thick and fast that I've cried until my eyes are too reddened and my head too painful to see any one. Someway I do not lift from the grief of Billie's going. I cannot. He passed to the great Beyond at midnight (11.50) January 7th in this house where I felt to remain. I bo't a half-lot at the Cemetery and had him buried here. I was at Fremont Nebraska and went to the Nye-Colson cemetery lot where Billie's second wife Charity V. Colson Huftalen is buried and ordered a stone exactly like hers for Billie. I wanted him buried beside her. I know of no reason why I should write in a diary at all as I so seldom have since ma died in 1888 but in the hopes of finding relief I will attempt it. There are some new friends but none but the Lord to tell one's suffering to.

Billie had been visibly failing and growing weaker since he failed in debt while keeping Second hand good's store in Manchester. He insisted on my signing the note and not letting the public know our circumstances which was right enough, but at the time it was a very hard thing for me to do. That must have been twelve or fourteen years ago. In a way it was a good thing for it put me in my realm of public school work.

Our friend, Mrs. A. B. Holbert of Greeley secured the grammar room for me in Greeley and we moved there and lived in a cozy brown square cottage for one year, then I took the Rector school in Oneida Twp for a term, driving one Lil horse of Holbert's four miles there to and from. Billie got the meals and tended the large lawn and garden.

Then the director (Geo. Myres) at Oneida wanted me to take that school. I did and remained nearly five years.

We lived 80 rds. east of the Junction (and school-house) and there ~~raised~~ grew $70.00 worth of onions and did all we could while teaching.

Billie and I were very happy in the home and doing the house duties and as he gradually failed, I would think and say to him, "Billie I cannot, I cannot have you grow old." It did not seem as though I could.

Then he would say, "we must all pass by," so quietly, so sweetly, with hands clasped and a dreamy far-away look in his eyes. Those dear eyes.—How they have watched for my coming.

The only thing I have to regret is: that I had to be absent from him and could not have it so that I could be with and care for the home and him; with nothing else on mind and heart during the past five years at least.

It took eight years of the most frugal living and saving to clear the debt. I gave up Summer vacation teaching as could not hold out.

After coming to Page Co. (Norwich) and receiving higher salary, the stress of living was not so great and yet it was hard, and self-denial had become a habit.

Billie never overcame his heart griefs—one he never told me I know. I wish he had. Charity's death, the loss of his hotel by fire, and his having me sign the note for debt to Simmons for store and house rent.

He wrung his hands, cried, begged forgiveness until I was very sorry. I would tell him not to mind and that it was all for the best.

Sometimes he would say that he could not see what life was for—"What is it all for anyway?".

We were at Norwich (Page Co.) nearly four years and Billie kept up the chores, got the breakfasts (always had since we were married) and the meals and did the dishes up to last Summer.

But last summer he had to give up mowing lawn, garden (although he dug the potatoes he & I had put in last spring 1913) and although he "puttered," as he called it, about the dishes until in November 1913 he finally had to give them up and on Dec. 6 Sat. evening when a severe pain came in his left side and he went to bed.

He sat up a few times only after that and was delirious a great deal and thrashed almost unceasingly much of the time until he died five weeks later.

I wish I could remember all the things he said when he was himself during this period of Death claiming its own. I did not undress during this time and took all care of him.

He called my name all the time and I scarcely left him. Along at the first he called loudly, "Help! Help! Oh, do help me! Chattie help me! God help me! It was terrible to hear.

At times he felt that he was falling. Then he seemed to be sheriff (once was) and would be handling some lawbreakers; then he would at other times plead Forgive me! Oh, forgive me! God forgive! Heaven forgive! until it was too pitiful to hear. The last such time when he had become so earnest he sank back saying calmly "This is heaven. Heaven is here," and seemed happy and contented in the thought and never plead again.

Then he would gather all the bedding and hold it in his arms and say so kindly, "Come Chattie let's go home," "I want to go home. Come on. Let's go." Then again he begged for his clothes, his coat, and pants and boots, wanted them on! This was really very hard to bear. At supper time the night before he died he said, "Come, Chattie, Let's go over to the hotel to supper." I raised him to a sitting position but he could not remain so and after eating a few mouthfuls of supper I had had brought over he said "Dear, dear Chattie" many times as he had a thousand times before and about ten o'clock became unable to raise the phlegm ? in his throat. I gave him the last olive oil thinking it might help but he said, "I can't do it." It grew worse. The last thing he said was "my dear Chattie, good bye."

One more mound on the sacred list.

One more grief in the chain of sorrow

One more life to eternity given
One more hope for the blessed to-morrow.

I called Dr. Powers who came and remained until Mr. Pfauder, Mr. Pruitt and Mrs. Creal came.

The feeling of a most terrible loneliness such as I had never known before came over me as his breath went out and the hand press I had known and loved so well was mine no more.

He began telling me a week before he died of his people and spoke of going to Delhi & Delaware and I thought he meant in Iowa. So he said he would wait and collect himself and tell it again. But he did not and I'm sorry I interrupted him for he was right as there is a Delhi in Delaware Co. New York where he must have been. He wished he could see his old house circle so I wrote (he never would let me before) and tried to find some of them. I finally got an answer from two nephews—one at Elmira and one at Unadilla but not until after he had passed away.[2]

Billie's sisterinlaw Carolyne (Mrs. Theron Nye) with whom we have corresponded for 22 years but never had seen (I never had) until I went to Fremont, Neb. where she lives June 13th, & stayed until the 16th, said Billie gave to her an old-fashioned deguerotyped photograph saying it was his wife and that she had died at or near Elkhorn.[3]

Carolyne said they were under the impression that they had married East and were going west over the plains (1858 or '59) and she had taken sick with fever and died a few months after marriage; that she may have been buried along the Elkhorn—there were no cemeteries in those days. She did not know where she was buried.

She said Billie was always very secretive about his people and she was surprised to learn after his death that he was 86 years of age.

Carolyne gave me Billie's and Chattie's pictures when they were married 1860 ? and the one of his first wife. I always knew Billie did not give his correct age at our marriage, but and I've known he had a secret but he never could tell it. It seemed such a great grief. I did pity him the past three years—He plead forgiveness so much when by himself. And he was so lonesome while I was away during the day. We would talk it over and try to think of some way different to do so I could be at home, but we could never come to the point of undertaking any thing else; he would say, he would get along and for me to come as soon as I could, and was anxious for me to be on time. I was not away a great deal at night. Had to be some times.

During his sickness he said: "If I give you all I've got it will be all

I have won't it?", and he seemed quite anxious about it and repeated it seemingly fearful lest he make himself not clear. At another time he said: "I have lived a life full of years." At another: "One thing I want to tell you, Chattie, one thing you must know." Again, "I have never done any thing criminal anyway."

Billie had a few keepsakes only, and I sent his clothing, except a few, to the two nephews. There is another nephew and a niece and I may send the scarf and something to them. I recall Billie told me much about his people and his trip west and of how he came with two men as far as Minneapolis but got Diarrhea and had to let them go on and he came back as far as Dubuque and there remained to recover and later come on our land as far as Denver. He had a trading post then and freighted to it back and forth from Omaha. It was on one of these trips that he stopped at Colson's log tavern and then met Charity whom he later married. 1861. She died in 1874. I have the Utica N.Y. paper that has her obituary in it, for she died back there near her old home.

Sometimes I think I could weave a story based on the facts of the pioneering days of Billie's life, but I don't know. I do know he idolized me and was precious of my life. I am sorry to have suffered so much pain and caused him so much worry therefor. How tenderly he nursed and cared for me as but few men would have done.

It was too much—three invalid wives. His sympathies were deep and tender and lasting.

I can understand how it doth hurt when the affections between those who are one are severed. One feels so lost, so lonely and a longing to wander away, away. I can see what Pa meant when he said he had cried days and days and nights and nights. Poor dear Pa. I never fully understood him. I do not see how Henry ever stays alone on the old farm and batches it as he has during the past two or three years, and more.

He and Pa were never reconciled to my marriage to Billie, so I never feel like saying any griefs to Henry.

It has now reached noon and I've wept the forenoon through.

This has been a hard ordeal and yet there is a degree of satisfaction in it. It is evening and this has been the hardest of days for me. I can understand how Billie used to mourn in silent grief over the loved and lost. I have a nervous headache and my eyes are swollen and painful. I can understand as never before how Billie always wanted to go "beyond the mountains, wanted to travel. "Only to wander away" runs the verse and again it says to the bleeding heart:

"Bury them here, my friend; here where the green plumed willow over the prairie bends."

The sunset glow falls on the calm of the day and the hush of stillness settles down on nightfall. We can but trust that the sorrowing of to-day may bring a greater hope, a truer faith and make life richer and a greater blessing.

SUNDAY, JULY 12, 1914. At home—five P.M. A very warm day. Have slept the most of it away. Had breakfast at home but go to hotel for dinner.

Mrs. Rankin occupies the two rooms up stairs and the living room, cellar, pantry, etc. down stairs. Came July 18th of June. She and her son have a clothes cleaning shop.

I walked out to the cemetery last evening. Only a silent mound away out to the new west part.[4] For the first time I turned away without a tear—he is risen. Mrs. Rankin and her daughter went with me.

How the death words and scenes linger. I waken in the night time and live it all over and over. It was so with Ma's going, then pa's was the same and now it is so with Billie's. One comes e'er the other has vanished. Life is one long day made gentle and tender by hallowed memories of sadnesses.

I wanted Billie's funeral service at the house and it was so and I selected a beautiful gray casket of pressed velvet,—half couch. I did not have the body embalmed and I helped dress him and combed his hair. I loved to do it—I felt that he rather my hands would than strangers. He had plenty of clothing, so I had his black pants that he has had for dress up for some years. And the sack coat to the suit that was new in the spring of 1913 and which he had worn a very few times, and the vest belonging with it, not worn any. A tie Cal [Carolyne Nye] had sent him. The under garments and linen, buttons and cuff links were new and nearly new that he had. And the socks were a pair that I had knit of saxony wool the first winter we were married. He always had kept them. I had knit love into every stitch, for him and felt glad to put them on.—Mr. Pruitt did, put them on, those dear cold dead feet that had never been too tired or feeble to go on the slightest pretense of an errand for me, offered so many times. Even when he could neither walk nor stand he wanted to help me about the house duties. Can I forget him and his undying love. Can I refrain from tears and loneliness. Can I help longing to see him once more as he used to be and we could visit once more—only once more. Can I help yearning for the touch of those hands,

Billie Huftalen, from his memorial card, January 1914. Sarah's poem is next to the portrait of Billie: "One more mound on the sacred list, / One more link in the chain of sorrow, / One more life to eternity given, / One more hope in the blessed tomorrow." SHSI.

the mild look in those eyes, and the voice that never spoke a harsh word or complaint. I've been so very busy with office duties and it's a blessing so to be. But it comes again and again on Sundays and crushes my bleeding heart.

Yet I know it is better so and I would not call him back to have him as he was the past three years.

Last summer and at Chautauqua time and when I was in the country (at day) visiting schools, he would go up town and could not find the way back. Then he would get bewildered and ask many strange questions of strange people. He was invariably searching "for my wife." I felt very anxious and worried over him, fearing he might get run over by autos, or that some people might be annoyed (Mrs. Duke the deputy auditor led me to think so), or that he would say queer things to people. At one time Mrs. Lee who lives next door said two men told her that if she knew where I was that I better come home (I was at Yorktown 7 mi. w. of Clarinda) as he had stopped them while passing by and told them he had cut up his wife and put her in a bundle on the table, and that he wanted to find his wife. She phoned me & I drove home that night getting here about 11 P.M. to find Billie in bed and perfectly calm and said what made me come when he was alright & I so tired & late—better staid & come home in morning, he said.

I never felt angry at him. But he was not himself and a few times I do not yet understand why he talked so untrue. "pretty girls," "my wife would she be true," "would have her investigated," would have the house searched for his things—old coins, etc. His memory was going I could plainly see, yet I did not and would not see. And he got things greatly mixed. I could usually get them straight for him, but he talked and mixed things up I never heard of, nor thought of. I never had been with old age before and did not understand. But I am so glad I could do the little I did in his declining years.

And now if I knew the name of this deguerotype picture that Cal gave me and which I conclude must have been taken in New York State, and if she was his wife, when they were married & where, when and where she died and was buried. If he was a father. Once when he was sick he said "If I could only see Ben" very impressively and wished to find him. I spoke that maybe we could, who was Ben. He quickly caught himself saying he did not know, he did not mean it.

I am so sorry Billie did not tell me whatever his secrets or life tragedies were. I dont suppose it would do much if any good yet one cannot help feeling a desire to know.

I think the picture was taken back east because it must have been in the fifties—and the style of dress is such as to show the time. She looks in poor health. I wish I could go back to where he was born and the places he lived.

He came west to prove out before there was any railroad in Iowa.

He had told me of how he rode on the very first R.R. in the U.S. and of just how the cars were pulled up over the mountains one at a time, and of his trips on the Hudson river, and of going to New York City, and of his trip west. He also said he went back a few times.

He took care of his mother when she died and he always seemed to feel *so overcome* when he spoke of his brother and family where he seemingly made it home part of the time.

I always felt that he had had some disagreement or grief and had left his people, and he would never let me write to find any of them. I now wish I had without telling him. I believe it would have been better and I could have helped to make him happier.

He said he had a team and began going with the girls when but fifteen, was pretty foxy young stripling, as he termed it. Said he worked in a tannery.

There are some real old people where he was born (Acra) and I should like to see them, and the Unadilla hotel where his brother LaFayette and brother in law—Gilbert—kept hotel.[5] It is there now. He must have been there. As I figure it out Billie was 48 yrs. old when his wife Charity Colson died in 1874. They were married in 1860 when he was 34.

Billie died when I was 48. We had been married 22 yrs. he was 67 & I 27 when we were married. = September 14, 1892. Does not that seem strange. If I were to wait 20 yrs. from now and then marry some one 20 yrs. younger than I now am? That is what Billie did.

Billie's uncle Charlie Huftalen came as far west as Rock Island Illinois "out on the prairie 3 yrs" and Billie was there, so Charlie's son Wm. H. writes.[6] This son was named for Billie (Wm. H.) and is the one to whom I sent the clothes (Summer) a box of good underwear and other clothing. This nephew has a wife in the hospital to have a cancer removed now at Elmira.

This nephew wrote that they lived in Ill. for 14 yrs. 3 yrs. on the prairie out from Rock Island and 11 yrs. at Moline Ill. He was 15 yrs. old when they moved back to York State. Billie was at R. Is. at this home when this nephew (Wm H) was 4 yrs. old. So Billie must have been well, I cant tell, will ask the nephew.

"Copy"

The following was written on a piece of paper I had in my grip on June 16, 1914, at 9.15 A.M. while I was on my way from Fremont to Clarinda at Red Oak—awaiting a train at depot.

It is cool and cloudy and beautifully serene but a spirit of sadness has stolen over me unawares and on the train all the way from Fremont here the old lines: "Bury them here, my friends, here where the green plumed willow over the prairie bends" has run through mind and heart; while mental pictures of the scenes of the past few days still remain fresh and vividly near and dead. The courtesy of Mr. C. F. Garrett, the generous and homy hospitality of Mrs. E. O. Garrett and her sweetest and dearest sons and daughters, the gladness of Mrs. Nye because of my presence, the kindly nurse who took me and the bundle of flowers that I might place them on the graves of those I've loved and known only in spirit this score of years and more. Yes all these come thronging and fill the heart full and overflowing.

The trip has been both joyous and sad. I stood by Chattie's grave where Billie stood, and mourned where he mourned. I did so want him laid beside her, I thought she was his first love and it should be so. I saw Hodges and Baldwin and ordered a stone like hers and turned away.

Billie had been married before he married Charity V. Colson. Cal (Mrs. Theron Nye, Fremont) said her impression was that she only lived a few months; that they had been married in the East and were going west over the plains when she took the fever and died near Elkhorn river,—does not know where. Cal said that Billie gave her her picture (the deguerotype she now gives to me) but not her name and she never knew more.

Cal is aged and frail but bright and hopeful—makes me think of Ma.

Yes, and she gave me tin types of Chattie's and Billie's when they were married. Billie had a post of some kind and freighted from Omaha to Denver. It was on one of these trips that he stopped at Colson's inn and met Charity and later married her. The inn was of logs.

Both these wives were invalids but look good and sincere, and so was I invalid at marriage. Fate it seemed would have it so. It undermined the financial ability and success of one of the tenderest and gentlest of men. Sympathetic and devoted as but few husbands are.

SUNDAY. AUG. 2, 1914. Beautiful day. Resting from holding three days examinations at Shenandoah. Sunday is my sorrowful day. I am unable to lift from under it. I can better understand why Pa cut the grand trees, removed the shrubs and seemingly tried to efface or destroy the familiar things that Ma's dear hands had placed. They all prompt tears in spite of you.

I had some copies of the photos made and have sent some of each to Billie's nephews: Carrington and Wm.H.

Carrington's brother Jay has gone to Unadilla. They are both painters. Wm.H. is a shoe repairer at Elmira, N.Y. I've looked the map of New York over and traced them all—and Pa's and Ma's folk too. They must have been acquainted away back there in time, place, and history.

Grandfather Hiram Gillespie was born in 1798 or 99 at Goshen, Orange Co. Billie's father was born at Esopus, Ulster Co. in 1795. Billie was born at Acra, Green Co. in 1826. Colsons were born near Earlville, Madison Co. The Hawleys, Bakers and Gorlicks (on Ma's side) were all about there. Huftalen's married Crandall, and Hyatt. Pa had relations named Hyatt—I guess we are all kin.

Brother Henry Gillespie writes good letters often. He is batching and running the farm. I wish I could go up and stay a month and tidy the house. Help is scarce and high priced. It cost a hundred dollars to get hay and grain cut. I wish I were well and strong. I have always been a sufferer—pain. It will surely cease. I always believe it will pass away. Mr. and Mrs. Garrett have kindly invited me to spend a month's vacation in their Jonesboro, Ark. home. It has been more than I can remember since I've had a vacation and I scarce dare think of such a happiness. I do not see the way. I need to go away "to the woods" as Jms. G. Wooley said one time in a lecture of his and rest from the long hours and days. I go to my office in the early morning and there before the grime and greed of the world is astir; drink deeply of the sublime beauty and purity of the depths above and of the peace and quiet below and thus secure a closer touch, a firmer hold of the Diviner powers and love above that sustains and guards and guides through the day.

The old earth is parched and dry, the grass is brown and withered. We need rain. I've looked over the cards that were attached to the beautiful and many floral tributes that were sent at the time of Billie's funeral. [. . .]

JAN. 1, 1915. At the office all day. Cleaning out the draws and trying to get things cleaner. Do not have files and shelf room as need badly. . . . Had a girl (old maid) Amelia Driftmier for 6 mo's, preceding but she was incompetent—and was virtually hypnotized by the Bows [Bowers] who had the appeal case last spring or winter at Sams No. 5. Valley township. I decided in favor of the board. He was vindictive and after I had generously made a home for he and his sister from the first of Dec. 1913 to the last of February 1914, he turned and sued me for housework at $5.00 per week and nursing at $25. It was very carefully understood when they came that there was "to be no pay either way" they to just call it home and do as they liked. She helped about the meals and dishes and brought in some fuel. She did not help care for Billie. But unjust as it was I turned it over to F. Fisher and he settled it with them it costing me $55. This was the meanest I was ever treated but come to find out this sister had been in the asylum, also a brother. So its no wonder people thought him insane. He was terrible. The sheriff had to take him out several times during the appeal. He was so uncontrollable.

Mrs. Theron Nye died in early fall. Ray and Annie sent card at Xmas, also when she died. I do not now believe the old daguerotype was a picture of Billie's first wife although it may be. Billie's nephew Carrington writes that his father told him that Billie married an Indian girl for his first wife and that she died soon after. So it may be that the deguerotype is of a sister or another wife—I know not. I'm sure it's not an Indian girl. It could be a half breed but she is white sure. I sent copy to Carrington. I sent Billie's watch also to Carr's. Thinking it should go down to his people and this nephew Carrington has a grandson. Sent Billie's last every day coat and shirts to his nephew William at East Smithfield, Penn. to where they have moved.

We are having much cold weather. Sleighing past two weeks or more. Am arranging for Teacher's Institute—for Jan. 14–15. Am to have Dr. Sumner who was my instructor at Normal in 1884 at Manchester, but who is now Sec'y. Exec. State Board of Health. Am to have Frank D. Joseph once a Co. Supt. of mine, now deputy State Superintendent.

JAN. 15TH, 1915. Saturday evening and tired. Have been out two nights during the week, the 5th at Yorktown to arrange for Community Center meeting for the 13th, and last night at E. Winters at Sam's school. Took Page Co. maps and other supplies for the schools. Attended the literary and served as judge on debate "equality of suffrage. Unanimously for aff.

Am changing and decorating courtrooms for the Institute.—Heap of work. Roy Herren and Claude Frey voluntarily helped in afternoon. Appreciated. So many in too—fifty or more—am tired.

I. H. Taggart signed as witness for me on the receipt of Carolyne M. Nye deceased. She willed me $100.00. I scarce can believe it. It is good to be a friend and to have friends. She and I have corresponded for more than twenty years. How I miss her although saw her but the once. So glad I did though. She always wrote her all and she bravely met so many heart griefs. I loved her and wrote and she always said my letters were bright and good and did her so much good.

Since I began to know her thru Billie, her mother, brother, and husband died, not so very many years apart. Her eldest son Ray's only child died—a son of a year I judge, Billie said. A nice baby picture. . . .

Had letter from Carrington Huftalen saying he has received the watch. He says that Billie's people moved from Caro and or Acra, New York to Sidney, New York in Delaware county, then to Unadilla where both his father and mother died. Carrington has pictures of Billie's father and sister Mary of which he says he will send copies.

Henry sent me some wheat meal and corn meal which he had ground himself. Also some whole wheat, some beans and walnuts. They were mixed as the sacks had broken in transit. Snow gone. Warm, chilly.

SUNDAY, JAN. 10, 1915. Dark gloomy day. rained and is now snowing. Nasty it is. I heard my S.S. boys (17 there to day) at the Christian church, then attended services at the M.E., then to Vesper service 5 P.M. at Presbyterian. Intended going to Christian this evening but had to bathe and go to bed instead and try to get rested for the week before me. It is a full week getting ready for banquet and Institute.

A year ago to-day, one year, memory of it floods my soul and in memory's vivid realness I live over the services and the everlastingness of the scene that was to be pictured but once in life's experiences. I can see the friends gathering, see the undertaker moving softly about, hear the whispered words, see the good pastor as he spoke the comforting lines, see the pall bearers seated as though waiting themselves for summons, see the beautiful tributes of flowers and their perfect arrangement and then the dove gray velvet casket with all that was mortal of him whom I had loved, him who had worshiped and idolized me as none other—all all indelibly impressed on heart and brain never to be effaced.

The dress I wore that day is in the draw[er] unfolded, the hat I've worn three or four times. ah well, life is lonely and tears will unbidden flow on Sundays especially when there are so many things to bring it all up. I can see now why pa effaced so many dear things, not that he loved ma less but that the sight and presence of them were constant sources of days gone by that brought genuine grief to think about. He could not endure it. I can see why Billie left the dear home scenes as he said after his parents died and of why he disposed of everything and wandered away from the scenes of familiarity that were constant reminders of the tender love of the wife he had loved and lost. I can see why he wanted to go beyond the mountains and begin anew as he so often plead. This is the most pitiful part of his life to me. my health was poor and we were in dire distress for means of subsistence so that I could not see the way to do other than as we did, and he was so brave and gallant to try to help in everything I proposed when he was all too frail and I did not know enough to know the demands of creeping age, how he was growing weaker and yet knowing it hiding all for my sake. How he would try to straighten up and walk spry without a cane and how it did worry him to not have his clothes look spick and span and wrinkleless. I can see him before the glass as he was wont to do. Sometimes I feel his presence and once he has spoken distinctly. I only wish that we had had a son like him. I cannot understand why childless I had to roam but I expect it is all for the best someway. Sometimes I wish we had married when I was twenty two. That was the time though that I was bloodless from loss of blood caused by the years of heavy lifting until I would fall and my voice and sight were nearly gone from the long continued strain of years of ceaseless care and toil. Dr. Sherman said he was afraid I could not last—to hold out before ma would go. Thank God I did. But from the years to twenty-two were given entirely to the duties and cares and anxiety of her who had given me life and the awful care and stress of those years in her behalf all but took mine. Billie asked her on bended knee by her bedside at the farm for me and told her in his way that I must have care and that he would care for me as I needed so much and she told him he could have me, but I would not outwardly yet I had inwardly known since the first time I met him at the age of sixteen in his store that I was his.[7] Then finally when I talked it over with ma that winter before she died in March and I was to tell him when he came to noon day meal for he boarded with us in town then, and of how overjoyed I was in the thought and eager for his coming and when he did come and I told him and he took my hand and said if I so wished it so should it be. I was in bliss in mind and heart yet no emotion on either part—almost silently were we. Then when Henry came and I was sad and glad to tell him but he said it must not be and then I broke it to Billie and broke our hearts, and suffered it for ~~six~~ 4 years and then again I told him, this time it happened to be in Des Moines where I was writing for Jesse B. Herriman and he had come from the Hot Springs in Ark. on his way to any-where. We were married at the Savery annex and remained there a month and then to the East side at 1022 12th, where we remained until spring and then went to Manchester to live. But why all this—I could go on and on for twenty more years and think and live it all over but no use. This writing is a comforter in a way like speaking to an unseen friend.

SUNDAY JAN. 15, 1915. Cold and bright. Have been to hear my S.S. boys. One of them Robert Pennington had cleaned the walks of snow last evening for we had a blustering storm yesterday. But when I returned from church he and Leonard Gebbie were here putting on the finishing touches fearing lest the wind had blown more on in the night. They thought to surprise me, the good boys that they are.

I am tired from the week's duties. Had institute Thursday and Friday Jan. 14–15.[8] Very largely attended, most came on the evening of the 13th, so we waited trains until after 10 P.M. Then on Thurs. evening had a banquet at the New Linderman 150 sat at table and then after a three course luncheon toasts were given by Frank D. Joseph, Des Moines, E. C. Bishop, Ames, Dr. Clark, A. H. Speer, D. B. Woolson, E. B. Delzell and Frank Henderson. It lasted until 12.20 midnight.

On Friday had lectures in forenoon and the County reading and spelling contests in the afternoon. They were great and a great crowd gathered. The record of the ages was broken as we had some school-officers at the Institute and banquet. fine. Everything was a success. The weather was warm and springlike. windows open. My speakers this time were Frank D. Joseph, E. C. Bishop, Arthur E. Bernet (Highland Park Coll.), Prof. LaFayette Higgins (State Health Board), Frank Henderson, J. C. McGlade and Wm. Orchard. Had conferences for Rural and high school sections. Splendid.

The following entry is on loose-leaf letterhead stationery imprinted with "Page County Schools, Mrs. Sarah Huftalen, Superintendent, Clarinda, Iowa." The pages have been inserted into the diary.

SEPT. 14, 1915.—At the old farm in kitchen. Dark and rainy. Dark everyway. I fear I have made the mistake of my life in coming to the farm. Henry has been batching and working the place alone for the past three years and when my term was out on Aug. 31, 1915 in Page Co. I had built up great hopes of coming to keep the house and have a vacation and rest from the strenuous duties of all the years of my life and be doing a Christ's deed to my brother and help all I could. I was all too happy in the thought of it last April when I was

"The Old Home Place," August 1910. SHSI.

here two days, I felt so sorry for him here alone doing the way &
living the way he is. I thought I would come as soon as possible
although in need of rest and relax.

All I have to show for fifty years of toil is a few household goods
and a buggy. The latter I had bo't 2nd hand, a splendid one it is.
Henry said for me to sell it & to sell or give away a number of my
things, the most of them, it would have been, & he wanted me to
send a few things at a time by local freight so he could haul them
with the one horse & little wagon.

I thought this the best way and so began but I could not part with
things that we'd need and I felt were precious to me. I sold some
almost for nothing and could not sell some at all. And I soon found
I could not send a few at a time as I had begun and beside it would
cost more in the end than to get a car,—at the rate those had cost to
send,—so I prayed God to guide and I'd follow and I did and I cannot
see where I sinned.

But Henry has been angry and very much in a spirit and words
that have caused me more grief than I've ever experienced in any
one week of my life. He tries to argue that I did so very wrong because I brought a piece of linoleum for the kitchen floor, & the
buggy & stove & etc. etc. etc. that I don't need any things, that he
knows what I need; that I don't know; that I should have asked him;
and that—and that—and that until he drove me to nearly lose my
senses and to feel and speak as I never have, nor ever felt. And to

cry as I never, never cried. I could not and cannot help this sorrow. I do not nor can I see any wrong or injury due to what I have done. Any man or woman would have been glad and kind surely when I felt as though I was doing all for his sake.

It is a terrible blow. Hardest I've had, yet I trust that He will show the way.

It just seems as though Henry is overdone and then instead of feeling as some might he rather evidences a revengeful spirit that would crush the life and heart and hope out and then press yet more. It makes me think of that harassing persistent E. Harold B——.

I've tried to lift under it but its brought out several nervous head-aches and back ache as well as undue menstrual flow and a pain in my heart all one night. I am sorry I came and brought my hard earned things. I told him so. Then he will say he is glad I came & here is the place of all places for me to rest. He said it was an impo-sition for me to come and bring the things causing him worry & work to get them here, at this time when he is so very busy. "I feel imposed upon." I have tried to look on the sunny side and I never prayed much harder & although we had both worried beyond telling of how to get the stuff hauled it was so good to have a neighbor Hempstead boy stop Sunday & then Henry asked neighbor Henry Herman & they both came Monday (yesterday) morning & hauled it out.

I just stood before pa's & ma's pictures & could all but hear them speak their gladness while a tear stole from my eye and dimmed it. It was too heavy for Henry & I would gladly have rubbed & bathed him last night but scarcely dare utter a comforting word & stole off up those awful stairs with a heart of gladness that the terrible bur-den of getting the things out here (by 48 hr. limit—only got word Sat. P.M. limit was 7 P.M. last night) and in the silent voice that said it was right and a heart also aching with sadness because Henry feels as he does. I did so hope 'twas all over but he began at breakfast & I could not eat nor think & likely said things that should & would not—I feel that it is the devils own work to argue and quarrel. I've never done it and God helping me I will not begin now. Henry al-ways did both pa & ma. Pa would get mad & Ma & I would weep. I thought now he is a man he would not any more.

AT MANCHESTER, IOWA. 10-13-1915. Came to the old farm home on Sept. 4, 1915 arriving in the afternoon. I was not re-elected to su-perintendency of schools of Page. Co. last April owing to the fact that Miss Field wanted a Y.W.C.A. Co. Supt. and thru strategy and dirty politics succeeded in finding a tool candidate.[9] I needed a rest and change and so refused several teaching positions that were offered and above all I felt it a duty to come & keep house for Henry who has been living on the farm alone and batching. I was in high hope and joyed at the thought of coming but I fear the change is too radical. I did all my packing and hired a car and brought some wood and the new buggy I bought of G. F. Crist at Shenandoah last Spring. Henry did not want me to hire a car or bring the buggy, my large bookcase, the wood and some other things. This has caused me much grief. Strange as it might seem I'm not at home here either in mind or heart. The duties difficult and beyond strength, such as have not done since lived here in girlhood thirty years ago. I wrote some notes on scratch paper which will copy. I have had to do all the unpacking and I've worked very hard for me in trying to clean the rooms. Henry scrubbed the kitchen walls and woodwork & floor, very black with smoke. I did it as high as door tops but he had to do mine over. I feel like giving it all up and going away. I must try to get well and God will yet show the way. I'm sure he will.

I left Clarinda on Sept. 1st stopping in Des Moines to look after school exhibit and copy the Annual Report if need be. Saw the state Department people who said very nice things to me, A. M. Deyoe, Mr. Joseph, Mr. McGlade, Mr. Woodruff, Mr. Fuller, Mr. Mahannah, Miss Schell, Mr. Hollingsworth and then down stairs was Dr. Sumner, Sec'y of State Board of Health and Mr. Paul across the hall. Dr. had an exhibit at the State Fair—Health Exhibit. I met him by calling at his office last spring when at Co. Superintendent's meeting at Ames. No, it was before this I think and I accidentally saw him then April? on the street—on East Locust when I was sauntering along on the north side. He spoke the third time before I turned. Had met him but did not recognize him, and as he spoke after my passing I feared to turn around thinking it a stranger. I was greatly penitent for not doing so. It was an event in my life as it proved to be, he came into my life and gave me freely and unconsciously the food my soul hungered for, yea longed for as only the lonely and bereft can realize. I have seen him once since at the fair and once when on the Board of Review at the State Department. He too has suffered the loss of a noble wife, and it was his unrestrained freedom in telling me of their private life that touched my heart and soul, so like my own and Billie's, in many ways exactly. He first poured out one of the most eloquent soul sermons there on the street for over an hour quoting the immortal "Thanatopsis." How it divinely stirred, thrilled and awed me thru and thru. He did it so unrestrainedly, so unconsciously, while I listened and listened. Speechless, silent. Conscious at intervals of the leaping and stirring of the soul within causing the muscles to contract at times. I never can forget it and it reminds me often of the "Gordon" who once stirred my spirit similarly only in a different sense,—entirely religious that was.

I would not wish to forget it. It did a blessed thing for me, more than one. It came at the very time I so needed it. I had become habituated to stop at the Savery when in Des Moines and always to saunter to the Locust Street bridge and across it and reflect and meditate on how Billie and I used to walk there and talk there and in a way it was a self comforting satisfaction, and then out to 921 E. 12th when we had a store out there 23 or more years ago. Dear Mrs. Cully died in Aug. 7th (1915). How I miss her.

Well, then after this outburst of sermonizing that made me dumb we stood and talked awhile then he took my arm and we walked about the streets looking in the windows at the displays, one of which had his new masonic charm of which he was proud I know. He passed the 32nd degree the four days previous he explained. The charm was attached to the gold chain and knife that the Colesburg pupils gave him as their Supt. 30 yrs ago?

He was instructor at Normal Institute where I first knew him at Manchester. He then studied medicine practicing later at Waterloo. He has grown somewhat stouter. We walked until 10.30 when he bade me goodnight at the Savery steps. It seemed as though his pent up feelings and sympathies and evening lonelinesses found vent and he by unveiling his own did not know that it was comforting me more than himself. It makes one think of Beatrice Harraden's "Ships that pass in the night and speak to each other in passing."

To day it has rained nearly all day. I pared and put up three pecks of peaches—24 mason jars—the parings are now 8.30 P.M. singing their jelly boiling tune. I am some tired and must go to bed. Mrs. Morse and Luella called to let us know that Charley Van Alstyne's wife is dead, funeral tomorrow at 2 P.M.

I guess we do not understand each other. Henry has lived here so long alone and in such a way that thus far I've felt the least at home of any place I've ever been. I did so crave some grapes and as it was not so he could go for them during the past two weeks I wrote to S. & McC to send out some and a 1/2 bu. of peaches. This morning it

rained so he would not go to Herman's and so could go. He thought
it was a great mistake to write and I sh'ld not have sent for the
grapes & kept on 'till I cried. It is so with every thing I do to such an
extent that scarcely dare suggest anything for fear I'll be told I don't
know what I want. It has been the hardest situation I've ever experienced. My back suffers much pain and I have nervous headaches,
something I've never had, nervous chills, menstrual periods irregular caused by these nerve shocks and the most tears I ever knew,
and he criticized everything I've brought in one way or another until
I wish I'd never come or brought them.[10] I cannot help it. I fear it is
the mistake of my life. Sometimes the darknesses have proved dis-
guised blessings. Maybe this will.

THURSDAY, NOV. 24, 1915. Stayed at home for Thanksgiving day
seemed like a funeral. Six years ago on Thanksgiving morning at
9 A.M. I sat on pa's bedside holding his hands until their press faded
and he was no more. The farm was then rented to a Mr. Yager but
when his time expired, Henry came here and has since been here
alone. One scarcely keep from eccentric ways to live alone so long
in such a way. I really believe he rather tho than to have the change
and restraint of living like people who are people do. It needs a
tough, strong virile woman here. I fear I am not the one for the place
but I was so tired of public service and had built up such high hopes
of this being just the place for me and I thought too that it was right
and duty and I came,—to suffer the hardest ordeal of requirements
and to be misjudged and misunderstood by Henry who killed my
spirit and took all heart & hope of enjoyment out of it until I really
wish I had not come,—and yet I cannot help but hope a little in the
thought that it is right for me to have at least a place to sleep at the
place. It is as much mine in reality as it is Henry's but he has idolized it so long that it causes me to feel a fear to touch any thing
unless he says to. . . . I don't dare plan or anticipate any thing here,
feel myself going away all the time more than remaining. . . .

I am trying to scrape the paper off the walls so can paint them.
There are so many hard tasks to do here. Very hard. I could do better
if I were happier and felt at home. Henry means all right but he
never lived with woman and has different ideas than he otherwise
might. . . . When anyone has asked me what I have received from
the farm for my share since pa died,—I can only say nothing. I have
said it during the past 5 years to a number & they have looked blank.
Now I could say I've had board since Sep. 4, 1915. . . . I wish he

were married and I were too and in homes of our own. Dark &
Lowry. [. . .]

*Sarah's diary entry dated February 2, 1916, was written on loose-leaf
paper and inserted into this volume of her diary.*

FEB. 2, 1916. I'm boiling an old fashioned corn meal pudding. Stirring
with a wooden paddle. It is cold weather and brother wanted it. Said
he'd rather have it than anything else tonight. I'm keeping house
for him. Bless him. He's batched it all his life. Jilted lover he. The
shame of it. If there is any unforgiveable love business I think jilting
is the limit. It crushes life; hope, and spirit out and antagonizes if
not destroys true conceptions of the opposite sex. I believe it is worse
than divorce, has a blasting effect anyway. But it seems to me I'd go
after another. Most women are worth having. Most are fair cooks,
and fair house makers. These things are the inherited instincts of
divined law and naturally are every woman's. There are plenty of
good noble women who will marry & live with men and not jilt nor
divorce them even unto death in many instances when they know-
ingly sacrifice unto it by abiding to their truth and vow.

FEB. 12, 1916. Well, life has gone on and I am still here trying to do
my best to become accustomed to the conditions and requirements.
It is the hardest ordeal I've ever experienced and it looks as though
I better teach. It is easier and I feel that my efforts & love are appreciated & that I do good beyond mere tutelage. I am very thankful
to sleep well & for all the blessings of friendships and the memories dear and pleasant. I just about live on them & the good letters received. The tasks here make me unwell every two or three
weeks. At first the awful nerve strain thrust upon me at coming
here stopped the periods from Sept. 15 to Dec. 27–31. Then again
Dec. 17–20 & Jan. 8–10. I pray & think & hope. I try not to hear
the sarcasm but oh, how it stabs. I've been reminded of being
babied, walking on a board, being a helpless invalid, & no time for
them around here, and so many many such remarks that I try to
steel myself to forget. . . . Henry does not realize how he drives me
from him. I can see the impress of the way he has lived all his life.
It is pitiful and I wish he were as cultured as he is learned, wish
he were more sympathetic and had a purer or truer attitude toward
woman. I expect his being jilted has had something to do with it. I
have never gotten down to having the blues and have always been
trustful, cheery & hopeful thru all trials & duties and have received

strength & guidance in time of need. I cannot but believe all will be well yet. If not here then I must elsewhere for it is the hardest place I've ever been in to keep up spirit, life or ambition. . . .

FEB. 21, 1916. Monday morning. I am very unhappy and cannot help crying. Henry all but drives one to despair. He always was given to argue and argue and drove ma & me to many tears and much worriment. I remember about our trying over & over to iron a shirt to suit him & after our doing it a half dozen times & into the night to please him he would still find some wrinkle & send us to bed in tears.

No matter how hopeful you are or cheerful he would crush it out. I don't think he intends to so aim, but is his way & then living all his life as he has has added some.

I've stuck to it 6 mo's & ate on the oilcloth covered worktable with the dirty dishes & utensils just to please him & do so wish I could set table and eat as I have always done & like to & I feel a fear all the time of the meals not pleasing him. And he reminds me about every so often of using the parlor for a bedroom, and daily of ventilation. . . . Dear me. The house looks like a barn all thru. About the only thing I could do to make it look as though some one lived in it was to put shades at the windows up stairs & shades & curtains down stairs except in large middle room & I suppose he would be remodelling that during the winter. But there it is cold bare room. The stove and my large book case & roll of linoleum & a few sacks of corn are its imposing & inviting contents.

I cannot think he appreciates a woman in any way. I know it causes me nervous headaches, tears and a dread of his presence. I am sorry indeed, very sorry. I've given up every plan or aspiration and tried to apply myself to his every wish & word. So far I've not felt at home here, nor any feeling of possession. The ideal of a happy home and housekeeping that are in my heart never can be entirely crushed out. I love a home & housekeeping, and take great delight in all its details. I long for it. I had hoped against hope to have such here. I am tenacious and clinging but it is like battling the rapids to stem the conditions. Try as I will. I've lived so differently so many years & now when I need it best of all to have it hardest of all. I've always had my house neat & nice enough to ask any one to come. I cannot the way it is here. Henry thinks that all bosh. Seems as though he just feels determined to grind one to "rough it"—the hardest way possible. I do not believe I can stay with him always. And he still hints about the buggy taking the room on the barn floor.

He seldom hints about Billie, but on the very anniversary of Billie's death he said the one that danced must pay the fiddler. . . .

I pray God not to let hate or anger come into my heart. The trials cannot always last. There is hope beyond. . . .

FEB. 26, 1916. Sunday evening unwell again. Dear me it seems as though my life would be crushed out trying to get used to conditions here. Henry has brought in most the coal during the past two weeks for the kitchen. Have had none in other room for two weeks. It did not seem as tho I could carry the coal for it. But when I spoke of its being cold to undress I was told "there is the stove & there is the coal." It has been cold & snow 6 below and more. Doors all open tho nearly all day each day to "air" the rooms. Sometimes I feel as tho could not endure it. "put on more clothes then." "Get some. you've got the money to." He dares me to run out in the snow barefooted. I have been driven to tell him that he does not deserve a woman once but I usually keep silent and endure and suffer until tears come & a nervous headache follows. I pray never to cause anyone the mental suffering and heart ache he causes me. It is the hardest 6 mo's I've ever known. . . .

I've been used to living with a kind husband who watched every way & did everything to prevent my chilling or suffering at all times as tenderly and thoughtfully as a mother her child. And whose heart was full of sympathy. It is the dearest of memories. And its being just the opposite here makes it seem hard indeed.

MAR. 5. SUNDAY. The dentist finished putting in bridge work (four on left lower jaw—two dummies between two he crowned. They are quite troublesome as he left them higher than others which he said was the way to do. It is painful to chew especially on the upper molars. I went to sewing circle at Luke Scanlans Friday. It seemed good to get away and to forget the sorrows for a little while. Luke thought my buggy fine & a good bargain. I never use it that I do not think of how hateful Henry was because I brought it here. He is spiteful about my things. Most anyone would have thought he would have been glad & thankful to have the house furnished and a buggy. And I never suggest a thing that is welcomely received. If it is a comfortable chair or couch "there's enough rockers and a bed cot." If it is planning and improving any part of the place or grounds "your ideals and ideas are wrong." Actually I get so I question myself if I have any sense or know any thing at all. . . .

THURS. MAR. 9, 1916. Unfit to do anything have nervous headache—entire head, feet & legs up to knees numb and chilly, heart pressed and painful. It cannot always last. Such nerve shocks and so many. I am indeed sorry that we have trouble. . . . I have always felt that he & pa were so dissatisfied with my marriage that they were ashamed of our presence. That was the hardest to bear,—I couldn't— it tore my heart out this morning. I have been so comforted by the memories, living memories of his Billie's gentle ways and words of his abiding devotion at all times, and he comes to me in dreams bringing peace into my grieved heart and troubled anxious mind. God is good and I live and trust in His promises. . . .

Evening has come and Henry has gone to town. The seed oats he sent to Ames for were lost in a wreck. Now we want to get some more from there. My headache is no worse but oh, how the *loud* voice, the stamping, the gesturing, the mocking of my grieving and mockings of my disposition & other things how they hurt. twitting of my "marriage to an old man." my! my! dear brother! Says I abuse and insult him, impose upon him. And had tell me to get out if I were not his sister. I cannot & do not want to quote it but he used the word damnable with such vengeance and stamped and gesticulated furiously. I just prayed to endure.

FRI. APR. 14, 1916. It is bright and beautiful outside. I have suffered much the past week. It seems as tho the lifting would kill me. Am unwell so often. But this is not as hard to bear as the frictions. Henry continues his fiery scoldings, stomping the floor with furious claps and determined to make me "see." Oh, his cruel mockings; one of which was of my "going up stairs in hysterics and yelling." The truth of it was I cried in agony the night thru and the awful crushing blows of his sarcasm and ugly words of fault finding and condemnation of me and my ways and disposition, of my "scorning his mandates," of my marriage and life broke my heart not only figuratively but literally. I tho't of Christ on the cross and Christ before Pilate. That night and many such since have caused my heart to be pressed and painful and I've wakened many times by its awful beating & gurgling as tho it would fly out, and I've held it and my side hard with my hands and thought I must make disposal of my things to those who will appreciate and value & care for them after I am gone. For if I remain & he continues his cruelty it will take my life. I realize it. And I've held my breath in suspense and dread so much of the time that the lower part of my lungs are often painful.

I am so sorry I came, and that I allowed my things to be brought here. I hope never to misjudge and ill treat anyone. He seems revengeful and to harbor prejudice and bitterness of real or imagined wrongs. Is resentful and crushing. I could not sleep after midnight last night because of my heart throbbing so and its been painful all day. Had nervous backache all day yesterday & day before. He administered a scolding lecture & said in conclusion he hoped I'd sleep well & get a good breakfast. Ah me. "when thy father & mother forsake thee turn to God." Something will come for me yet if I am to live for I felt it duty & right to come & make it home for Henry. . . .

I should like to remain and rest here in the country but unless it is very different by fall I shall expect to begin teaching again. Even a Rural school is not so hard as this. Not as much lifting and not a thing unpleasant—except the outhouses. I have been thinking and praying much these 8 months.

OCT. 26, 1916. A year has passed, the saddest and most miserable year of my life. I wish pa had given me one half the property and Henry the other half. It is very hard for me here and I feel that it is best for Henry to get a woman who will be a help meet for him. He may mean all right but he tortures the life out of me. I never can stay with him always. I've tried to keep silent and prayed God to help me so to do and not to hear his faultfinding, scolding, sarcasm and constant chiding. All unnecessary all uncalled for. He always was so but I hoped against hope that he had found a better way. It is hard on the nerves and causes head aches and heart aches. . . . One gets so at times you scarcely know where you are at, one cannot succeed even in the things that have before been able to do well. . . . And now am reconciled to believe I am not the right kind of woman for him and am truly hoping he may find one who is suited to him and his words and ways. It is hard in a way to realize I must leave the old place and go forth to earn and to toil and to save again. I do so feel the need of a house and the house spirit of gentleness and tenderness and companionship. I miss the freedom of thought and conversation that I've always enjoyed so much. . . .

SUNDAY, DEC. 24, 1916. Quite a fall of snow after a week of cold (16 below) weather makes it seem like Christmas. During the week have walked to town and back twice. To the dentist on Monday & to Mrs. Elder to take vapor bath on Friday. The Osteopath Dr. Beyer says I have a lesion and a twisted vertebra and 2 other sore spots between the shoulders. It is painful, has not ceased night nor day since first of November. Henry ran my buggy out of the barn and so left it during two days and two nights of rain and I had to find storage for it at a neighbors—Ransom Arnolds. He drove in the old wagon with a few bushels of corn in the front end of the box—all

possibly worth 15 or 20 dollars. my buggy cost $135. I was glad had
even a muslin cloth over it but I wept half the night thinking what
to do. Johnny Herman took it to Arnold's for me. Henry is determined I spend $900.00 as he wishes it for stock alone. I do not feel
that it is right. He does say the meanest things and threatens to sell
the place. I endured much then I told him that I would go out and
earn the money rather than to spend the little I had saved, that from
conditions to be endured here I had long ago seen that I am not the
one for it, the work is harder than I can do and that all I could see
in it for me is suffering, sorrow, my board and a grave. That is not
the blues nor being discouraged. Just facts conclusive from conditions. . . . But I have decided to go away, I can see no other course
for me. I never have quarrelled nor will I. I rather be in a little house
and get it cozy and comfortable and feel that I could pass an entire
day without fear of demands and sarcasms and scoldings. I have
sold my linoleum which I bo't in Clarinda to put on the kitchen floor
but Henry will not let me put it down. It has never been unrolled. I
got the same as I gave. . . . Inwardly God tells me it is my right to
remain here and to have my things here but for me to have to feel
and to know that my name (Huftalen) is hated, that my things are a
bore, that I am thought of as lazy and unprincipled. These are hard
to endure. I pray for strength sufficient.

JAN. 11. THURSDAY. 1917. Ready for bed in my room. Warming my feet
by the little stove I brought and which Henry wanted me to sell. It
comes very good indeed. I start the fire every night & it helps to go
to bed by. It is 10 below zero today. Very icy. Christmas day was like
a cloud all day burdening the soul. I could not stay a day were it not
that I feel Pa & Ma would want me to and that it is right I should. I
suffer pain in my back between the shoulders continuously has been
so night and day since first of November only about 3 or 4 hrs. after
taking a treatment of Dr. Beyer. I've spent all the chicken money
Henry gave me and much more of my own on treatments and baths.

Henry is determined I must put $900.00 in the place stock mostly.
It comes very hard for me to give up my hard earned savings. I am
in a corner now and scarcely know what best to do, but the Lord will
show me yet the way. . . .

Sometimes I think it would be better to sell the old farm and divide
up. I thought I saw it so before I had been here a week. I feel it. I
can see no possible chance for me to see any happiness here. I am
sorry but to think of spending the few or many years that may be
mine as it has been during the past year makes me shudder. If I

could be free from physical pain it would seem a relief and helpful. There is much lifting of this thing and that even tho Henry now brings in the water for the most part and a little of the fuel. I know he thinks I could if I would from both attitude and remarks. . . .

FEB. 10. SAT. EVENING. In my room trying to get warm before going to bed. Have been cold all day. The stack is frozen full of snow or water and hard to keep fires such cold weather. 12 below & has been 26 below—pretty steady during past week. . . . Scarcely a day passes that [Henry] does not hurl some cutting words. I do not reply, and I try not to cry. Cannot help it. I can feel the venom creep over my nerves as tho hate fills his heart.

To night he said he hoped I'd be better morally and physically tomorrow, better than I had acted to day. No one could say I had done anything to merit this and the many other like speeches he makes. Is constantly inferring & saying I have no mind. "about like a six year old child." Says I'm unprincipalled and unrighteous and he doesn't want anything to do with such folks nor work with them nor have them around him. And not long ago he said that he would work pretty hard for me to have a S.S. class but my religious principles were such that he feared I would not get very far leading a class. Says I am dishonest. Says there is a streak of evil in our ancestry which he inferred was in me. . . . I rather have a small house & have it comfortable and what I could take care of. It seems so bleak & bare and no telling when it ever will be settled & in shape to live in. . . . It is hard to me to think of getting my things packed and move. My books have never been unpacked and that will save a lot of work. I intend having hair flowers and keepsakes put in shape and have them put in the Historical Building at Des Moines. I will try to sell my buggy, the large book case and library table. My, how hard I worked to have these. Billie gave me the book case. How eager I was to possess these needs. It does not seem right I should have to dispose of them.

MONDAY FEB. 12. Nearly collapsed from effects of nerve strain of last evening. I had felt badly all day as result of waking in the night sobbing over the hurt of Saturday evening. . . .

Henry has gone to town. He is seemingly peaceable today. He said so much last night. I kept still all possible. When he said I had not tried to do the work here, I replied I had. He contradicted and I should not have said a word but I had endured the other false accusations and it did not seem as tho I could this where I have tried to do his every suggestion and command even when I knew I could not. I said it was a lie for I had. My! My! how enraged shaking his fist in my face again and again threatening to "throw me out of the door," or "through the window if its the last thing I ever do under heaven" he said. I cannot tell all the bitterness and anger and raving at me. I hit his hand away from my face telling him to throw me out if he wanted to that I would go without his doing it, that I am not afraid to die. Accused me of being stingy and avaricious, said my affections and sexual organism are abnormal and it has affected my mind is what ails me. Scarcely a day passes that he does not give some inference that I have no mind, do not think, no power of concentration etc.etc. Says he'll sell the place and divide up and I can go my way and he will go his and I will be as dead to him ever after. Told me to go and see any one I wanted to and something about dividing that I did not understand. He said he was grieved to have worked here five years past in the hope to make a home for us and that I do not appreciate it. Said it was an imposition the way I came inferring there was some scheme or mystery. How far from true. He said "*I intend you shall do your part.*" How unnecessary. I've always been a willing, faithful, conscientious worker in every way. I rather he would stay on the farm if he likes it best and I will go away and praying health and strength sufficient ask God to guide will yet hope to make my way as I ever have done. I pity Henry and it is my greatest sorrow to have any trouble with him. I am not given to quarrelling. I never was and I've never had any such criticisms and sarcasms to meet. I do not know how to meet it. I literally give up. It tries my nerve force so intensely that the re-action all but collapses me. Limp, lifeless and weak do I feel all over. Seems as tho energy and vitality were gone. . . . The way he has lived alone and batched it has left its impress and it would seem that when home making influences have come in that he is not ready for such. And altho I say nothing anymore I do so need and long for a cozy, comfortable home. I need it, I do, and peaceful and congenial environs. I have been in suspense ever since being here, and the house torn up and dirty and unsettled has been a constant weight. I cannot but believe all will yet be well and hope and pray that whatever is best will be. . . .

APR. 18, 19. Two very very hard days—seemed as tho death was trying to lay her seal upon me all day, my back in hollow very heavy pain and lower limbs unable to support me,—similar to that of the "grip." But I have no cold nor grip. Have felt badly all along back, have no strength to get a purchase on any task. Drag thru the days. Hope be better tomorrow. Could get along with it better if Henry could only get along without scolding & finding fault because of my not doing more. He says I could if I "wanted to," "just stubborn and willful." Oh how untrue. It hurts, hurts!

APRIL 20. Spine still continues trembly and painful. Weak and as tho recovering from a long illness. So weak. But some better. Have managed to get the meals and pray to have grace to endure the scoldings. Will have to see a physician and go away I think for rest of mind and body. [. . .]

Sarah wrote that Dr. Dittmer had recommended she rent a room and get away from Henry and the farm. Henry, however, wanted Sarah to go to Rochester, Minnesota, for tests to determine whether she had mental problems. A break in diary entries occurs from April 27 until August 21, 1917.

AUG. 21, 1917. At the kitchen table 2.15 P.M. dishes done and put away. Had Mr. Seymour who is helping Henry haul hay for dinner. I am tired though after having overhauled and repacked my books and household things. It undoes my back which aches hard constantly.

I had four very serious days in June, and went to Hinsdale Sanitarium on June 12th, was there five weeks then went home with Mrs. H. D. Fulton at 444 Englewood Ave. Chicago and remained one week. She is a melancholic and nervous wreck. Had a card from her maid Mrs. Mitchell to day who said that Mrs. Fulton has been in bed with a trained nurse since I left. I came back to the farm July 22nd and in less than four days was suffering much. two to four to cook for & on my feet all the time.

On Aug. 6, I went to Willard Hall at Chautauqua Park Beach, Waterloo where the State College of Cedar Falls is conducting a Method's Conference for their critic teachers and associate professors of which I am now to be one.[11] There are twenty of us. I came back on Friday the 10th, and have been sorting and packing since. Jennie Brown has bought the rugs, bedstead, mattress, lawnmower, etc. Will Noble bought my buggy. I felt so sorry and grieved and wronged to have to sell it. He gave me $40.00. And now I am searching for a horse, harness and buggy to use in my work. The shame of it, and yet—the goodness of it.

Last spring prof. J. C. McGlade of the Iowa State College, Cedar Falls, phoned me to come over on the following day which I did. He had been called from the office but Macy Campbell was there and took me to four of their Demonstration schools. Asked me which I preferred—one of these or a Township Supervisorship and to state my salary. I told him to place me in the one they most wished me to take and to pay me what they pleased. He said no one ever talked that way and insisted that I state but I refused & he then said they meant business when they called me over there & w'ld do best possible & an increase. I am to have the Supervisorship of the 9 Rural Schools of Bennington Township in Blackhawk County and $105 per mo. which includes the $160 voted by the township board for the care & feed of the horse. $20 a mo. for 8 mo. The College pays me 85 per mo. to start on. This is the next step to what I was trying to work out in Page Co, i.e., township leadership.[12] A "circuit teacher I thought. I tried it by having the strongest teacher hold meetings for which I arranged programs for the year & for the 16 twps. The College tried it similarly last year but had the teacher visit the schools going 2 days ea. week. I suggested to Mr. Campbell this would not work leaving my school in the hands of a fresh student teacher (a new one each month) Miss Cortz has told me since it did not, Miss Cortz has Lincoln township. We are the only ones in the State or U.S. to try out the new plan. . . .[13] Crops are wonderful in yield. Oats 45 to 100 bu. Corn great if frost holds off. Henry has been helping neighbors thresh. I guess he means all right but I cannot overcome the fear, dread and suspense. He does say cruel, cutting things continually. . . . Jennie Brown is helpful and has been out often. Some of my things are there ready to ship and I have trunk and several goods boxes packed, ready of books & school supplies. Macy Campbell said over the phone this morning to ship all to the college. Jennie & I think of driving over to Waterloo the last of the week. Not decided fully yet on the horse. Have looked at several. It is beautiful weather. Mrs. Tom Elder took the linoleum. My heart hurt all night. I was so fearful of what Henry might say when he learned I was looking for a horse. He is so hasty, excitable and wrathy. I cannot understand him. I am sorry so sorry for him. Now I will put this in Billie's trunk. Am leaving my pictures, furniture library and other things in the old parlor. And hope they will not be destroyed.

CHAPTER NINE

"What Is the Criterion of a Teacher?": 1922–1935

What is the criterion of a teacher, man or woman,
married or single, young or mature, experienced
or inexperienced?
—from Sarah's essay, "Why a Teacher?"

FEB. 2, 1922. Rec'd. a pair of very nice gray wool blankets from Henry. I fell on ice in the dark on Feb. 1, when coming from supper & cracked the humerus bone & tore the ligaments in my right arm. It is now Feb. 26 and I am doing my first writing with my right hand.[1] I missed 6 days of recitations being unable to dress. I dress with the left hand even to lacing & tying my shoes. It is more painful than humorous. I cannot comb my hair yet. Lora Wharton does it. I had Dr. McLean and nurse Miss Sylvia Samson. My students sent me a perfectly beautiful white cyclamen—having 14 large blossoms. Ruby Roberts and Grace Shaffer gave me a home made box of candy, many called. It is very painful yet and but little use. [. . .]

SEPT. 10. SUNDAY. Returned to Fayette Sat. 9 by way of West Union. Mrs. Bopp bringing me to Miss Whartons. I went to Iowa City July 23. Sat. Enrolled July 24 as a graduate student for 5 weeks. Room & board Currier Hall Aug. 24. Convocation. 47.50. Dr. Seashore presiding. Dean Russell address. 3 of us remained at Currier Hall boarding ourselves for a week. Cost nothing for the room our food cost—2.00 ea. Sept. 2 I went to Manchester arriving at 6 P.M. It cost 96¢ to Cedar Rapids. I called at College to get data for my thesis. I went to Mt. Vernon for the same purpose car fare & return 1.50. . . .

At farm all day Saturday. Saw Henry. He did not act as though he saw me. He was in town most the day on his milk route. He said he was well. I went to Ruth Herman's to dinner & to town with them in the evening. Stayed at Jennie Brown's 3 nights & at Mrs. Holberts one night. To West Union Wed. visited Mr. & Mrs. Tirrill, supper at

Jennie Shelders, dinner at Geo. Keys, sup & break, Holberts. Fred was there Sunday. Tom's wife & Eldred & Lonnie & his wife, Glen Baker & his wife. I went to West Union to visit Mrs. Graham & Mrs. Bopp. . . .

SEPT. 11. MON. Helped enroll students in P.M. I made my silk dress at Ia. City entirely by hand, cut it without any pattern whatsoever & it is very well received. Looks well on me. [. . .]

In September 1922 Sarah began teaching in the Rural Education Program at Upper Iowa University (UIU) in Fayette. While teaching at UIU, Sarah went back and forth to Iowa City to gather data for her master's thesis. She continued to be active in the state rural teachers' association. After Dr. Colgrove left UIU, Sarah's lifetime position there was rescinded.

APRIL 21, 1923. . . . The Pres. wrote a letter saying the Executive Board could not provide salary for extra professors any longer, so I am free. I am glad although have not the slightest idea where I will be or go. It has been Providential for me. The position was created for me & now will be discontinued. Dr. V. said I was receiving a mere pittance. I am going to Iowa City to study at the Summer School. And will hope to find a position through the University placement bureau. [. . .]

MAY 15. This is more than 4 wks have cold & sore throat, very sore throat. I am sorting & packing all possible. Am having library table & sewing table crated & shipped to Henry. Am advertising rug & birds eye maple furniture which hope to sell. I sent curios, shells, coins & some of Billie's keepsakes to Carrington Huftalen, Unadilla, New York. [. . .]

JUNE 7. I take leave of thee, my dear old room #1 College Hall, where I've toiled the past 5 years. I have no regrets at parting, I feel glad to go, feeling I have done what I could & was glad to teach everything & anything while working for degrees. The college does not need the extra teacher, & I am ready for a position to which I am better fitted and adapted. I have enjoyed my work, mixed as it has been. I am very tired. Mr. Finsh opened the bank & let me in to get some money. My goods are at Platt's residence. It was very hard to leave them in a barn but they would not go up stairs. . . .

JUNE 8. . . . Saw Henry at restaurant. His eyes have turned from hazel to steel gray. It grieves me very much to know how he lives and feels. He seems to have a fixed notion that I am evil in spirit, unrigh-

Sarah's graduation portrait, Upper Iowa University, August 28, 1920. SHSI.

teous, I wrote him a good long letter to try to disabuse his mind of its false ideas. It will be made right some day. . . .

JUNE 9. Came last night to Ball Cottage, Currier Hall Annex, Room No. 7.[2] Miss Gray, chaperone. Room is at N.W. Corner, up stairs cot, table, wardrobe, dresser, extra mirror, 2 chairs & wicker one, wardrobe. I have my trunk & valise & type writer. Saw Miss Searl (Maud) from Clarinda, Also Anna Cortz, Cedar Falls, and from U.I.U.— Mead, Resser. . . . [. . .]

AUG. 21, 1923. Room 214 Currier Hall. 9 P.M. I am bothered because Miss Harlow may decide to chaperone some fraternity house. We had planned to room at Miss Hughes 112 N. Capital St., she taking undergraduate work & I to complete Master's. We engaged the room today, to pay 1 mo. rent 20.00 tomorrow. This would leave me alone & I do not feel that I can afford it. She may not but I fear she will take the work as she needs to save all possible. She coaxed me to stay. I gave up trying to get a position. I have no place to go. It must be for some good. I thought I could get my thesis done during vacation & then rev. my subjects & enroll for one or two courses & take the exams in January or whenever it is customary—Oct or Jan, is what Professor Green said.

I also want to write a book in Educ.—one for college text, & one for elem. grades in Rural schools. And I should like to do Institute work & lecture on Chatauqua. I looked forward to a happy year. Never mind; it will surely be all right some way.

THUR. AUG. 23. 9 P.M. Cool & splendid day. Miss Harlow has decided to take the sorority girls' house. I saw Wendell Knill yesterday & he is glad I will be here & gave me good advice. He was a student in my geology class at U.I.U. & is now asst. in Biology & is working for his Master's. I will be glad to complete mine. I saw Dean Paul today & he said for me to wait until School then to enroll for thesis. He said a Dr's Degree was not worth the price. [. . .]

FEB. 15, 1924. I have been at Iowa City all first semester and expect to the Second & possibly summer until secure a position. I received Master's degree Jan. 1924 in New Science blgd. auditorium.

I am now taking 15 hours. . . . I am feeling the reaction that naturally comes from five such strenuous years as my last five have been. Taking a full four year college course & a Master's course and teaching nearly all of the time, summers included.

Now I am eager to be earning. Positions are scarce at this time of the year. I am praying much these days. Miss Harlow is very comforting. We reciprocate almost daily in cheering each other on. [. . .]

JAN. 1, 1927. Listened to 6 hrs. of radio California—Alabama football at Pasadena, California. 7-7.

Damrock, New York.

Jas. McCormack.

At home all day. Rest & read, church & S.S. Sunshine.[3]

SUN. 2. Atwater—Kent radio hour.—Louise Homer & Louise Homer Stereo. "Whisperings of Hope." walked 3 miles.

MON. 3. School begins. Splendid day. Rain.

TUES. 4. Pleasant classes. Grammar class are correcting their slang & vulgarity.

WED. 5. At school 8:00 A.M.–5:45 P.M. nearly every day.

THU. 6. Organizing material in files on shelves girls helping.

FRI. 7. Sunshiny. A satisfactory day's work.

SAT. 8. At school forenoon. Letters from Henry & M. Y. Chin.

SUN. 9. Church & S.S. Blow & snow.

MON. 10. Teach & work at school from 8:00 in A.M.

TUES. 11. until 5:45 every day this week.

Every day a busy, happy day. [. . .]

1934. SEPT. 6. SAT. In my room at 921 W. 3rd St.[4] Sunny and clear and serene. Began teaching in the Lincoln Bldg. Park Ave. Tuesday the 4th. 29 pupils. Grade 6-B. Nice room, upper floor, S. W. corner of old part. Door (fire escape stairs also used at recesses) & 2 windows at west & 3 at south. cream painted walls & shades, cupboard for library, blackboard, & door to hall at north (front of room) 2 doors at East to boys, & girls' halls. also blackboard spaced at East. Jacqueline Goetz (last year pupil, "A,") brought medallions Tues. A.M. to give me, & Ruth Weirscheuser (last yr. p.) flowers. Two boys brought apples. I like them all as ever and everything goes like a song. 2-3/8 mi. each way & I walk.

Mr. Walters & Reba Bushnell brought me & my baggage Sunday, 2nd Sept. We ate picnic lunch at Weed Park. I pd Mr. G. $4.00 for bringing me.

Thursday evening there was a called meeting at the church. Accepted the resignation of the pastor, Rev. R. W. Merrifield. It is a tragedy to do as the church has. It was a spiritually dead church when he came & he & his family have been untiring in their efforts to build a church. S. S. from 0 to 134. Y. P. organized. Jr. choirs (2) etc. Scholar, minister in every sense. Preached gospel truths & a few couldn't absorb it. There are 154 members. 6 (pastor's family) withdraw. Others think of withdrawing. It would seem that the churches everywhere are at the testing point. 30,000 closing, I read in the

Pathfinder. The Devil & his cohorts are on top in this liquor besotted country. We are inviting degeneracy & decay as all other nations that have gone down ~~have~~ did.

Rec'd check Sept. 7. for 1st month of school. 102.00. [. . .]

SUNDAY 23RD. Have gotten entire out of the way of writing in a day journal, or Keeping accounts. Every day goes along about the same; much disciplining & fitting in the "system" some days & little others. I pity the children, especially those poorly born, & those from broken homes.

Supt. C. K. Hayes, now at Berkeley, California, asked me to come as a Normal Training supply for a teacher who was in hospital, for three weeks, in fall of 1924. He said he wanted me to remain permanently but was ashamed of salary. I have been here since that time; the first year as supply & part time, & then in High School as Normal Training teacher until last fall when the Supt. ~~removed the~~ discontinued my loved department & placed me in grade. 1933–1934 the first semester I had all the 6A & 6B classes except 4 (1 Arith. 1 Hist. & 2 Eng.) There were 49 pupils in 6A & 6B. Seating filled the room, could not use the blackboard. When these classes (4) went to other rooms, 4 other classes came in for me to hear: 7A & 7B, 8A & 8B History. There were 89 of these pupils. Total daily 138. It was not much like school to me; impossible to do good work. I cannot think it was right. The supt. said he discontinued Normal because of expense, but they hired another coach, and the second semester a part time teacher to take the History classes, giving me 6-B, & Miss Phillips 6-A, pupils alone. This year I have 6-B alone. The county supt. E. D. Bradley, said the supt. worked me hard so I could not help the Normal Trainers on the side. They were greatly disappointed & several left school.[5]

I walk 5 miles daily,—to & from school 2-3/8 each way. Sometimes more when have errands.

I will copy from statements what have spent during the summer vacation and since returning the second of September as near as can. In the spring at close of school—June 8, I cashed $22.00 of my last month's salary & got Traveler's checks for $80.00 all of which I have spent & some besides. I went to the Central State Bank yesterday and received the 10% payments on the closed first National & the Hershey State Bank. Also 62¢ in Normal Training Fund. Also September salary, also coupons on U.S. bonds. Kept out $40.00 cash & deposited the balance. Sept. salary 102.00, Hershey State 63.81 coupons 94.48, first Nat'l. 129.60. cost 40¢ fee. Ate dinner at Y. W.

31¢. 3 doz. fruit jars 2.30, basket & groc. .76 (to send Henry) postage 12¢. P. O. 6¢. Sent 1.95 to Marshall Field for canvas & zephyr. Bo't a lined denim jacket for Henry $2.02.

Sarah continued her entry, commenting on her recent visit to Manchester:

... I worked hard at the farm, my hands are stiff, swollen, & lame yet. I mended the board gate that the calves broke. Had Reba keep me 3 or 4 days, to can fruit, clean the cellar of *many* pails of plaster, dirt that had washed in, old rubbish, rotted cupboards, which I broke into kindling, old cans, etc., etc, a hard job, & Reba cleaned the kitchen walls. I, alone, took bbls. & seed corn, tool chests, bags of mineral feed, all to the store house. It helps if I go every summer. The screen doors which I repaired & put wire on; the window glass (many) I puttied in, etc. & the 2 w. rooms are pretty good shape, & the linoleum on their floors. I got a large piece to put on top of other in parlor to save it. My! My! When I think of what I have done there it does not seem possible hardly. It is hard. I lost 9 lbs. this summer. I picked up & split all the fuel used it is hard on one's back. But I like the out-of-doors, air & freedom to breathe, etc., & the ozone of the meadow and wood lot.

Am working on the genealogy which is interesting & fascinating. Will be glad when finished. Want to do other things. I read Ma's diary 1858–1888. It sorrows my heart & I once again go with her through the trials & sorrows that were so heavy to bear. It was not right. I had never read it before. Many articles & possibly a story c'ld be written.

Vacations[6]

AT THE OLD HOME FARM.

Ma named it "Pleasant Valley Farm." Henry called it "Golden Rule Dairy Farm." I call it The Old Home Farm.

It was eleven or twelve years that I had not been there. Henry having taken possession & management a year or so after Pa died (Nov. 25, 1909), & backing it. I had promised Ma I would care for her heirlooms. Have been going summers & am getting things in better order & shape, trying to. Will copy from little memoranda which is quite accurate.

"At the farm" July 11–Aug. 31, 1930.

Aug. 4, 1931–Aug. 29, 1931, July 29, 1929–Aug. 31, 1929. June

21, 1932–Sept. 4, 1932. July 7, 1933–Sept. 2, 1933. June 21, 1934–Sept. 2, 1934. June 8th, 1935–

1929. JULY 29–AUG. 31, ~~1931~~ 1929. One month.

After returning I sent box with woolen blanket Henry gave me, pair of sheets pa gave me to Henry. They are needed there now at the farm more than I need them here which is none at all.

The house is in quite dilapidated condition. Kitchen window falling to pieces. Screens ragged, out, etc. glass out & covered with different materials, walls black, floors a mass of litter knee deep. Cannot describe it. It seemed as though ma & pa wept loudly through my tears. Cried! See later page several leaves over.

1929. at farm. 5 wks. July 29, 1929 ticket to Chicago 7.59. Exp. valise .49. Chic. to Manchester 8.43. Left Muscatine 2:15 A.M. Arrived Tues. July 30 at 5 P.M. Stayed at Jennie Browns overnight; Earl Seeley took me to the farm Wed. July 31. I never would have believed a human could live in conditions such as I found Henry living in. Returned to Muscatine Aug. 31, 1929, by bus from Cedar Rapids, via Ia. Cy. Arr. 9:30 P.M. [. . .]

AUG. 28, 1930. . . . Henry was at State fair. Reba helped me clear barn floor of machinery, boards, etc, also put heavy boards on W. end of shed so could stack straw.[7] Also put boards on posts high to keep stock from stack. Reba & I did this alone. [. . .]

1930. This time I fed calves, took care of Chevral [sp?] while Henry was at the fair 1 wk. at Des Moines carrying water nearly floored me. Helped with chores, fed cows, scalded oats & 1 qt. oilmeal in the pasture & hay in the stable. Put linoleum & piece down alone on parlor floor. Scrubbed the floor many times & nailed tins over holds etc. Painted Parlor walls & ceiling. Had to scrape off old paper, one coat on parlor, & 2 coats on bedroom. Pulled patch of velvet weeds in cornfield—walked every 3rd or 5th row through the field on the knoll S. W. corner farm. Sweltering heat. Had threshing done from 12:00 noon to 4:10 P.M., splendidly done, oats while & clean & all good enough for seed. Reba & Julia helped me. I did everything I could so Henry could shingle the house & do other things needed. I got up at 4:00 to 4:30 A.M. Had hired men part of the time to cook for. Put screen netting on doors & windows. This was quite a job! & it won't be lasting. Cared for milk things in milk house. Fed calves in barn & also in pasture. The porch has fallen off! [. . .]

1932. JUNE 11. Had 40.00 on arriving at farm, sent to 1st Nat'l. Muscatine for $50.00 more & had to draw $18.00 more after returning.

Sarah with one of her groups of oratory students. Reba Spitler Bushnell stands at right with her hand on Sarah's shoulder. Courtesy of Forrest and Charlene Scanlan.

Sarah in her office at the Normal School, Muscatine. Her caption reads, "Saturday, December ?, 1931, end of first semester. Mrs. Huftalen at her desk, Home Room, B-16, recording psychology grades for 63 pupils." SHSI.

Had but 2.00 of the 90.00 left. It disappears fast. Henry says it's like putting it in a hole. He does not want me to do it but I see no other way. So much needs to be done there. . . .

copy June 1933 & on. "Little Essays on Life's Invisible Realities"

I had a small gift booklet published summer 1933. It cost me over 60.00 for 250 copies because of Lyman Grew's dishonesty. He was printing teacher in the high school & arranged with the Midwest Press to set it up, charging the account to me which I paid—over 24.00. He turned the work over to one of his pupils. The work was so poorly done that books were unfit to give away so I burned them.

I went to the white print shop & hired it done at a cost of over 30.00. This did not include the covers. I have old rose, green, & gray & tied them with complimentary colors in silk cord. *"Little Essays on Life's Invisible Realities"* is the title which brother Henry says is a good title.

I have given away some copies and Mrs. Smith & Miss Stelgner sold a number of copies at 35¢—giving me 30¢ each. . . .

[APRIL 1935] . . . I sent some farm machinery to Henry, bought it of the Farmer's Supply Co (Snyder Willits) who handle John Deere Implements here. It is expensive but I couldn't endure it any longer to see Henry trying to get along with virtually nothing, old mower with more rotting & breaking & he trying to mend & mend, & mend old hay rake & a spring tooth harrow & older corn cultivater, all I could see he had. So I got a corn planter, a side-delivery hay rake, a corn sheller, and a mower, & some (2) Jack screws. $300.00, $15.00, $6.00. $321.00. . . .

I do not feel right to get things to repair house unless Henry has machinery to work with. It may be foolish at best but we are well & good workers. I enjoy my walks to & from school. . . .

APRIL 30, 1935.[8] Am having the class copy the leaflets on Alcohol & its effects. Some are graphs. Each bears its facts & data that are convincing. I gave a dollar for the leaflets.

MAY 8, WEDNESDAY—I have been coming at 6:00 A.M. (leave house at 5:15 A.M.) or earlier so might keep materials for building a model house & yard in readiness for boys to work on in spare time, at noon, & sometimes after school. Miss Stocker asked each 6th grade teacher to do this project. We are making ours of pine shingles, clay, moss, rock garden, swing, bird house, etc., a job! But pretty, & a pleasure. Painting house (a bungalo) white, green trim.

There is a circus—Schell Bros.—pitching tents 2 blocks south of school—can see activities from south window. For my room is on second floor. If I could I would take all pupils this P.M. [. . .]

MAY 29, 1935. Adv. in Muscatine Journal: wardrobe trunk, electric one burner plate, Remington Portable typewriter, 50 copies of "Little Essays on Life's Invisible Realities" By. Mrs. Sarah Huftalen. Telephone 1157 R. [. . .]

To the Faculty, M. H. S. May 31, 1935.

Whenever we come to the signboard that tells us we are at the crossroads the mind is prompted to reflect as well as to project. So at this glad June time, I want you, individually & collectively, to know that I've stored up & am treasuring the good will & good fellowship you have so generously & graciously given. I do not know which road to take nor where it may lead but the pleasantest of memories will abide and make the burden light. . . . After all is said & done there be some things that are not the criterion of a teacher: degrees, chronological age, poverty, relation, "needing a job," etc. When contracts expire, they expire. I know of no law that will compel a board of education to re-elect for any reasons outside their own wish & will. They may select whomsoever they will.—married or single. . . .

To the Board of Education:

I wish to thank you for whatever you have done in my behalf during my tutelage in the schools of Muscatine. You will recall I have never lost a day by illness, never asked a favor, never been later than 7:15 A.M. to any class room, and always done more than required in whatever duty assigned.

I am well, having walked a thousand miles during last school year & expect to accomplish as many or more, this present year. I have never been tired of my work, never felt "old," never seen a "long day." As it has been & now is the custom to extend a year or two to those approaching the age limit as ruled by the board here may I not expect the same courtesy be granted me. It will be appreciated. After all is said & done there be some things that are not the criterion of a professional educator: chron. age, degrees, married or single, poor or rich, etc. [. . .]

MAY 30, 1935. MEMORIAL DAY. No school. Misses Viola & Elizabeth Smith invited me to go with them to Buffalo where Rev. Viola S. had a part in the services at the cemetery. Eliz. & I sat in car & visited. Then we drove to Davenport & had dinner at the "Lend-A-Hand," then back. It is 3:45 P.M. Now I will pack more books, etc.

I adv. in yesterday's Journal wardrobe, trunk, typewriter, electric plate, & 50 copies of my "Little Essays." Sold the typewriter to a Mr. Graves last evening for $10.00 cash. Had 6 calls for it.[9]

CHAPTER TEN

"God Is My Refuge":
1937–1944

God is my refuge & I can trust in His promises.
Were it not for this I never could have endured
what I have suffered here.
—from Sarah's diary, October 13, 1941

SEPT. 1, 1937. Very dry weather,—one rain. Having tomatoes to eat &
a few to can. 10 qts. carrots O. K. turnips sown a month ago coming
up.[1] [. . .]

OCT. Rec'd. 3 arbor vitaes from Burgess Co and set them out. Look fine
now. Little fellows! I carried 3 pails & more fine earth to put in holes,
planted carefully, watered, carried 2 bu. baskets leaves & mulched
all around 5 ft., then put on brush. [. . .]

JAN. 1, 1938. Usual housework, fuel, chickens (24), ducks (4). Bake
fruit cake from recipe of 50 yrs. ago. Roasted 2 ducks, cranberry etc.
Gray, lowry, not cold. [. . .]

JAN. 30. Had cold snap, 3 below, Wed. & 2 days & 2 nights of heavy
wind with some snow. Blew spark arrestor partly off kitchen chimney, & one of the window shutters w. parlor window. I had mended
all broken ones, & painted all of them green & hung them even to
putting on hinges on several. And I had put hooks & eyes on every
one so thought they wouldn't (& couldn't) be blown off & broken
more. But this one is badly split off both hinges & part way down
the side! I have some wood glue & will mend & put it on again first
opportunity.

I have worked on the Hawley genealogy almost every day since
Christmas when Mrs. Hawley, Clarinda, sent the book. It is interesting, fascinating, and at times disappointing & vexing; with the
everlasting missing link just ahead. [. . .]

MAY 14, 1938. Took several years copies of Journal of Educ., Geographical Magazines, Heredity, and Primary Educator to Public Library. [. . .]

JUNE 1, 1938. Let Reba have 65 [chicks]—3 die—12 die—12 die—now have over 80 chicks, & 13 hens. Old coops rained & drowned a number. Lumbago in my back & feel worn out. An old horse can be lashed up & do much but eventually the limit of latent energy is reached & one is fatigued. June 20 have 66 only. The Osteopath treatment was extremely severe, suffering yet June 3, pain going into thighs, spine, etc. [. . .]

1939

SUN. JAN. 1. U. B. church with Mrs. Luke Scanlan.

MON. 2. Called on Ward Walston family. Thawing. Warm like spring. [. . .]

JAN. 30–31. Painful back, canker gum.

Have been working on the Hawley genealogy; writing letters for information, data, etc. Received some. Each bit makes it more complete. Frank Royce paralytic. 6 strokes. Where I visited in Ripley N. Y. in 1889–1890 winter. Sorry. [. . .]

FEB. 28. *Heavy snow* fall last night & today. Blustery but not cold. Have spent Feb. 27.99 + 1.06 & this not include the bulk of postage. Had envelopes & stamps on hand. I walked down yesterday afternoon & rode back with Julia Lane.[2] Raw wind. I am so thankful to believe my ankles can be cured of threatening palsy. [. . .]

WED. APRIL 26. Cleaning wood & windows Kitchen. Dentures troublesome. roof of mouth black & blue & inflamed. Tonsils & palate gorged with black red blood, sore throat, papilla on base of tongue like little volcanoes of red & pus. I think it the poisonous injections in the gums that causes all this. feel sick. [. . .]

WED. MAY 3. Work outside & inside, 3/4 qt. walnut meats picked out & cracked from Henry's trees. Sick stomach for a mo. bad today. Warm. [. . .]

MAY 28. SUNDAY. Had dinner at noon, & for supper had cottage cheese, baked beans, whole wheat bread & butter, milk, corn bread, cake, egg, & put on jar of peanut butter, as just out of bananas. Henry said: "I'm not eating this (peanut butter) because I like it but because there's nothing else on the table." I get all the groceries & it costs a lot & when he makes such sarcastic remarks it wounds deep. It haunts my rest & sleep. [. . .]

MAY 31. Strawberries begin to ripen. Begin to take seed corn down in kitchen—heavy job. back pains much. 6 bu. baskets ready to take to store house. Began to put store house in order. Take down the bedstead, etc. hard task. Beautiful day. [. . .]

FRI. JULY 7. *Hard* rain half the night. Wind lodged corn & oats.

74 years ago this morning at 5 o'clock I was born prematurely with a twin bro. too small to dress. 2 1/2 lbs.? one side of head overlapped other the thickness of my mother's hand (no. 3 glove) covered with 3 in length of black hair. C'ld put coffee cup over my head. 74 *busy* years. [. . .]

THURSDAY, JULY 20. cheese & yeast. 25.

Henry took 3 young cows to Waterloo—Bang's disease they said.[3] Seemed like a funeral pall all day. And so stiff & lame did little outside or inside. Beautiful day. Corbin only to dinner. He is piling lumber. [. . .]

WED. JULY 26. Reba help can 29 jars of sw. corn. Looks nice & hope it keeps. A hard, & very hot job. Gives me the head ache,—a sun head ache to get overheated. Used gas & range both. Fire in range from 5 A.M. till 5 P.M. so very warm. Picked up fuel last night. [. . .]

AUG. 1, 1939. TUESDAY. Threshers came at 10:30 and were through at 2:30, stopping at 12:15 for dinner. I did it alone, not a single chore done for me. There were 10 men besides Henry. I walked to Julia's & borrowed her coffee pot. . . . Then I pared the potatoes, & picked 2 doz. ears corn, put cheese, pickles, honey, bread & pies on the table and covered them with clothes that could snatch off quickly as men sat down. I had cooked pan of beans yesterday so just had them to bake. Then I processed the rump roast from 11:00 to 12:00 & used the gas stove. Made very rich gravy. My bread & biscuits were very nice & pies good. I poured glasses of water & put the hot dishes—potato, beans, meat, gravy, & corn on table as men were sitting down; snatched off the cover cloths, & poured the coffee & it all went off fine. Henry had to wait as only 10 could sit at once. I finished washing the dishes all but the cooker at 2:30. Then I took a large dish (casserole) of beans & the coffee pot to Julia. She brought me back so as to get the dozen ears of corn I had left from dinner. I was oh, so tired & back painful all day. 8 coops to put boards over, & table leaves to take out, etc. Commode & water pails to move from w. door etc., made a pretty full day, & not a particle of help.

They got the threshing (oats & ~~barley~~ rye) done at 2:30 & went to neighbor Bockenstedts & brought the machine back & got it in the shed just as it began raining.[4] And I got the last coop closed ditto. It was 6:00 or after. [. . .]

TUES. AUGUST 22. Work inside most the day, rained nearly all day. Work in garden some. A man & his Mexican wife hitchhiking from Wis. to Cedar Falls slept in little house, gave her pr. stockings. Gave them breakfast. . . .

WED. 23. Usual work. garden. house. Beautiful.

FRI. 1ST. SEPTEMBER. Sprained ankle when running all over the north half of pasture to get neighbor Gearhart's hogs out.[5] Very painful & swollen all day. Canned 8 qts. plums. Did usual work. pain caused nausea & I vomited. Henry turned water in, & emptied slop pail. I ran & ran after those hogs—have for 3 wks, every morning but not so unruly as this time. We circled the corn barn & it was then I stepped in hole turning my right foot. I went down quickly. Warm today. I got dinner etc. Irvine helping Henry. [. . .]

WED. OCT. 4. Wrap more trees, wash E. windows in the kitchen & put S. storm windows on South. Painted sash & puttied in panes & planed the window to fit casing. Pulled 5 rows of sw. corn, ears not developed enough to eat. Give some corn stalks & all, to calves in barn yard, & in lumber yard every day. Pick up boards & coops, & pile old boards by E. fence, pull weeds. Hunt around to pick up cobs & sticks, etc. Back still lame from bringing 6 large coal buckets & 2 bu. baskets chips from mill Sunday evening so to bake Mon. Today I scoured the barn yard & grounds around buildings & found enough for tomorrow. Windy & sunny & warm. [. . .]

FRI. OCT. 13. Reba help a couple of hrs in P.M., wash ceiling & walls in living room, put on E. Kitchen storm door & my W. storm window. Cold & windy all day. [. . .]

TUES. OCT. 24. More wind, very strong S. W.

National Voice copies.

Thumb getting healed [cut while paring a squash]. Shoulder & chest muscles still painful. Work in house mostly, canned 100 lbs. potatoes to the cellar & 2 bu. baskets of apples in the closet. Went to W.C.T.U. both yesterday & today.[6] [. . .]

SAT. NOV. 11. Armistice Day. Reba took me & came for me afternoon to attend Bert Crosein's funeral 2 P.M., Presbyterian Church. Beautiful & many flowers, church filled & good sermon. . . . [. . .]

MON. 20. Genealogy a little, wrote to Lyle & Alice, not financially situated at present to make loans, made myself a cap—just enough pieces of my cloak which I shortened & mended to make it. Chilly.

TUES. 21. put strips (had to fit them at bottom of cupboards & at side), and painted them green, painted the cupboard doors & the E. living room storm sash, & screen sash, put the screen behind the closet door. Put the storm sash on, pick up around yard—debris to dump. Chicken house nearly ready to fall down, but I tried to put boards on, etc. Baked up piles of book & chips at log yard and brought up a lot. Hard on my back. Aches! Brought chunks for the heaters. Swept all lower floors, painted the looking glass frame & tin cans for flowers—had a little green left & used it. I am very tired & back aches hard. [. . .]

SUN. DEC. 10. Attended Universalist church services at Waterloo. Edna Bruner is the pastor. Her sermon was "God's Kingdom is man's kingdom too." Very good. I was glad to be there. Pd. Martha Rowe 1.00 & our dinners at the Club Cafe, Independence .87. Contribution .10. Perfect day. Sunny, warm. [. . .]

MON. DEC. 25. I went to Scanlans to dinner. nice day—warm. mend, etc. Sunday P.M. I baked fruitcake & 3 pies. [. . .]

MONDAY, JANUARY 1ST, 1940. Cold.

45 in Kitchen, same as it was yesterday. 20 in morning at 7:00. My feet are chill blained. No fire in middle room until evening when Henry wants it. I keep fire in my oil burner heater but it is a cold room,—N.W. Finished catching the chickens,—7 last night & 2 to night & put in henhouse—That makes 8 old hens & 1 old rooster & ~~4 18~~ 16 pullets & 4 young cockerels. I typed on genealogy some. Cold. [. . .]

THURS., FEB. 1. Have had lumbago & lame back yet. Very disagreeable pain all of the time. Have done usual work but not any on genealogy until today did a little—letters mostly. Has been as low as 25 below zero for a few days but warmer this week & thawing today. Went to W.C.T.U. at Belle Baileys.[7] Rode with Scanlans. Have pieced 2 silk cushion tops & bottoms & mended etc. Neighbor Gearhart died . . . [. . .]

FRI. MARCH 1ST. Henry to town all day. Put evergreen wreath on monument—pa's 102nd birth day had he lived. . . . [. . .]

WED. MARCH 20. scrub kitchen chairs—6—back aching job, sew none until evening, storm brewing. Snow last night.

THURS. 21. finish crib quilt 40 x 60 inches. 70 blocks, pieced 35 & plain (figured blossoms) 35 very pretty nine patch 6 1/2 in square. Sew on jacket in afternoon. *Deep* snow last night. 4 inches. [. . .]

SUN. 24. Ch. & S. S. Aster .06.

Ma died 52 yrs ago this morning. Precious memory. She lives. [. . .]

TUES. 26. It is said that Easter will not come again as early as March 24 for 116 years. It is very chilly, snow, sleet, cold, raw wind.

Reba came & spent a half of the day. We visited. Too cold to do anything. She took the washing. She said eggs are 13¢ only.

WED. 27. cloudy & chilly. Thaw.

Attended Colesburg W.C.T.U. in P.M. Splendid meeting. Martha Rowe took me. We went in the Petersburg Catholic church—Most elaborate carving & gorgeous decorations I have ever seen—dozens of statues & statuettes. [. . .]

FRI. APRIL 5TH. Rev. Morrow called, candidate for Senator. I felt palsied in right leg so kept off feet. I think nerve shock in dread and fear causes paralysis. . . . I've felt these nerve tremors chilling & deadening from sarcasm, twitting, falsely judging, calling me mad & crazy looking, unrighteous, etc., from Henry. It has all but killed me at times. But we must forgive & forget & trust and hope & pray.

Laura Tutles in Miss Roff's said she remembered me as a wonderful woman, referring to when I had private kindergarten & how the children liked to come, & of my giving her two baby ducks when she was ill, etc., & Jas. Burbridge said he never would forget my finishing him off for 8th grade examinations & his birthday. He is pres. of our Bank now. So there are joyous things along the way as well as sad. Being misunderstood & harshly treated by the ones we give our lives for is hardest of all. [. . .]

THURS. MAY 2. Sew & mend all day.

Henry went to Artazna's funeral in afternoon. Rebecca stopped this evening to tell me they held W.C.T.U. meeting at Mrs. Platts after the funeral. Strange they would go to their cousin's funeral & then to any kind of a meeting. They did not inform me of it so, of course I could not attend. I sensed something was being done—out of order. "My ears burned," as the old saying is. A very strong west wind all day—quieted to night. Bright sunshine all day.

The tiger Kitty starved to death, sorry to have that happen. It came last fall but was so afraid one couldn't get near it until a couple of days ago it came to house & door and cried piteously. I gave it milk but it didn't know what it was & too weak to eat. Last night before last it came to store house & I got it to eat a little; then put rags & old sack (clean) in bu. basket & put it in when it tried to rub its head on my hand & purr its thankfulness. It cuddled up & I partially covered the basket as it would be warm but it was virtually a skeleton & was dead in the morning.

Such things are very unpleasant to me. It should have been fed all winter some. Henry objected. [. . .]

SUN. MAY 12. Mother's Day—memory day of a dear mother who sacrificed much and endured much. Windy and sunny today. My nose has been "blocked" sore & very disagreeable for a week. Blood on hdkf., affected ears & throat. Some better & I pray gets over it soon. Looks like rain. [. . .]

FRI. JUNE 7. men here. I feel so sorry for the horses, *they are old.* The one all sore mouth, raw nose, stiff & aching muscles. (I know for I was so all the 1st year was here, work so hard on weak muscles.) She was too worn out to eat her oats, Irvin [Heyer] said, & coltie (black 25 yr. old) so tired tongue hung out of her mouth, kept stopping. I never thought Henry would treat a horse like this. Cecil [Dunham] tearing old henhouse down. Irvin & Henry hauling manure. [. . .]

SUNDAY 7TH JULY. My 75th birthday anniversary. Sleep & rest. Sort Temperance material, write letters and yesterday I sent 75 or 80 of my Birthday rhyme cards to old friends and some students, and relatives, from Florida to Minn., & from Boston to Los Angeles. Hope they like them. Warm. [. . .]

THURS. JULY 11TH. . . . Still receiving cards & hdkfs from friends for my birthday, & letters. . . . Had driver stop at Daltons & they brought me home, picked the berries & had supper & to bed. I sleep best ever. Sunshine & beautiful & rain. [. . .]

SAT. 13TH JULY 1940. Reba Bushnell & Julia have got up a surprise party in honor of my 75th birthday anniversary and 23 neighbors came last evening from 7:45 to 11:00. Had program, served cake, ice cream, & coffee. Mrs. Bessie Scanlan made an angel food cake with lettering in red on white frosting "Happy Birthday, 1865–1940 to Mrs. Sarah Huftalen. It was very nice of them to come. We visited a lot. I somehow sensed it when Julia came up in the morning & saw Henry. I asked him what she wanted, & he said they "talked about Elmer Kehrli," which I tho't an evasive reply. But it was my "6th sense" that really told me.

Have done usual work today besides getting things in order— chairs folded etc. & the dishes used washed. Reba called & sent for groc & daily—.65¢. Have bought bread & cake this week of Mrs. Huston. .60 Had a qt. of raspberries for dinner. Birds like them too.

It is a relief to have had my feet treated,—no pain & comfortable so far. Julia came & got the chairs this morning. [. . .]

FRIDAY, 26TH. Glorious downpour last night and this morning. Slough full of water. How very good it seems—& cooler. Several hard showers,—real dark each one. And a veritable cloud burst in late afternoons. Hurry in it after the cows. Could only see a few rds from house,—sheets of water. Slough like a fast flowing mountain stream. Air clear & fresh, sun shining now at 6:00. Everything smiling. Roof leaks up stairs. Caught in dishpan & other vessels. Rain & Sunshine. [. . .]

SAT. AUG. 31ST. Type most all the day old deed 1833 etc. in the Baker family. This week I have canned 2 qts pieplant, 4 qts plums, & made 5 cups plum jelly, pulled grass & weeds, etc. and worked on the genealogy a lot every day. Beautiful day. [. . .]

WED. SEPT. 4. Swept & picked up all the down stairs etc. Reba stopped for me to go with her to town. . . . Henry 77 today. I cannot account for his uncouth sarcasm so cruel & cutting. He tied the young bull to the plow which somehow dragged it 2 or 3 rds into the gate. I only remarked how could it. He replied, "He's like you; he wanted to go somewhere." He has called me crazy, mad, glum, unrighteous, & now its like a bull,—what next. [. . .]

MON. SEPT. 9. Went to town—walked down the railroad—jumped the slough filled with water from an all night's rain, met no train or person,—nor automobiles! Geo & Maud Durey brought me from edge of town. I only got bak. powder & 10¢ meat. Jo Walters drove in just as I got off Georges car & I went to town with him & got more groc. 1.70 meat 10¢ graham, oatmeal, cheese 1.80, envelopes, & 40¢ for W.C.T.U., yearbook 1.00. [. . .]

SUN. SEPT. 22. One restful day. Refreshed by morning bath and change of clothing, read, slept and meals was all. Rain hard shower this A.M. for an hour,—clear air & sunshine so fine.

Butterflies & lady bugs on the gorgeous zinnias. Grapes more ripe and tasty—in abundance this year for the first time after 4 or 5 yrs. of careful pruning & care. Sweet briar rose bush most fragrant today. I "called" on all the trees & shrubs I have set out and they looked their best and are growing tall & beautiful to me. Perfect day. [. . .]

OCT. 8. . . . All toil & expense clothes & food,—all with the thought of making home for Henry,—to be comfortable & have enough to eat & to wear and live as one should & then to be told he "would get rid of me out of here in a hurry if he didn't pity me." That I am a crazy woman. But I forgive him; he seemingly has a spirit of revenge, or spite. Never a word of commendation, adverse criticism only,—even the way I sit or eat or dress,—nothing goes unnoticed & commented on. "When did I learn to eat with a fork?" "Why hold your left hand in your lap while you eat?" & so on & on & on. I cast out all possible & seldom let it get on my nerves. Says I'm the "biggest problem he has & its a very great trial to have me here but thinks it better for me to stay here. . . . Every about so often he has a streak about eating. Yesterday I had chicken & gravy, sw. potatoes, cottage cheese, prunes, gems, ~~prunes~~, onion, carrots. He got up immediately after sitting down; put hands on edge of table; looked all over the table so I asked him what he was looking for thinking I had not put salt or ? on the table. He said he was looking for something to eat & got the raw oatmeal from the cupboard & ate it with milk—nothing else. Kept that up for 4 meals.

It worried the life out of me & kept me in continual suspense but I am praying & God is answering to never mind and not fear whatever may comme. For it seems the harder I try and more I do;—only that much more to be censored for. [. . .]

WED. OCT. 23. Picked up boards & sticks in barnyard & lane so as to have fire in evening & to get breakfast. Have gathered all used this week & part of last; Have no wood pile whatever. Henry brings up a sliver of bark occasionally. Perfectly beautiful day. [. . .]

SUN. OCT. 27. Henry brought a bedstead down from upstairs for me to sleep on.[8] Moved davenport out in middle room. I have slept on the floor, on a 2nd hand couch (too short) & on our davenport—all hard places but every time I would set up the single bed he would take it to the storehouse for some transient to use. . . . So I got a davenport,—nice to rest on. The bed surely looks good tonight. The old mattress will do. One Billie & I had in Des M. Used 23 yrs. Was on floor upstairs with debris when I came & found it & cleaned it best I could. Edith Scanlan called. [. . .]

TUES. NOV. 5. Presidential election. Voted straight Prohib. ticket "Babson & Moomian" for P. & V.P. rode up & back with Hoffmans.[9] Henry walked on R. R. all the way to Masonville, 6 mi. to vote, & 1/2 way back. Mop & wax kitchen floor, & pick up in general expect bride & groom tonight or in morning, bake bread, carried in 10 bu. baskets wood & cobs—bark, etc., a big job. Squally and cloudy day. *I am tired.* mop & wax floor, etc. [. . .]

SUN. DEC. 1. Work all day. Shame! Wash 27 cans, usual work, cobs out doors, etc. [. . .]

WED. DEC. 4TH. canned 27 qts beef. Looks fine. snowing this evening—
thaw.[10]

CHRISTMAS 1940. Five and one half years since coming to the old farm
to try to make a home for Henry. Besides the several summer vacations working here before June 1935 and which taxed my mind,
heart & body to the uttermost, (one of which virtually laid me about
half alive all the teaching year following) these five and a half years
have been years of heavy toil and pain. God has been good to spare
my life; to give me grace & patience to endure; hope to sustain and
faith to believe and trust & pray. I never would have believed that
any one could hold so much bitterness toward anyone as has been
shown me by Henry. I have been fatigued & prostrated several
times. Never a word of commendation but ever adverse criticism;
sarcasm, cruel and cutting, mocking me in pain & being so very
tired, twitting me of being like child; hypocritical to attend Dr. B.
church & have a class of poor little west side girls; calls me unrighteous & scolding severe; says I've transferred my dislike of pa to
him. I never disliked pa but was afraid he might kill us all when in
his tantrums & threats to hang himself, & moods. I really believe
ma's paralysis was caused by the constant intense fear & dread of
his terrible temper & spells. It paralyzes one to be under constant &
intense nerve strain,—numbs the extremeties, unbalances the circulation, muscles get rigid, spinal cord aches its length like an aching tooth. The large nerve centers—plexus & abdominal, brain continually aches in a dull way. I think I am safe in saying there has not
been 6 continuous days & 3 would be nearer correct it has not been
inferred or insinuated in one way or another; direct or indirect that
I do not use my mind; says he knows just how my mind works, that
I don't know but he does. One day when I spoke about going to town
he said I was like the bull; I wanted to go somewhere. This was
when I casually remarked I didn't see how his young bull could have
pulled the plow a rod or so to which he was tethered. And when Rev.
Morrow came for me to speak at Buck Creek Missionary meeting &
I was so happy to feel had done a little bit to uplift & cheer the large
group he said I was tired on my return by Rev. Morrow. Why, no, I
said, I wasn't. He said very decidedly that I was but didn't know it
& said "Sarah, you are a crazy woman. I'd rid you out of here in a
hurry if I didn't pity you." It took all the nerve force I had to reply to
him that he is a crazy man to argue & argue and that I w'ld go
anytime he said & would not stay at all if I did not pity him. He said
it is a very great trial to have me here.

He makes one feel as tho you were just tolerated & ever in suspense to stay or leave. No possibility of feeling settled & at home. I seldom ask about anything; not answered, or evaded, or answers in such a way that makes the soul shrink and crushes the spirit. Pray God gives me grace & strength to endure.

I met Mr. Carr a few times on the street last summer & he gave such a searching piercing look that I sensed it enough so that my spirit quaked.[11] I do not understand why he should have. I scarcely know him other than to speak. Not long after when I was speaking about having Reba Bushnell help me, Henry said I was an invalid; then modified it to "semi-invalid & would get worse and worse, couldn't lift a pail of water."

Not so long afterward I noticed in the paper that Mr. Carr is one of the committee of examiners for the insane, so I believe Henry had said something to him in some way. And it was likely my fault for I unthinkingly said one day to some one who was here to eat & we were talking about the hospitals, etc., that there were those committed who should not be & told about the case Mr. Oats & I know about when I was Co. Supt. at Clarinda, Iowa. Mr. Oats said the old lady was not insane but that as soon as her soninlaw got the deed in his name, Grandma was in the way & it was easy to have her placed in the asylum. I saw the soninlaw, a great swarthy man carrying the mother off the train to the ambulance, tears coursing down her cheeks. She was nice looking & sane looking. So Mr. Oats traced it, & said there were others same way & that they did not live long after being there & that it was pitiful. I recall Henry said he did not believe it very emphatically & so I put two & two together & think he went to Carr to inform himself.

I never mean to let anything he says or nags about get on my nerves but five years & more of continual inference & remarks it does once in a while. It would seem he has a "mental set" in regard to me & I pray for him that God touch his heart & bring him to a better way. He lived alone so long, habits are deep set—both in the way of living & doing & whatever does not be in full accord therewith is wrong in his estimation. Everyone, especially me, lacks judgment. "There is a place he says for such as our good neighbor Julia Lane." She told me how Ed treats her & I do not wonder she is nervous. Sometimes it looks as though farmer men think of a woman only as a chattel, estimate her worth by what amount of physical labor she can perform & wait upon them.

I had faith to believe that I could make a home for Henry, my only brother, whom I was taught to revere & be a serf for from early childhood & ever have been. When I resigned my profession in 1915 & came here to make a home for him it was because I kept hearing he was "off"; was unbalanced & I could not & would not have it so. Just thought if I were here & settled the house which badly needed it & get meals etc., everything would be all right; I just knew it would. So I came, & brought furnishings & a new carriage— morocco dash, leather cushions, rubber tire—resigning several of- fers for positions & generous salaries. He did not speak for 6 months— and would not allow me to place the things—all bare floors & very soiled. Had to leave these things piled in a room & there they were for two years until I could endure it no longer & as God would have it a position for life at the State Teacher's College came out of a clear sky & I accepted it. Henry raved at me at times & finally threatened "to throw me out of the house if it was the last thing he ever did under Heaven." I became afraid & consulted Dr. D. who said it was not safe for me a single day & offered to send a dray for me & my things at once. I prayed mightily for guidance & felt that when the position came it was divinely sent.

My life has gone so smoothly & happily that makes it hard for me to nerve myself to meet the conditions. Some desultory remark about this or that every day. Gives one no peace of mind of content- ment of spirit. Trying to do everything suggested & so he sug- gests—sometimes opposites—makes one feel as tho he were going in a circle & accomplishing little or nothing.

Irregularities of eating & sleeping when regular habits in these respects have been ingrained in one's system for years disturbs di- gestion & circulation. Manure covered milk pail is nauseating the winter through & then to be told its all in your mind!

Treats me as an enemy, dishonest, a foe or a villain; asked me what I came here for. Censors everything I do, ought to wear floor length dresses of gray or brown; my voice, "when did I learn to eat with a fork?" "why hold my left hand in my lap while eating," "doesn't look nice to see me walking on the road" & so on & on ad infinitum. Not a day passes that some desultory remark is made about one thing or another until I have gotten so it makes me feel limp or as though my knees would fall out from under me; I pray God give me courage and strength to endure. When speaking of Aunt Edna's marriage, he said she didn't deserve anything from her father's estate. Insinuating by tone of voice that I shouldn't & as though her marriage was a disgrace. He has ever been very bitter because I married Billie against his will & a man whom he disliked. He cannot understand that love goes where sent & woman's love is her life. A man looks at marriage more as a business transaction,— of what a woman can do in labor & do his bidding. Maybe I should go away; I've been tempted to a thousand times and not try any longer to make a home for him. He rather be alone. There is no home spirit or atmosphere. [. . .]

1941

[. . .]

SAT. MAY 31, 1941. Had cloud burst yesterday late afternoon. Such a heavy down pour as seldom have.

Today is heavy fog & *moist*, work in house. Glad had garden in good shape—It is very large. Peas in blossom. Strawberries a quart, old bed, needs new.

There are ten little lambs. Sheep pastured in dooryard; eat off every spirea, hollyhock, & little tree I went above Ry. & got. Discouraging. Henry keeps saying to have flowers in front to share with others,—says it is selfish to have them in the garden. I have spent a number of dollars for flowering shrubs, planted seeds, & bulbs but all destroyed. Only one rosebush & that is very fine. It is the sweet briar that I planted seed balls fall 1939 & is as tall as I now. 4 came up & are in one bed with lilac I am trimming for tree shape. It is small now,—4 ft. 2 yrs. since set it out. I do like to work out door but it is pretty hard on my back. Am sawing off dead limbs from trees & those killed by rabbits. And today the horses are pasturing in dooryard,—breaking branches & lilac bush. [. . .]

MON. JULY 7. 76th birthday. Up at 4:15, pick peas, ride to edge of west side town with Mr. Fogel who is tearing porch off. walked most the way back. Bank 20.00. Got back at 10 & got dinner. Milo come at 11:00 thinks much about eating & watches clock called it 4 hrs. helping hay. 3 1/2 it was. groc. 37¢. Daily 4¢ . . . . [. . .]

SAT. JULY 12. Typed 8 pages on Genealogy. Usual work. no extra men today. Rec'd. cheques from Muscatine Central State Bank 8th dividend 80.78. Went above R.R. searching gooseberries, none. Saw the disk harrow that horses ran away with. A wreck, all 1/2 of it in pieces by the catalpas S.E. corner field. All disks off on ground. [. . .]

MON. OCT. 13. Today I baked bread, and moved a pile of boards, & did odd jobs outside, finished putting wire screen around trees so rabbits cannot gnaw them. Also staked a roll of fence around the spirea near the road. I am tired. Rains. Fred Mahannah died yesterday at his home in Des Moines. I am so sorry. I shall miss his help and goodness when I go to Des to see about my keepsakes that are still there. I was there in May 1940 & he said I could have all returned & do whatever I wished. Things were in a turmoil & he was working hard to get things adjusted. I wrote Miss Jessie Parker this morning for advise, etc. And then when Henry brought the Leader in P.M., there was the obit of Fred Mahannah. I should have written sooner, —Had him and Musgrove on my mind but I have been very poor in spirit so accomplished nothing. Dehn 2 meals. Cool but pleasant. Jesus said, "Blessed are the poor in spirit for they shall see God." God is my refuge & I can trust in His promises. Were it not for this I never could have endured what I have suffered here. [. . .]

SAT. OCT. 18. Accomplish little. Mr. Dehn who works for Henry spade tulip bed. I feel very poor in spirit. I never told Henry before the reason I came here in 1915, nor why I came this time. I told him Wednesday. He seemed surprised & said he would investigate that. Poor man! Little he realizes what I have suffered trying to make a home for him. I thought my duty. Rainy.

SUN. OCT. 19. Make out program for W.C.T.U. Institute.

I am beginning to question if it is my duty to try longer to stay here. Possibly I should not have tried to make a home for him. Cannot feel at home or settled,—always in suspense. I pray God show me the way. Half afraid all the time. [. . .]

THURS., NOV. 27. . . . Did not seem much like some of the old Thanksgiving Days when Uncle Henry Baker came in sleigh in raging blizzard & we had turkey & a big dinner.

Pa died 31 yrs. ago the 25th which was on a Thanksgiving Day. I should like to have attended Union Services but did not feel like walking down. A beautiful warm summer-like day all day. Kept no fires. Sunshine. [. . .]

CHRISTMAS 1941. type on genealogy all time could get. Henry does chores most all day every day. I received 70 Christmas greetings & letters. All so fine. Dr. Starbuck's sinks deep into my heart. My muse did not work this time.

This year has gone swiftly, & sometimes painfully. I wonder I am alive & concluded to try to save myself a little for no matter, what it is or I do; it is never right.

Irregular hours of eating and sleeping,—scarcely two days the same only when has men working there meals more regular. This week breakfasts have been at 11:00, 8:30, 11:00, 10:30, 11:45, &

10:45. Maybe will come in to eat at 2:00 P.M., 4:00, 3:00 or 7:00, once after 8:20 P.M. So it is all year. I have finally tried to eat more regular & not wait. It disrupts digestion. Keeps one in suspense.

I have been invited to become a member of the New England Historical & Genealogical Society, Boston, Mass. Have not yet but think I will.

Henry has not been quite so mean since I told him the reason of my coming here in 1915, again in 1935. He "supposed I had no other place to go." I was offered positions at 1200.00 & 1400.00 as prin. in 1915 but refused to accept for he was living in such a terrible way & I kept hearing he was "daffy" and "dippy" & I couldn't have that. I just knew if I could be here & make a home for him he wouldn't let me unpack my furniture, negative things & didn't speak for 6 mos. I toughed it out on bare floors & fearful conditions for 2 yrs & the good Lord called me to the State College to teach & demonstrate at Cedar Falls.

I was so worn out for loss of sleep & the terrible suspense & fear that I went to Hinsdale to rest & recuperate before beginning my year's work.

And when I came again in summer vacation it took all the nerve force I could muster to come & I would not had it not been that I promised ma I would take care of the heirlooms. And every year I've thought would not try to stay another. It has cost me a lot of money, & a slight stroke of my right side. I've trusted & hoped & prayed from day to day & tried to be brave & endure,—resting in the promises of God. And I've overcome the most of the worry & fear & dread.—These paralyze the nerves.[12]

Wants me to get some notions out of my head & to "think," "think," wants me to educate myself up to feeding the hens a dead calf; to churn butter for market, to raise poultry. . . .

I can see the psychology of his attitude but one would naturally think when he has lived in the conditions he was in that he would appreciate having meals & housework done. He eats irregularly,—I never know when he will come in sit down to the table & say: "I am ready to eat now." Any & all hours of the day.

My shoulder bothers a considerable where the ligaments were torn loose when I fell on ice at Fayette. And my back in lumbar region, hips & thighs ache a dull dragging down lifeless ache more than is comfortable. Takes the pep out a lot at times.

Prayer & hope & faith sustains although do get poor in spirit once in a while. "Blessed are they who are poor in spirit and who endure."

I am so thankful to be as well as I am despite the pain and to keep up courage, & as pa said the day before he died: "Sarah, you must be brave." And I try to be. I never was a fighter or quarrelsome nor combative. . . .

The last of December & first of January were fearful cold 15 to 36 below zero. House cold. He said if I had to do what he did I'd see. I said I couldn't do it. He said I could do it as well as he could. There was a raging N.E. blizzard one whole night & day. Stinging, drifting deep etc. I fear to take care of 30 head of stock is beyond me even if he does say I could & either infers or says "if you wanted to."

1942

THURS., JAN. 1, 1942. Blizzard all last night & all day today. Drifts large & deep.

I shoveled on 4 ft deep that covered the distellate bbl. so could get cars filled. Also shoveled at henhouse door so could get in. Fed chickens, brought in coal, emptied ashes & slops, etc. Quite a job, snow above knees some places had to wade. Wrapped legs with towels to shoetops. Then was covered with snow. Stand by stove to day!

Baked bread. Henry wanted to know why I didn't make Johnny cake. I did yesterday. I usually make it once a week. Then he chided me for not roasting the sheep's quarter instead of making it into chops. Always tells me I "don't think; just do anything that comes into my head, etc." I ought get used to it for its been virtually every day for 6 1/2 yrs. But I don't get used to it. Nothing is ever just right. It is 7:30 P.M. still snowing & blowing & drifting to getting colder. [. . .]

TUES. JUNE 16TH. A week gone,—too busy to keep tab. hoeing garden yesterday & some before. Hoed the raspberry & strawberry rows; peas, 2 rows, 35 melon hills & far out over all ground, yesterday. Today hoed corn, 5 rows, 4 rows potatoes, Swiss chard, Salsify, beets, lettuce, etc., a big hard job. Have to weed each row by hand; mostly grass in the rows. Have mended some & made nightgown & usual house duties. I am very tired & back aches hard tonight. yesterday the Geneal. books (3) came from Boston & I have made 8 pp. of notes & ready to send them back tomorrow. Get up at daylight & no idle minutes. Henry mowed alfalfa yester. below barn & began clover above Ry. [. . .]

SUN. JUNE 21. Beautiful & clear & bright. no rain yesterday or last night, my head aches some yet and the back of my head & neck feel some bruised. I am grieved to say from a hard vicious blow by my brother Friday morning.

He came in & wanted to know where the glass pitcher was & to use it in well house. I said I w'ld get something else to put the milk in that I did not want to use the pitcher as I prized it. He flew angry & raved about my not having reason, etc. I tried to reply but he was so furious I kept still; got the white granite kettle which he took out; soon returned for me to pour the milk into the fruit jar with funnel & went out saying he was afraid he'd spill it. I poured it in & started down the steps to take it out to wellhouse—met him at the steps when he said very angrily about my lack of reason and struck my head on the back with his flat hand which pained & shocked me greatly. I never had been struck in my life. Some of the milk spilled & I couldn't speak for a second so stunned but I didn't go over nor let the milk fall. I asked him what he meant,—fearing he might strike me again. He said he meant what he said I am void of reason,—never had any from a child. He appeared mad—his tone evidenced it. My head hurt & I could not help crying as a reaction & came in my room. He said he did it on the impulse of the moment & to be forgiven & he never would again. I said I would not stay with any one who would strike me.

I do not know what I ought to do. He ought not be alone but I am greatly moved to leave for he may do the same thing again, & I am not strong enough to endure such experiences. [. . .]

WED. JULY 8. Rec'd. nice birthday card from Jno. & Helen Meuller. Very pretty & stanza. Also from Dora & Agnes Stewart, and Mrs. Ruthenburg. Reba's most beautiful.

—Had parsnips & tomatoes—hard.

—Work on geneal. books. Tired but glad head did not ache to-day—1st time in 3 weeks. Pains some on top & I am praying what I should do. Henry said he would never strike me again but he may have other uncontrolled "impulsive moments." I do not get over it—hard nerve shock for me to bear. I've never felt at home a single day since I came here. [. . .]

SUN. OCT. 25. . . . Letter from Robert Hawley—Clarinda saying his mother passed away June 15, 1941. Saddens my heart. She was ever so dear to me. My deputy Co. Supt. schools of Page Co.—We always exchanged letters at Christmas time,—none 1941. I grieved because of not receiving her good message.—Couldn't think why. So I wrote her a few days ago & Robert answered with the sad intelligence. I have all her letters so precious they've ever been. [. . .]

1943

SAT. JAN. 9, 1943. copy Grace Baker notes 11 pp. usual work, side rib
pretty same from getting corn from crib, ladder 3rd step & rake to
reach it in 2nd story of old crib, sheep below all open & racked badly.
Hold long pail in left hand & get ears with rake & right—sheep bent
ladder. Thaw some. snow again last night. Drifts getting deeper.
[. . .]

SAT. MAY 22. plant corn & peas & hoe most all day. Moles are *bad*. Set
out 12 raspberry. First time this spring have had 2 pleasant days in
succession. Beautiful day. [. . .]

MON. MAY 31. Another unhappy day. It gets on my nerves once in
awhile—8 yrs. of constant reminding & inferring my mind. I said I
w'ld like to have 2 good posts in front gate & asked him what would
he think of it. He finally replied "The few short years we have to live
it wouldn't pay." I said Pa & Ma w'ld like to have the farm put in
shape. He said when I got my balance, etc. So I asked him what he
meant by that, he said he could tell me but I wouldn't like it. I was
very indignant and tried to argue which made me tremble & talk in
a loud key. He wanted to know what I thought of pa that I had said
he was a demon. I denied this & said it was not true; pa was a good
& honest man but he had terrible spells his own mother saying she
didn't know what would become of him, etc. I have thought all day
what I should do or go where. He is too old to be alone. But it is a
very unhappy place for me with such an attitude as he has. [. . .]

TUES. JUNE 29. hoe potatoes, melon vines, & old peas that died, also
some corn, & weeded parsnips & one row onions by hand, transpl.
tomatoes. Cool & nice to work. Feel better. . . . [. . .]

SAT. DEC. 25. Christmas Day. presents from Archie Hawley family =
cotton figured table cloth, 3 rosy cakes soap fr. LeRoy & Luverne,
window (horse) ornament, 3 framed flower pictures (small), plant
root of a "spider" plant, too dry to grow I fear, from Mrs. Garlick =
bath towel & cloth & 2 hdkfs. in box. from Evelyn Paul print (blue
figured) & rick-rack for apron, 60 or more beautiful Christmas cards
from friends. Warm today enough to let my oil fire out for the day &
balmy out of doors. Beautiful Day. [. . .]

1944

SUN. JAN. 16, 1944. Go through "Baker" notes & write to Mr. Phillips,
who is also working on the Baker's family. Henry accuses me of

"hiding" an old aluminum kettle that he used at the barn. I haven't seen it for a yr. or more. It was at the lumber yard when Mr. Jordison ran the sawmill engine & that is the last time I've seen it. I was minded to bring it to the house but hesitated fearing Henry wouldn't like it. I thought it might be stolen. It was large, no bail but had a handle on the side. There was a small light aluminum kettle that I bought for the kitchen. He filled it with carrion fat for me to try out on the range which I did, & vomited to pay. Disinfected the house with sulphur; covered the kettle & took out doors to wellhouse. It was there some time & when opened was full of maggots so I took it out by the chicken coop & that is the last I've seen of that. He wanted me to use it but I had no desire to. It must have been a yr. ago. I had cast it out of my memory—unpleasant. Beautiful day. [. . .]

WED. JAN. 19. Just as I had gone to bed I heard an auto & some call Henry abt. "fire." I got up & dressed & looking out saw the Ry. right of way for nearly the 80 rods burning furiously—flames much higher than a man. It proved to be neighbor Chas. Bockenstedt who drove Henry out to the fire & they "spaded" it out where it caught in the pasture. Lucky the wind had veered to the west or they couldn't have stopped it, might have burned across the 50 to the highway. We did not see it. . . . [. . .]

WED. APRIL 26. Work out doors all afternoon. Pick up 6 bu. cobs & put in storehouse; uncover raspberry bushes; pick up branches over the yard; pick up corn stalks & bank evergreen trees with them; etc. typed 4 pages only. Pleasant. [. . .]

SUN. APRIL 30. Tidy my desk, write a letter to Mrs. Baker, & cards to state leaders. Slept an hr. Down pour & then clear sunshine—trees budding, grass vivid green. yesterday I pruned grape vines & raspberry bushes; uncovered strawberry bed; drove stakes at edge of bed entire length. I finished putting "Universalism & Lodges" of Henry's in the cupboard & put the filing cabinet (both parts) upstairs in the NW bedroom. It was very hard to get it up the stepladder & 3 board step pieces. Baking potatoes & have lamb roast for supper. [. . .]

THURS. AUG. 10. Pull much grass in multiplier onion row; cut some corn for horses & sheep; prepared & canned 4 qts beets—mild pickle; go to the wood lot to look for dewberries,—found 4 bushes & got a sauce dish full. Exceedingly hot in wood lot. Kept inside Railroad fence on a/c of young bulls in pasture; tore dress much in getting through Ry. fence & just about ran below the knoll to keep out of sight of our cattle & get to wood lot,—another barbwire fence to tear through. Came back same way along east line fence for cattle stayed beyond the knoll near Railroad gate. The new highly pedigreed young fellow pawed & saluted. I am very warm.

Henry got up at 2:00 moonlight this morning to get sheep into west pasture. I thought it must be morning upon hearing him and so got up & dressed.—It was 2:30 so I waited till he came in at 4:00 & went back to bed. [. . .]

FRI. NOV. 10. Work all day—carried manure on garden using bu. basket & little wagon. Finish 6 substantial nests. Arm (weak one) some painful from sawing the old boards. Swept sides & floor clean. Put on straw. Turned oil heater off. Took old nests all down. Cloudy. [. . .]

WED. NOV. 15. On feet entire day cooking for Henry to have while I go to Muscatine to dentist tomorrow, dressed & processed a rooster; bake rye bread; 2 apple & 1 peach pie; beans; corn meal mush to fry; prunes & I am tired. He always wants something different "would be glad if I had or would bake gems & make gravy." I did not make gravy because had no milk & there wasn't enough fat in cooker to make gravy. Rainy day. Not cold. The groceries came so I think he will not need to go hungry. But when I am so tired it all but unnerves me to never have a satisfactory meal & for supper we had fresh rye bread & butter, potato couldn't be nicer; beans; chicken; prunes, catsup, cheese (40¢ a lb.), milk, onions, peanut butter, & noodles. I haven't sat down today from 6:30 A.M. & its 8 now & I just finished milk pail & strainer & dishes. Now I must pack my little grip to be ready to go early A.M. [. . .]

SUN. DEC. 31. Sort & collect Baker data—Cloudy.

Had a considerable. Now to get the rest that have begun in shape as well as punch & fasten this one I have collected together.

I do not know of anything to add to this year's closing. I have done all I could & more many times to make home. I am thankful for the blessings God has granted & for the happy & congenial fellowships of the years from July 7, 1865 to date.

CHAPTER ELEVEN

"All Will Yet Be Well":
1945–1952

I shall continue praying that all will yet be well.
—from Sarah's diary, October 3, 1948

1945

[. . .]

TUES. MAY 8, 1945. [To] Belle Bailey's to type an article for her. Wind so strong had to brace all strength I had to keep upright. N. West wind. Had to go 2nd time to Express office as he not in first time to send Baker Record to N.E.H. & G. Soc. [New England Heritage and Genealogical Society] Boston.

The War in Europe (except guerilla) was announced by Stalin of Russia, Truman of U.S. & Churchill of England to be stopped. Germany to Surrender unconditionally. Terrible tragedy,—the horror of murdering millions of captives by the Germans in their prison camps is beyond belief. Starved 1000's; burned 1000s alive, etc. [. . .]

SAT. JULY 7. My 80th birthday anniversary. Received a box of choice maple candies from Reba & card. I baked rye & graham bread & mopped yesterday. Up at 5:30. Built fire in range; empty slops & ashes, feed & let out chicks; chop old boards into 3 bu. baskets fuel; sickle a rd. of grass 2 yds. wide; get breakfast; look over gooseberries; prepared ground on S. side & plant turnip seed; ditto short row of peas. . . . Got supper,—chard, potatoes, eggs, gooseberry sauce. Then I hoed watermelon patch till dark 8:30 P.M., typed some out of little primers of my childhood. Beautiful day after slight morning shower. [. . .]

MON. JULY 9. Wrote to Reba. I got up at 5 & it is now nearly 8 in evening & I've worked outside all day. Sickled a lot in SW garden among raspberrys; the eleven walnut & maple trees I set out; & planted a row of beets, radishes, & parsley. I gathered a large pile of old boards in lot W. of barn; the ones on the bottom rotted badly; &

kept sheep away from barn all P.M. till 6:00 while Mr. Chrystal was drawing alfalfa in. Margaret drives the tractor to load & unload. *I am tired.* Nice day after a threatening morning. I typed some from my old school books also. [. . .]

SUN. JULY 22. Wrapped & packed my old school books & primers to send to the State Hist'l. Society of Iowa, Iowa City. Very warm. [. . .]

MON. JULY 23. Did not get to sleep until after 4 this morning. So grieved at the way Henry treats me. A sheep died that he gave too much milk to,—bloated *very rapidly.* Poor lamb calling for her. He dragged the body into the garden paying no attention to my plea not to & offering to help haul her away on my little wagon. When I couldn't help crying & begging him not to he said, "Don't act silly." So my heart pained all night. He never has buried the sheep & he's lost from 1 to 3 each year since I've been here. Just let them rot & carrion beyond enduring. He put some on ground in SW corner of garden once & millions of maggots & stench. I tried to throw dirt on daily but had to give up the West 1/3 & more of the garden; later hiring Tom Dalton & Billie to dig out the grass. I feel mistreated & ill dealt with & wish I could leave here & have a little place of my own. He surely has been the meanest of anyone I've ever known. I fear it will kill me sometime. I've worked like a slave to make a home for him & been treated worse than a slave. I packed my old text books ready to send to Hist'l Soc. of Iowa, Iowa City, & typed a list of them. Someway I couldn't rest, very warm. He did dig deeper hollow to put the sheep in but the dogs always dig everything out. hope not. I asked him not to bury a lamb in garden a week ago but he paid no attention & put it in the melon vines. I've had to cover it daily & finally put a board on top but it is off today.

I've had to endure carrion ever since came here & have dug deep hole 4 ft. deep & buried some but it is too hard for me.

I am beginning to question if it was my duty as I thought to try to make a home for him. He was never taught to have any consideration for a woman. So no need to expect it. He dragged the body over the row of beets I have sown & over the turnips & radishes. He is self-righteous to the nth degree. And puts me through 2rd deg. trial. I wonder at myself staying here; the work so heavy. And then he'll say I don't have to do it. Dear Heavenly Father lead thou me. [. . .]

MON. SEPT. 10. Clean up shop room; harness to the barn; old carpet taken outside, swept & laid down in middle room. Went with Gretchen to her garden, velvet & other weeds high as one's head.[1]

She gave me a pan of tomatoes to can. It blew *hard* this P.M. & a cold sleety rain. I got soaked getting chickens in coops. Scarcely walk against the wind. This was last evening. Cards from Reba. So sorry for her boy Edgar died in Japanese prison camp in Siam (Thailand).[2] The cruelties are beyond belief: steel bits in mouth, some beaten to death. Over 1000 died on the 140 mile march to the camp. Edgar was purser on the SS Houston sunk in Java Bay July 30, 1943. It is cold today. I cleaned the house & put on garden where I have the corn cut off. Mrs. Arnold tells me via card that I was honored at W.C.T.U. Co. Conv. at Colesburg on Aug. 24 by being made a Life Patron. I am already so now what? I became a Life Patron at Mason City State Conv. "in memory of my sainted mother." [. . .]

WED. NOV. 21. Had first snow fall—a lot of it. Had a great time trying to get a leghorn rooster & a pullet. Finally got them in the coop & got the rooster & put him in henhouse. The pullet got away & went everywhere about the yards & bldgs. She crouched in the snow in the East field & I chased her to the coop & fastened her in. Didn't accomplish much,—days too short. Henry still has a cold & cough. Worries me.

THURS., NOV. 22. Supposed to be Thanksgiving Day acc'd. to the Roosevelt regime. I think most people rather the last Thurs. in the month as has been the custom for 400 years. Roosevelt wanted it changed for commercial purposes.—The shame of a greedy few in high position & all already wealthy. Henry rested & slept most the forenoon & boarded up the west door of the barn in the afternoon. I thought he w'ld be in at noon but not so,—came in at 4:30 to eat, dark. I cooked beans, chicken, potato, squash, & had cranberry, etc. Kept it on stove until he ate. Mr. Chrystal got the pullet out of the coop for me. I was very glad for I had kept trying to get her all day & it has been, & now is, a blustery, snowing day. I went into the East field & husked out of the shock a pail of ears of corn for the hens. I have been writing to Mrs. Donovan, Iowa City, who asks permission to give me a write up in the Palimpsest magazine.[3] A snowy, windy day.

SAT. 24. Wrote & typed letter in answer to Mrs. Donovan. Dug a bu. of turnips in snow & frozen ground. Have more to dig. Gave them to Mr. Chrystal,—he & Kehrli gathering the corn. Corn is poor this year. Thaw. [. . .]

WED. 28. Typed March 29–June 30 inclusive of Ma's Diary 1858. Portrays the life of the Baker Settlement in those early days. Very interesting. Usual work & dug a bu. of turnips out of the snow & mud, cold job. Dragged 2 cartons of them over the garden to the house,— too heavy to carry. Pleasant.

FRIDAY, DEC. 7. So warm let the hens out,—happy chicks! Finish reading diary 1858/59. What a busy life ma led, & social, charming, intelligent, industrious. Beautiful day.

1946

SUNDAY, JANUARY 14, 1946. Thaw some, writing ma's diary, dear mother o' mine. Baked 1 loaf bread, 1 tin of biscuits, coffee cake, 1 peach pie & 4 pumpkin pies. built or rather put fresh straw in hen nests, usual care of them daily, milk & feed (oats & corn) & usual house work. Miss Elkins called.

SAT. JAN. 19. Very chill strong wind all day & now in evening. copy some more diary. finished mending Pa's clothes to send to foreign peoples devastated & impoverished by the war, 2 pr linen summer pants, 2 light shirts & collars, 1 dark plaid gingham shirt, 2 all wool winter shirts & 2 pr wool (all) drawers. 1 undershirt (summer), 1 pr. suspenders, 1 winter cap, 1 summer cap, 1 pair of shoes, 1 heavy double breasted dress coat & 1 heavy winter overcoat, and I am going to make a child's dress &c.

SUN. FEB. 24, 1946. Usual work daily during the week & copying Diary. Weather almost like spring part of the time, snow off. Yesterday morning there was not enough water to cook sufficient oatmeal for both so I cooked for Henry & ate wheat shred for my breakfast, so remarking. He said "you are very unselfish in some ways & very selfish in others." I only wonder what next he can call me; if he were not my brother I wouldn't stay & try to make a home for him. I have all but sacrificed my life for him—God has helped me to endure his abuse so far although at times it did seem as though the burden was heavier than I could bear. Henry came in to eat breakfast at 7:30 an hour or more earlier than usual. I got it as fast as I could. he ate, then lay down & slept 2 hrs, then out to chore. 9 o'clock P.M. I just got in from catching 5 pullets & 2 cockerels nice brown leghorns & put in coop. Mrs. Chrystal brought. quite a jog & got stepladder out of stable (bull & calf) & get it into the henhouse part & get 3 from under the roof I do not like to let them go but rather have buff rocks or Rs Reds. [. . .]

OCT. 29, 1946. Tuesday. *Warm.* iron, bring in 4 bu. baskets bark & break up boards, etc, bake bread & cake, hang curtains, do all could to get ready to go to W.C.T.U. State Conv. tomorrow. I let hem out of dress (purple) that Mrs. Chrystal gave me & Julia Saterlee altered. Roy Hatfield got the puppy dog that was left here. So glad to have him in a good home,—friendly & playful.—"helped" me pick berries & chips—

OCT. 30. WED.	Bus to Waterloo———	1.15
	Street car "Williston" to Bapt. church	.10
	Dinner at Lamson Hotel	1.28
	Collection plate Colvin appeal	1.00
	Cab from Hotel to Church	.15
6.70		
	Collection———	.05 +
	Lodg. & breakfast (25) room 75——	1.00
	Lunch Kresge 25 + 4 apples .26	
	6 pears .30	.82
	Bus to Manchester (to farm)	1.15

Reba & I went together & roomed together. Nice day. Poor breakfast. She went before on 7:30 bus. I at 12:30. Mrs. Colvin's address was on "Courage, go forward." Attitude toward liquor traffic, as changing. Radios & Daily's are asking her for interviews & addresses. The Thank Offering was over $1200.00 & Mrs. Colvin's special appeal over $1000.00. Large auditorium of church more than filled, around 300 delegates. 250 plates at banquet best of all one table of 75 Y.T.C.'s who had charge of dinner program. [. . .]

TUES. NOV. 5. Election Day—clear & sunny. I rode with Mr. Elkins to the Ry. Station when he came for milk 5:45 A.M., only to learn the passenger train does not stop at Masonville so I walked back home thinking to go on the bus. When Julia Lane came for milk she said I could ride with Mr. & Mrs. Harte Allyn & her & Mrs. Judson Lane so I did & voted the Prohibition ticket as far as it went (State) then marked for Henry A. Talle, U.S. Rep., & for Mr. Senz. for Sheriff. We attended the Cemetery Ass'n. luncheon in the Methodist Wes-lyan Hall @ 60¢ a plate. I bought a plate for Henry & 45¢ of brown bread, beans, & pieces (5) of pie—lemon & 4 pumpkin. $1.65. Harte Allyn gave me a check for 10.00 for W.C.T.U. I picked all the huckleberries after got home 2:30, hard white frost last night & *cool* to night. Saw Frank Sullivan 90 yrs & 3 mos. of age, old neighbor of years agone. Henry did not go, worked on fence & slept. It worries me to have him failing. Reba went to Seattle, Wash., Sun. night at 11:00 to son Lester. [. . .]

TUES. NOV. 14. To town—rode with Mrs. Gibbs & back with Mrs. Hoffmann. Called on & collected dues for W.C.T.U. . . . Henry had on
Nov. 6, 1946 deposited 190.00 in the Bank on my acct without my
knowledge. I could scarcely believe it & asked him. He said it was
what I had sent him in 1933 that he put in P.O. & int. & he thought
I would rather have it in the bank. Beautiful day. [. . .]

SUN. DEC. 1. Colder but clear. Bull tore evergreen tree about to pieces
yesterday & again today. It grieves me to have things I've bought to
try to make a home for Henry, destroyed. The side-delivery rake I pd
130.00 for has stood in slough for 2 mos. most the time in water.
Now I must try to get a stove to heat more than the little cookstove.
Henry says we'll have to have more heat, but refuses to say what or
how. [. . .]

MON. DEC. 16. Mr. Kline set up heater & cook stove in middle room.
Victor McCarthy came in evening to clean oil heater in my room. Pd
him 3.00 for it & gave him $2.00 bonus for his trying to clean it 2
yrs ago. Snow flurries. [. . .]

WED. 25. DEC. 1946. Christmas, wrote letters, etc. the day, a pleasant
day,—a wind just a little chilly. [. . .]

1947

[. . .]

THURS. JAN. 9. To Mont. Ward for pail & pan. 2.33 +.11   2.44
To Nat'l Voice for sub. to Mrs. Ruthenberg & books   5.00
To Hawley Society dues Southburg Com.   1.00
 A nice winter day.—snow about gone, sun bright. cleaned up desk
of letter writing for most part. [. . .]

THURS. JAN. 23. Walked to town, rode part way back with Will Scanlan. . . . It helps much these past several months since Henry eats
more regularly 3 times daily. He makes queer remarks now & then
but not every day. Says it keeps me in better balance to go somewhere. Says if I want to get out & walk to go up on the hill instead
of to town or neighbors; doesn't look well to see a woman walking in
road, has been told by one of my best friends that all that ails me is
my mind, not my back,—a secret told to him, etc. He has gone to
Howard Scanlan's 20th wedding anniversary this evening. Snow
nearly gone, muddy. [. . .]

FEB. 26. WED. Have been working on Academy record & doing the
daily round. See Acct book for February & 25 yesterday went on bus
to W.C.T.U. Institute in Baptist Society, joined it. A group of bird

lovers & Home spirit. Chilly wind. Groceryman brought me & groc. home. The last time (Feb. 21) I was 1 3/4 hrs in Dentist chair from 11 : 15 on, tired, no lunch & started home vs. *strong, cold* west wind, carrying mdse & holding hat on. too much. Clarence Boardway overtook me from near Lanes so rode a little way. Thankful. Heart pumping & palpating when got in house. Will not do that again. [. . .]

MARCH 14, 1947. Have been working on Academy (1879–1882) record & making a scrap album of clippings, photographs of students & Kissell, Butler, Randall & Mrs. Webster, & typed considerable & pasted in. Jno. Arbuckle sent letter & his autobiography, from Waterloo. His wife died Feb. 8 & he is broken & lonely. I know,—my sympathy goes out to him.

Have done the daily round of duties & cleaned the down-stairs rooms except for the shop. The weather has been mild for the most part with rain & much water. It is frozen this morning. Henry got $4.39 groceries yesterday & meat. He does not find so much fault as he always has daily the past 10 years & he eats more regularly 3 times daily. Instead of sitting down at the table at any minute during the day & saying "I'm ready to eat now" he waits until called most the time.

He smells as he does every winter,—puts on drawers & does not take them off or change until spring or summer & they are black & in shreds. And he has not bathed for four years that I know of, for he said he hadn't for 3 yrs. a year ago last fall. He combs his hair before eating for the first time this winter since I've been here. He got some apples & fried cakes to treat the thresher crew who are to meet here soon,—saying he wants to make them feel good when they go away. He says he wants everyone to know how kind he is to me. He does not say he has been abusive,—denies it but he hisses at times that sounds exactly like a serpent.

He did not so long ago when I remarked that Mr. & Mrs. Rule would enjoy the near-by roadhouse. He said she caused her father sorrow by marrying a jail thief; "mean, cruel, wicked,—lust of the flesh." He, of course, inferred the same to me as he has so many times because I married at all. He was determined I shouldn't marry at all. [. . .]

APR. 17. Stamps 40¢. 30 addresses to Ethel Hubler. I have been & still am working on old Academy record all spare time 2 mo's. No use to chronicle the usual household work: mop, sweep, mend, wash the dishes; put things in order, bake, etc., etc. Weather chilling only 2 or 3 warm days. Much rain, slough full all the time. [. . .]

SUN. JUNE 22. Has not rained except light shower for this the 3rd day. Wrote letters & wrapped Records I have compiled ready to mail. [. . .]

SAT. JUNE 28. This week I have put in potatoes, sw. corn, radishes, peas & beans & hoed the garden, cut 30 large thistles today out of E. alfalfa field (*overheated & tired*) so very warm. Englehorn served Henry a dirty deal after all arranged to cut alfalfa & hay came this A.M. & tried to put him off & finally said he couldn't do it. It is ready in full bloom nice & heavy crop. Cyclonic storm this evening. Sent Hawley Record to Conn. State Library. [. . .]

THURS. JULY 3. *Rain on alfalfa. Too bad, too bad.* Cleared by 10 A.M. Bus to Dr. Byer & ret. 40¢. daily 5. thread 20¢. 1 yd. calico 60¢. pr. combs 50¢. tax 2¢. candy 10. bananas 61¢. hair washed & pins .10 .55. Drew from bank 15.00. lunch .30. Got my watch at Lewis. no charge.

FRI. JULY 4. Mend 5 suits winter underwear & make an apron. Rainy. Mrs. Rann call to see about Audubon picnic. [. . .]

MON. NOV. 3. Henry sold the horses, 8 & 9 yrs. old and only halter broke. I knew when they were 2 & 3 yrs. old he wl'd never train or use them but said nothing. I would have hired a trainer & sold them then, cried to see them go, Prince large Percheron & intelligent & gentle. Dapple gray. Daisy, bay, the other nervous & flighty & ever afraid. It is wisest to let them go on a/c of feed & care. Would have been wiser my way of thinking, if had long ago. I do not know who got them nor what received. The Rendering truck was here a few days ago & maybe they will be humanely killed. Things like this are very disagreeable to me. Rake & put leaves around little peach trees & etc. in garden. Do very little on Baker record. Did not accomplish much today. A day like May,—beautiful, sunny & warmer. Hauled one load of wood from wood yard saw mill.

TUES. NOV. 4. Dark, chilly day. Slept little last night thinking abt. the horses.—Prince looking wistfully for food asking with lips on my hand, & pawing the gate. Poor dumb beast! Got ready to go to Audubon Soc. in P.M. waited 20' for bus at gate, began to rain & concluded to stay at home.—I slept an hour this forenoon. Henry naps both A.M. & P.M. he said he hated to see the horses go. Did nothing outside & little inside. Colder wave. [. . .]

1948

THURS. JAN. 1ST. New Year's Day. Blizzard. I bring in & saw old boards etc. Usual work, do a little on record & write letters, put Temperance papers & Prohibition platform in to mail tomorrow. Hope do some good. [. . .]

FRI. JAN. 30. Not accomplish much. The living room is too dark. Keep my room closed days to save oil. Chilly. I bring in old boards & saw enough for kindling for mornings every day. [. . .]

SUN. FEB. 1. Beautiful day, warmer. I worked on Baker Record, read the History of Bean Creek Valley & made notes to copy. [. . .]

TUES. FEB. 3. Typed 80 "Kitchen Shower" lists for Mrs. Chrystal. She brought a doz. eggs. I have a lame back. Henry says its a shame to have furniture—infers again to dispose of dining set. He complains of my not using the pressure cooker to cook meat in. Wants John Daker to come here. Daker wants to. . . . [. . .]

THURS. FEB. 5. wrote to the "Doolittle House" to see if could get info on Gillespie record. Henry wanted to know if I thought of going there. I said I had not thought of so doing. He read the material they sent & remarked their discipline was like a poison; later saying it would be a nice place to live among those old ladies. I said that would be a great note for me that I had a house here a 1/2 interest same as he,—that I wished Pa had left it as he & Ma intended. He said I could have the west 50 or the East fifty whichever I wanted. It made me feel not at home he suggestion [*sic*].

FRI. FEB. 6. I didn't get to sleep until 3 A.M. He asked why & I said I was thinking of his suggestion abt. my going to that home. He denied it & raved, stomping his foot. I am sorry I said anything abt. it & kept still. It paralyzes my ~~neve~~ nerves to see him so mad & the spirit. It is terrorizing to me. I felt as though my legs would go out from under me. Guess better not tell him everything abt. the family tree project,—or—I do try to keep still for he always taboos everything I do, or say. I rested a little while; I overheard Mr. Wolf & Henry talking so I think he is to rent the farm land. I will be glad when through here. [. . .]

WED. JULY 7. 83 yrs. ago this A.M. at 5:00 Ma welcomed me into her heart & home,—a homely prematurely born with twin bro. died. Helped Mrs. Chrystal what I could to clean the middle room. She washed the walls & ceiling. Not so hot as yesterday, but plenty warm. Rec'd. Birthday letters & cards,—Abiah, Evelyn, Jimmie D., Evelyn, Howard, & Anna, Mrs. Ruthenberg. Thankful for friendships, for life & its manifold blessings. [. . .]

SEPT. 4. Henry 85 today, working on the spring above R.R. Mr. Wolfe & son helping.

THURS. AND FRI. 3RD. SAT. 4TH. As above. I've been going through old U.I.U. School scrap book material, photos, etc. & bake as usual, etc. Had a heavy rain Tuesday night. Pleasant weather,—fall is before us. [. . .]

TUES. SEPT. 30. making green tomato preserves. Didn't get to sleep last night until after 3.00 o'clock. Up at 5.30. Clear & cold. needs a fire. I guess I'm getting indignant. Henry says I need a guardian. What next! guardian. "use force." Old-fashioned Millers rec'd. receipt for whole wheat flour. [. . .]

WED. OCTOBER 1. Henry go to Waterloo on bus in morning 9:25. Reba came to spend the day. She & I rebuilt the kitchen door steps & hauled 4 loads (little wagon) chips & chunks from sawmill lot. Put on 2 storm windows & visited. I had just finished 4 pts tomato preserve & had hat on to go out doors to work when the bus came. I put the sheep in & fed & watered the calves. Fall day—cool. [. . .]

FRI. OCT. 3. *Following a foot treatment, Sarah's infected foot was gradually healing.* When I told Henry what Dr. Byer said about my foot he scolded me to keep off of it, have "no sense or judgment" etc. last evening after came home. And this morning again & said I was "off" & had always been; that Pa & Ma knew it. I made myself brave to say that wasn't so and that he had twitted me about my mind for ten years; that there was not 3 days running in which he did not until I got tired of it, & that he has called me everything but a decent woman since my being here. I said he was as "off" as was I; that it was shameful disgrace to have the attitude toward each other as we do. He insisted I am willfully stubborn not to do a lot of things that I could & it wouldn't hurt me a bit. He threatened selling the farm & he go his way & I go mine. It is a pitiful state of affairs only the two & on the old home farm where I came to make a home for him as he never married or had a home. I've tried very hard to provide for the house in every way, & have worked outside until I actually fell down. I shall continue praying that all will yet be well. made preserves—watermelon 4 pts. can 2 qts, Jonathan apples & 3 pts. huckleberries—hope they keep. Chilly wind. [. . .]

WED. OCT. 14. trim black raspberry bushes, & prune grape vines, scatter manure on garden, gather limbs & rubber tires off E. lot along road fence. Beautiful day,—too nice to stay in. Break a lot of Kindling, cleaned the henhouse,—a hard big job, have 5 bu. droppings & put on the garden. And so am very tired,—fatigued. Pleasant. [. . .]

SAT. OCT. 17. When I started to close the henhouse door, Henry said not; he had a sheep & lamb in there. I was so surprised I exclaimed

"My," at which he blew up. I tried to answer but no use; he looked very ugly & threatened to sell the farm, etc., so I kept still, all in a tremble,—seemed as though paralyzed & would fall. I just prayed. I had worked very hard to clean & repair the henhouse,—not only tired but fatigued, & the sheep knock nests, feed rack & everything to pieces,—hard for me to repair. I think many times I will have to leave,—think he would be happier for me to be away. I have spent 13 yrs; 4000.00 in money, and a lot of work & seemingly to no avail in trying to make a home for him. I am beginning to question if it was, & is, a duty. [. . .]

THURS. NOV. 25. Thanksgiving Day. Pa died 39 yers. ago this morning also Nov. 25. Usual work—all days alike it would seem. Dark. Dues to S.U.I. Alumni 3.00. stamps 1.00   4.00

Rains a drizzle but not cold. I wrote letters & little else.[4] Henry chore. [. . .]

FRI. DEC. 24. 1948. mopped, cleaned doors & etc. tidied up. Took all forenoon. The threshing crew met here in afternoon, came at 1:00. Belle Scanlan came so we visited. Beautiful winter day. Not thawing.

SAT. DEC. 25. 10 above zero, clear & bright, write letters & usual work. Seems like Sabbath. Ed Lane brought box—cake, etc. [. . .]

MON. DEC. 27. . . . Baby card announcing birth of John Leslie Huftalen, born Dec. 16, 1948, 10:37 A.M. Far Rockaway, N.Y. 1st child of Agnes & George Huftalen. 6 lb. 6 oz. 2017 Cornaga Ave. This will insure the Huftalen line if he lives & eventually has a home.[5] Cold.

FRI. DEC. 31. Copy Baker data to send to Eugene [Baker]. Cold. Last day of year.

1949

WED. MARCH 30. strong chilling wind & rain all day until nearly 5:00 P.M. Wind continuing Prepared cans for canning but Henry thought to wait so did not. I put some of Ma's items together & indexed it.

"Excerpts from diary with my quotations thereon, also Educ. & Industries of Emily E. Hawley; Accounts from 1858 to 1885; Her scrapbook clippings 1858 on, began with a clipping of 1858 Message of Queen Victoria over Atlantic Cable, poems & articles she had saved, & copies of pieces Henry spoke when a young boy "I Remember" & "Carry the News to Hiram," also a prisoner's poem to his mother because of crime committed by liquor (sad & pathetic selection)." [. . .]

WED. APR. 6TH. Collect & read my Oneida School a/c book & the scrapbook of the Column I edited during the 5 1/2 years I taught there.[6] At this distance it sounds like a book and if published might be helpful to teachers. Henry to town.

I wrote to Retha Wright Baker data & song, motto, etc. Windy but sunny. Grass turning green. [. . .]

MON. APRIL 11. . . . Rake grass, etc., beds & around asparagus row & grapes. Warm. Sort papers, mend on blanket for Henry's bed. This is Ma's birthday. Wolf sowing oats west field. Henry help. Meadow lark has nest East of house. [. . .]

AUG. 1949. State Agr. Society under control & management of I.S. Ag. Coll. Forestry Dept. at Ames, Iowa. I do not know what will come of it but I did not think they were very favorably impressed,—will take it up with the Forestry Dept.

Beautiful day. Henry to town get groceries. The State Ag. has just rec'd. via Emma Brayton will, 310 acres of timber so they are all thinking & planning about it. [. . .]

MON. AUG. 8. Finish picking corn in garden except 4 ear. Dry it on platters = 1 qt. Cut grass with sickle, usual work. Very warm today. Henry & 4 men haying on alfalfa field. [. . .]

MON. AUG. 15. Type all day on Gillespie record.[7] Henry is pitching over 7 tons of hay & opening 169 bales to keep from combustion. He gets fagged out. Up at 4:00 worked in hay, then milking & chores & breakfast at 10:00 then slept 2 or 3 hours. He has been at the hay several days—mow, beams & all over has hay he's pitched over. I went after the cows—at 5:00 P.M. [. . .]

THURS. NOV. 17. Henry get groc. the 1st of the week 8.95. Finish Devotion Index for 336 pages—8 pages of it. Henry go to town to get rubber boots. Colder.

Geo. Browning called Mon. to talk about our giving the farm to the State Forestry Dept. of Agr. College at Ames. I do now know what arrangement could be made & it may be an unwise act. Do some mending etc. Henry is very anxious to arrange with the State Agr. Society in connection with Forestry Dept. I. S. Ag. Coll. to have our farm given as a perpetuity with security as a memorial to our parents. The points I noticed in Mr. Browning's talk were like this if I understood correctly. The farm would be an experimental farm of various things including perhaps some trees. When the farm was brought to its maximum possibilities it w'ld be sold & another bought elsewhere by the state also for experimental purposes.

They would want to operate the farm on a paying basis—"Possibly some plan could be brought about & arrangements made."

The more I think & pray over the proposed project the more skeptical & reluctant I become to think of parting with our farm as a gift to the state or anyone.

We are not in debt but we are not financially able. Pa said the day he & I visited all day—the day before he passed away for us to "live on, rent, or sell it, he was through with it."

Henry says it needs 2000.00 now to repair & paint & put the farm in needed shape—fences & buildings. He thinks the state would do this. He has little concept of what it costs to keep house in bare necessities. [. . .]

1950

SAT. FEB. 25. Distellate oil of Farm Service—

I nearly swooned over after building the fire & sweeping off the steps. *no pulse beat* & then very it was fast [*sic*]. I have had always a slow pulse, was bothered all day as tho would go over. didn't do much. Sent a number of previously written letters & cards with data to Eugene etc. Cold.

SUN. FEB. 26. Henry built fires this morning. I rest the day & pulse getting more normal. he went to town yesterday & got groceries 10.49¢. I do some house chores—empty slops & keep oil stove going, bring in oil was about all. Began Fri. to take heart Vitamin B. complex, swept my room, & etc. Snow last night again.

MON. FEB. 27. Do usual work. Henry built fires this morning. I take care of my stove. Beautiful sunshine but cold. I asked him to criticize the Gillespie record as I want to send it to State Archives at Lansing, Mich. He said the worst thing was the name Huftalen in it & he wanted it left out—the greatest disgrace that had ever come into our family; the worst thing that ever happened to me etc. etc. He was terribly upset. I kept still, & as always pray to God my refuge. I tremble all over when he is so irate. There never was any disgrace in our family. Our home was a most unhappy one, Ma living in constant fear and dread of Pa. He was abusive; they incompatible. There is no good in harboring bitternesses, losses, hate. rained last night. [. . .]

SAT. APRIL 1ST. Work on record some. Mr. McComb & Mr. Lee, Ames College Forestry professors called in late P.M. 5:00. Yesterday stood outside to talk with Henry who did not invite them in. I finally went to the door & did so. Mr. McComb came inside & we talked about the campus & the proposition Henry seems determined on that our farm shall go to the I.S. Ag. C. to be entirely planted to trees; for us to receive an annuity "enough to keep us from going to the poorhouse." Mr. McComb said they had no money,—couldn't say what an annuity would be at all. Said we could will it, that then they could buy another farm suitable for forestry; that this section was more suitable for agricultural purposes. Mr. Lee would have come in, too, but Henry made no move for him to & continued stating his wish etc. about his wanting the farm in forestry for a memorial to Pa. Pa said to me the day before he passed away for us to "live on it; rent it, or sell it." & I think he was right. Henry ignores me altogether & this morning "didn't see why I didn't keep the range magazine filled with coal, that I could do a lot of things as hard etc. Probed to the nth degree about my arms etc. If I "were an invalid better go to bed or to the hospital."

APRIL [?] 1950. Has kept speaking & questioning about my arms— "use my left one & hard to work with," "there are exercises to strengthen the hands," "Have an x-ray," "what's the matter with you anyway?" It takes a lot of prayer & grace to endure. A tremor comes over me when he begins these probings, what ailed me. "that man influenced me against him."

I said then to disabuse his mind of that thought for Billie never said aught against him in any way, that the only thing he ever said was that Henry liked to read. I am sorry he is so bitter, can feel it. This time I did not let it affect me.—should these fears & tremors continue it would eventually paralyze me. It has already begun in my feet so I pray to keep close to my Divine refuge.—

Did not accomplish much other than usual work. Neighbor men came P.M. & sawed the pile of boards I had gathered last summer & I was so glad almost to joy—have wanted wood to burn so long. It is rotted some but makes quick fire so good to get supper with. *no carbon.* [. . .]

THURS. JUNE 22. Elmer Kehrli stop after 9:00 P.M. to pick up my gift of a doz. qt. jars for the "shower" for Dean Walston & bride this evening. Mrs. Hoffman & LaVerne Bockenstedt also call to offer to take it & us.[8] We did not go. Shoes—Ground Grippers—received from Des Moines store, "Heggers"—512 Walnut. [. . .]

WED. JUNE 28. Heggers Shoe Store, Des Moines, for shoes. check 13.41. Wilma Kehrli stopped for me to attend Presbyterian Ladies

Henry Gillespie, ca. 1950. Courtesy of Wilbur Kehrli.

Club at Howard Scanlans 2–5 P.M. Sat. 3 hrs. & was tired & knew so few. . . . [. . .]

FRI. JULY 7TH. Mrs. Chrystal brought washing and mopped floors— my foot so painful yesterday—little sleep & still so sore & aching. Treatment severe, too. Beautiful day.

The neighbors gave me a surprise Birthday shower, spent the P.M., served ice cream and cake, cards, hdkfs, towels, aprons, candy, stationery, pretty & useful.[9] Mrs. Geo. Chrystal, Mrs. Howard Scanlan, Retta Scanlan, Julia Satterle, Frances Squires, Mrs. Geo. Skinner, Mrs. Ed. Hoffman, Mrs. Leslie Gibbs, Mrs. Ward Walston, Mrs. Dean Walston, Mrs. Geo. Skinner, Mrs. Ray Jaycox, Mrs. W. N. Bawden, Mrs. Frank Beye, Mrs. Ed Lane, Mrs. John Herman, Mrs. Earl

Sarah with her friends and neighbors at her eighty-fifth birthday party, July 7, 1950, on the Gillespie farm. Sarah is at front left, Reba Bushnell at front center, and Wilma Kehrli at back right. Courtesy of LaVerne Bockenstedt.

Kehrli, Mrs. Elmer Kehrli, Mrs. Chas. Bockenstedt. Each one gave a greeting card & a gift. Reba wrote a lovely letter as she couldn't be here. Members of the Audubon Society sent cards. Also lovely letter from Marie Ruthenberg, cards from Mrs. Jake Gearhart & Mrs. Vernon Gearhart, Eva Cloud, Mr. & Mrs. Wayne Bushnell, Jimmie Burbridge, Mrs. Leslie Gibbs.

It was very nice of them. Beautiful day. [. . .]

SUN. JULY 23RD. Foot so painful until 1:00 o'c. I got up & renewed the cold pack, not seem to help. And today I'm keeping off of it all can after putting beans in closet (now pantry) shelf, & morning work. The soreness & aching seem to center in the ball & under the toes with terrific torturing, griping, dagger-like stabs. But on the whole it is improving for those pains were all through the foot & toes & the swelling goes down & comes up in instep, not so much in the leg only by spells, & no cramps under knee. I typed a letter to C. G. Salisbury, Supt. of the Ganado Mission, Arizona. *Came near fainting away* & steeped cup of postum, feel better but shaky. [. . .]

WED. 30. AUGUST. Mrs. Hoffman brought 4 pieces of chicken Mon, all ready to fry. Some yet. It is cold enough to have fire. Foot continues improving but painful yet. Work on I.S.T.A. Rural Section material. [. . .]

SAT. SEPT. 2. Cleaning up desk, answering letters, etc. Slept an hour in forenoon. Some typing & some pasting photos & pictures of Rural Section. Beautiful day & I "shut-in" 6 mo's! I did cry yesterday—a long siege of pain. I cannot believe it will get well. It is so good of Mrs. Hoffman to take me to the Dr. & good of him to bring me home. Henry rode back with him yesterday. [. . .]

MON. SEPT. 4. Henry 87 today. I had no present this time. Same last night—little sleep, but foot no worse. Less pains in day except big toe & joint & 3 small toes. Soreness on ball continues. Right foot continues swollen on top. So I put both feet in cold pack every night. I work on I.S.T.A. about finished. Beautiful day. [. . .]

FRI. SEPT. 8. Mr. Jordison came to see about repairing henhouse & I told him to do it & I would pay for it. I slept from ten until after 5 first time in 27 wks. Mrs. Hoffman took me to Dr. Byers. He brings me home. Swelling on right foot painful. Treatment painful on both feet. So thankful no worse. Beautiful day but cool, so cool. Accomplish nothing today. [. . .]

THURS. SEPT. 14. Mrs. Chrystal took me to see the "Centennial" Parade, bought carrots, cabbage, beets, and tomatoes. I canned 3 pts. tomatoes. Nice day. [. . .]

SAT. SEPT. 30. Mr. Scanlan brought me to the Memorial Hospital at 1:45 or 2:00 P.M. at the treatment at Dr. Byers Friday A.M. he said he didn't like the looks of the toe next to the little one on the left foot. It was very dark purple, swollen & looked like a big blister on end. He took me home & at 4:30 came for me to meet Dr. Willard for counsel. I thought they were thinking to amputate it but Dr. Willard said he thought there was a chance to save it, & in a few days could tell if amputate it & possibly a part of the foot. So the Dr. took me back home.

Pain began early March; went on painful foot 10 wks, then to Willett & Becker & Waterloo to no avail. Then to Dr. Byers. The pain & soreness have been beyond describing.—Many sleepless nights; near fainting & agony. Swollen to knee etc. Dr. Byers telephoned and made arrangements Fri. evening to send me to Iowa City Monday morning. This I dreaded & prayed to God not to go there.

Sat. morning he sent Miss Lewis to bring me to Mem'l. Hospital. I was writing my will & told her I must get dinner for Henry. [. . .]

SUN. NOV. 5, 1950. Still on the bed, foot much better, not swollen, less soreness & burning; fewer sliver-like pains, needle & pin pricks, & so thankful have had none of those terrible spasmodic, jerking pains for 2 wks today. The Dr. & the Lord be praised. I voted yesterday in absentia. Mrs. Byers notary pub. posting the ballot for Tues. 7th. Archie & Vining Hawley, my dearest cousins came yesterday to see Henry & me, from Webberville, Mich. Have many visitors & many flowers. Indian Summer all of Oct. I love it. [. . .]

MON. NOV. 20. It sure is a paradox to come to the Hospital well & regular except for foot affliction & then to be sick for over a week. It is my fault to have physically sinned to try to eat indigestable viands,— paying the penalty !!! now. . . . Stomach feels as though had had a hard time but is on the mend. Have sat up nearly all day on the bed. Wrote letters. Sent to Montg. Ward for Henry a coat, moleskin kind with lambskin. Beautiful day after snow last night. 10 above zero. Thankful to feel stronger. Have lost some flesh. [. . .]

1951

MON. 8 JAN. 1951. I am at the Home of Jane. . . .[10] My ankles almost broke when came in the uneven snow path. Dr. Byers supported me, ankles extremely painful but better too. Reba gets the meals & takes care of the furnace. Jane is at Del. Co. Mem'l. Hospital from 3 P.M. until 11:00 P.M. daily. Reba came from San Diego to be with me. 18 below zero. She went to farm & surprised bringing my bed, clothes, & commode, and stuff to work on. I slept well, awake from 3 & 4 first time have not slept all night. She brought comforts from farm. . . . Reba went to town, got cooking & table utensils, dishes, etc. [. . .]

FRI. JAN. 12. Type a few pages on I.S.U. material that Mongold demanded to lay on his desk both before & after classes in Gen. Psychol, App. Psych., Sources, Projects, Hist. of Educ. VIII, Princ. Methods.

Dr. Byers came A.M., gave treatment all over. Beautiful winter day. Whole body racked getting into house.

SAT. JAN. 13. Back, legs, ankles & feet aching so laid down a considerable, a dark, damp, foggy day. Mr. Hoffman brought Henry this forenoon. He brought 2 pts my canned tomatoes, 2 cans pears, 1 can pickles apples, & 1 can ? also 2 qts. of milk. He looks well. He spoke abt. the farm for forestry. I told him what McComb told me & that I was not in accord to give it to the state. He said he had $1000.00 saved. I told him that wouldn't go very far if he were hospitalized. I also told him as I have before that Pa said we could "have it & live on it, rent it, or sell it" & I think Pa was right. There are other ways to make memorials. We may sorely need the farm. McComb told me to will it to the state if we do wished. Then they would sell it, buy another, put a tenant on what they bought, bring it up to standard & sell it.

Our farm is not a tree-growing farm but grain growing, he said. [. . .]

WED. JAN. 17. Toe painful again 2 hrs. early morning before seven. Jane has gone to work at 2:30 & Reba to town at noon. Sunshine and beautiful & warmer. I sent pkg. mail by Reba. Peterson, Ia. Cy., my hist. of Rural Section I.S.T.A. 1909–1910. Clippings to Mrs. Chas. Chamberlain who loaned them to me; 200 Christmas cards to Piney Woods School, gave her 2.00 for postage.

Maggie Schmidt Evans called & brought cactus blossoms. Rec'd. beautiful card & letter from Mattie Duffey, & letter from Ensign. I wrote Henry yesterday, also Forestry Dept., Ames. [. . .]

FEB. 15, 16. Sorting & organizing data. Type some. It has been a long, painful siege for me. Jan. 6, 1951, came [to the] home of Jane, at 35.00 rent per month, no arrangement to furnish meals, gas, or other. She told Reba she was to have 2 meals and pay for gas. Nothing said to me. Will not have trouble with her but will change to betterment when can. I am thankful to be here, rooms pleasant. Reba keeps our part, gets meals & puts coal in furnace. The Dr. comes once a week—on Fridays, my feet are no worse, ankles still painful but better. That was a terrible painful; body-breaking thing to get into the house over that rough snow, after not walking for 3 months in hospital, fog, rain, snow. [. . .]

THURS. IST MARCH 1951. Not accomplish much, wrote letters. Reba to town with Eunice & husband. He has piles, too. Her daughter Helen came & they visit in the car.[11] Icy & colder. My ankles least painful yet. [. . .]

MON. APR. 9. Bathed in forenoon & washed hair, tired me out to have to lie down. But it was 2 wks & I did so want & need it & clean clothes. Reba wash my underwear & hose & her things. She went to town. Beautiful but cooler. Abbie Hennessey call, sells monuments. Reba to town. [. . .]

MON. JUNE 11 & TUES. JUNE 12. Reba came this evening Mon. after supper. Helen (her dau.) brought her from Cedar Rapids. She wash her clothes, bathe, etc. etc. until 11 o'c. then at noon go to Cedar Rapids with Mary Ortberg & Mrs. Putnam to get tickets to California. I type & organize Gillespie Record (finish typing so now will punch holes to string in a scrap book cover). There are 77/8 pp. single space. Nice warmer (yet cool) day. Heavy shower 4:30 to 6:00 A.M.

WED. JUNE 13. Reba says when she comes back from Calif. she "is going straight to Cedar Falls to work at the College Commons. Says she will come down often & if I am as well as now she is not needed here. I am hoping & trusting but somehow it saddens me.

I finished typing Gillespie Record & am anxious to get all things cared for, my toe is no worse.—scales off & sore but better—using Iodex.

Beautiful day all day. Reba at Blosches for supper, was at Ritz for Beulah Ludley shower—home 12:30 midnight. I am tired, fingers bother (stiff) some. Letter from Henry abt. Gillespie record. [. . .]

SAT. JULY 7. 86 yrs. today. I went with Gretchen to her garden out at "Uncle Henry Bakers Inn house where we so loved to go.[12] She gave me beans, beets and lettuce. We stopped at the gate & Henry happened to be out for the mail. I gave him some papers & a banana. Gretchen gave him 2 onions and lettuce. He is haying—baled w. field, 2 men helping. He is old & looks worn, I do pray some way present itself so he can stop. I was very tired, typed a few pages only. Warm. Sat in car 2-1/2 hrs, hot sun, picked white clover. [. . .]

SUN. JULY 15. Make, or rather put together Family scrap book, Pa & Henry & some of mine, & made excerpts of my diaries of 1877, 78, 79, 80, 81, 82, only kept in 2 books. Pretty mussy, quill pen & walnut, & purple, & red inks, many drawings of dresses, wrap, hood, apron, etc.—warm today. Jane gone to Winthrop.

MON. JULY 16. Henry came this A.M., but not time to come in. He looks poor & unkempt & uncared for. I couldn't help crying & have accomplished nothing today. I wish I could buy a place here but if I did he might not come & live in it. He looks so old & feeble; it is pitiful to live the way we are while going down the valley from which there is no return. I thought I could make a home for him, was all the thought I had in mind & heart when I came there, June 1935. It was too strenuous an undertaking after 70. I did my best. . . . [. . .]

WED. AUG. 1ST. Heart still bothering a little this morning. Did a little yesterday morning after May [Mead Ryan] phoned for me,—Sldnt have but guess was overjoyed at going [to May's home]. Rested some. Mrs. Fred Traver call until 6 P.M., so we had beef & noodle soup & crackers & were satisfied. [. . .]

MON. SEPT. 3. Type some. Jane has today (Labor Day) off so is here. Her sister doing her washing will be glad when I can leave here. She said my towel smelled. One was not yet used & the other I washed yesterday also the wash cloth = pure imagination. She is a queer body to live with. I am tired so not accomplish much.

TUES. SEPT. 4. Henry 88 today. I wrote him. Mrs. Camadus came & got 23 more of the [M.E.] booklets & pd. me $4.00. I gave her a receipt. I sorted photographs so as to get some ready for Henry to keep & some to send to relatives, etc. Mr. Reth brought some green corn to Jane. She had the Dr's sign washed off his window by the cleaners while he was away on vacation & she is worried about it. I pray she keeps her job.

SAT., SEPT. 8. Typed 28 pp of Ma's Diary. I rec'd. letter from Frances Waugh, Ruth's dau. It contained 2 cloths religiously anointed to wear in slippers for seven days. Acts · . She is very religious "Christ is coming soon." says 7 is the Lord's number of healing. I rec'd. it the 6th & tears came to know someone thought of me in such a way. She said & told of cases who were thus cured. I've held it & said it a thousand thousand times. "The prayer of faith will cure the afflicted. The Great Physician is ever near & God cures all diseases, heals all wounds. But we must remove the causes & cooperate. To be in fear & dread all of the time will thwart God's purpose. I shall ever think such constant nerve strain caused Ma's paralysis & early death. It causes hardening of the arteries etc. Article on "worry &   " in the "Today's Health" explains this fully. There is a limit to strength & endurance.

It is not pleasant for me here & I want to change if can better myself. The room & convenience could not be better but a temperamental person who has hallucinations to live in with is not the best. Henry wrote a most plausible sounding letter to arrange for me to come to the farm. But I have grave fears & no desire to try to live there again & in the condition I am in. [. . .]

FRI. SEPT. 14. Treatment. letter from Henry last Saturday proposing to modernize the house & put in repair. It makes me sad, I should like to be home but am not strong enough to do the needed work & no one to live with us to do it. Dr. Byer says I must not go there for I would get back as if the way with this affliction, caused by being on nerve strain etc. I surely was weary & worn from fear of not doing enough & nothing to please Henry & I tried so hard with making myself entirely subservient in every way. It's pretty hard to be mocked & told you could do things if you wanted to when you are using every atom of strength willingly and trying so hard. It is pitiful my marriage so embittered & upset him.[13]

I asked advice of the Dr. He says better to stay here in pleasant & convenient rooms than to change. I had decided although it would be less expense. . . . [. . .]

TUES. SEPT. 18. finish copying Book 3—of Ma's Diary to Aug. 18, 1865, covers our births & all daily happenings & doings. I am tired. Pleasant day. Cool morning. [. . .]

SAT. OCT. 27. Jane abusive, said I lied that she had proof of my telling some (didn't name) she was lazy said so much I cried; my legs shook; it was a terrific thing I couldn't endure so abusive. She put her arm out & said "In the name of the Lord etc," & wanted me to same way. I replied we were in the presence of the Lord all the time. She took my bowl of oatmeal, dried it on dish towel, & put it in plastic dish & set it in refrigerator. I see she was mad & then she surely did say very abusive language. I didn't accomplish anything all day thinking what to do. Several have said she was lazy but I never have & have defended her; it seems as though she has few friends & my sympathy & love has gone out to her but I fear I will have to move. Beautiful day but too cool without any fire from 1:00 o'clock none evening, pretty chilly. I go to bed 7 o'clock. [. . .]

THURS. DEC. 6. Reba here an hour in forenoon. Says she will retire in 3 mos. & then we will see what we can do in the spring at the farm— too late now as I was beginning to plan & prepare to put the two bedrooms in shape etc. My stomach better think it was the truss too loose. I've shortened the belt an inch—feels better. rain squall. [. . .]

TUES. DEC. 18. Began to rewrite will in P.M. put little disks to reinforce record of Hawley. Mr. Nieman came & put ribbon on typewriter.[14] Thanks. Reba sent 6 boxes (100 ea) & Phillips 3 boxes stickers @ 5¢ each, postage 2¢ & 3¢ to pay for. Glad to have them, too dark to do but little. Reread letter rec'd. yesterday from Forestry Dept. Ames Coll. I can't think it the thing to do,—to will our farm as a gift. No knowing what we may need in care & comfort.—Expense, etc. May have to sell it for necessities. Pa said for us "to live on it, rent it or sell it, to do as we pleased with it,—he was through with it." [. . .]

TUES. 25. CHRISTMAS DAY. *deep snow.* It is nice to be remembered. Jane gone to family dinner.

May Mead Ryan	large box of fruit
Mildred & Vining	apron & head scarf (blue wool)
Mrs. Earl Kehrli	candy, fluffy slippers

Wilma Kehrli	eggs, brown bread, biscuits & cookies, apples
Mrs. Retz	cake, cookies, apples
Henry	wool slippers, too small
Kno. & Millie Herman	stationery
Ruth Hall	stationery
Jane	night gown
Eva Rector Cloud	2 cups jelly

Cards & letters scores of them from everywhere. Mrs. Strait 95 yrs the 15th of Dec.

1952

TUES. 1ST. Like Sunday, work on vol. 1, Baker Record, getting pages ready to cover—punching holes & sticking on reinforcements. Cold all day. Jane's window open last night 20 below so house got cold and did not get warm all day. She home. [. . .]

MON. JAN. 7. I came here 1 yr. ago today. Did not think would be here this long. How I long for a home of my own. I should have bought one when I went to the farm & intended to & rent it until such time as wld. need it. I wanted Henry's consent but he didn't answer at all so I dropped it. Chill & damp. [. . .]

SAT. JAN. 12. . . . I've worked on Henry's scrap book all day, typed some. from scraps about Pa's passing, will have to do over.[15] Wish could do more every day & get all in order to preserve etc. Feet & back feel much better today. I cannot lose faith & pray yet to believe will recover completely. I am badly needed to make a home for Henry. [. . .]

THURS. JAN. 17. Head feels bad yet, aching when woke up. Did a little on my personal scrap book, pasted articles I wrote also that May Mead wrote on School. . . . [. . .]

WED. MARCH 5. Beautiful day, wish I could move tomorrow. Jane ordered me to leave—says I laugh at her & that I lie. I've phoned Dr. Byer, for she has gone to her pastor for a little while. She gives me 30 days . . . poor girl. I never laughed at any one.

32883—Mrs. S. Neurotics are hard to live with. She gets an imagined idea & works her self up to a mad spell.

THURS. 6. Another beautiful day. Jane began again this morning & said she was trying to bring me to repentance & confess my sins to the Lord. I told her I had a long time ago & that every day was a repentance day. She said I better keep about moving in my mind, said how good she has been as is always her custom, etc. I told her I would move today if I had a place to go. She rented the her [*sic*] house today to Dr. Willett for his wife's folks. I have track of a place to live with an elderly woman & also an apartment 2 room & bath on ground floor. I tried to answer Jane this morning but she was so fierce & pounded the chair arm with her fist saying I lied it made me tremble. I told her to forgive me & it was my first quarrel & I would not again. She tells how good she is etc. etc. God could not change her of her mental set unless she evaporated. At 5 o'c. P.M. She brings her sister in to testify she has given me 30 days to leave. Calls me a "little devil & fibber" & wish I could leave now, hates to see me around.

Sarah added this note in the margin: "She brought her sister to swear me to leave in 30 days."

FRI. 7. . . . I paid rent yesterday to Apr. 5. 35.00 with the understanding of refund should I move before. How mad, abusive, spells wear me out. I am looking for a place all I can. There is an apartment of 3 rooms, bath, & kitchen with cupboards on the ground floor no 437 Brewer St. S. of the Ry. & a place to live in with an elderly M.E. woman on E. Main. I will take one or the other I think. Dr. B. interested. [. . .]

SAT. 15. I packed box of records, data, & genealogy material. Took diaries, books, papers etc. out of the commode & put in carton. Can't do a great deal in a day but do some & rest some. Jane says she wants a husband & to buy this place. She is very nervous & unsettled, poor girl! Wants everything her own way. It looks as tho she gave her affection to "her doctor," would go back if called.

This was the final entry in Sarah Gillespie Huftalen's diary.

Conclusion: The Diary as Cultural Text

We only learn a little from books. There are three
other sources from which we learn more:
Associates, observation, and experience. And the
beauty of it is we are learners all the way as we
journey along life's pathway. I was not blessed
with being a mother although have been called so
by a number of children who have come under
my care and training.
—Sarah Gillespie Huftalen, 1942[1]

"Why a teacher?" Sarah Gillespie Huftalen no doubt asked herself this question many times during her long career as country school teacher, county superintendent of schools, instructor of teaching methods, and supervisor of novice teachers. For Sarah, the question had no simple answer. As she wrote in 1942, she viewed teaching as a vocation, not a job. It was an opportunity to learn as well as to teach, an opportunity to set an example and to "mother" her students. Glenda Riley discusses the importance of teaching as an acceptable enterprise for nineteenth-century American women:

> Teaching, in particular, was considered a natural concomitant of women's domestic duties because of the inherent qualities that women supposedly possessed in the areas of child care and nurturing. Advocates of women as teachers stressed women's innately high character; their capacity for affection, which would make students anxious to respond to them; and maternal instincts that would allow a greater rapport with students than would be proper for the "other sex," as men were often called. On their part, women who were committed to exercising their moral responsi-

bilities, farm girls who were interested in escaping the drudgery of farm work, single women who wanted to earn money and fill time before marriage, and women who needed to support themselves and family members—all welcomed the opportunity to become teachers. (*The Female Frontier*, 103–104)[2]

For many women, teaching was not only an extension of their culturally prescribed role as conveyor of moral values, teaching was also a practical career born of economic necessity. Until access to more than a common school education became available to women in the mid-nineteenth century, teaching remained a male-dominated field. During the industrial era, however, the field of teaching opened up rapidly for women, in large part because "men discovered that they could earn better pay and have steadier employment on farms and in factories, stores, and offices. As men left teaching, they created a void that women were willing to fill, so that in some prairie regions, women teachers accounted for 55 to 60 percent of the employed teachers" (Riley, *The Female Frontier*, 104).

In November 1883, when Sarah Gillespie began teaching at the District No. 1 School in Coffins Grove Township, Delaware County, Iowa, it was because she had been asked to substitute for another teacher who had unexpectedly resigned. During her years as a teacher, Sarah often found that the politics of school boards and county superintendents strongly influenced not only where she was hired to teach but also whether she was hired at all. Certainly, for Sarah, as for many other women teaching in midwestern rural schools during the late nineteenth and early twentieth centuries, teaching was not a glamorous, highly lucrative profession. In fact, female teachers were routinely paid less than their male counterparts. As Madeleine R. Grumet points out, "Lower salaries for women hardly required the myth of transience for justification. The very figures who led the common school movement and supported the employment of female teachers are on record as supporting their recruitment with the argument that they were less costly than men" (38). Wayne E. Fuller adds:

> The notion that teaching was women's work was supported, perhaps inadvertently, by the educators themselves. For years country-school directors on the Middle Border tried to employ male teachers at least for the winter school, as they were directed to at their annual school meeting. But when it became obvious that women teachers could always be employed for an average of

ten dollars less per month than men, the necessity of employing male teachers, even in the winter term, began to dim in the directors' minds and virtually disappeared when the educators themselves began to argue, sincerely or otherwise, that women were better teachers than men. (160–161)

Despite her low pay, Sarah's diary reveals that she took her work as a teacher seriously and that she saw herself as a role model who could encourage her students to excel. At the same time, she recognized that her income would provide much-needed economic support for her family, both prior to her mother's death and in the years that followed.

The country school system in which Sarah began her teaching career was based on the belief that every child was entitled to a basic common school education consisting of classes in reading, spelling, writing, history, literature, arithmetic, and geography. In Delaware County, Iowa, during the early 1880s, each of the fourteen townships organized its own country schoolhouses, and township school boards hired teachers one term at a time. When Sarah was hired in 1883, Horace G. Miller was Delaware County superintendent of schools. Teachers were required to make monthly reports to him on such subjects as the condition of school property, the comfort level of classrooms, the grading and classification of students, and the maintenance of school records (Aurner, Vol. 1, 104–105). Although townships maintained a good degree of control over daily school operations, teachers' organizations continued lobbying for compulsory attendance. Many students came to school on a sporadic basis; most country schoolhouses had only one room and one teacher, whose task was made all the more difficult by not being able to count on regular attendance on the part of the students.

Throughout her teaching career, Sarah worked hard to create a rigorous curriculum as well as a sense of community among her students and their parents. She believed in the goals outlined in the brochure that she prepared while teaching at the Arbor Vitae Summit School:

> We want to have the best school in the state, nothing short of it will satisfy us, we are determined to reach the summit of excellence that is founded on workers. We want and need supplies and apparatus. We seek your co-operation and helpfulness, such only as parent, patron and friend can give. We solicit your visitation, interest and suggestions. We are glad at all times of your counsel and advice. We thank you for all past kindly favors and expres-

sions. The parent, the pupil and the teacher form the trinity of the schoolroom—of education. Let us work together to raise its standard of excellence.

Whilst we as learners are gleaning knowledge and storing it in our minds that we may have it to use in the future that continually lies before us, so that our lives may be more useful, more worthy, such as will please Him who created us; whilst we are thus laboring to acquire understanding and wisdom and intelligence, we as pupils and teachers invite you to enjoy this school year with us in our efforts and remain yours loyally for the advancement of the individual and the betterment of all.[3]

It was during the Arbor Vitae Summit School years that Sarah began writing in earnest about her experiences as a teacher. She published newspaper articles in the Greeley, Oneida, and Manchester newspapers; she also contributed essays to *Midland Schools: A Journal of Education*, commenting on the correlation between a beautiful educational environment and effective teaching and learning. In her memoirs summing up her experience at the Arbor Vitae Summit School, Sarah spelled out the basis for her philosophy of education:

When children are happily busy and interested in a united effort in their studies, projects and games one need not worry about the so-called problem of discipline. There is none to worry about. With a beautified yard that all hands help make possible establishes interest akin to ownership. And what child does not but enjoy the sensation of ownership; his very own. Complete trusting and confidence between teacher and child serves as a strong tie when allowing the sitting on of stumps & lying on the grass to study on hot July days. ("I Remember This and That," Brown Scrapbook No. 2, Box 8, Vol. 11, Huftalen Collection)

This philosophy was to serve Sarah well throughout over fifty-two years of teaching, and it sheds light on the difficulties before her when she faced mandatory retirement in 1935 and had to return to live on the farm. Teaching had become her life; what was she to do, now that that life was over?

During her final years on the farm, Sarah turned her attention to chronicling her family history. Sarah's diary entries reveal that she worked tirelessly to compile and interpret this history. As her neighbor, LaVerne Bockenstedt, observed, "She was always typing whenever I went down there. She sat by the typewriter, and she was always typing. . . . And she told me one time, 'If you live long enough, you'll go back to your childhood' " (interview with author, August 14, 1992).

By February 1952, Sarah had finished compiling genealogical information, photograph albums, scrapbooks, and scores of typed explanatory pages. She boxed up all these materials and mailed them to the State Historical Society of Iowa (SHSI) in Iowa City. In an accompanying letter to William J. Petersen, the SHSI superintendent, dated February 25, 1952, Sarah wrote: "I am sending a carton of Historical-Genealogical materials including deeds, papers, childhood diaries that I am ashamed of, my Mother's diary from March 29, 1858 to March 24, 1888, and old almanacs, etc. today by Railway Express, C.O.D. I thank you for this privilege" (Acquisition File, Huftalen Collection).

Not quite three months later, Sarah suffered a massive stroke, which left her right side paralyzed. She was unable to write in her diary again, and she entered the Dehn Nursing Home in Manchester, where she spent the last two and a half years of her life. By August 31, 1952, however, she had recovered sufficiently to type this brief note and send it to Petersen: "A stroke May 7 1952 afflicted the entire right side, useless. please do not enlarge mistakes; i a I am beggining to try with left hand; one finger" (Acquisition File, Huftalen Collection).

As Sarah's diary reveals, she and Henry disagreed vehemently about whether the family farm should be donated to the Iowa State Agricultural College in Ames. Sarah preferred that the farm be sold to someone from the Manchester area who would continue to live on it and work it. Henry's death on July 13, 1954, made the decision Sarah's alone.[4] That September, she asked her attorney, Thomas H. Tracey, to invite Elmer and Wilma Kehrli to visit her at the Dehn Nursing Home. Then she asked the Kehrlis if they would like to buy the Gillespie farm so that their son, Wilbur Kehrli, could farm it. Wilma Kerhli relates the story of how Sarah sold her farm to the Kehrlis:

> [In her younger years, Sarah] was away from home quite a lot. That is, she went to college, and then she went to teaching. And when she was teaching, she just loved young boys and girls. She wanted to teach them the value of the farms and how to stay on the farm, and it was the root of civilization for, you know, feeding the people. In her teaching she wanted to even help the boys get so interested. Then when she got older and Henry was gone. . . . I think she must have asked the doctor if she had long to live. Then she had to have a lawyer come and get everything lined up

"Manchester Pioneer Notes 90th Birthday": Henry Gillespie's photograph in the Manchester Press, *September 1953.*

because Henry was gone, you see. . . . She wanted a young farmer to have it, and she wanted somebody that she knew to have it. . . . (interview with author, July 28, 1992)

The Kehrlis agreed to buy the Gillespie farm for $12,500.[5]

Sarah's decision to sell the farm to the Kehrlis had not been made lightly. For many years, Sarah had lived across the road from the Kehrlis. She had watched the three Kehrli children grow, and she had been especially pleased when one of Wilbur's 4-H projects yielded surprising results.

On February 22, 1952, Wilbur's sow farrowed eighteen piglets, a record size for a litter. The entire Kehrli family pitched in to bottle-feed the piglets on two-hour shifts, and all eighteen survived and thrived. The August 1952 issue of the *Farmers Hybrid Hogs* featured Wilbur's eighteen pigs and quoted his mother, Wilma Kerhli, on her part in the project: "I have lost more sleep with this litter of pigs than I did with all three of my children, but it was worth it to see the boy succeed" (4). After a year, he sold the hogs for $100 per head. The $1,800 generated by the sale of the litter provided the down payment for the Gillespie farm. As Wilma Kehrli explains:

> . . . Wilbur had this $1,800, don't you see, from the eighteen pigs, and that's what he used. . . . And if you'd have seen the farm at that time—there was this house—no running water, no electricity. And Henry, when they'd built it, he'd put in wire, before they put the ceiling in, don't you see? But you see, that had been how many years. And the electrician says, "Elmer, we won't do anything with that stuff." He says, "It's rotten." And furthermore, it wouldn't stand the power that would come in on the electric wires that we were using then. So we had to rewire it, so that meant a little more money. And then get water in, you had no idea. . . . No bathroom or anything. . . . It was just a house—and no running water, no lights, and no cupboards or anything. . . . And then you see there was just the barn and one or two little other buildings, but, you see, Wilbur was going to have pigs, and so we fixed the house up so that he'd have a little rent coming in. . . . We put in cupboards and running water and a bathroom and lights. Then he had to go and start outside, too. . . . The reason that old barn is there—it's well built, and it's put together with wooden pegs, not nails, and that's as sturdy as a rock. . . . Of course, in those days $1,800 was quite a little, and then Elmer and I just kind of helped him along. . . . (interview with author, July 28, 1992)

When she died on February 11, 1955, Sarah knew that the home place was in good hands.[6]

"MEMORIES"
When I think of the years agone
And trace the sunny side,
The dearest thoughts that come to me;
That lend the sweetest charm,
Are those that hallow my memory
Of the dear old days at the farm.
And oft in fancy I wander
To the place where I was born;
The wood, the orchard and meadow,
And fields of tasseling corn;

Sarah's grave in the Gillespie family plot, Oakland Cemetery, Manchester.
Photo by Suzanne Bunkers.

> Just a lowly home by the wayside
> That to youth could give no harm;
> So my heart goes back without divide
> To the dear old days at the farm.

This poem is included in a typescript collection of Sarah's poetry entitled "Poems of the Prairie." In her preface to the collection, Sarah explained, "These poems, written at the prairie home where I was born, are lovingly dedicated to the memory of my parents, James Fawcett Gillespie and Emily Elizabeth Hawley. The lines breathe of the very atmosphere of the prairie home where the cool, flowing stream in the old pasture seemed to say to my child mind and heart: purity, plenty, peace" (Box 11, Vol. 6, Huftalen Collection).

A careful reader of Sarah's diary cannot help but be puzzled by this dedication. Given Sarah's detailed descriptions of discord and discontent on the farm, what accounts for the sanitized and romanticized vision of farm life in "Memories"?

Perhaps it was the same impetus that led Sarah's mother, Emily, to add this comment near the conclusion of her March 4, 1886, entry in Sarah's diary: "No Sorrow so great, but there is somewhere a pleasure mingled in." Perhaps it was the same impetus that led Sarah to maintain, in the face of ample evidence to the contrary, that "all will yet be well."

I believe that Sarah's impetus was all this and more. If Emily Hawley Gillespie's diary reflects her internalization of the cultural ideal of being the perfect wife and mother, Sarah Gillespie Huftalen's diary reflects her internalization of the cultural ideal of being the perfect daughter and sister. Clearly, Sarah tried to be the kind of "good girl" about whom she had written in her childhood copy book and the kind of "good woman" that her mother—and her culture—had trained her to be.

True, Sarah's horizons were broader than her mother's. Sarah was well-educated, widely traveled, and a public figure. Despite her success as an educator, Sarah continued to place a high premium on making a home—first for her abusive father, James; then for her docile husband, Billie; and finally for her recalcitrant brother, Henry. In this respect Sarah was like many women coming of age in nineteenth- and twentieth-century American life. Economics dictated that she earn a living throughout her life; at the same time, she intensely needed to feel that she had done her duty as daughter, wife, and sister, especially in her retirement years, when she knew she was no longer valued as an educator. But, as determined as Sarah was to make a home for her brother, Henry was just as determined not to let her.

The ideal of creating and sustaining a home—a central tenet of what Barbara Welter has termed the "Cult of True Womanhood" in nineteenth-century America—was as important for Sarah as it had been for her mother, Emily. Based on a review of American women's magazines, gift books, religious tracts, and cookbooks during the 1820 to 1860 period, Welter attributes four traits to the Cult of True Womanhood: piety, purity, submissiveness, and domesticity. Welter also notes that "corroborative evidence not cited in this article was found in women's diaries, memoirs, autobiographies and personal papers, as well as in all the novels by women which sold over 75,000 copies during this period" (151). In analyzing the effects of such cultural prescriptions on women's lives, Welter concludes: "The American woman had her choice—she could define her rights in the way of the women's magazines and insure them by the practice of the requisite virtues, or she could go outside the home, seeking other rewards than love. It was a decision on which, she was told, everything in her world depended" (173).

At the same time as they conformed to culturally prescribed models of proper womanhood, Emily and Sarah rebelled against the strictures of those models. Their diary entries reflect their conformity and rebellion, set against the backdrop of their shared inability to break free of destructive family patterns within the home. During the years before Emily's death, the Gillespie family, like many others, worked hard to keep the family unit intact, even if doing so took precedence over the safety of individual family members.[7] As is the case in many dysfunctional families, Emily and Sarah continued to exhibit certain attitudes and behaviors not necessarily because they wanted to but because they had no viable alternatives.[8]

Emily and, in turn, Sarah came of age in the midwestern United States during an era when women had few rights; their economic security depended on maintaining good working relationships with fathers, uncles, husbands, brothers, and other male relatives and friends. Like Emily, Sarah supported the Universalist, suffrage, and temperance movements—all of which advocated additional rights and public recognition for women. Yet in her own life, Sarah felt keenly her own lack of power and influence. Her efforts to place her trust in God and her hope that dark clouds would yield a silver lining were shaped by the fact that her daily survival depended on accommodation, mediation, and sometimes silence. Like her mother's diary, Sarah's diary embodies both her sense of powerlessness and her struggle for empowerment. Sarah's painstaking work in preparing all of her and her mother's papers for donation to the SHSI indicates a certain desire, perhaps both conscious and subconscious, to make public her mother's and her own perceptions of their daily lives, warts and all.

Sarah's diary weaves a rich, vital, colorful tapestry of a life. Her diary is anything but miscellaneous, haphazard, sterile, or tedious. It illustrates how the diary as a form of autobiography can follow the daily rhythms of housekeeping to inscribe what Ann Romines refers to as "domestic ritual." Romines defines what she calls the "home plot" as a "complex of narrative strategies" that "respond to, replicate, continue, interrogate, and extend the repetitive rhythms of domestic life, which emphasize continuance over triumphant climax and often subordinate the vaunted individual to an ongoing, life-preserving, and, for some women, life-threatening process" (293). Romines has noted that one reason why women writers have a "special affinity for the journal form" is because it "replicates the daily rhythms of housekeeping; its ongoingness precludes a dominant, completable plot" (295).

Diaries such as Sarah's represent an attempt by a writer to establish a pattern of writing, a "home plot," and sustain it. Such texts do not emphasize traditional patterns of exposition: rising action, climax, falling action, and denouement. Rather, they reflect life's continuity, its complexity, its paradoxical nature. They open up narrative possibilities, for, in a diary, loose ends are not always tied up; everyone does not live happily ever after.[9]

As Carolyn Heilbrun comments in her conclusion to *Writing a Woman's Life*, "We women have lived too much with closure" (130). Texts such as the diary of Sarah Gillespie Huftalen are important because they illustrate the value of "household words" in establishing "diary cycles," meeting women's discursive needs, and sustaining communication networks.[10] Just as important, such texts challenge us to continue our reassessment of what constitutes history as well as what constitutes autobiography.[11]

When I ask myself why I am so intrigued by this Iowa woman's diary and life, I realize that there is no one easy answer. I was first drawn to her diary because, like Sarah, I am a teacher, and I was curious about what a nineteenth-century teacher's life might have been like. I now realize that I continue to be fascinated by Sarah's diary because she kept on writing, despite formidable odds, *and* because she worked so hard to see that her writings were preserved. After all, if Sarah had not donated her diary to the SHSI, I would not be reading it today.

Like Sarah, I keep house. While working on this Conclusion, I spent some time on domestic ritual: I got up at 6:00 A.M., made coffee, did three loads of laundry, washed a set of dirty dishes, gave my daughter breakfast, got her off to play, fed our cats and changed their litter boxes, scrubbed the basement floor, went to the store to buy the week's groceries, and vacuumed the living room carpet. All of these aspects of domestic ritual have helped me get ready to sit down at my computer and write what you are now reading. Like Sarah, I use daily tasks and words to make a house a home. When I write in my diary, I continue Sarah's project:

The more I put pieces together, the better I understand who Sarah was & what made her tick. Quite an intelligent woman with an intense need to be useful—and to be acknowledged for her efforts. That's not unusual for a person to desire, but in the times when Sarah lived, it was very difficult for a woman to achieve. I think that Sarah did about as well as any woman could do.

—from Suzanne Bunkers's diary, July 30, 1992

Notes

Introduction: The Diary as the Tapestry of a Life

1. This entry is in a hardbound book (4 by 6 inches) with a red marbled cover, reinforced corners, and lined pages. On the inside front cover, Sarah wrote: "Diary of Sarah Gillespie, Jan. 1, 1877–Dec. 31, 1880. Finish attending Country School. Begin attending Manchester Academy."

Sarah's first writing exercises are contained in a tiny (3 by 5 inches) hand-sewn booklet with this note in Sarah's handwriting on its back cover: "Pre-school, Sarah Gillespie. Ma made this book." This booklet includes spelling exercises, multiplication tables, and handwriting practices such as "I am a good girl" and "Learn your lessons well." Next, Sarah wrote in a cut-down version of a school record book (4 by 6 inches). Its spine is hand-stitched, and it contains additional exercises, sketches of flowers, and this sentence: "Be gentle Ever be kind Miss Sarah Gillespie." On the book's first page, Sarah wrote: "Sarah L. Gillespie. First attempt at Diary & school. Ma made this book, about 4-1/2 to 5 yrs. of age." Sarah's note places the starting date for her first attempt at diary-keeping in the early 1870s. Her entries became more detailed beginning about 1873. This edition begins with Sarah's January 1877 entries.

The sentences which Emily gave Sarah for handwriting practice sent two messages from mother to daughter: the first was that Sarah should achieve; the second was that Sarah should be a "good girl." These contradictory messages, like those sent by many mothers to daughters, helped to shape Sarah's attitudes and experiences; later, these messages became motifs throughout Sarah's diary.

2. Judy Nolte Lensink's superb book, *"A Secret to Be Burried": The Diary and Life of Emily Hawley Gillespie, 1858–1888,* has influenced my study of Emily's and Sarah's diaries.

3. In fact, Roy Pascal asserts that an "autobiography proper" must be a narrative that involves the "reconstruction" of a life and that renders a "coherent

shaping of the past" (5–9). According to Pascal, a diary cannot be defined as autobiography because a diary "moves through a series of moments in time" and "its ultimate, long-range significance cannot be assessed" (3).

4. Although Fothergill's work is based entirely on his study of published diaries by individuals who considered themselves writers, his concept of the "book of the self" is useful in studying manuscript diaries, such as Sarah Gillespie Huftalen's, which clearly indicates that the diarist shaped her diary into a life narrative.

5. Lensink's edition of Emily Hawley Gillespie's diary has been the source for a good deal of my information on members of the Gillespie family. In addition, unpublished papers in the Sarah Gillespie Huftalen Collection, State Historical Society of Iowa, Iowa City, have provided a wealth of information on family lineage as well as biographies of individual family members.

6. Family deeds indicate that Lorindia Gillespie bought the 200-acre farm (Section 35, Coffins Grove Township) in 1859 for $3,500. In her diary entry for December 29, 1862, Emily explained: "Pa was here to dinner. Ma *gave James a deed of one half of her* (James Mother) farm the *east* half.—one hundred acers, today" (Lensink, *A Secret*, 107).

7. Both Hiram and Lorindia Gillespie are buried in the Gillespie family plot in Oakland Cemetery in Manchester, Iowa.

8. For a detailed analysis of this support network, see Christie Dailey's unpublished paper, "The Family on the Farm: A Case Study of Rural Exchange Networks." As Dailey explains, "From each farmstead radiated myriad lines of exchange which augmented each individual family's resources and formed overlapping networks of mutual aid and support. Each member of a farm family defined his or her interactive community individually, based on personal values and needs or societal expectations. Thus exchange took place in several categories—social, economic, and ideological" (3–4).

9. Excerpt from "Personal Reminiscences," Brown Scrapbook, Personal #2, Box 8, Vol. 11, Huftalen Collection.

10. In "Purely Personal," Sarah wrote that in 1879 "a Commercial Institute and Normal Training College was organized in town this being commonly known as the Manchester Academy. It ceased operation in the spring of 1882. This owing to an epidemic of measles. Brother and I lacked but two months of graduation for we had pursued a double course of study" (Green Scrapbook, Box 9, Vol. 4, Huftalen Collection).

11. In her examination of violence against women in the literature about western American families, Melody Graulich asserts that social critics (e.g., Mari Sandoz, Agnes Smedley, Meridel Le Sueur, and Tillie Olsen) have treated violence against women "as the widespread and inevitable consequence of the common belief that men have the right to dominate women and to use force to coerce compliance with their wishes" (113). Graulich explains that the causes for men's brutality "are embedded in their society's attitudes

about women and marriage and in its sanctioning of male power and authority" (113).

In her analysis of Jules Sandoz's pattern of abusiveness, Betsy Downey notes that "Sandoz apparently never resorted to actual physical violence with his neighbors, preferring verbal abuse and warning or harassing shots, and withdrawing from public confrontation before it resulted in physical exchange or bodily harm" (36). While Jules Sandoz had "remarkable control over his public outbursts," Downey acknowledges that only "within his family did he actually go over the edge and lose control. This public control and private loss of control is frequent behavior with wife beaters" (36–37). Evidence from both Emily's and Sarah's diaries demonstrates parallels between the attitudes and behaviors of Jules Sandoz and James Gillespie.

In her introduction to the new edition of the memoirs of Abigail Abbot Bailey, first published in 1815, Ann Taves links the Anglo-Catholic emphasis on marriage as "a sacramental union for the purpose of procreation," the Calvinist tradition of conformance to the will of God, the Congregationalist belief that "nothing occurred by accident," and the sanctioning of violence against women by many Christian religions (9–12). Taves discusses the relation between cultural mores and Abigail Bailey's passive reactions to her husband's physical and emotional violence, manifested in his incestuous relationship with their daughter, Phebe. Abigail's text provides another careful reading of domestic violence in historical perspective.

Although neither Emily's nor Sarah's diary contains overt evidence of incest within the Gillespie family, each extends our historical perspective on the complex nature of family violence. As Elizabeth Pleck points out, even though the problem of family violence began to receive more public attention during the latter 1800s, it was unusual for a wife to file charges of abuse against her husband, who often elicited sympathy from other family members while she received the blame (12).

12. Sarah later reminisced, "There were Normal Training summer schools in Manchester each year of six or eight weeks and these I attended thus being in readiness to teach should opportunity come to the longing desire of my heart" ("I Remember This and That," Box 8, Vol. 11, Huftalen Collection).

13. County superintendent of school records, stored in the Delaware County Historical Society in Hopkinton, Iowa, indicate that on August 25, 1882, Sarah L. Gillespie, aged seventeen, took the examination for teachers but did not pass. Her average score was 71.4; with one exception, her individual scores ranged from 65 to 88 (e.g., orthography, 71; reading, 74; writing, 70; arithmetic, 70; geography, 65; grammar, 65; physiology, 88; theory and practice, 79; appearance of papers, 85). Her score in U.S. history, however, was a dismal 47, and her candidacy was rejected.

On April 28, 1883, Sarah again took the examination; she scored 95 in U.S. history and did well in her other subjects. This time she passed, receiving a second-grade teaching certificate, which permitted her to teach until August 1, 1883. On August 20, 1883, Sarah once again took the examination, scoring highly in every subject except American history (score: 46). On August 18, 1884, Sarah took the examination for the fourth time; her scores averaged in the nineties. She was granted a first-grade teaching certificate that would permit her to teach for two years (Superintendent's Records for Delaware County, Delaware County Historical Society, Hopkinton, Iowa).

Keach Johnson notes that, given the uncertain quality of the education and professional training of Iowa's teachers, few were able to earn first-grade certificates: "From 1882–1883, when the system of state certification began, through 1900–1901, the state board of examiners issued 3,103 certificates, 348 diplomas, 287 primary certificates to teachers of the first, second, and third grades, and 3 special certificates to specialists in such subjects as drawing, music, and penmanship" ("The State," 42–43).

14. Twenty years after Sarah began her teaching career, the situation remained about the same. Keach Johnson explains: "Calculating the average annual salaries of teachers in Iowa in 1903 to be about four hundred dollars for men and less than three hundred for women, the Educational Council, the policy-making body of the ISTA [Iowa State Teachers' Association], stated that teachers, male or female, could not support themselves, let alone families, on such meager incomes" ("The State," 50).

Writing in 1914, John F. Merry commented, "There are but sixteen male teachers in all Delaware County; on the other hand, 216 females are employed. The average compensation per month for males is $82.18; females, $42.38. The great discrepancy between the two classes of instructors is largely accounted for in that the higher positions in the high and graded schools of the towns and villages are filled with men, who demand salaries that will, in a measure, be commensurate with their ability" (365).

15. Excerpt from "I Remember This and That," Box 8, Vol. 11, Huftalen Collection.

16. In *Who Cares for the Elderly?*, Emily Abel comments on the tensions inherent in situations where children are caregivers for elderly parents:

> Parent care involves a constant tension between attachment and loss, pleasing and caring, seeking to preserve an older person's dignity and exerting unaccustomed authority, overcoming resistance to care and fulfilling extravagant demands, reviving a relationship and transforming it. Some of these contradictions are built into the experience of caring for any person at the end of the life course. When adult children are the caregivers, however, services are rendered within the context of relationships that already are characterized by deep ambivalence. (112)

In her analysis of the relationship between Emily and Sarah Gillespie, Abel explains that Sarah's role as caregiver for her mother "was simultaneously gratifying and stultifying. She was able to demonstrate her love for her mother and meet the cultural definition of a good daughter. But she had to confront the loss of her primary source of support and abandon a satisfying career, while becoming submerged in domestic obligations" ("Dependence and Autonomy," 45).

17. In his study of nineteenth-century diarists and twentieth-century theories about grief, Paul C. Rosenblatt defines grief as "expressed feelings of sorrow, loss of interest in work, depression, being unable to eat or sleep, or other signs of distress about the specific person or persons lost, or expressing either a desire to reunite on earth with the lost or joy at hearing from the lost" (25). In analyzing how an individual works through the grieving process, Rosenblatt explains that the process demands one's willingness to face up to the pain and one's ability to detach in order to complete the grieving process (33). Rosenblatt notes that working through the grief goes more slowly if one is out of contact with important reminders of the loss (39). Over the years, Sarah learned how to use her diary as an aid to working through her grief following the deaths of loved ones; in fact, her diary became an important reminder of her losses, and its presence may have expedited her grieving process.

18. Linda Gordon cites the following statistics on incestuous relationships, 1880 to 1960: the relationships were primarily heterosexual; forty-nine out of fifty of the older perpetrators were male; the perpetrators were on the average twenty-five years older than their victims. Of the younger victims, ninety-three out of ninety-seven were girls, and the average age of victims was ten. Most incestuous relationships continued for several years; the relationships were never voluntarily ended by the older males. The incest usually ended only when the girl moved away from the household or became pregnant (210).

Contemporary researchers are analyzing the many kinds of incestuous sexual abuse, such as that perpetrated by a father on a daughter or that perpetrated by an older brother on a younger sister. Kristin A. Kunzman defines childhood sexual abuse as "a physical violation of a child's body through any sort of sexual contact or a psychological violation of the child through verbal or nonverbal sexual behavior" (2). Kunzman views sexual abuse as covering "a wide range of behavior from covert episodes such as a father staring at his daughter's breasts and saying, 'You're really pretty. It's too bad your breasts are so small,' to the overt action of an older brother raping his preteen sister over a period of years" (2–3). While neither Emily's nor Sarah's diary entries state that incestuous sexual abuse occurred in the Gillespie family, one cannot help but wonder about the nature of Sarah's fear of her father—and about the nature of Emily's "secret to be burried."

19. Emily Hancock defines the reckoning process in this way:

> What women want to do in relation to their mothers is perhaps best summed up by the many dictionary meanings of the word *reckoning*. They want to render the account, settle the debts that left them owing.

They want to loosen the grip of old entitlements, to calculate the value of the relationship. They want to balance the ledger by figuring themselves into the equation as adults so that they carry equal weight. They want to count on the tie, to rely on it, not as dependent children but as full participants in a mutual, reciprocal attachment. They want to rectify it, put it to rights, bringing its edges together so that the fit is flush. They want to make the relationship hardy, strong, substantial. They want to take a reckoning by it, to set their compass and find their position from that relationship. (205–206)

20. Emily's legacy as a mother was the proverbial double-edged sword. As Lensink explains, "The most successful female role in Emily Gillespie's life was that of mother. In the diary one can trace her methods for raising educated, thoughtful children. Sarah became much like Emily Gillespie, eventually keeping a diary with language and viewpoint that paralleled her mother's." Yet Lensink also acknowledges that Emily's "characterization of her life as selfless, especially given the talents and insights she demonstrated in her diary, may strike modern readers as frustratingly narrow" (*A Secret*, 372, 376).

1. "I Am a Good Girl": 1877–1879

1. Uncle Jerome was William Jerome Doolittle, who was married to James Gillespie's sister, Margaret. The Doolittles had four children and lived in Manchester, where Jerome was a partner in a wagon shop.

2. George Trumble was the son of Patrick Trumble, who came from Massachusetts in 1855 to farm in Coffins Grove Township.

3. Willie Scanlan, the son of William and Isabella (Anderson) Scanlan, was Henry and Sarah Gillespie's neighbor and friend.

4. The North School was located in Section 11 of Coffins Grove Township, about a mile east of Henry Baker's Stagecoach Inn.

5. All of these families were neighbors of the Gillespie family. H. P. and Jane (Furbush) Chapman and their sons, Charles and Fred, farmed in Section 36 of Coffins Grove Township. James Van Alstyne, his wife, and their children lived near Henry Baker. E. H. Sellens, his wife, and their family lived directly west of Emily and James Gillespie. J. A. Morse, his wife, and their four children farmed in Section 25 of Coffins Grove Township.

6. Ella and Victor Esty lived with their parents (the Silas Estys) in neighboring Delaware Township, where their father ran a boardinghouse and delivered milk.

7. References to "uncle" in Sarah's diary are to Henry Baker, Emily Gillespie's uncle, who lived in the Stagecoach Inn in Section 22 of Coffins Grove Township.

8. Quite likely this date marked Sarah's first menstrual period. Unlike her mother, Sarah did not encode her menstrual periods in her diary by using exclamation points (see Lensink, *A Secret*, 19, 401). Sarah customarily referred to that time in her menstrual cycle as "being sick," "feeling unwell," or "coming around."

9. The December 7, 1877, issue of the *Manchester Press* contains this item: "Maggie McCormick, teacher of the school in District No. 6, Coffin's Grove township, reported her star pupils for the term of Luella Morse, Charles and Fred Chapman, Henry and Sarah Gillespie, Earl and Ida Beal and Mattie Van Alstyne."

10. Aunt Harriet (whose nickname was Hattie), Emily Gillespie's younger sister, was married to John McGee. They farmed near the Gillespies. Dennis Gillespie was the younger brother of James Gillespie.

11. The Universalist Church in Manchester and its Sunday school were first organized in 1864, although no regular services were held until 1868, when Rev. Jewell became pastor. In May 1871, a brick church was completed and dedicated. The church remained active under pastor E. R. Wood until September 1873, when he left. From 1873 to 1877 the church was inactive, until Mr. Wood returned and reorganized the society. The church dissolved several years later, and its building was leased to the Manchester Grange Society. Today the building houses the Golden Age Activity Center (Merry, Vol. 1, 360).

12. Sarah appears to be referring to her aunt Edna Preston, Emily's sister. If so, there is a major discrepancy between her diary and her mother's. In 1884, Emily traveled to Michigan to visit her family. Her diary entry states: "it is 18 years since I saw Edna. she scarcely knew me, nor I her" (Lensink, *A Secret*, 280). Emily does record seeing Edna in 1866 but makes no reference to an 1878 Thanksgiving-day visit. It is not possible at this point to resolve this apparent discrepancy in the two diaries. The Ryans, neighbors of the Gillespies, were unable to attend.

13. Sarah's reference to "Lizzie" is to Mary Elizabeth Griffin, the daughter of Ray B. and Sarah (Coffin) Griffin, the sister of Henry Baker's late wife, Elizabeth.

14. Florence and Bertha Bailey were the daughters of Joel Bailey, one of Henry Baker's brothers-in-law. Loring R. Loomis was the youngest child of A. R. and Phedora (Parmalee) Loomis, who lived near Quaker Mill, just outside Manchester. Mr. Loomis organized the First National Bank in Manchester.

15. "Cousin Sarah" was Sarah (Sadie) Griffin, the daughter of Sarah (Coffin) and Ray B. Griffin.

16. Luella Morse, the daughter of Mr. and Mrs. J. A. Morse, and Hattie Beal, the second youngest of Mr. and Mrs. Louis Beal's nine children, were Sarah's classmates.

17. The Manchester Normal College and Commercial Institute, established

by former State Superintendent Abraham S. Kissell, employed three instructors: Mr. Kissell, Mrs. M. A. Chapel, and Miss Amelia Ames. Seventy pupils attended the first session in fall 1879. Two years later, the enrollment had reached 200 students (Aurner, Vol. 3, 97).

18. An item in the *Manchester Press*, dated December 26, 1879, noted: "The pupils of the Manchester Academy gave an entertainment in charge of Herbert Conger and Russ Clark. Among those on the program were Verda Kelsey, Miss Wilson, Miss Mary Kissell, Arthur Denio, Mr. Kerr, Miss Lottie Robbins, John Pentony, Chas. Van Anda, Carrie Conger, Sadie Kissell, Mabel Burnside, Florence Chapel, Miss Gillespie, Mr. McEnany, Mr. Mcgirl, Austin Brown, Miss Platte, Jennie Brown, Mertie Sherman, Miss Brayton, Miss Todd, Carrie Toogood, Genevieve Parker, and a male quartet composed of Messrs. Granger, Stevens, Dunham, and Conger."

2. "A Perfect Woman Nobly Planned": 1880–1882

1. Sarah's next diary (Box 7, Vol. 3, Huftalen Collection) is a 6-by-8-inch hardbound, lined notebook containing 238 pages, with twenty-four lines per page. At the right-hand side of each page are small columns which could be used to record amounts or numbers. On the inside front cover Sarah has written classmates' names, and on the first page of the diary Emily has written this dedication.

2. Walter H. Butler succeeded A. S. Kissell in overseeing the Manchester Academy.

3. Alexander G. Alcock, a neighbor, lived near Masonville with his wife, Elmira (Zerfass), and their five children.

4. The Luke Scanlan family lived on a farm about a mile west of the Gillespie farm in Section 34 of Coffins Grove Township.

5. In her diary entry dated March 29, 1881, Emily noted: "*John & Harriet* have rented Mrs. Carpenters place & moved there to day, about 80 rods east of our house" (Lensink, *A Secret,* 243–244).

6. Sarah is referring to her maternal grandparents, Sarah and Hial Hawley, who sold their Michigan farm. This news greatly upset their daughters, Emily, Harriet, and Edna, because it proved that their brother, Henry Hawley, was not adequately taking care of their parents. In her diary entry dated April 5, 1881, Emily wrote: ". . . I received a *letter* from Edna yesterday she is very much offended because Father & Mother sold their farm, says they have trouble, *trouble* all the time. *I* am sorry, & do wish they might spend the last of their lives in happiness, if [brother] Henry has all they have for taking care of them he ought to make them comfortable, & do all he can to promote their well-fare, long as they live" (Lensink, *A Secret,* 245).

7. John Arbuckle was another student at the Manchester Academy and a good friend of Sarah's.

8. Clement, a son of Sarah (Coffin) and Ray B. Griffin, was another cousin of Sarah's and Henry's.

9. President James A. Garfield, a Republican, had been elected in November 1880. Although the president was shot by Charles Guiteau on July 2, 1881, Garfield did not die until over two months later, on September 19, 1881. On June 30, 1882, Charles Guiteau was executed.

10. In her diary entry dated May 21, 1882, Emily expressed similar sentiments: "James has another freak of being *ugly* to his horses. *'tis too mean* to tell. I—well I did get very angry at him—am sorry tis so, yet I can not endure the seeing of kind animals abused" (Lensink, *A Secret*, 253).

11. Sarah is describing Henry's phrenological chart, which he had just received from Nelson Sizer of Fowler and Wells, New York City. Phrenology was defined as "discourse on the mind." It was based on the principle that, just as each bodily function had its organ, so did each faculty of the mind. Phrenologists believed that one's mental faculties could be assessed by studying the shape of the skull and noting such things as the size of the forehead and any unusual bumps. Like Henry, Emily and Sarah Gillespie believed in phrenology, and Sarah had her phrenological chart done on January 30, 1883.

12. In her diary entry dated July 19, 1882, Emily Gillespie wrote: "Tis four P.M. Alas, our Mother is dead and gone. Ere this they have laid her away in the silent tomb. Mother fare you well—you can be with us no more" (Lensink, *A Secret*, 256). Emily did not travel to Michigan to attend her mother's funeral.

13. "Aunt Aggie" was Agnes Hawley, the wife of Henry Hawley, Emily's only brother, who lived in Michigan.

14. Emily's cousin Elisha Hawley lived at Rose Hill, and Henry, who had just turned nineteen, went there to stay with him and peddle merchandise to earn money. Henry's leave-taking, which was urged upon him by his father, was especially hard on Emily and Sarah.

15. Jerome Alcock was the eldest child of Alexander and Elmira Alcock of Masonville.

3. "I Question Myself": 1883–1884

1. The Congar (sometimes spelled Conger) family ran the Conger Dry Goods store in Manchester.

2. In her diary entry dated May 31, 1883, Emily wrote: "James has one of his crazy spells again. he has got the idea into his head that he wants a deed of the place. I think I had not best to give it to him, but Ill try to do right about it, I want it so we will all have a home while together. then if Henry & Sarah both outlive James & me it shall belong to them equal . . ." (Lensink, *A Secret*, 265).

3. Henry's intention was to attend Adrian College in Adrian, Michigan, to

learn the carpentry trade. He remained there for nearly a year, then returned to work as a carpenter in Iowa, Missouri, and the Dakotas from 1883 to 1889.

4. In her diary entry dated November 26, 1883, Emily noted that Sarah's wages would be $32.50 per month, compared to $6.00 per month, Emily's wages when she began teaching in 1855.

5. The Tripp, McGee, and Cook families all had children attending Sarah's school, which was on Isaac McGee's land in Section 23 of Coffins Grove Township. Apparently, not all the parents wanted the school to be open the next term, and Sarah refused to close it. Some parents responded by pulling their children out of the school. Emily's assessment of the situation was that the McGees wanted to spite her and let her know that "she was no smarter than anyone else." But the McGees could find no fault with Sarah as a teacher (Lensink, *A Secret*, 277).

6. In her diary entry dated May 15, 1884, Emily used much the same language to describe her father's arrival:

> I think a great deal of him and respect him though I feel it an imposition upon us all (after Henry [Hawley] has squandered all he had, then leave him, poor old man, in the streets.) we will trust that it will be all right. I will do the best I can and see what we can do about it, most surely I do not feel able to take care of him. my health is too poor and I can not concienciously keep Sarah at home to do the work. she wants to teach and earn something for herself, & it would cost more than we could earn to hire help. (Lensink, *A Secret*, 282–283)

7. This is a reference to Emily's and Sarah's menstrual periods. Emily, who was forty-five at the time, was nearing menopause. Sarah's reference to the "toupad" was a slang reference to her having such a heavy menstrual flow that she needed two pads to staunch it.

8. After the Universalist church disbanded, the Gillespies began attending the Congregational church in Manchester.

9. Charles, born in 1865, was the oldest son of H. P. and Jane Chapman, who farmed in section 36, Coffins Grove Township. One other son, Fred Chapman, survived.

10. E. A. Seger, born in 1837, came to the Manchester area in 1854 with his parents. In 1857 he married Sylvia Cates, and they farmed 140 acres near Earlville, Iowa. As the *History of Delaware County* puts it, "He became identified with farming interests in Oneida township and for many years carried on general agricultural pursuits, his persistency, determination and energy being manifest in the excellent appearance of his place" (Merry, Vol. 2, 97). E. A. and Sylvia Seger were members of the Congregational church in Earlville, where he taught Sunday school. He was employed as an insurance agent for State Fire and Tornado Insurance and the Continental Insurance Company during the 1880s, during which time he and his wife built a new home.

11. The October 10, 1884, issue of the *Manchester Press* carried a lengthy account of Henry's accident:

> Last Friday, while Henry Gillespie, a young man of about eighteen, a son of J. F. Gillespie of Coffins Grove, was at work on the steeple of the new Methodist church, he lost his footing, and he fell from the scaffold on which he and another workman were standing. He first struck on the roof of the church, and went off that to the ground, fortunately striking on a pile of loose lath and rubbish, by which his fall was broken. This doubtless saved his life. He was severely injured on the hip and back of the head, but is doing well and is now thought to be in a fair way to get well. The height from the ground to the scaffold from which he fell, is about seventy-two feet, and he may congratulate himself on having a very fortunate escape. (Lensink, *A Secret*, 424)

12. Harry Jeffers, a schoolmate and friend of Henry's, began courting Sarah about this time, although her interest in him appears to have been platonic.

13. In her diary entry dated December 13, 1884, Emily wrote: "Father is about to sue me for his things, my bureau, too. I will have to let it go . . ." (Lensink, *A Secret*, 291).

4. "This World Is Not So Bad a World": 1885–1886

1. Mr. Alcorn served as director of the York Township school, located one mile south of Edgewood and eleven miles north of Manchester. While she taught at the school, Sarah boarded with Mr. and Mrs. Alcorn and their family.

2. Andy Alcorn and his wife, Edna, oftened visited in his parents' home while Sarah was boarding there. As Sarah noted in her diary, an Alcorn daughter was married to Jud Breed, another teacher in the Edgewood schools.

3. Grover Cleveland served two terms (1885–1889 and 1893–1897) as president of the United States.

4. According to Michigan law, a child could be held accountable for the support of an aged parent if the child had "sufficient ability" to pay. Iowa law held that a woman could be held accountable for family expenses if she had property in her name. James Gillespie's consultations with Mr. Sumner and Mr. Bronson, Manchester attorneys, reinforced his belief that Emily could be held liable to support her father, Hial Hawley, if she kept the deed to the farm in her name. Emily and her children feared that, if the deed were returned to James, he would turn them out and they would have no home (Lensink, *A Secret*, 424–425).

5. Emily Gillespie's interpretation of Sarah's failure to "come around" (i.e., start her menstrual period on time) reflects the culture's high premium on a

young woman's virginity as well as the near-hysteria that could develop from her having been placed in any "compromising" situation.

6. Sarah's reference is to James's siblings: his younger brother, Dennis, his older sister, Margaret, and his younger sister, Mercelia.

7. Emily's diary entry for April 1, 1885, stated: *"I gave James a deed of the farm. indeed I felt as though it was signing myself out of a home.* I said to Mr. Bronson 'it seemed pretty bad to be *compelled* to do such a thing as this, that I should *never* had done it had I not been *obliged* to.' he said a deed was good for nothing if one was compelled to give it" (Lensink, *A Secret,* 296).

8. Emily's diary entry for August 10, 1885, stated: "I have never seen a happy day since less than two weeks after we were married. he told me how he had been tempted to kill himself as far as to get a rope & go to the barn to hang, he has threatened it many time since" (Lensink, *A Secret,* 303).

9. Sarah was attending a summer normal institute, the purpose of which was to provide guidance for teachers in the areas of methodology, school organization, and discipline. During the period from 1885 to 1896, attendance at the annual summer institute rose to nearly 23,000 teachers (Aurner, Vol. 2, 172–186).

10. Emily's diary entry for September 18, 1885, noted: "Sarah & I seem to have friends among the other sex—more friendly than we like, or rather more than most *they says* would approve" (Lensink, *A Secret,* 306).

11. Joseph Hutchinson, the son of Henry and Elizabeth Hutchinson, came to Delaware County in 1857 and worked as a cashier in his father's bank.

12. Part of Harry Jeffers's prophecy came true: in later years, he did hold several patents and was a talented inventor.

13. Emily's diary entry for November 8, 1885, indicates that she either had read Sarah's diary entry for that date or had spoken with Sarah about Mr. Seger's behavior: "Segar—last night—took advantage of Sarah standing near him when he started—and kissed her. he must never do it again, for Sarah is pure & innocent" (Lensink, *A Secret,* 308–309).

Once again, Emily's and Sarah's diary entries reflect the ideology of the times: a young woman's virginity was a highly prized possession, and she was to be protected from potential sexual predators. As Sarah's mother, Emily had the primary responsibility for protecting her daughter. Robert M. Ireland states:

> Nineteenth-century American women, especially those who were young and unmarried, carried a great sexual burden. On the one hand they were supposed to be models of chastity, while on the other they were preyed upon by increasing numbers of men eager for pre-marital or extra-marital sexual relations. The need for them to marry to survive economically and socially and the realities of their sexual drives (as opposed to their theoretically restrained sexuality), coupled with the presence of an abundance of male sexual adventurers, meant that certain of them would become

involved in pre-marital sexual liaisons that would result in pregnancy, abandonment, and societal ostracism. (95)

Apparently Emily Gillespie saw to it that Mr. Seger did not threaten Sarah's chastity again. Around 1890, Mr. and Mrs. Seger moved to Sioux City, where they lived until Mr. Seger's death six years later. An obituary in the *History of Delaware County* notes: "They traveled life's journey happily together for almost four decades but were separated by the hand of death on the 14th of November, 1896 . . ." (Merry, Vol. 2, 97).

14. Sarah's fears for her mother's health were well-founded. Emily's diary entry for April 11, 1885 (her forty-seventh birthday), stated: ". . . I have tried with all my might to overcome the great strain imposed upon me by him who promised to protect and support through life. but my nerves broke down, my strength failed & now I scarce can walk. however I can not be too thankful I have been permitted to retain my mind." Emily's diary entry for April 18, 1885, concluded with these words: "My strength is gone" (Lensink, *A Secret*, 331, 332).

5. "Murmur Not—It Must Be Right": 1886–1889

1. Katie Pheyton was the new hired girl in the Gillespie home. She replaced a Mrs. Day, who had been working there. According to Emily's diary entries made during January, February, and March 1887, Katie and Henry Gillespie had struck up a friendship of which Emily did not entirely approve. After Katie and Henry had spent some time out in the barn, Emily wrote: "Henry took Katie home yesterday (8 miles): she has been a little offended because I did not approve her going and staying so long at the barn. *not* that I thought it wrong but did not look well" (Lensink, *A Secret*, 339).

2. As Lensink has noted, "Magnetic physicians, also known as 'magnopaths' and 'electropaths,' saw the human body as a receptacle and emitter of currents. They recommended application of mild electrical charges for correcting physiological imbalances that caused disease" (Lensink, *A Secret*, 426).

3. William (Billie) Huftalen, in his early sixties, was a pawnbroker in Manchester. Twice widowed, Huftalen befriended Emily, Sarah, and Henry, eventually boarding with them. Emily's diary entry dated May 2, 1887, wryly notes: "Mr Huftenlen came up for a ride, told Sarah 'if she would ride with him he would take her to school' she went. it saves Henry 18 miles drive this morning but she rather it be the Banker instead. 'indeed it *was* a perfect sell'" (Lensink, *A Secret*, 341).

On August 30, 1887, Emily added: "Mr Huftenlen came here the 10th to board & make his home, last *monday he asked Sarah to marry him too old*, about 60, she 22. he pay us [to board] ever liberal" (Lensink, *A Secret*, 343).

Interestingly, Sarah's diary contains no entries from late May through early

November 1887. Thus, we cannot ascertain her early impressions of Billie Huftalen. Many years later, after Billie's death, Sarah did write in her diary about his proposal (see chap. 8).

4. Emily's diary entry for November 7, 1886, stated: "The Children could not make a bargain with James to rent the place. they rented ahouse [*sic*] in Manchester I came with them, so they could take care of me" (Lensink, *A Secret,* 343, 346). William (Billie) Huftalen was also boarding at the Loomis house. Along with the hired girl, Paulina Shaw, Huftalen helped Henry and Sarah care for Emily.

5. Sarah wrote this entry, dictated by Emily, in her mother's diary on January 12, 1888: "*Blizzard* of drifting snow. * * * Sarah is here and cares for me the best she can. Dear Daughter it is to Ma more than words or pen can tell. It is not always to last. Ma's work nearly finished And all is well. Snow" (Lensink, *A Secret,* 347).

6. The house to which Sarah is referring is located at 501 East Howard Street in Manchester, one block east and one block north of the old Universalist church (later the Grange, and now the Golden Age Activity Center).

7. Scrofula refers to swelling of the lymph glands of the neck.

6. "Nobody's Wife": 1890–1891

1. Sarah's diary covering the period from 1890 to 1892 is a hardbound account book (6 by 12 inches). It contains 167 lined pages in account book format. At the front of this volume are several blank pages marked A–Z, apparently for indexing accounts. Loose-leaf pages have been inserted at various points in this volume.

2. Sarah's reference is to a first-grade certificate, which would permit her to teach for two years and would show that she had already taught successfully for thirty-six weeks. To gain such a certificate, Sarah had to take a written examination over the subjects commonly taught in the schools. As Keach Johnson points out, "Second-grade certificates were good for only one year and generally required only one term (three months) of successful teaching at most. Third-grade certificates were limited to one or two terms at the discretion of the county superintendent" ("The State," 44–45).

3. Sarah was feeling especially alone because Henry had left for Galesburg, Illinois, a few days earlier, to attend Lombard Seminary and prepare to be ordained a minister.

7. "The Parent, the Pupil and the Teacher": 1900–1914

1. James Gillespie's letter to Sarah (in "I Remember This and That," Box 8, Vol. 10, Huftalen Collection) reflects his grudging acceptance of his daughter's marriage.

Manchester   Oct 15 92

Sarah Huftalen

I cannot call you mine any more, I sapose. it seems to strange that I have
a soninlaw by that name. My friends sends greetings & much Joy & I
wish you that happiness which you deserve may your life be one of sunshine & yours the same is the wish of your Father.

My health is good this fall have been to Meads making syrup made
1,500 this fall come home today & had stay some time I guess. what are
you going to do with those things in town, hear from Henry very often is
making a success I think. The weather is very warm this fall. Lane not
been to meeting much this summer. Harry Minkler is very low & will be
no better. They say

Bought a suit of black today. do not no what to say to Huftalen only
success in life trusting that he will care for you as a lover & a husband
should

do you take the press or the Democrat if you would like it will send
pleas let me here from you oftener is the wish of one that will call blessings on you.

From a loving father & thinks of you often.

J. F. Gillespie

2. This volume of Sarah's diary (Box 11, Vol. 7, Huftalen Collection) is a
5-by-8-inch lined book labeled "Composition Book. Property of Mr. and Mrs.
W. H. Huftalen, Manchester, Iowa." Its diary entries begin on January 1,
1900, and continue sporadically through 1906. Sarah also made several diary
entries in tiny 3-by-5-inch ledgers during the period from 1905 to 1908 (see
Box 11). In addition, she kept separate diaries while teaching in the Arbor
Vitae Summit School near Oneida, Iowa, from fall 1904 to spring 1909 (see
Box 10, Vols. 2–5, Huftalen Collection).

3. The July 17, 1902, issue of the *Manchester Press* reported: "Mrs. Sarah
Gillespie was keeping house at the A. B. Holbert home in Greeley while Mr.
and Mrs. Holbert were in Europe." Since Sarah always referred to herself as
Mrs. Huftalen, it is doubtful that she submitted this item to the newspaper.
The Holbert family, one of the most prosperous in the area, imported and bred
Belgian horses. A. B. Holbert, Jr., had come to Iowa in 1854 with his parents.
He married Elma Baker, the daughter of Jerome and Sarah Baker (not related
to the Coffins Grove Bakers). A. B. and Elma Holbert had six children: Tho-
mas, Fred, Benjamin, Charmion, Warren, and Marjorie.

4. Superintendent Frank D. Joseph hired Sarah to teach at Oneida, located
nine miles north of Manchester. At that time, it was unusual for a teacher to
sign a contract for more than one year in a particular school, so Sarah was
pleased to have been offered an extended contract. Years later, when Sarah
recalled her first days at the Arbor Vitae Summit School, she wrote: "Not un-

like other country school districts the building was located on the summit of a long, sloping knoll at the far eastern outskirts a block north of the main street. The physical conditions of the grounds and buildings presented the customary problem of "cleaning up"; the grass-covered yard being littered with stones and debris. There was also a large, deep mudhole close to the steps, unsightly and unavoidable."

Sarah also reminisced about the first beautification efforts at the school, and she concluded: "We felt something like the mother who has put everything to rights for the night and sits down in the rocker to do some knitting and mending" (from "I Remember This and That," Box 8, Vol. 11, Huftalen Collection). Sarah often used maternal metaphors in her remarks on her teaching (see Conclusion).

5. C. R. Scroggie was the editor of *Midland Schools: A Journal of Education*, published in Des Moines. Sarah's article, "The Use of the Hand Book in Rural Schools," appeared in the June 1910 issue (Vol. 24, No. 10). In her article, Sarah noted the correlation between the educational environment and effective teaching and learning: "Beautiful and appropriate surroundings impress themselves on the lives and hearts of the young. Transform the schoolyard and it transforms every home in the neighborhood" (300). She urged parents to work together with teachers to ensure that children would attend school regularly. Sarah's remarks in her article alluded to the *Hand-Book for Iowa Schools*, first published by State Superintendent Henry Sabin in 1890. The *Hand-Book* was distributed across the state and it was revised in 1895, 1900, and 1906 (Johnson, 909). It laid out a course of study for rural schools in an attempt to replace the haphazard approaches often used (Johnson, "Roots," 909, 910). Sarah's article outlined ways in which sections of the *Hand-Book* might be used by rural teachers to improve their school settings.

Sarah's article also noted the values of compulsory education. In 1902, Iowa had become the thirty-third state to pass a compulsory education law. Up to that point, such a law had been resisted strongly by those who believed in the tradition of local control over education. By 1909, the minimum period of attendance had been increased from twelve to twenty-four weeks per year with the provision that school boards in cities of more than 20,000 could require attendance for the entire school year (Engelhardt, 60, 71). Although Sarah's article expressed her hope that "the age limit therein may be raised to sixteen years" (300), it was not until 1913 that an amendment to the compulsory education act set the age limit at sixteen or completion of the eighth grade (Engelhardt, 72).

6. The Norwich school was Sub-District No. 9 in Tarkio Township, Page County, Iowa. Sarah had originally been offered a teaching position there in summer 1907, but she had already promised to teach at the Arbor Vitae Summit School until the 1908–09 school year had concluded. In August 1909, she signed a contract to teach at the Norwich school. In her reminiscences, Sarah wrote: "The Norwich community received us favorably; not only the patrons

but the citizens of the district cooperating with us in our endeavors to standardize the school but also in improving and beautifying the school grounds . . ." ("Norwich School, Page County, Iowa," Brown Scrapbook, Box 10, Vol. 8, Huftalen Collection). See also Ginalie Swaim's "An Acre of Hill," a photo essay, including Sarah's photographs and diary entries, that details Sarah's years at the Norwich school.

7. The *Manchester Democrat* carried James Gillespie's obituary. It noted that he "had been ill but two weeks and his death was due to heart disease." The obituary went on to describe James's life in the laudatory and sentimental language common to obituaries of the era.

> James Gleespie [*sic*] was a man of excellent habits, fine moral character and sturdy constitution and he continued to be active in his accustomed pursuits till long past the age at which men ordinarily drop out of the ranks of the workers. To this end there is no doubt that his sunshiny disposition largely contributed. This cheery spirit remained with him to the last and he met his fate with calmness and fortitude. He was invariably a good neighbor, and there was no happier family circle than his, when the members of his family were together. When he died, full of years, and ready to be gathered to his father, the grief that was felt over the close of his long career was widespread and sincere. . . .

When reading this account of James Gillespie's life, one is hard-pressed to recognize the same man whose life is chronicled in the pages of Emily's and Sarah's diaries. The glaring contradictions in public and private accounts of James's life can, however, be reconciled, if one notes an important clue in this obituary. Curiously, James's surname is misspelled; had a family member submitted an obituary, he or she would surely have spelled the name correctly. Thus, James Gillespie's obituary was most likely prepared and typeset by someone who did not know the Gillespie family—or James—well.

8. During her years at the Arbor Vitae and Norwich schools, Sarah strove to standardize the school curriculum, beautify the school grounds, and involve parents in their children's educations. During the summers, Sarah often taught methods courses for aspiring teachers; she also supervised chautauqua camps for boys and girls, and she was active in the budding 4-H movement, founded by Jessie Field Shambaugh. Sarah worked tirelessly to establish a Rural Section of the Iowa State Teachers' Association (ISTA); when she succeeded in 1909, she became the section's first president, an office she held for many years. In its November 11, 1909, issue the *Manchester Press* reported:

> At the recent meeting in Des Moines of the Iowa State Teachers association, attended by Supt. F. D. Joseph as a representative of this county, a rural school section of the association was organized. Mrs. Sarah Huftalen of Oneida, this county, being made chairman. Mrs. Huftalen, who is one of the most capable teachers in this county, is the originator of the rural-

school section idea. She formulated it something over a year ago and was aided in carrying it into effect by Supt. Joseph. It promises to be a most valuable adjunct to the state association, and it is but proper that Mrs. Huftalen should be given this credit for its inception, particularly since efforts are being given in other quarters of the state to lodge the credit elsewhere.

In examining Sarah's leadership of the Rural Section of the ISTA, Cordier notes:

Starting with sixty members in 1910, Sarah was re-elected president of the Rural Department of the Iowa State Teachers Association every year until she resigned in 1927. At one point the membership had grown to six hundred members. This on-going professional network of rural teachers and superintendents brought encouragement and enlightenment to many school directors, as they too were invited to attend the rural education meetings. (228)

In January 1913, Sarah succeeded Jessie Field as Page County Superintendent of Schools. In that role Sarah supervised examinations for teachers, planned the annual teachers' institutes, inspected each of the hundred schools in the county, and wrote a regular newspaper column for the *Clarinda Herald*. During the summers, she continued to supervise chautauqua institutes and 4-H camps.

9. The remainder of this volume of Sarah's diary contains only a few short entries for the rest of 1914. Notes in the diary indicate that the Bowerses had brought suit against Sarah for money owed them for caring for Billie, who was in frail health. The case was heard and went to jury, which found for Sarah. The decision stipulated, however, that Sarah would pay the Bowers thirty dollars. Sarah wrote, "It's an outrage."

8. "I Do So Feel the Need": 1914–1917

1. These entries are taken from Sarah's diary covering the years 1914 to 1917 (Box 7, Vol. 5, Huftalen Collection). This first long entry, written five months after Billie Huftalen's death on January 7, 1914, recounts what Sarah knew of Billie's early life, his young adulthood, and their marriage.

Records in the Huftalen Collection indicate that William Henry Huftalen was born on September 21, 1826, in Esopus, New York, the fifth child of Pamelia (Crandall) and Joshua G. Huftalen. The Huftalen family was descended from the Huguenot and Dutch settlers who founded New Paltz, New York. According to Sarah's notes, Billie "came west with some business men. He had a trading post in Denver, Colorado, and transported goods from St. Louis to Denver. He held local offices in Fremont, Neb., and built its first hotel. This burned at a total loss in 1874" (Box 5, Vol. 7, Huftalen Collection).

Billie had been married twice before his marriage to Sarah. His first wife, a Native American woman whose name Sarah did not know, died soon after she married Billie and was buried in the Platt River valley, Nebraska. Billie's second wife, Charity (Chattie) V. Colson, whom he married on January 18, 1860, died of consumption on March 20, 1874, and was buried in Fremont, Nebraska. Sarah's notes indicate that Billie had no children from either marriage.

Sarah also explained that Billie "later became a dealer in furniture both new and 2nd hand" (Box 5, Vol. 7, Huftalen Collection). In Manchester, Billie was well known as the proprietor of the local pawnshop until his business failed around the turn of the century. As Sarah had earlier recorded in her diary, Henry had worked in Billie's store. Later, both Henry and Sarah were part owners, with Sarah being a "silent" partner. A January 29, 1925, news item in the column called "Remember Way Back When . . ." in the *Manchester Press* recalled Mr. Huftalen's store: "Uncle Billy Huftalen's second-hand store was a haven of refuge for every kid in town when he wished to raise a little change for a circus or some other unusual emergency. Uncle Billy would whistle softly to himself while examining the article for sale and would finally say he guessed it was worth 'about twelve cents,' which proffer was always eagerly accepted."

2. These unnamed nephews were Carrington (Carry) L. and Jay G. Huftalen, the sons of Billie's older brother, George J. Huftalen, and his wife, Clarissa (Hyatt) Huftalen, who lived in Unadilla, New York. Sarah stayed in touch with this branch of the Huftalen family through Carrington's descendants.

3. Carolyne (Colson) Nye, the widow of Theron Nye, was the older sister of Billie's second wife, Charity V. Colson. The Colson and Nye families had originated in Hamilton, New York. In 1853, according to Sarah's genealogical notes, both families "settled on the Platte River in Nebraska and dealt in lumber, coal and real estate" (Box 5, Vol. 7, Huftalen Collection). Carolyne Nye died on August 10, 1914.

4. Sarah's notes stated: "All that was mortal was laid to rest in beautiful Birchwood Cemetery, Lot 80, Block 5, in perpetual care." A newspaper clipping containing Billie's obituary (which apparently appeared in the Clarinda newspaper) is pasted into Sarah's genealogical files on the Huftalen family. The obituary reads:

> W. H. Huftalen. Son of Joshua and Pamilia [*sic*] Crandall Huftalen. Born at Acra, Green County, New York, Sept. 21st, 1836. Died at Clarinda, Ia., Jan. 7th, 1914. It has been a sacred obligation and privilege to walk down through the valley of the shadow beside one of the most devoted and sympathetic of husbands. A man who was one of the gentlest of men.
>
> The kindly thoughtfulness of the county officials and deputies, of teachers and pupils and friends and of our Ames boys and girls in their generous and beautiful floral tributes and letters will be treasured as a hallowed memory. One more mound on the sacred list. One more mound in the

chain of sorrow. One more life to eternity given. One more hope for the blessed tomorrow.

Rev. Williamson spoke comforting words from the 103rd Psalm second Corinthians at the service at the residence on N. 16th street, Saturday afternoon, Jan. 10th, at 1:30 o'clock and all that was mortal of him whom we had loved and lost was laid to rest in one of the most beautiful spots of Birchwood cemetery, there to await the glad resurrection morn when all shall be reunited forevermore.

The pallbearers were John Baker, Thomas Copeland, Thomas Snyder, Alva and Fred Miller and Frank Beeson. Henry Gillespie, my brother, returned to his home at Manchester, Iowa, Tuesday, after having spent a week with us.

In contrast to the uncertain authorship of James Gillespie's obituary, the authorship of Billie Huftalen's obituary is clear. Interestingly, Billie's obituary lists his birthplace as Acra, New York, rather than Esopus, New York (as stated in Sarah's genealogical files). Even more interestingly, Billie's date of birth is listed in his obituary as 1836, not 1826 (as stated in Sarah's genealogical files). Perhaps Sarah did not know Billie's actual date of birth until sometime after his death, when she compiled the genealogical materials; or perhaps, given the great disparity in their ages (he was nearly forty years older than she), Sarah misstated Billie's date of birth so that his obituary would make him appear ten years younger than he actually was. Henry Gillespie was apparently on good enough terms with Sarah in 1914 to stay with her for a week and attend Billie's funeral.

5. La Fayette Huftalen, born April 7, 1824, was another of Billie's older brothers. Sarah's notes on La Fayette Huftalen are sketchy, but they indicate that he died in a railroad accident at Livingston, New York. Two children, a son and a daughter, survived him. Billie's older sister, Mary Huftalen, born on May 8, 1817, married John Gilbert. Mary and John Gilbert had two sons. The Huftalen and Gilbert families ran the Unadilla Hotel in Unadilla, New York.

6. Charles (Charlie) Huftalen, Billie's younger brother, was born on March 20, 1829. He married a woman named Nettie (surname unknown), and they had two sons, William Henry, who lived in Elmira, New York, and Fred, who lived in Binghamton, New York.

7. On August 30, 1887, Emily Gillespie had written this in her diary: "Mr. Huftenlen came here the 10th to board & make his home, last *monday he asked Sarah to marry him too old,* about 60, she 22. he pay us [to board] ever liberal . . ." (Lensink, *A Secret,* 343).

8. Sarah's reference to "institute" was to the annual teachers' institute for Page County, which she as county superintendent was responsible to plan. The purpose of such an institute was to bring together county teachers and administrators to address issues and problems specific to that county. Such

institutes, typically a week or less in length, were held across the state during the break between the first and second term of classes. County teachers' institutes were different from normal institutes, which customarily met for two to six weeks, generally in the summer, and which offered more highly structured programs of study (Cordier, 53–60).

9. By 1915, approximately one-sixth (503) of the nearly 3,000 county superintendents in the United States were women (Cordier, 36). In Iowa, women had held the position of county school superintendent since 1869, and by 1915 there were 59 women serving as county superintendents. As Ruth A. Gallaher points out, women were "permitted to hold offices of some importance and yet were denied the right of voting for candidates for the same offices" (231–232).

Sarah, who ran for re-relection to the Page County superintendency of schools as a Democrat, was defeated by Agnes Samuelson, who served as county superintendent for the next eight years. Samuelson eventually served as Iowa State Superintendent of Public Instruction from 1927 to 1938 and was elected president of the National Education Association in 1935 (Cordier, 100). Jessie Field had moved to New York City in May 1912 to become the National YWCA Secretary for Small Town and Country Work. She was instrumental in the formation of the national 4-H program, sponsored by the U.S. Department of Agriculture. In 1917, she returned to Clarinda, Iowa, and married Ira W. Shambaugh. Jessie Field Shambaugh eventually became known as the "Mother of 4-H" (Friedel, 98).

10. Sarah was nearly fifty when she returned to the family farm in 1915. Some of her symptoms were doubtless attributable to menopause. Nonetheless, as Mary Hurlbut Cordier has noted, "Sarah's unrecognized menopausal symptoms were aggravated by her brother's criticisms, perhaps a return to the pattern of their childhood relationship. The shift from a position of leadership to that of the belittled and demeaned housekeeper took its toll on Sarah's fragile physical and mental health" (233). In many ways, Henry's abusive behavior echoed that exhibited by his father fifty years earlier. Ironically, Sarah's responses—and the complaints entered into her diary's pages—echoed those of her mother.

11. In later years, Sarah wrote about having been offered a position as a member of the Rural Section of Iowa State Teachers College (ISTC) at Cedar Falls. Her first assignment was to supervise teachers in nine rural schools in Bennington Township in Black Hawk County; her goal was "to bring each up to standard as far as possible" ("I Remember This and That," Box 8, Vol. 2, Huftalen Collection). Cordier has written that "Huftalen's position at Iowa State Teachers College was part of the on-going effort to upgrade rural schools under the leadership of College President Homer Seerley and Dr. Chauncey P. Colgrove, chair of the Department of Education" (235).

In 1918 Dr. Colgrove moved from ISTC to the presidency of Upper Iowa University (UIU) in Fayette, and he offered Sarah a lifetime position teaching methods courses at UIU. She resigned her position at ISTC. Colgrove encouraged Sarah to begin college coursework at UIU, and she did. Sarah later noted, "I remained at U.I.U. and took a four-year course in two years and taught ~~a full course~~ during that time. How savagely and furiously I worked day and night with never a holiday or respite" ("I Remember This and That," Box 8, Vol. 2, Huftalen Collection). While taking courses, Sarah continued teaching natural, physical, social, and mental sciences, along with education courses. In 1920, Sarah received her A.B. degree from UIU. She continued teaching there until 1923.

12. Wayne E. Fuller notes that "by the time the United States entered World War I, a part of the county superintendent's work had been parceled out to teaching supervisors and rural inspectors in some Midwestern states" (227). Their duties included not only supervising teachers but also meeting with rural school boards, condemning school houses that they deemed unsuitable, and making suggestions to the county superintendent concerning how to improve the schools. By this time, the growing movement toward consolidation of schools, which had originated in Massachusetts in 1869, had spread to the Midwest. But the movement was still meeting strong resistance from rural communities that wanted to keep control over their children's education in their own hands.

13. As Mary Hurlbut Cordier has observed, "This year of leadership through on-site teacher education rescued Sarah from the unhappiness of trying to live with Henry and propelled her into full-time teacher education for the rest of her professional years" (235).

9. "What Is the Criterion of a Teacher?": 1922–1935

1. The account book entitled "Ledger" (Box 11, Vol. 6, Huftalen Collection) contains a few entries from 1912 but primarily entries from 1921 on, during which time Sarah was supervising teachers at Upper Iowa University in Fayette. These entries are mainly lists of accounts and expenditures; however, an occasional lengthy diary entry is interwoven with the lists.

2. In June 1923, Sarah began the summer session at the University of Iowa, where she lived in a dormitory, Currier Hall. Her plan was to do research for her master's thesis and to prepare to take her master's examinations the following January.

3. The next several entries are taken from a small notebook (4 by 6 inches) entitled "The Universal Students Expense Book" (Box 11, Vol. 9, Huftalen Collection). In it Sarah recorded her expenses while a graduate student at the University of Iowa. In fall 1924, Sarah secured a position as supervisor of novice teachers in the Muscatine, Iowa, high school. She wrote sparingly in her diary during the period from 1924 to 1935; excerpts follow.

4. The next several entries are excerpted from Sarah's diary found in Box 7,

Volume 6, of the Huftalen Collection. This diary includes additional entries made during Sarah's years in Muscatine.

5. Sarah was bitterly disappointed that the Normal Training Department had been discontinued. As she later wrote in her reminiscences, "It nearly broke our hearts and not a few tears oozed out from sadness." She continued: "Many people are saying it is a grave mistake; that the teachers from the department are the best they have in the country schools. They ask why not discontinue some of the unnecessary departments such as Domestic Science and Printing etc. It is a fact that country bred boys and girls who take the Normal Course do become the most efficient country school teachers. They are familiar with country life and conditions and with the country school system and its needs" ("Normal Training Department, June 8th, 1933," Box 9, Vol. 4, Huftalen Collection).

6. The following entries were made during Sarah's summer visits to the Gillespie farm from 1929 through the 1930s. Each year's entry lists such things as amounts of money spent, work done, and travel plans. Sarah's descriptions of her chores on "The Old Home Farm" indicate that her work there continued to be as rigorous and demanding as it had been during her younger years. Viewed in this light, Sarah's choice of the heading "Vacations" for this portion of her diary carries an ironic weight.

Although Sarah used her diary to keep track of her arduous labors on the farm, those labors might well have gone unrecognized and unacknowledged by outsiders. Deborah Fink addresses this issue in her analysis of the paradoxical nature of women's "invisible" work:

> How does one assess reports of women who picked corn, made hay, milked cows, and tended hogs, horses, and chickens, yet did not do any farm labor? How does one understand a report of a woman who managed a dry goods department well, yet did not work in the store? Obviously, the people operated under a different conceptual system from that of today. Women did specific activities that we tend to call work, but that, within the family economy, were not considered work. Had nonfamily people been hired to do the same tasks, they would have been called workers. Women's work might have been invisible in the family economy, but it was a factor of production and it shaped relations both within the household and among households. (*Open Country,* 35)

To make matters worse, the Gillespie farm had fallen into disrepair. The "dilapidated" condition of the house, the machinery strewn across the barn floor, the broken-down fences—all became metaphors for the condition of Sarah and Henry's relationship, which was as complicated and dysfunctional as ever. Even though the siblings co-existed in the farmhouse, they did not share it, and their relationship continued to be deeply troubled.

7. References to Reba (Spitler) Bushnell, a neighbor of the Gillespies, be-

come more frequent in Sarah's diary during the 1930s and 1940s. Reba, who was born on December 21, 1883, on a farm two miles south of Ryan, Iowa, was the youngest of nine children of Amos and Martha (Talmadge) Spitler. According to Helen (Bushnell) English, Reba's daughter, Reba "attended the first eight grades of school at West Manchester and while there became friendly with her teacher, Mrs. Sarah Huftalen." Reba followed in Sarah's footsteps and taught for several years in country schools (letter to author, October 20, 1992).

In 1906, Reba married Earl H. Bushnell, and they had ten children. After her husband died in 1922 from complications after an emergency appendectomy, Reba raised the children on her own. In later years, Reba and Sarah were neighbors. Reba often helped Sarah accomplish her daily work, and the two women became close friends. As Reba's son, Lloyd Bushnell, remembers, "Sarah told us that her parents had given her strict orders to always look after Reba. She then remarked that it was now Reba who was looking after her" (from *Reba*, personal recollections by the Bushnell children, privately printed).

Sarah valued Reba's friendship so highly that she left Reba a portion of her estate: "I give and bequeath a one-fourth portion of said rest, residue and remainder of my estate to my good friend, Reba S. Bushnell." Court documents indicate that Reba received approximately $4,400 from Sarah's estate (Delaware County Probate File No. 5768, November 14, 1955).

8. The next several entries are from a 6-by-9-inch university composition book dated "1935, Muscatine, Iowa" (Box 7, Vol. 7, Huftalen Collection). This volume contains a few diary entries, along with Sarah's class notes during her final year of teaching hygiene and biology courses. It also contains copies of letters that Sarah planned to send to fellow teachers at the Muscatine high school and to the Muscatine board of education in May 1935, when Sarah was about to reach the mandatory retirement age of seventy. Clearly frustrated and deeply hurt at being forced to retire from teaching, Sarah let others know how she felt.

9. This was the final entry in this volume of Sarah's diary (Box 7, Vol. 7, Huftalen Collection). Upon her retirement, Sarah reluctantly left Muscatine and returned to the family farm to live with Henry. Of her years in Muscatine, Sarah later wrote:

Somehow I never could refuse a request to teach unless the postman brought several in the mail at the same time, then I had to think a bit. Disliking to take a vacation from the work I was revelling in, yet knowing that degrees were not a necessity so far as teaching ability was concerned I went to Muscatine to supply for three weeks. This was in October 1924 and where it was my happy privilege to remain until 1935 when the Board of Education had made a ruling to automatically discontinue the services of those who reached the age of 70 years. Be it said that chronological age is not a criterion of professional ability. ("I Remember This and That," Box 8, Vol. 11, Huftalen Collection)

10. "God Is My Refuge": 1937–1944

1. From 1935 to 1945 Sarah and Henry, both in their seventies, were trying to weather the Great Depression and World War II. Sarah's diary entries indicate that her days continued to be filled with heavy labor, visits with friends, and letter writing. She kept gathering genealogical materials and preparing biographical information on her mother, Emily.

Sarah's diary entries reveal that she was following national and world events closely, yet she did not often use her diary as a forum for expressing her feelings about those events. This aspect of Sarah's diary seems to corroborate Elizabeth Hampsten's findings about the private writings of North Dakota women: namely, that such writings constitute a "literature of omissions" in which little or nothing is said about local or national politics, cultural events, or scientific activities; however, Sarah's diary does not bear out Hampsten's assertion that such texts exhibit an "inevitable self-assurance" and forthrightness (*Read This*, 88–89). Rather, Sarah's diary entries often reflect the kind of uncertainty and self-doubt characteristic of someone living under extremely stressful conditions.

In this sense, Sarah's diary resembles that of Emily French, a working-class divorced woman keeping her diary in Denver during 1890. In Janet Lecompte's assessment, "poverty was the matrix of [Emily French's] life in 1890, and the source of constant anxiety. But her deepest fears were centered, in this first full year after her divorce, on loss of family and of 'home.' Her expression of these fears becomes the most poignant part of this most expressive diary" (12). The loss of Sarah's identity as an educator, a loss occurring during the worst economic conditions in twentieth-century America, might have produced enough anxiety that writing in her diary about the horrors of World War II was more than she could do.

2. Julia and Edward Lane were neighbors who farmed next to the W. L. Scanlans, just across the road from the Gillespie farm.

3. Bang's disease is slang for brucellosis, a disease which causes spontaneous abortion in cattle.

4. Sarah's reference is to Charles and LaVerne Bockenstedt, who farmed across Highway 20 from the Gillespie farm. Along with Wilma and Elmer Kehrli, the Bockenstedts provided generous assistance to Sarah and Henry during their later years.

5. The eighty-acre J. F. Gearhart farm adjoined the Gillespie farm to the east.

6. The Women's Christian Temperance Union (WCTU), founded in 1874,

advocated abstinence from alcohol. Frances Willard, its second president, tied temperance to other causes, such as women's suffrage. By the turn of the century, the WCTU had become a broadly based social service organization (Sochen, 180). By 1911, the WCTU was the largest women's organization in the United States, with a membership of 245,000 (Cordier, 96). By 1920, it had over 800,000 members (Ryan, 204).

Emily Gillespie had joined the WCTU in the mid-1870s, and Sarah took the Temperance Pledge as a teenager. Sarah remained an active member as an adult, serving as president of the Delaware County WCTU for nine years and as treasurer for five years. During the late 1930s and early 1940s, Sarah often wrote in her diary that she had gone with Reba Bushnell to WCTU meetings, which became her most important activity outside the home.

7. A contemporary of Sarah's, Belle Bailey was born in Manchester in 1869. Like Sarah, Belle attended the Manchester schools and later the Iowa State Teachers College at Cedar Falls. In later years, she became well known as a local historian, and she published a three-volume work, *A History of Delaware County, Iowa, 1834–1934*. Belle Bailey died in 1946 (Bailey, Vol. 1, 3).

8. According to Wilma Kerhli, the Gillespie farmhouse had no steps joining the upstairs to the downstairs. The only way to go from one floor of the house to another was to climb a ladder. Knowing this helps one appreciate the importance that Sarah attached to having a bedstead brought downstairs for her (interview with author, July 27, 1992).

9. The Prohibition party ticket of Roger Ward Babson and Edgar V. Moorman received 57,812 votes in the 1940 election. Babson (1875–1967) was a businessperson, statistician, and author.

10. This entry concluded Sarah's diary for the years 1939 to 1940 (Box 7, Vol. 8, Huftalen Collection). The Christmas 1940 entry begins a different volume of her diary (Box 8, Vol. 1, Huftalen Collection).

11. Hubert Carr was a well-known Manchester attorney from a prominent and wealthy family. No doubt his occupation as well as his position on the board of examiners would have made him an influential voice in decisions regarding sanity and insanity.

12. Sarah's concerns parallel those of her mother, Emily, fifty years earlier. As Carroll Smith-Rosenberg and Charles Rosenberg explain, many nineteenth-century doctors believed that "in males the intellectual propensities of the brain dominated, while the female's nervous system and emotions prevailed over her conscious and rational faculties." The uterus was assumed to be connected to the central nervous system, and paralysis and headaches were assumed to be linked to uterine disease. In fact, many physicians "contended that far greater difficulties could be expected in childless women" who "thwarted the promise immanent in their body's design" (13).

In analyzing prevalent nineteenth-century medical views on educated women, Vern Bullough and Martha Voght note that many doctors believed that "higher education left a great number of its female adherents in poor health for life" and that "overstimulation of the female brain" would cause "stunted growth, nervousness, headaches and neuralgias, difficult childbirth, hysteria, inflammation of the brain, and insanity" (30, 31). Such beliefs carried over into the twentieth century and, apparently, into the Gillespie household.

11. "All Will Yet Be Well": 1945–1952

1. Gretchen (Evans) Kuhlman, born in 1898, was the daughter of Ada (Hersey) and William Evans. A cousin to Sarah, Gretchen was the great-granddaughter of Elizabeth (Coffin) and Henry Baker, proprietors of the Stagecoach Inn. Gretchen lived in the Stagecoach Inn from 1907 until 1922, when she married Edward Kuhlman. According to Kris (Kuhlman) Saba, her granddaughter, Gretchen Kuhlman rented out the farm for several decades and eventually sold the Stagecoach Inn during the 1960s (letter to author, August 13, 1992). During Sarah's later years, Gretchen often visited and helped her.

2. Edgar Bushnell had a career in the navy and was aboard the USS *Houston* when it was sunk during the battle of the Java Sea in 1942. At the time, he was reported missing in action. Nothing further was known about his whereabouts until the end of the war, when his family learned that Edgar had succumbed to tropical ulcers resulting from an injury incurred while he was a prisoner of war, working on the Burma railroad (Helen English, letter to author, February 10, 1993).

3. Sarah's reference is to Josephine Donovan, a young writer from Granville, Iowa, who planned a story on Sarah's childhood books for the *Palimpsest,* the State Historical Society of Iowa's (SHSI) popular history magazine. "Schoolbooks of Sarah Gillespie" (April 1947) describes Sarah's primers, readers, spellers, and arithmetic and geography books. At the end of her article, Donovan observed: "These books used by Sarah Gillespie in the seventies and eighties preserve something of the mother's interest in her daughter's education. On many of the fly leaves, in fine Spencerian handwriting, are inscriptions such as the one in the arithmetic—'A present to Sarah for trying to learn. October 8, 1874. Thursday By E. E. Gillespie'" (120–121).

4. One of the letters that Sarah wrote on November 25, 1948, went to her Michigan cousin, Eugene Baker, whose aid she hoped to enlist in compiling the Baker genealogy. In that letter, Sarah reminisced about having visited Eugene's home in 1891 and finding him and both his parents sick. Sarah asked Eugene to help her trace the Baker line back to Boston. Toward the end of her letter, she turned her attention to life on the farm:

> Now we are well (brother and I) on the farm busy and hoping for a mild winter. He leases the land and has 16 or 17 head of P. B. Guernseys and 35 to 40 Shropshire sheep. No hogs or horses. I have one hen and when

she stops laying will likely put her in the pot. We are having spring-like weather, but never can tell when it will turn cold and blustery. . . . My brother will be 86 on the 4th of Sept. next and I will be 84 July 7th next. I was born July 7 1865 on the farm where we are living but not in this house which was built in 1876. . . . (letter privately held by Lee C. Baker, the great-nephew of Eugene Baker)

5. John Leslie Huftalen was the great-great-great-grandson of Joshua G. and Pamelia (Crandall) Huftalen. His great-great-grandfather was Billie Huftalen's brother, George J. Huftalen.

6. Sarah spent countless hours compiling her teaching records, reminiscences, photographs, and scrapbooks from her years at the Arbor Vitae Summit School in Oneida Township. Shortly before her death, she donated all of these materials to the SHSI in Iowa City. Sarah also donated detailed records of her teaching experiences at the Tarkio Township school in Page County and of her term as Page County superintendent of schools. Her papers also include records and reminiscences of her years supervising Bennington Township schools, her work at Upper Iowa University, her work at the State Teachers College in Cedar Falls, and her years supervising the Normal School in Muscatine (see Inventory, Huftalen Collection).

7. Sarah also spent a great deal of time contacting Hawley, Baker, and Gillespie relatives in Michigan and New York concerning genealogical records. She became a member of the New England Genealogical Society and was able to trace her parents' ancestries back several generations to their roots in England and Scotland. Her genealogical records are also included in her papers at the SHSI (see Inventory, Huftalen Collection).

8. These individuals were all farming neighbors. Elmer and Wilma Kerhli farmed across the road and a half mile east of the Gillespie farm. The Walstons, Hoffmans, and Bockenstedts farmed just to the west of the Gillespies.

9. In July 1950, the *Manchester Press* reported on the surprise birthday party:

No one need ever tell Mrs. Sarah Huftalen that women cannot keep a secret. This was proven to perfection on Friday afternoon when her neighbors came to help her celebrate her 85th birthday anniversary. The previous mails had been delivering letters, gifts and cards from Muscatine, Oneida, Cedar Falls, Des Moines and other places, also from the members of the local WCTU and Audubon society, of which she is a member.

One of the ladies came early as a prelude for a visit she long had been wanting to make, but soon cars filled the lawn and the women came by twos and fours. They heaped the dining room table with gifts both beautiful and useful, sang "Happy Birthday," spent a couple of hours in social jollity and served delicious ice cream and cake.

Mrs. Huftalen tried to muster a suitable response, but her usually fluent speech center was out of commission. She said she had been surprised and serenaded a number of times, but this event beat them all, so all she could say was "Thank you, each one, and may you have many more birthday anniversaries than I have," and she quoted a few lines from a poem she composed on July 7th, 1890, which were:

> And to you, my friends, I tender
> Warmest sympathy and love;
> Kindest thoughts for thee
> And comfort till God calls
> Us from above.

Snap shots were taken, good wishes extended and the happy guests departed to their homes in time to get supper for their waiting husbands. . . .

10. In order to protect her privacy, I have substituted the name Jane for the person's real name throughout this chapter.

11. Helen Bushnell English is the fifth of Reba and Earl Bushnell's ten children. Helen now lives in Cedar Rapids, Iowa.

12. In recent years, Ann and Steve Baumgarn bought the Stagecoach Inn and restored the first floor to look as it did during the mid-nineteenth century, when Emily Hawley first came from Michigan to live in her uncle Henry Baker's household. On March 20–21, 1992, the Baumgarns hosted a workshop for teachers at the Stagecoach Inn. The workshop, "In the Daily Course of Human Events," featured discussions of Emily's and Sarah's diaries and lives.

13. Henry Gillespie fits the profile of an emotional abuser provided by Kay Porterfield in *Violent Voices*. Porterfield explains that "not all men who are verbal and psychological abusers handle their anger inappropriately in every situation. . . . Frequently he discharges his rage only in the relative safety of his home and only when he views his target as smaller and weaker than himself" (3). Porterfield outlines explicit and implicit threats of violence, violence against property, extreme controlling behavior, isolation, extreme jealousy, and mental cruelty as common emotionally manipulative techniques used by an abusive individual.

In many ways, Henry Gillespie's behavior toward Sarah resembles that of emotionally abusive husbands described by Porterfield. His belief that Sarah, by marrying Billie Huftalen, had brought dishonor on the Gillespie name echoed nineteenth-century mores: by defending the "sexual honor" of female family members, male family members were protecting and maintaining the patriarchal structure of the family. Entries in Sarah's diary reveal that, as the years passed, the relationship between Henry and Sarah became emotionally incestuous—and that Sarah understood the nature of abusive relationships.

14. Mr. Nieman is Robert Nieman, clerk of court for Delaware County, Iowa.

15. Sarah compiled a good deal of information on Henry's life for donation to the SHSI: photographs, school papers, phrenological chart, letters, sermons, newspaper clippings, and other memorabilia. In biographical notes that

Sarah prepared for Henry's scrapbook, she described him as a writer and editor, a stockman who had won many "premiums and Guernseys and Shropshire Sheep at Fairs," and as an effective farmer: "Keeps our 100 acre farm virtually free from weeds and takes care of 30 head of cattle and about as many sheep. at 88 yrs." (Box 4, Vol. 1, Huftalen Collection). This public portrait of Henry, shaped by Sarah for the historical record, contrasts sharply with the private portrait that emerges on the pages of Sarah's diary. Like many members of emotionally abusive families, Henry and Sarah were enmeshed in a love/hate relationship throughout most of their adult lives.

Conclusion: The Diary as Cultural Text

1. This information is excerpted from Sarah's "Membership Information, New England Genealogical Society," dated March 9, 1942 (Box 11, Vol. 12, Huftalen Collection). This four-page document includes genealogical information, an outline of Sarah's education and teaching experience, and information on her public service experience.

2. Riley explains that it is difficult to gauge the number of female teachers prior to 1870 because, before that time, U.S. census records did not differentiate between male and female teachers. Iowa had 5,663 female teachers in 1870; by 1880, that number had risen to 10,157 (*The Female Frontier*, 104).

3. This information is taken from a brochure that Sarah prepared to describe the Arbor Vitae Summit School schedule for 1908–09. The schedule included information on "entertainments and socials" as well as this note: "Visitors are welcome. School officers and parents are especially invited to visit the school during the week days' regular sesions" (Box 10, Vol. 3, Huftalen Collection).

4. On September 4, 1953, Henry celebrated his ninetieth birthday, and Clarence Cox of the *Manchester Press* published a profile entitled "Manchester Pioneer Notes 90th Birthday." In that profile Cox noted: "After his father died, Gillespie settled on the home farm. For more than 40 years, he has raised Shropshire sheep and Guernsey cattle. For many years he operated a steam fired boiler and sawmill on his farm near here. He never married. His sister, Mrs. Sarah Huftalen, has made her home here with her brother for many years."

Accompanying Cox's article is a photograph of Henry, wearing a dress hat. His long white beard, stringy white hair, and stern expression are explained in this way: "Henry Gillespie, one of Manchester's pioneers, said he decided to have his picture taken before parting with his hair and beard, which he has been accumulating for protection against the coming cold weather.

'It gets pretty cold out here in the winter,' Gillespie said. He is one of the third generation in his family to own the original 200-acre farm on Highway 20 west of town."

Henry Gillespie's death certificate, filed on July 15, 1954, by attending physician H. B. Willard, listed cause of death as "endocarditis, chronic" (Delaware County Death Records). Henry was buried in the Gillespie family plot in Oakland Cemetery, Manchester.

5. This information is listed in Delaware County Probate File No. 5768 for the estate of Sarah L. Gillespie Huftalen. The property owned by Sarah and sold to Wilbur Kehrli is described as follows: "The East Half (E1/2) of the Northeast Quarter (NE 1/4) and the North Half (N1/2) of the Northeast Quarter (NE 1/4) of the Southeast Quarter (SE 1/4), all in Section Thirty-Six (36), Township Eighty-nine (89), North, Range Six (6) West of the Fifth Principal Meridian."

6. Sarah's obituary in the *Manchester Democrat* stated: "Funeral services for Sarah Gillespie Huftalen, 89, who passed away at the Dehn Nursing home in Manchester Friday following an illness of 5 years, were Sunday afternoon at the Gill Funeral home. Mrs. Huftalen had retired from teaching to Manchester in 1935 after devoting over 51 years of her life to teaching in Iowa. . . . Mrs. Huftalen was the last of one of Delaware County's pioneer families. Her brother, Henry, 90, died last July. Survivors include four cousins, Archie Hawley of Webberville, Mich., Henry Hawley of Morenci, Mich., Charles Hawley of Adrian, Mich., and Frank Gillespie of South Sioux City, Neb. Preceding her in death besides her husband and older brother, were her parents.

7. In *Iowa Pioneer Foundations,* published in 1940, George F. Parker emphasizes the primacy of the family unit as society's foundation. According to Parker, the isolation of pioneer life strengthened and preserved the family unit (116). Parker delineates different types of pioneer family scolds. The shrewish "female scold" was best exemplified by the isolated, overworked wife who would be quiet only when worn out and ignored by the community (194). The patient "husband-victim" generally had to suffer for years. Yet Parker notes, "Even wife-beating was forbidden as a relief because this was permissible only in the lowest quarters" (195). The foil for the "female scold" was the "male grumbler," who overworked his family, mistreated his stock, and made life "a burden to all around him" (196).

Parker's analysis reflects the prejudices of the era in which it was formulated as well as the era about which Parker was writing. For this very reason, his analysis is useful in understanding how prevalent attitudes might have shaped interactions among members of the Gillespie family.

8. My working definition of *dysfunctional family* is a family that suffers from the effects of chemical dependency, sexual abuse, and other forms of physical, emotional, and/or verbal abuse. Paradoxically, the dysfunction seen and felt by family members is often carefully hidden from those outside the family unit. This "invisibility" is one of the hallmarks of the dysfunctional family.

9. As Alice Van Wart observes:

... flexibility is a distinguishing feature of the diary form. In the hands of women it points to a potent form of rhetoric different from the conventional modes of discourse based on inductive or deductive thinking and organization. Unlike the framed, contained, and closed thinking revealed in the conventional (or male mode), the writing in women's diaries generally proceeds by indirection and reveals female thinking to be eidetic (presented through detailed and accurate visual image reproducing a past impression), open-ended, and generative. The diary's form is capable of an endless flexibility, a quality well suited to encompassing the multifarious nature of women's lives. (22)

In her analysis of the journals of Elizabeth Smart, a twentieth-century Canadian writer, Van Wart describes the "gradual shift in [Smart's] writing from closure, a style characterized by being framed, contained, and closed to indirection" to a "generative, eidetic, and open-ended" style (26). I would assert that the diary of Sarah Gillespie Huftalen follows a similar pattern.

10. Cinthia Gannett comments on "diary cycles"; that is, "multiple generations of women keeping diaries in the same family," cycles that "speak to the ways in which diaries were preserved and diary writing handed down from one generation of women to the next" (133). Gannett concludes that, while diaries "certainly performed important verbal housekeeping in accordance with women's muted discursive responsibilities, they also appear to have served women's discursive needs and networks and their sense of self as well" (133).

11. Susan Stanford Friedman hypothesizes that women's stories often trace female psychological development by portraying a woman in relationship with others rather than as an individual. In drawing on the work of Nancy Chodorow, Friedman presents an especially cogent analysis of the "autobiographical self" that "does not oppose herself to all others, does not feel herself to exist outside others, and still less against others, but very much *with* others in an interdependent existence that asserts its rhythms everywhere in the community" (56).

The recent work of Carol Gilligan, Nona P. Lyons, and Trudy J. Hanmer uses the metaphor of *soundings* to illustrate the ways in which psyche develops like a fugue, in relationship rather than in stages (314–328). Drawing on this metaphor, I believe that the diary of Sarah Gillespie Huftalen develops very much like a fugue, one in which "self" is dynamic rather than static and one in which relationship with others evolves into the music of a life.

Bibliography

Abel, Emily K. "Dependence and Autonomy in Mother-Daughter Relation-
ships: Emily Hawley Gillespie and Sarah Gillespie, 1865–1888." Unpub-
lished paper, 1990.
———. *Who Cares for the Elderly? Public Policy and the Experiences of Adult
Daughters.* Philadelphia: Temple University Press, 1991.
Alexander, Ilene, Suzanne Bunkers, and Cherry Muhanji. "A Conversation on
Studying and Writing about Women's Lives Using Nontraditional Method-
ologies." *Women's Studies Quarterly* 17 (1989): 99–114.
Andrews, William L., ed. *Journeys in New Worlds: Early American Women's
Narratives.* Madison: University of Wisconsin Press, 1990.
Aptheker, Bettina. *Tapestries of Life: Women's Work, Women's Consciousness,
and the Meaning of Daily Experience.* Amherst: University of Massachusetts
Press, 1989.
Armitage, Susan. "Aunt Amelia's Diary: The Record of a Reluctant Pioneer."
In *Teaching Women's Literature form a Regional Perspective,* edited by
Leonore Hoffmann and Deborah Rosenfelt. New York: Modern Language
Association, 1982.
Arpad, Susan, ed. *Sam Curd's Diary: The Diary of a True Woman.* Athens:
Ohio University Press, 1984.
Aurner, Clarence. *History of Education in Iowa.* 3 vols. Iowa City: State His-
torical Society of Iowa, 1915.
Bailey, Belle. *A Three-Volume History of Delaware County, Iowa, 1834–1934.*
Monticello, Iowa, 1932, 1935, 1946.
Beauchamp, Virginia Walcott, ed. *A Private War: Letters and Diaries of Madge
Preston, 1862–1867.* New Brunswick: Rutgers University Press, 1987.
Benstock, Shari, ed. *The Private Self: Theory and Practice of Women's Auto-
biographical Writings.* Chapel Hill: University of North Carolina Press, 1988.
Brodzki, Bella, and Celeste Schenck, eds. *Life/lines: Theorizing Women's Au-
tobiography.* Ithaca: Cornell University Press, 1988.

Bullough, Vern, and Martha Voght. "Women, Menstruation, and Nineteenth-Century Medicine." In *Women and Health in America*, edited by Judith Walzer Leavitt. Madison: University of Wisconsin Press, 1984.

Bunkers, Suzanne L. "Diaries: Public *and* Private Records of Women's Lives." *Legacy: A Journal of Nineteenth-Century American Women Writers* 7 (Fall 1990): 17–25.

———. *The Diary of Caroline Seabury*. Madison: University of Wisconsin Press, 1991.

———. "'Faithful Friend': Nineteenth-Century Midwestern American Women's Unpublished Diaries." *Women's Studies International Forum* 10 (1987): 7–17.

———. "Midwestern Diaries and Journals: What Women Were (Not) Saying in the Late 1800s." In *Studies in Autobiography*, edited by James Olney. New York: Oxford University Press, 1988.

———. "Reading and Interpreting Unpublished Diaries by Nineteenth-Century Women." *A/B: Auto/Biography Studies* 2 (Summer 1986): 15–17.

———. "Subjectivity and Self-Reflexivity in the Study of Women's Diaries as Autobiography." *A/B: Auto/biography Studies* 5 (Fall 1990): 114–123.

———. "What Do Women *Really* Mean? Thoughts on Women's Diaries and Lives." In *The Intimate Critique: Autobiographical Literary Criticism*, edited by Diane Freedman, Olivia Frey, and Frances Murphy Zauhar. Durham: Duke University Press, 1993.

———. "What Do Women *Really* Mean? Thoughts on Women's Diaries and Lives." In *The Intimate Critique: Autobiographical Literary Criticism*, edited by Diane Freedman, Olivia Frey, and Frances Murphy Zauhar. Durham: Duke University Press, 1993.

Bunkers, Suzanne L., and Judy Nolte Temple. "Mothers, Daughters, and Diaries: Literacy, Relationship, and Cultural Context." In *Nineteenth-Century Women Learn to Write: Past Cultures and Practices of Literacy*, edited by Catherine Hobbs Peaden. Charlottesville: University Press of Virginia (forthcoming).

Cassidy, Jessie J. *The Legal Status of Women*. National American Woman Suffrage Association, 1897.

Chodorow, Nancy. *The Reproduction of Mothering: Psychoanalysis and the Sociology of Gender*. Berkeley and Los Angeles: University of California Press, 1978.

Cordier, Mary Hurlbut. *Schoolwomen of the Prairies and Plains*. Albuquerque: University of New Mexico Press, 1992.

Cott, Nancy. *The Bonds of Womanhood: "Woman's Sphere" in New England, 1780–1835*. New Haven: Yale University Press, 1977.

Culley, Margo. "Women's Diary Literature: Resources and Directions in the Field." *Legacy* 1 (Spring 1984): 4–5.

———. ed. *A Day at a Time: The Diary Literature of American Women from*

1764 to the Present. New York: Feminist Press at the City University of New York, 1985.

——. ed. *American Women's Autobiography: Fea(s)ts of Words*. Madison: University of Wisconsin Press, 1992.

Dailey, Christie. "The Family on the Farm: A Case Study of Rural Exchange Networks." Unpublished paper, State Historical Society of Iowa, Iowa City.

di Leonardo, Micaela. *Gender at the Crossroads of Knowledge: Feminist Anthropology in the Postmodern Era*. Berkeley and Los Angeles: University of California Press, 1991.

Donovan, Josephine. "Schoolbooks of Sarah Gillespie." *Palimpsest* 28 (April 1947): 113–121.

Downey, Betsy. "Battered Pioneers: Jules Sandoz and the Physical Abuse of Wives on the American Frontier." *Great Plains Quarterly* 12 (Winter 1992): 31–49.

Egan, Susanna. "Changing Faces of Heroism: Some Questions Raised by Contemporary Autobiography." *Biography* 10 (Winter 1987): 20–37.

Engelhardt, Carroll. "Compulsory Education in Iowa, 1872–1919." *Annals of Iowa* 49 (Summer/Fall 1987): 58–76.

Faragher, John Mack. *Women and Men on the Overland Trail*. New Haven: Yale University Press, 1979.

Fink, Deborah. *Agrarian Women: Wives and Mothers in Rural Nebraska, 1880–1940*. Chapel Hill: University of North Carolina Press, 1992.

——. *Open Country, Iowa: Rural Women, Tradition and Change*. Albany: State University of New York Press, 1986.

Foote, Edward B., M.D. *Medical Common Sense: Applied to the Causes, Prevention and Cure of Chronic Diseases and Unhappiness in Marriage*. rev. ed. New York: 110 Lexington Avenue, 1867.

Fothergill, Robert. *Private Chronicles: A Study of English Diaries*. London and New York: Oxford University Press, 1974.

Frank, Gelya. "'Becoming the Other': Empathy and Biographical Interpretation." *Biography* 8 (1985): 189–210.

Friedel, Janice Nahra. "Jessie Field Shambaugh: The Mother of 4-H." *Palimpsest* 62 (July/August 1981): 98–115.

Friedman, Susan Stanford. "Women's Autobiographical Selves: Theory and Practice." In *The Private Self*, edited by Shari Benstock. Chapel Hill: University of North Carolina Press, 1988.

Fuller, Wayne E. *The Old Country School*. University of Chicago Press, 1982.

Gallaher, Ruth A. *Legal and Political Status of Women in Iowa*. Iowa City: State Historical Society of Iowa, 1918.

Gannett, Cinthia. *Gender and the Journal: Diaries and Academic Discourse*. Albany: State University of New York Press, 1992.

Geertz, Clifford. *Works and Lives: The Anthropologist as Author.* Palo Alto: Stanford University Press, 1988.

Gillespie, Emily Hawley. Unpublished Diary Manuscripts, 1858–1888. Sarah Gillespie Huftalen Collection. State Historical Society of Iowa, Iowa City.

Gilligan, Carol. *In a Different Voice: Psychological Theory and Women's Development.* Cambridge: Harvard University Press, 1982.

Gilligan, Carol, Nona P. Lyons, and Trudy J. Hanmer, eds. *Making Connections: The Relational Worlds of Adolescent Girls at Emma Willard School.* Cambridge: Harvard University Press, 1990.

Gillikin, Dure Jo. "A Lost Diary Found: The Art of the Everyday." In *Women's Personal Narratives: Essays in Criticism and Pedagogy,* edited by Leonore Hoffmann and Margo Culley. New York: Modern Language Association, 1985.

Gluck, Sherna Berger, and Daphne Patai, eds. *Women's Words: The Feminist Practice of Oral History.* London: Routledge, Chapman, and Hall, 1991.

Gordon, Linda. *Heroes of Their Own Lives: The Politics and History of Family Violence.* New York: Viking Press, 1988.

Graulich, Melody. "Violence against Women: Power Dynamics in Literature of the Western Family." In *The Women's West,* edited by Susan Armitage and Elizabeth Jameson. Norman: University of Oklahoma Press, 1987.

Grumet, Madeleine R. *Bitter Milk: Women and Teaching.* Amherst: University of Massachusetts Press, 1988.

Gwin, Minrose C., ed. *A Woman's Civil War: A Diary, with Reminiscences of the War, from March 1862, by Cornelia Peake McDonald.* Madison: University of Wisconsin Press, 1992.

Hampsten, Elizabeth. *Read This Only to Yourself: The Private Writings of Midwestern Women, 1880–1910.* Bloomington: Indiana University Press, 1982.

———. *Settlers' Children.* Norman: University of Oklahoma Press, 1991.

———. "Tell Me All You Know: Reading Letters and Diaries of Rural Women." In *Teaching Women's Literature from a Regional Perspective,* edited by Leonore Hoffmann and Deborah Rosenfelt. New York: Modern Language Association, 1982.

Hancock, Emily. *The Girl Within.* New York: Fawcett Columbine, 1989.

Heilbrun, Carolyn. "Women's Autobiographical Writings: New Forms." *Prose Studies* 8 (September 1985): 14–28.

———. *Writing a Woman's Life.* New York: W. W. Norton, 1988.

Hinding, Andrea, Ames Sheldon Bower, and Clark A. Chambers, eds. *Women's History Sources: A Guide to Archives and Manuscript Collections in the United States.* London: R. R. Bowker, 1979.

Hogan, Rebecca S. "Diarists on Diaries." *A/B: Auto/Biography Studies* 2 (Summer 1986): 9–14.

———. "Engendered Autobiography: The Diary as a Feminine Form." *Prose Studies* 14 (September 1991): 95–107.

Huff, Cynthia. *British Women's Diaries: A Descriptive Bibliography of Se-*

lected Nineteenth-Century Women's Manuscript Diaries. New York: AMS Press, 1985.

———. "From Faceless Chronicler to Self-Creator: The Diary of Louisa Galton, 1830–1896." *Biography* 10 (Spring 1987): 95–106.

———. "Text as Process: Learning How to Read the Unpublished Diary." Paper presented at the 1987 Modern Language Association Convention, San Francisco.

———. "'That Profoundly Female, and Feminist Genre': The Diary as Feminist Praxis." *Women's Studies Quarterly* 17 (Fall/Winter 1989): 6–14.

Huftalen, Sarah Gillespie. "Care and Training of Children." *Home Life* 1 (September 1899): 1–2.

———. *Little Essays on Life's Invisible Realities*. Privately published, 1933.

———. "School Days of the Seventies." *Palimpsest* 28 (April 1947): 122–128.

———. Unpublished Diary Manuscripts, 1873–1952. Sarah Gillespie Huftalen Collection. State Historical Society of Iowa, Iowa City.

———. "The Use of the Hand Book in Rural Schools." *Midland Schools: A Journal of Education* 24 (June 1910): 300–302.

Hunter, Jane H. "Inscribing the Self in the Heart of the Family: Diaries and Girlhood in Late-Victorian America." *American Quarterly* 44 (March 1992): 51–81.

Ireland, Robert M. "Frenzied and Fallen Females: Women and Sexual Dishonor in the Nineteenth-Century United States." *Journal of Women's History* 3 (Winter 1992): 95–117.

Jelinek, Estelle. *The Tradition of Women's Autobiography: From Antiquity to the Present*. Boston: G. K. Hall/Twayne, 1986.

Johnson, Keach. "Roots of Modernization: Educational Reform in Iowa at the Turn of the Century." *Annals of Iowa* 50 (Spring 1991): 892–918.

———. "The State of Elementary and Secondary Education in Iowa in 1900." *Annals of Iowa* 49 (Summer/Fall 1987): 26–57.

Juhasz, Suzanne. "Towards a Theory of Form in Feminist Autobiography." In *Women's Autobiography: Essays in Criticism*, edited by Estelle Jelinek. Bloomington: Indiana University Press, 1980.

Kadar, Marlene, ed. *Essays on Life Writing: From Genre to Critical Practice*. Toronto: University of Toronto Press, 1992.

Kagle, Steven E. *Late 19th Century American Diary Literature*. Boston: G. K. Hall/Twayne, 1988.

Kaufman, Polly Welts. *Women Teachers on the Frontier*. New Haven: Yale University Press, 1984.

Kelley, Mary. *Private Woman, Public Stage: Literary Domesticity in Nineteenth-Century America*. New York: Oxford University Press, 1984.

Kerber, Linda, and Jane DeHart-Mathews, eds. *Women's America: Refocusing the Past*. 2nd ed. New York: Oxford University Press, 1987.

Kolodny, Annette. "A Map for Rereading: Or, Gender and the Interpretation of Literary Texts." *New Literary History* 11 (1979–80): 451–467.

Kunzman, Kristin A. *The Healing Way: Adult Recovery from Childhood Sexual Abuse*. San Francisco: Harper and Row, 1990.

Langness, Lewis L., and Gelya Frank. *Lives: An Anthropological Approach to Biography*. Novato, Calif.: Chandler and Sharp, 1981.

Lanser, Susan S. *Fictions of Authority: Women Writers and Narrative Voice*. Ithaca: Cornell University Press, 1992.

———. "Toward a Feminist Narratology." *Style* 20 (Fall 1986): 341–363.

Lecompte, Janet, ed. "Introduction: Discovering Emily." In *Emily: The Diary of a Hard-Worked Woman*. Lincoln: University of Nebraska Press, 1987.

Lensink, Judy Nolte. "Expanding the Boundaries of Criticism: The Diary as Female Autobiography." *Women's Studies* 14 (1987): 39–53.

———. *"A Secret to Be Burried": The Life and Diary of Emily Hawley Gillespie*. Iowa City: University of Iowa Press, 1989.

Lerner, Gerda. *The Female Experience: An American Documentary*. Indianapolis: Bobbs-Merrill, 1977.

Lionnet, Francoise. *Autobiographical Voices: Race, Gender, Self Portraiture*. Ithaca: Cornell University Press, 1989.

Marcus, Jane. "Invisible Mending." In *Between Women: Biographers, Novelists, Critics, Teachers and Artists Write about Their Work on Women*, edited by Carol Ascher, Louise DeSalvo, and Sara Ruddick. Boston: Beacon Press, 1984.

Mason, Mary. "The Other Voice: Autobiographies of Women Writers." In *Autobiography: Essays Theoretical and Critical*, edited by James Olney. Princeton: Princeton University Press, 1980.

Merry, John F., ed. *History of Delaware County, Iowa, and Its People*. S. J. Clarke, 1914.

Miller, Nancy K. *Getting Personal: Feminist Occasions and Other Autobiographical Acts*. London: Routledge, Chapman, and Hall, 1991.

———. *Subject to Change: Reading Feminist Writing*. New York: Columbia University Press, 1988.

———, ed. *The Poetics of Gender*. New York: Columbia University Press, 1986.

Motz, Marilyn. "Folk Expression of Time and Place: 19th-Century Midwestern Rural Diaries." *Journal of American Folklore* 100 (1987): 131–147.

———. *True Sisterhood: Michigan Women and Their Kin, 1820–1920*. Albany: State University of New York Press, 1983.

Myerhoff, Barbara, and Jay Ruby. "Introduction: Reflexivity and Its Relatives." In *A Crack in the Mirror: Reflexive Perspectives in Anthropology*. Philadelphia: University of Pennsylvania Press, 1982.

Olney, James, ed. *Autobiography: Essays Theoretical and Critical*. Princeton: Princeton University Press, 1980.

Parker, George F. *Iowa Pioneer Foundations*. Vol. 2. Iowa City: State Historical Society of Iowa, 1940.

Pascal, Roy. *Design and Truth in Autobiography*. London: Routledge and Kegan Paul, 1960.

Personal Narratives Group, eds. *Interpreting Women's Lives: Feminist Theory and Personal Narratives*. Bloomington: Indiana University Press, 1989.

Pleck, Elizabeth. *Domestic Tyranny: The Making of Social Policy against Family Violence from Colonial Times to the Present*. New York: Oxford University Press, 1987.

Porterfield, Kay. *Violent Voices*. Deerfield Beach, Fla.: Health Communications, 1989.

Rich, Adrienne. *Of Woman Born: Motherhood as Experience and Institution*. New York: Norton, 1976.

Riley, Glenda. *The Female Frontier: A Comparative View of Women on the Prairie and the Plains*. Lawrence: University Press of Kansas, 1988.

————. *Frontierswomen: The Iowa Experience*. Ames: Iowa State University Press, 1981.

Romines, Ann. *The Home Plot: Women, Writing, and Domestic Ritual*. Amherst: University of Massachusetts Press, 1992.

Rosaldo, Renato. *Culture and Truth: The Re-making of Social Analysis*. Boston: Beacon Press, 1989.

Rosenblatt, Paul C. *Bitter, Bitter Tears: Nineteenth-Century Diarists and Twentieth-Century Grief Theories*. Minneapolis: University of Minnesota Press, 1983.

Ryan, Mary P. *Womanhood in America: From Colonial Times to the Present*. 3rd ed. New York: Franklin Watts, 1983.

Schlissel, Lillian. *Women's Diaries of the Westward Journey*. New York: Schocken Books, 1981.

Showalter, Elaine. "Piecing and Writing." In *The Poetics of Gender*, edited by Nancy K. Miller. New York: Columbia University Press, 1986.

————. *Sister's Choice: Tradition and Change in American Women's Writing*. New York: Oxford University Press, 1991.

Simons, Judy. *Diaries and Journals of Literary Women from Fanny Burney to Virginia Woolf*. Iowa City: University of Iowa Press, 1990.

Smith, Sidonie. *A Poetics of Women's Autobiography*. Bloomington: Indiana University Press, 1987.

Smith-Rosenberg, Carroll. *Disorderly Conduct: Visions of Gender in Victorian America*. New York: Alfred A. Knopf, 1985.

————. "The Female World of Love and Ritual." *Signs: Journal of Women in Culture and Society* 1 (Autumn 1975): 1–30.

————. "Writing History: Language, Class, and Gender." In *Feminist Studies, Critical Studies*, edited by Teresa de Lauretis. Bloomington: Indiana University Press, 1986.

Smith-Rosenberg, Carroll, and Charles Rosenberg. "The Female Animal: Medical and Biological Views of Woman and Her Role in Nineteenth-Century

America." In *Women and Health in America*, edited by Judith Walzer Leavitt. Madison: University of Wisconsin Press, 1984.

Sochen, June. *Herstory: A Woman's View of American History.* New York: Alfred Publishing, 1974.

Spelman, Elizabeth V. *Inessential Woman: Problems of Exclusion in Feminist Thought.* Boston: Beacon Press, 1988.

Stone, Albert E. "Modern American Autobiography: Texts and Transactions." In *American Autobiography: Retrospect and Prospect*, edited by Paul John Eakin. Madison: University of Wisconsin Press, 1992.

———, ed. *The American Autobiography: A Collection of Critical Essays.* Englewood Cliffs, N.J.: Prentice-Hall, 1981.

Superintendent's Record for Delaware County. Delaware County Historical Society Archives, Hopkinton, Iowa.

Swaim, Ginalie. "An Acre of Hill." *Palimpsest* 68 (Spring 1987): 22–31.

Taves, Ann, ed. *Religion and Domestic Violence in Early New England: The Memoirs of Abigail Abbot Bailey.* Bloomington: Indiana University Press, 1989.

Taylor, P. A. M., ed. *More Than Common Powers of Perception: The Diary of Elizabeth Rogers Mason Cabot.* Boston: Beacon Press, 1991.

Ulrich, Laurel Thatcher. "Martha's Diary and Mine." *Journal of Women's History* 4 (Fall 1992): 157–160.

———, ed. *A Midwife's Tale: The Life of Martha Ballard, Based on Her Diary, 1785–1812.* New York: Random House, 1990.

Van Wart, Alice. "'Life out of Art': Elizabeth Smart's Early Journals." In *Essays on Life Writing: From Genre to Critical Practice*, edited by Marlene Kadar. Toronto: University of Toronto Press, 1992.

Walker, Alice. *In Search of Our Mothers' Gardens: Womanist Prose.* San Diego: Harcourt Brace Jovanovich, 1983.

Welter, Barbara. "The Cult of True Womanhood, 1820–1860." *American Quarterly* 18 (Summer 1966): 151–174.

Wilkinson, Sue. "The Role of Reflexivity in Feminist Psychology." *Women's Studies International Forum* 11 (1988): 493–502.

Index

*"All Will Yet Be Well": The Diary
of Sarah Gillespie Huftalen,
1873–1952*
By Suzanne L. Bunkers

A Cook's Tour of Iowa
By Susan Puckett

The Folks
By Ruth Suckow

*Fragile Giants: A Natural
History of the Loess Hills*
By Cornelia F. Mutel

*An Iowa Album: A Photographic
History, 1860–1920*
By Mary Bennett

Iowa Birdlife
By Gladys Black

Landforms of Iowa
By Jean C. Prior

More han Ola og han Per
By Peter J. Rosendahl

*Neighboring on the Air:
Cooking with the KMA Radio
Homemakers*
By Evelyn Birkby

*Nineteenth Century Home
Architecture of Iowa City:
A Silver Anniversary Edition*
By Margaret N. Keyes

*Nothing to Do but Stay:
My Pioneer Mother*
By Carrie Young

*Old Capitol: Portrait of an
Iowa Landmark*
By Margaret N. Keyes

*Parsnips in the Snow: Talks
with Midwestern Gardeners*
By Jane Anne Staw and
Mary Swander

*A Place of Sense: Essays in
Search of the Midwest*
Edited by Michael Martone

*Prairie Cooks: Glorified Rice,
Three-Day Buns, and Other
Reminiscences*
By Carrie Young with
Felicia Young

*Prairies, Forests, and Wetlands:
The Restoration of Natural
Landscape Communities in Iowa*
By Janette R. Thompson

A Ruth Suckow Omnibus
By Ruth Suckow

*"A Secret to Be Burried":
The Diary and Life of Emily
Hawley Gillespie, 1858–1888*
By Judy Nolte Lensink

*Tales of an Old Horsetrader:
The First Hundred Years*
By Leroy Judson Daniels

The Tattooed Countess
By Carl Van Vechten